AI Ethics, Governance, Equity, and Safety for Responsible Organizations

Darrell Norman Burrell
https://orcid.org/0000-0002-4675-9544
Marymount University, USA

IGI Global
Scientific Publishing
Publishing Tomorrow's Research Today

Vice President of Editorial	Melissa Wagner
Director of Acquisitions	Mikaela Felty
Director of Book Development	Jocelynn Hessler
Production Manager	Mike Brehm
Cover Design	Jose Rosado

Published in the United States of America by
IGI Global Scientific Publishing
701 East Chocolate Avenue
Hershey, PA, 17033, USA
Tel: 717-533-8845 | Fax: 717-533-7115
Website: https://www.igi-global.com E-mail: cust@igi-global.com

Library of Congress Cataloging-in-Publication Data

LCCN: 2026017107 (CIP Data Pending)
ISBN13: 9798260010167
Isbn13Softcover: 9798260010174
EISBN13: 9798260010181
British Cataloguing in Publication Data
A Cataloguing in Publication record for this book is available from the British Library.

Table of Contents

Detailed Table of Contents

As predictive analytics becomes central to modern hiring, it raises serious ethical concerns around fairness, transparency, and accountability in decision-making. This chapter examines algorithmic hiring through a multidimensional lens, drawing on over 25 peer-reviewed studies across human resource management, artificial intelligence, and ethics. Using a qualitative case study methodology, it explores how historical data biases, opaque model design, and limited applicant recourse can reinforce systemic discrimination. Strategic frameworks, such as the Balanced Scorecard and Kotter's 8-Step Change Model, are used to assess ethical integration from both planning and implementation perspectives. The chapter identifies key ethical risks and offers actionable strategies, including fairness-aware machine learning (FAML), algorithmic audits, participatory design, and regulatory reform. Bridging technical systems, organizational behavior, and governance, the chapter provides a blueprint for embedding ethical resilience into predictive hiring and shaping a more equitable future of work.

This perspective style article proposes a comprehensive ethical framework for the responsible deployment of artificial intelligence (AI) in healthcare, grounded in a synthesis of philosophical ethics and practical governance principles. As AI technologies, particularly generative systems, become integral to healthcare operations, their implementation raises complex moral challenges related to bias, equity, transparency, and trust. The paper introduces Ethical AI Deployment Framework, which integrates deontology, utilitarianism, virtue ethics, the ethics of care, practical wisdom, moral particularism, social contract theory, stakeholder theory, and corporate social responsibility.The framework emphasizes inclusive design, lifecycle-oriented impact assessments, ethical leadership training, and continuous feedback mechanisms to ensure that AI-driven innovations serve all patient populations equitably and humanely. This multidisciplinary approach advances a

This management consulting case study examines how organizational culture and employee behavior contributed to prolonged misuse of corporate purchase cards at Quest Wellness Consortium (QWC) and how artificial intelligence (AI) can be leveraged to detect fraud and reshape ethical conduct. Drawing on a qualitative, three-phase focus group methodology involving auditors, organizational development specialists, and AI implementation experts, the study translates expert recommendations into actionable consulting deliverables. Findings demonstrate that unethical behavior among skilled employees emerged from normalized deviance, moral licensing, and low perceived accountability, exacerbated by reliance on manual controls. Results show that AI-enabled anomaly detection, behavioral nudges, and transparency dashboards function not only as fraud detection mechanisms but as behavioral interventions that increase ethical salience and accountability.

The rapid evolution of artificial intelligence (AI) is reshaping workforce dynamics, organizational culture, and ethical norms, demanding new models of human-AI collaboration. This work examines the intersection of AI and human capital, emphasizing trust, bias, and workforce readiness. Special focus is given to aviation, aerospace, and infotainment systems, where AI drives safety, efficiency, and user experience but still requires adaptive human oversight. Integrating human talent and AI necessitates actionable frameworks, building trust, mitigating algorithmic bias,

psychology, criminal justice, cybersecurity, and human factors, the study explored offender strategies, organizational decision-making, and guardianship effectiveness. Findings indicate that cybercriminals systematically exploit cognitive overload, authority bias, and normalized risk behaviors within healthcare environments, while organizational fragmentation and short-term risk perceptions weaken defensive capacity. Participants emphasized that cybersecurity failures are rarely technical in isolation but emerge from predictable human and cultural vulnerabilities.

The rapid expansion of e-commerce has introduced significant challenges in the detection and prevention of financial fraud. As fraudulent techniques evolve in complexity and coordination, traditional rule-based systems have proven increasingly inadequate. This study examines the effectiveness of machine learning models, specifically Random Forest and XGBoost, in detecting fraudulent transactions within highly imbalanced credit card data representative of online commerce environments. The analysis focuses on the impact of resampling methods, including Synthetic Minority Oversampling Technique (SMOTE) and random undersampling, in addressing class imbalance. Results indicate that both techniques improved model performance, with SMOTE yielding higher F1-scores and recall. Among the models evaluated, XGBoost trained on SMOTE-balanced data demonstrated the most effective performance. The study also incorporated interpretability analysis through SHAP values to identify key contributing features, thereby enhancing model transparency.

Hospitals face rising threats from ransomware and phishing attacks which reveal both system vulnerabilities and staff security weaknesses in their medical record systems. Healthcare sector has faced tremendous cyber-attacks since the inception of Electronic Health Records (EHRs) - digital versions of a patient's medical history, stored and accessed electronically. Healthcare environments face regular attacks from malware like ransomware, adware, spyware, trojan horses, worms, viruses, botnets, and rootkits, so organizations need to identify these threats. Attackers use system and network weaknesses to launch phishing email attacks and distribute harmful email attachments. Healthcare organizations need to establish both technical and

Preface

Artificial intelligence is redefining the architecture of decision-making across organizations, industries, and governments. Yet, as its capabilities expand, so too do the ethical, social, and governance challenges that accompany its use. *AI Ethics, Governance, Equity, and Safety for Responsible Organizations* was developed in recognition of a fundamental truth: innovation without responsibility is unsustainable. As editor, I have assembled this volume to explore how organizations can move beyond technical adoption toward the intentional design of AI systems that are ethical, equitable, transparent, and safe.

This book is grounded in the belief that responsible AI is not a peripheral concern—it is central to organizational legitimacy, public trust, and long-term resilience. The chapters that follow reflect a multidisciplinary effort to confront some of the most pressing questions of our time: How do we ensure fairness in algorithmic decision-making? What governance structures are required to manage AI risk? How do we embed equity into systems that are often built on biased data? And how can organizations balance innovation with accountability?

CHAPTER OVERVIEW

We begin in Chapter 1 with a critical examination of predictive analytics in employment and hiring. This chapter sets the tone for the volume by exposing how algorithmic systems, when built on biased historical data and opaque models, can reinforce systemic inequities. By integrating strategic and ethical frameworks, the authors provide actionable pathways—such as fairness-aware machine learning and algorithmic audits—for embedding accountability into hiring practices.

Chapter 2 expands the ethical conversation into healthcare, presenting a comprehensive framework for responsible AI deployment grounded in both philosophical theory and practical governance. The chapter emphasizes that ethical AI must be designed across its entire lifecycle, incorporating inclusive design, continuous evaluation, and leadership accountability to ensure equitable outcomes for all populations.

In Chapter 3, the lens of industrial and organizational psychology is applied to the risks of AI in hiring. Through a rigorous, consensus-based methodology, the authors reveal how overreliance on automated systems can amplify discrimination, particularly when organizational cultures prioritize efficiency over fairness. The findings reinforce the need for interdisciplinary oversight and human-centered design.

Chapters 4 and 5 address the persistent issue of gender inequity in AI. Chapter 4 introduces a conceptual framework for understanding how AI systems impact women, linking gender inclusion to organizational agility and innovation. Chapter 5 deepens this analysis within healthcare, highlighting the structural barriers that limit women's participation in AI-related roles. Together, these chapters underscore that equity in AI is not only a moral imperative but also a driver of organizational performance and resilience.

Chapter 6 offers a compelling case study on the role of AI in detecting and mitigating financial misconduct. By examining organizational culture and behavioral dynamics, the authors demonstrate how AI can function not only as a monitoring tool but as a mechanism for reinforcing ethical behavior through transparency and accountability.

In Chapter 7, the focus shifts to the evolving relationship between AI, cybersecurity, and the workforce. The chapter explores how organizations can align human capital strategies with technological advancement, emphasizing trust, continuous learning, and ethical safeguards in building resilient, AI-enabled workforces.

Chapter 8 situates AI within the broader context of public policy and governance. It challenges traditional models of authority, arguing that digital transformation requires more adaptive, transparent, and participatory governance frameworks. This chapter highlights the need to rethink how legitimacy and accountability are constructed in a digitally networked society.

Chapter 9 provides a sobering case study of AI governance failure in healthcare. Through a multi-framework analysis, the authors reveal how the absence of oversight and accountability can lead to discriminatory outcomes at scale. The chapter offers a practical roadmap for governance reform, emphasizing the integration of fairness metrics and cross-functional accountability into organizational strategy.

In Chapter 10, the focus turns to digital equity in education. The authors examine how institutions can leverage technology and agile strategies to bridge the divide between urban and rural learners. This chapter highlights the importance of leadership, collaboration, and inclusive design in ensuring equitable access to digital resources.

Chapter 11 explores the psychological dimensions of cybersecurity, emphasizing how human behavior and organizational culture contribute to cyber risk. The findings challenge purely technical approaches, advocating for strategies that address cognitive and behavioral vulnerabilities.

In Chapter 12, the application of machine learning in fraud detection is examined, demonstrating how advanced models can improve accuracy and transparency in financial systems. The inclusion of interpretability techniques highlights the importance of explainability in building trust in AI systems.

Finally, Chapter 13 addresses the growing cybersecurity threats facing healthcare organizations. By analyzing ransomware and phishing attacks, the chapter underscores the need for integrated security strategies that combine advanced technologies with workforce training and regulatory compliance.

Taken together, these chapters reflect the complexity and urgency of governing artificial intelligence in contemporary organizations. They demonstrate that ethical AI is not achieved through isolated technical fixes, but through the deliberate integration of governance, culture, policy, and design.

As editor, I see this volume as both a scholarly contribution and a call to action. It challenges leaders, researchers, and practitioners to move beyond reactive approaches and to proactively shape AI systems that align with human values and societal needs. The future of AI will depend not only on what we build, but on how—and why—we build it.

I extend my deepest gratitude to the contributors whose work has made this volume possible. Their insights represent a meaningful step toward advancing responsible AI. To the reader, I offer this book as a guide and an invitation: to think critically, act ethically, and lead responsibly in an age increasingly defined by intelligent systems.

Darrell Burrell
Marymount University, USA

Chapter 1
The Ethics of Predictive Analytics in Employment and Hiring Practice

Lord Dordunoo
http://orcid.org/0009-0007-7395-2677
Marymount University, USA

ABSTRACT

As predictive analytics becomes central to modern hiring, it raises serious ethical concerns around fairness, transparency, and accountability in decision-making. This chapter examines algorithmic hiring through a multidimensional lens, drawing on over 25 peer-reviewed studies across human resource management, artificial intelligence, and ethics. Using a qualitative case study methodology, it explores how historical data biases, opaque model design, and limited applicant recourse can reinforce systemic discrimination. Strategic frameworks, such as the Balanced Scorecard and Kotter's 8-Step Change Model, are used to assess ethical integration from both planning and implementation perspectives. The chapter identifies key ethical risks and offers actionable strategies, including fairness-aware machine learning (FAML), algorithmic audits, participatory design, and regulatory reform. Bridging technical systems, organizational behavior, and governance, the chapter provides a blueprint for embedding ethical resilience into predictive hiring and shaping a more equitable future of work.

INTRODUCTION

The rise of predictive analytics in employment and hiring practices represents one of the most consequential shifts in contemporary human resource management.

DOI: 10.4018/979-8-2600-1016-7.ch001

Leveraging advancements in artificial intelligence (AI), machine learning (ML), and big data, predictive analytics tools enable organizations to process vast volumes of candidate and employee data to forecast job performance, assess cultural fit, and identify potential retention risks (Binns et al., 2018; Gaebler et al., 2025; Geden & Andrews, 2021). These tools are often marketed as objective decision-making aids that reduce inefficiencies, enhance workforce planning, and minimize human bias. In practice, algorithm-driven systems are now widely used in resume screening, psychometric assessments, and video-based evaluations across industries such as technology, healthcare, and financial services (Raghavan et al., 2020). This trend signals a significant reconfiguration of talent sourced and evaluated, positioning computational systems as gatekeepers of employment access.

The evolution of predictive analytics in human resources dates to the 1980s when early talent assessments relied on manual scoring methods. By the 2000s, applicant tracking systems (ATS) introduced digital screening but lacked adaptive learning capabilities. The last decade has seen an explosion in AI-based hiring tools capable of learning from historical data to predict candidate outcomes, a shift fueled by advances in data science and intensified competition for top talent (Tambe et al., 2019). This rapid development has outpaced ethical and regulatory safeguards, raising urgent concerns about how these technologies influence access to economic opportunity.

While predictive analytics promises efficiency and scalability, it also introduces various ethical, legal, and social challenges. Key among these are algorithmic bias, data privacy, an approach that focuses on how people understand and shape technology, and limited accountability. Algorithms trained on historical employment data may inadvertently encode and perpetuate patterns of discrimination, especially when proxy variables such as educational background or location correlate with race, gender, or socioeconomic status (Cowgill et al., 2020). Moreover, using black-box systems models whose internal logic is opaque even to developers makes it difficult for applicants, HR professionals, or regulators to understand or contest automated decisions. Individuals affected by such systems are often unaware of their use or lack the means to appeal decisions, which raises critical concerns about consent, due process, and fair treatment in digital systems (Raji & Buolamwini, 2019).

Current scholarship emphasizes the need for ethical governance mechanisms that address these challenges through fairness-aware machine learning (FAML), algorithmic transparency, inclusive datasets, and stakeholder-centered design (Dordunoo, 2025; Radanliev, 2025; Veale & Binns 2017). This chapter builds on that foundation to provide a structured, interdisciplinary exploration of the ethical implications of predictive hiring systems. By bridging insights from human resources, AI ethics, and strategic change management, the chapter contributes to both scholarly discourse and organizational practice.

This chapter proceeds in four parts. First, it explores the ethical challenges of predictive hiring, including bias, privacy concerns, and lack of transparency. Second, it examines how predictive analytics impacts employees, leadership behavior, and organizational culture. Third, it applies the Balanced Scorecard framework to assess strategic alignment between ethical goals and performance metrics. Fourth, Kotter's 8-Step Change Model guides organizations in ethically integrating predictive tools into their recruitment practices. The chapter concludes with practical recommendations for ethical deployment and outlines a path forward for building trust and accountability in the future of work.

PROBLEM STATEMENT

Despite the promise of efficiency and objectivity, predictive analytics in hiring has exposed critical ethical and organizational vulnerabilities. At the center of these concerns is the risk of perpetuating historical patterns of discrimination encoded in training data. Predictive hiring models, especially those built using machine learning, often rely on datasets that reflect past employment decisions, many of which are tainted by systemic bias. When these models are not rigorously audited or designed with fairness constraints, they can replicate and amplify exclusionary outcomes, leading to the underrepresentation of women, people of color, older candidates, and other marginalized groups (Cowgill et al., 2020). These discriminatory patterns may not be explicit; instead, they manifest subtly through proxy variables like zip codes, college names, or gaps in employment, making their detection and correction even more challenging.

This issue is further compounded by the lack of transparency in how predictive tools function, often described as black-box models due to their opaque inner workings. These systems can produce difficult decisions to interpret, explain, or contest, creating a dangerous illusion of neutrality and objectivity. Affected individuals may not be aware that AI tools were used in their evaluation, let alone have access to mechanisms for appeal or redress (Raji & Buolamwini, 2019). Without accountability, organizations risk violating principles of fairness, due process, and equal opportunity under existing employment and civil rights laws.

To address this growing ethical dilemma, the primary goal of this chapter is to explore how predictive hiring systems can be developed and implemented in ways that are not only scalable and efficient but also equitable, transparent, and accountable to all stakeholders. Achieving this requires more than technical adjustments; it demands institutional reform, regulatory clarity, and interdisciplinary collaboration. Key questions include: Who designs and validates these algorithms? How are fairness and bias measured and mitigated in practice? What forms of redress exist for candidates negatively impacted by automated decisions? Moreover, how can organizations align their predictive analytics use with legal standards and public trust?

The problem is not just a matter of algorithmic bias; it is a broader failure to center human dignity, justice, and equity in the development and governance of digital hiring systems. This chapter argues that predictive analytics when used without ethical guardrails, can erode the foundational values of meritocracy, equal access, and inclusive innovation. Addressing this problem requires technological reform and a shift in organizational culture toward ethical accountability and democratic oversight.

SIGNIFICANCE STATEMENT

The ethical deployment of predictive analytics in employment and hiring is not merely a technical challenge. It is a critical issue with far-reaching implications for equity, civil rights, organizational legitimacy, and social trust in technology. Employment serves as a cornerstone of economic mobility and personal dignity. When access to job opportunities is mediated by opaque algorithms trained on biased historical data, the stakes extend well beyond recruitment. If left unchecked, predictive hiring tools risk reinforcing existing inequalities, undermining public confidence in the fairness of digital systems, and entrenching discrimination in automated decision-making (Raji & Buolamwini, 2019). These tools can shape life trajectories, making the ethics of their design and implementation a matter of societal urgency.

From a legal and regulatory standpoint, the use of algorithmic systems in hiring intersects with anti-discrimination laws such as Title VII of the Civil Rights Act in the United States and the General Data Protection Regulation (GDPR) in the European Union (Sartor, 2020; United States Equal Employment Opportunity Commission, n.d). Failure to proactively address algorithmic bias can expose organizations to legal liability, reputational damage, and public backlash. For example, Amazon discontinued its AI-powered resume screening tool after internal testing revealed that it systematically penalized resumes containing the word “women's” (Dastin, 2018). This incident highlighted how easily predictive models can encode and operationalize structural bias, even in organizations that position themselves as innovation leaders.

Ethically questionable hiring practices also have direct consequences within the workplace. Employees who perceive recruitment processes as biased or opaque are less likely to trust their employers, reducing morale, engagement, and retention (Kubiak et al., 2023). Conversely, organizations prioritizing ethical AI practices in HR tend to cultivate stronger employer brands, more inclusive workplace cultures, and greater alignment with social responsibility commitments. Importantly, research shows that trust in hiring systems influences job acceptance decisions, long-term commitment, and performance outcomes (Ajunwa, 2020).

Broadly, the misuse of predictive hiring tools threatens delegitimizing technological progress in human resource management. Public skepticism toward AI-driven systems is rising, particularly when such systems are perceived as violating human rights or exacerbating inequality. If industry leaders and policymakers fail to implement strong ethical safeguards, the resulting erosion of trust may stifle innovation and lead to reactionary regulation that limits the potential of AI. While U.S. regulations such as Title VII and the EU's GDPR have received significant attention, predictive hiring practices are expanding globally, including in developing economies. In India, for example, AI hiring systems are increasingly used in the tech and telecom sectors, which are often subject to limited regulation, thereby amplifying caste-based and socioeconomic disparities (Sambasivan et al., 2021). Similarly, in sub-Saharan Africa, multinational companies often use imported AI tools without localization, resulting in mismatches between system assumptions and local labor market dynamics. Addressing global inequity requires context-sensitive adaptations of ethical principles. Therefore, the need for ethical, transparent, and participatory approaches to predictive hiring is not only a moral imperative but a strategic necessity for sustainable organizational growth, regulatory resilience, and public confidence in the future of work.

METHODOLOGY

This chapter employs an exploratory qualitative case study methodology rooted in an approach that focuses on how people understand and shape technology to investigate the ethical implications of predictive analytics in hiring. This approach is well-suited for analyzing multifaceted, context-sensitive issues like algorithmic fairness and bias in organizational decision-making. Social constructivism emphasizes how meaning is co-created through social interaction, making it an ideal lens to explore how individuals and institutions interpret and respond to AI-based hiring systems. Rather than aiming for statistical generalization, this method allows for an in-depth exploration of values, perceptions, and decision-making processes related to the ethical deployment of predictive technologies in recruitment.

Historically, qualitative case studies have been widely used in information systems, organizational behavior, and science and technology studies to uncover emerging technologies' social, ethical, and political dimensions (Yin, 2017). In the domain of AI and employment, scholars have successfully applied case studies to analyze the adoption of algorithmic hiring platforms, the responses of HR practitioners and job seekers, and the institutional logics that shape AI governance (Binns et al., 2018; Raghavan et al., 2020). These studies highlight that predictive analytics do not operate in a vacuum but are interpreted, contested, and reshaped by diverse stakeholders, including software developers, HR managers, compliance officers, and candidates. Building on this tradition, the current chapter synthesizes insights from over 25 peer-reviewed scholarly articles published within the last seven years, including empirical research, theoretical analyses, industry reports, and policy papers.

This chapter's analysis unit is the predictive hiring ecosystem, including the technical models, organizational practices, regulatory frameworks, and cultural assumptions influencing ethical outcomes. The research draws from interdisciplinary literature in computer science, business ethics, human resources, and law to triangulate key themes and identify points of convergence across domains. Particular attention is paid to frameworks such as fairness-aware machine learning (FAML), explainable AI (XAI), algorithmic auditing, change management, and strategic planning models like Kotter's 8-Step Model and the Balanced Scorecard.

Using this methodological approach, the chapter can surface both technical and non-technical dimensions of ethical risk in predictive hiring systems. The case study format allows for flexible analysis of emerging ethical themes, stakeholder perspectives, and implementation challenges. Rather than providing a single-case narrative, the chapter functions as a combination of real-world examples from different studies, drawing from multiple documented instances, such as the Amazon AI hiring controversy, and synthesizing best practices from scholarly and practitioner literature. This design is intentionally aligned with the chapter's guiding research questions: How can predictive analytics be deployed in hiring ethically, equitably, and transparently? What strategies exist for mitigating algorithmic bias and ensuring accountability? How can organizational leaders integrate ethical principles into the design, adoption, and governance of predictive hiring tools? Through this lens, the chapter advances a human-centered, evidence-informed framework for ethical innovation in the future of work.

LITERATURE REVIEW

Overview

The adoption of predictive analytics in hiring has surged over the past decade, prompting extensive interdisciplinary inquiry into its benefits, limitations, and ethical ramifications. Scholars in computer science, law, organizational ethics, and human resource management have examined how predictive tools shape recruitment decisions, impact candidate experience, and reinforce or mitigate systemic inequities (Binns et al., 2018; Raji et al., 2020). While proponents highlight gains in efficiency, consistency, and scalability, critics point to rising concerns about lack of transparency in how AI systems make decisions, fairness, and data privacy. This literature review synthesizes findings from peer-reviewed studies published mostly within the last seven years. It is organized around four key themes: (1) ethical challenges of predictive hiring tools, (2) impacts on employees and organizational culture, (3) integration with strategic planning using the Balanced Scorecard, and (4) the role of change management frameworks such as Kotter's 8-Step model.

Ethical Challenges of Predictive Hiring Tools

A central theme in the literature is the potential for predictive analytics to replicate and even amplify biases embedded in historical hiring data. Studies show that machine learning models trained on prior decisions often reflect existing disparities related to race, gender, and socioeconomic status (Cowgill et al., 2020). These biases can be encoded through seemingly neutral variables such as zip codes or educational institutions that serve as proxies for protected characteristics. O'Neil (2016) describes this as a form of algorithmic redlining, where predictive tools create exclusionary outcomes while appearing objective.

The problem is further complicated by the opacity of many AI systems, commonly called black-box algorithms. These systems often lack explainability, making it difficult for users to understand decisions or detect errors and biases (Doshi-Velez & Kim, 2017). The absence of transparency undermines accountability and prevents applicants from contesting potentially unfair outcomes (Barocas et al., 2023). Scholars advocate for developing and adopting explainable AI (XAI) frameworks to ensure that predictions are interpretable and subject to oversight.

Privacy concerns also surface prominently in the literature. Predictive hiring systems may scrape data from social media, browsing history, or other sources not directly provided by candidates, raising ethical questions about consent and surveillance (Ajunwa, 2020. Regulatory responses such as the EU's GDPR and California's CCPA have established baseline protections, but enforcement and implementation remain uneven (Sartor, 2020; Wachter et al., 2017). Collectively, these concerns underscore the need for ethical governance in predictive analytics to safeguard fairness, autonomy, and legal compliance.

Impacts on Employees, Leadership, and Organizational Culture

Beyond technical concerns, predictive analytics also affects workplace dynamics, employee trust, and organizational legitimacy. For job candidates, algorithmic hiring can feel impersonal and unfair, particularly when they are not informed of its use or given meaningful feedback about their evaluation outcomes (Raji & Buolamwini,

2019). This lack of transparency can undermine trust in the hiring process and reduce candidate engagement. Ajunwa (2020) notes that when candidates feel reduced to a series of data points, it can result in emotional disengagement, increased attrition post-hire, and reputational harm to the organization. As job seekers increasingly share their experiences on public platforms, perceptions of unfairness may also harm the employer brand and deter high-quality applicants.

For organizational leaders, using AI in hiring introduces operational efficiencies and complex ethical trade-offs. While algorithmic tools can help streamline decision-making, overreliance on these systems may lead to automation bias, in which managers defer unquestioningly to algorithmic outputs (Glikson & Woolley, 2020). This deference can diminish critical thinking and weaken accountability, particularly when AI-generated outcomes conflict with core values or legal obligations. Raisch and Krakowski (2021) argue that excessive reliance on algorithms can erode managerial judgment and make it more challenging to detect discriminatory practices or rectify unjust decisions. Therefore, Leadership teams must balance AI's benefits with a commitment to ongoing oversight and human-in-the-loop governance.

At the cultural level, predictive hiring can significantly influence how employees perceive fairness, inclusion, and organizational integrity. Research by Kubiak et al., 2023 found that employees are more likely to question leadership intentions and values when algorithmic tools are deployed without adequate ethical guidelines or transparency. This perceived disconnect can result in lower morale, decreased psychological safety, and higher turnover among employees who value justice and inclusivity. Organizations that integrate diverse stakeholder voices into designing and rolling predictive systems, such as involving DEI officers, ERG leaders, or frontline employees, tend to foster stronger trust and internal legitimacy (Chamorro-Premuzic et al., 2019). These practices help transform predictive analytics from a compliance exercise into an ethically grounded strategy aligned with organizational culture.

Research has shown that marginalized communities, particularly racial minorities, individuals with disabilities, and formerly incarcerated individuals, face heightened risks when subjected to opaque AI hiring systems (Mullin et al., 2021; Raji et al., 2020; Turner et al., 2019). These groups often lack digital visibility or present nontraditional profiles that AI systems are not trained to interpret in an equitable manner. Including their voices in design, testing, and audit processes is critical to understanding unintended consequences and ensuring inclusive hiring practices. Intersectional analysis should inform algorithmic fairness benchmarks to avoid further entrenching historical disadvantages.

Strategic Planning: The Balanced Scorecard Approach

The Balanced Scorecard (BSC), developed by Kaplan and Norton (1992), offers a strategic framework for aligning organizational goals with performance metrics across four dimensions: financial performance, internal processes, learning and growth, and customer (or employee) satisfaction. Integrating ethical and operational goals, the BSC enables organizations to evaluate the broader impact of their decisions beyond immediate cost savings or productivity gains. Scholars suggest that applying BSC to implementing AI in hiring helps organizations balance operational efficiency with transparency, fairness, and accountability (Pierce, 2022; Tambe et al., 2019). This holistic approach allows leaders to assess the risks and rewards of adopting predictive analytics in workforce management.

Financially, predictive hiring tools may reduce recruitment costs, shorten time-to-hire, and enhance productivity by forecasting performance and employee retention more accurately than traditional methods. Automation can also help companies avoid costly hiring mistakes by identifying patterns in candidate success metrics. However, Binns et al. (2018) caution that these benefits can be negated by reputational damage, legal challenges, or regulatory sanctions when algorithmic tools produce biased or opaque outcomes. For this reason, organizations must incorporate ethical considerations such as fairness audits and bias mitigation strategies into their cost-benefit analyses and return-on-investment calculations.

From the perspective of internal processes, predictive analytics can improve consistency in candidate evaluation by reducing human subjectivity in early-stage screening. These systems can standardize assessments and eliminate some forms of overt bias. However, Raghavan et al. (2020) emphasize the importance of maintaining human-in-the-loop oversight to monitor for unintended consequences and contextual nuances that algorithms may miss. A hybrid approach that combines algorithmic efficiency with human judgment ensures that predictive tools remain adaptable, ethically guided, and aligned with broader organizational values.

The learning and growth dimension of the BSC underscores the need to build internal capacity for ethical AI usage through ongoing education and professional development. Training programs for HR staff, data scientists, and decision-makers should include algorithmic accountability, fairness-aware model design, and regulatory compliance (Chamorro-Premuzic et al., 2019). A well-informed workforce is better positioned to identify risks, correct issues early, and contribute to the responsible evolution of hiring technologies. Investing in ethical literacy protects the organization and cultivates a proactive and reflective culture that can sustain long-term innovation.

Finally, employee satisfaction dimension highlights the importance of trust, transparency, and communication in predictive hiring. Candidates and employees need to understand how AI tools are used, what data is collected, and how decisions are made. Providing clear, accessible explanations and offering avenues for appeal or feedback can significantly improve perceptions of procedural fairness (Ajunwa, 2020; Pierce, 2022). These practices strengthen the employer brand and contribute to greater engagement, lower attrition, and a more inclusive recruitment ecosystem.

Figure 1. The Balanced Scorecard Framework for Ethical Predictive Hiring

This figure illustrates how the Balanced Scorecard aligns ethical hiring goals across four dimensions: financial performance, employee satisfaction (instead of customer), learning and growth, and internal business processes, emphasizing fairness, transparency, and accountability.

Change Management: Kotter's 8-Step model

Successfully integrating predictive analytics into hiring processes requires more than technological investment; it necessitates thoughtful, structured organizational change. Kotter's 8-Step Change Model provides a widely respected framework for managing such transformation in an ethical and sustainable manner (Kotter, 1996). This model emphasizes the importance of building urgency, forming inclusive coalitions, communicating a clear vision, and embedding change into the organization's culture. Applying Kotter's framework to predictive hiring ensures that implementation reflects technical readiness, ethical responsibility, and organizational alignment.

The first two steps, creating a sense of urgency and building a guiding coalition, are foundational for change to take root. Ethical deployment of predictive hiring tools must be framed as a technological advancement and a response to pressing challenges, such as biased decision-making, compliance risks, and evolving societal expectations. Scholars have found that organizations that position ethics and equity as urgent concerns rather than afterthoughts are more successful in fostering internal buy-in (Raji et al., 2020). Building a diverse guiding coalition that includes HR professionals, legal advisors, DEI leaders, and technical experts ensures that multiple perspectives inform the implementation process and guard against one-dimensional decision-making (Binns et al., 2018).

The next steps in developing a clear vision and communicating it broadly are critical for setting expectations and reinforcing accountability. Leaders must clearly articulate how predictive analytics will improve fairness, efficiency, and candidate experience. This vision should be communicated through workshops, guidelines, and internal forums that demystify the technology and clarify the ethical guardrails (Chamorro-Premuzic et al., 2019). Ajunwa (2020) stresses that transparency and accessibility in communication foster organizational trust and reduce resistance, especially among those concerned about being displaced or unfairly evaluated by algorithms.

Steps five and six, empowering broad-based action and generating short-term wins, are essential for building momentum and demonstrating tangible benefits. Organizations should remove barriers that prevent employees from raising concerns, sharing feedback, or participating in developing and reviewing predictive tools. Implementing pilot programs with measurable outcomes, such as improved candidate diversity or reduced biased screening errors, can be proof points for the broader rollout (Tambe et al., 2019). Recognizing and celebrating these early successes builds credibility and fosters a sense of shared accomplishment across departments.

Finally, Kotter's last two steps, consolidating gains and anchoring new cultural approaches, emphasize the importance of sustained commitment to ethical transformation. Ethical AI governance must be embedded into hiring policies, performance reviews, vendor contracts, and compliance audits to ensure long-term integrity (Wachter et al., 2017). Organizations that institutionalize algorithmic impact assessments, ethics committees, and employee training programs are better positioned to respond to new risks and evolving standards. Anchoring these practices in the culture solidifies change and signals to internal and external stakeholders that the organization is committed to justice, accountability, and continuous improvement in AI.

Figure 2. Kotter's 8-Step Model for Ethical Change Management in Predictive Hiring

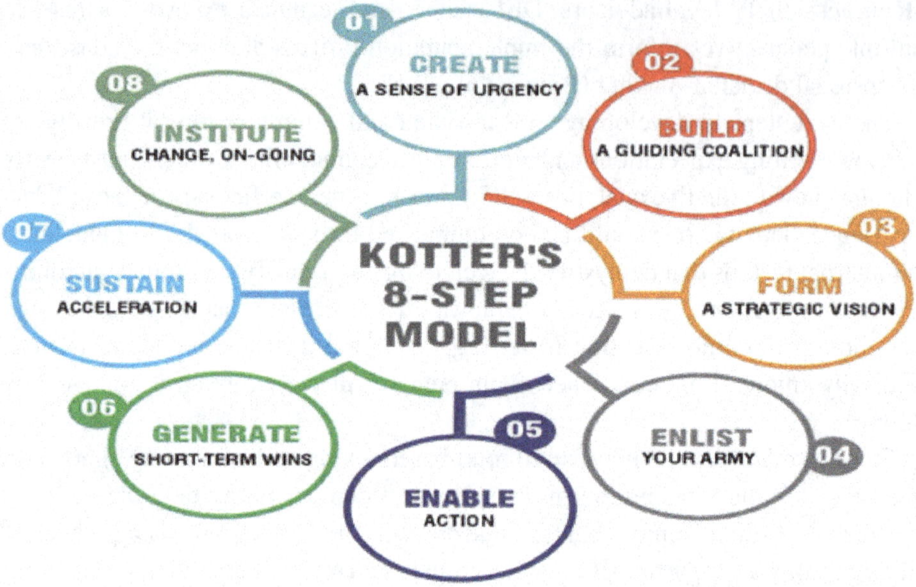

This figure depicts the sequential steps of Kotter's model, from establishing urgency to anchoring new approaches, highlighting how each step supports the ethical integration of AI tools in organizational hiring practices.

Recommendations

To ethically integrate predictive analytics into employment practices, organizations must take a multi-pronged approach that includes technical safeguards, policy development, stakeholder engagement, and continuous education. First, adopting fairness-aware machine learning (FAML) techniques is essential for reducing algorithmic bias. These techniques can include reweighting datasets, adjusting optimization functions, and applying post-processing corrections to improve equity in model outcomes (Dwork et al., 2011; Raji et al., 2020). Research by Caton and Haas (2020) demonstrates that properly implemented FAML can significantly reduce disparate impact without significant trade-offs in model performance. Embedding fairness constraints into the model design process, organizations can ensure that ethical considerations are not afterthoughts but core elements of their predictive systems.

Second, organizations should establish robust algorithmic auditing and accountability frameworks to detect and correct bias before harm occurs. These audits should assess performance across protected demographic groups and evaluate input data quality and outcome fairness (Barocas et al., 2023). Independent third-party evaluations should complement internal audits to enhance credibility and transparency. Wachter et al. (2017) emphasize that meaningful auditing must be tied to enforceable consequences and real corrective actions, such as retraining models or adjusting hiring criteria. Regular audits, supported by publicly accessible reports or impact assessments, also build trust with external stakeholders, including regulators and civil society organizations.

Third, organizations must prioritize transparency and candidate rights, particularly disclosure and contestability. Applicants should be explicitly informed when AI tools are used in the evaluation process and be given access to understandable explanations of how decisions are made (Ajunwa, 2020). This is where explainable AI (XAI) becomes crucial, enabling hiring systems to offer human-interpretable justifications for automated decisions (Doshi-Velez & Kim, 2017). Furthermore, a formal grievance process should be established to allow candidates to appeal or request reconsideration of algorithmically determined outcomes. These steps are essential for ethical compliance and aligning with data protection regulations like the GDPR and CCPA, which mandate transparency and the right to meaningful review (Sartor, 2020).

To support implementation, Table 1 summarizes key ethical "do's and don'ts" for HR professionals deploying predictive analytics in hiring. This guide consolidates best practices discussed in the chapter and serves as a quick reference for aligning AI-enabled hiring processes with ethical and legal expectations.

Table 1. Ethical Do's and Don'ts for Predictive Hiring in HR Practice

Disclose AI use in hiring to all candidates	**Don't deploy black-box models without explainability tools**
Conduct regular fairness audits across demographic groups	Don't ignore biases embedded in training data
Involve diverse stakeholders in AI tool design	Don't centralize decision-making to tech vendors without HR oversight
Train HR staff on ethical AI use and regulatory compliance	Don't rely solely on performance metrics without ethical review
Provide contestability and appeal mechanisms	Don't collect candidate data from non-consensual sources like social media

Fourth, organizations should invest in cross-functional ethics training and capacity-building programs for all stakeholders involved in the hiring process. HR professionals, data scientists, legal teams, and executive leaders should be trained on AI ethics, bias mitigation techniques, and regulatory compliance requirements (Chamorro-Premuzic et al., 2019). Training should be ongoing rather than one-off, integrated into leadership development and professional certification programs. Research has shown that ethical literacy improves employees' ability to identify issues early and promotes a shared vocabulary for discussing complex ethical dilemmas

(Raji & Buolamwini, 2019). In addition, organizations may benefit from appointing dedicated ethics officers or forming algorithmic accountability boards to provide guidance and oversight.

Fifth, organizations must adopt inclusive, participatory design approaches to ensure that predictive tools reflect diverse perspectives and social contexts. Involving affected stakeholders, such as employee resource groups (ERGs), advocacy networks, and candidates in developing and testing AI systems can uncover blind spots and improve system equity (Chang & Ke, 2023). Participatory approaches also increase adoption rates by creating a sense of ownership and legitimacy among end users. Binns et al. (2018) argue that stakeholder involvement leads to more context-aware design choices and better alignment with user needs. Feedback loops should be embedded throughout the system life cycle for continuous iteration and improvement based on real-world outcomes and user experience.

Organizations must also consult directly with marginalized groups through focus groups, advocacy partnerships, or employee resource groups (ERGs) to ensure that system design and ethical reviews incorporate their lived experiences. These individuals often possess valuable insights that can help identify blind spots and unintended consequences in algorithmic hiring systems. Engaging with these communities in a sustained and respectful manner moves beyond tokenistic gestures toward meaningful inclusion. Such participatory design practices not only promote equity but also enhance system legitimacy, trust, and long-term effectiveness.

Finally, policy and regulatory frameworks must evolve in step with technological developments. Industry leaders should proactively engage with policymakers to shape emerging standards, contribute to ethical AI benchmarks, and advocate for responsible innovation (Barocas & Selbst, 2016). Organizations can also participate in voluntary self-regulatory efforts, such as developing internal ethics charters, signing algorithmic impact pledges, or seeking certification from third-party bodies. As Wachter et al. (2017) point out, legal compliance is necessary but insufficient; ethical leadership involves going beyond minimum standards to safeguard fairness and dignity proactively. A consistent regulatory environment supported by clear guidelines, enforcement mechanisms, and inter-organizational cooperation will help establish norms that protect individuals while supporting innovation.

Ethical implementation must also account for transnational deployment, especially as multinational organizations increasingly adopt predictive hiring tools. Companies operating across borders should perform local context assessments before deploying these technologies, ensuring alignment with regional labor laws, cultural norms, and socio-political histories. Without such assessments, there is a risk of importing systems that unintentionally reinforce inequality or violate local ethical standards. The development of globally inclusive ethical AI standards, such as those outlined in the UNESCO AI Ethics Framework, can provide essential guidance for achieving cross-jurisdictional compliance, fairness, and culturally responsive innovation.

CONCLUSION

Predictive analytics in employment and hiring practices represents a powerful innovation and a profound ethical challenge. As organizations increasingly adopt algorithmic tools to assess candidate fit, forecast performance, and optimize workforce planning, ensuring these systems are implemented with fairness, transparency, and accountability is imperative. While predictive analytics can deliver measurable efficiencies and consistency, it can also entrench historical inequities, diminish candidate autonomy, and erode trust if deployed without appropriate safeguards. This chapter has examined the complex interplay between technological advancement and ethical responsibility, offering a framework for navigating this tension through scholarly insight and practical guidance.

Drawing on interdisciplinary literature and structured around four central themes, the chapter addressed the ethical risks of algorithmic bias and opacity, the organizational and cultural impact of AI-driven hiring, the strategic utility of the Balanced Scorecard, and the role of Kotter's 8-Step model in guiding ethical change. These perspectives demonstrate that predictive hiring is not solely a technical issue but a multidimensional challenge involving policy, culture, and human judgment. Each theme reinforces the broader argument that the ethical integration of AI tools must be guided by deliberate planning, continuous evaluation, and inclusive stakeholder engagement.

To support the responsible and equitable use of predictive analytics in hiring, the following actionable recommendations are offered:

1. Implement Fairness-Aware Machine Learning (FAML): Integrate fairness constraints into algorithmic design to minimize disparate impact and improve equitable outcomes (Dwork et al., 2011).
2. Conduct Regular Algorithmic Audits: Establish internal and third-party auditing protocols to evaluate model performance, bias, and compliance across demographic groups, with clearly outlined corrective action procedures (Wachter et al., 2017).
3. Ensure Transparency and Explainability: Adopt explainable AI (XAI) techniques that provide interpretable rationales for decisions, enabling HR staff and candidates to understand the logic behind outcomes (Doshi-Velez & Kim, 2017).

4. Disclose AI Use to Candidates: Inform applicants when AI tools are used in the hiring process and allow them to receive explanations or contest decisions (Ajunwa, 2020).
5. Develop Contestability Mechanisms: Create formal grievance and appeal procedures for applicants adversely affected by predictive systems, ensuring access to human review and corrective pathways.
6. Invest in Cross-Functional Ethics Training: Educate HR personnel, data scientists, legal teams, and leadership on AI ethics, algorithmic bias, and regulatory compliance as part of ongoing capacity-building (Chamorro-Premuzic et al., 2019).
7. Establish Ethics Committees or Accountability Boards: Form dedicated groups within the organization to provide oversight, approve AI systems, and review ethical risks before implementation.
8. Engage Stakeholders in Participatory Design: Involve diverse voices, including job seekers, DEI leaders, and advocacy groups, in the co-design and testing of predictive tools to ensure inclusivity and social relevance (Mullin et al., 2021).
9. Align AI Use with Strategic Objectives: Use frameworks like the Balanced Scorecard to balance efficiency goals with ethical performance metrics and integrate fairness indicators into organizational KPIs (Kaplan & Norton, 1992; Kaplan & Norton, 1996; Pierce, 2022).
10. Advocate for and Comply with Evolving Regulation: Monitor and influence policy developments at local, national, and international levels while proactively adhering to data protection and anti-discrimination laws (Barocas & Selbst, 2016).

These ten recommendations provide a strategic, ethical, and operational blueprint for embedding accountability into predictive hiring systems. They reflect best practices from scholarly and industry literature and a commitment to centering human dignity and social justice in the digital transformation of work. In conclusion, the future of work depends not only on the sophistication of our technologies but also on the values that guide their use. Predictive analytics can widen or close the opportunity gap depending on how they are designed, governed, and evaluated. Employers, technologists, and policymakers must collaborate to ensure that these tools expand access, promote justice, and uphold the dignity of every applicant. Embedding ethical foresight into the DNA of predictive hiring systems, organizations can lead not just in innovation but in fairness, accountability, and long-term societal value.

REFERENCES

Ajunwa, I. (2020). The paradox of automation as anti-bias intervention. *Cardozo Law Review*, *41*(4), 1671–1742. https://cardozolawreview.com

Barocas, S., Hardt, M., & Narayanan, A. (2023). *Fairness and machine learning: Limitations and opportunities*. MIT Press.

Barocas, S., & Selbst, A. D. (2016). Big data's disparate impact. *SSRN*, *104*(3), 671–732. DOI: 10.2139/ssrn.2477899

Binns, R., Veale, M., Van Kleek, M., Lyngs, U., Zhao, J., & Shadbolt, N. (2018). 'It's reducing a human being to a percentage': Perceptions of justice in algorithmic hiring. *Proceedings of the 2018 CHI Conference on Human Factors in Computing Systems*, 1–14. https://doi.org/DOI: 10.1145/3173574.3173951

Caton, S., & Haas, C. (2020). Fairness in machine learning: A survey. https://arxiv .org/abs/2010.04053

Chamorro-Premuzic, T., Polli, F., & Dattner, B. (2019). Building ethical AI for talent management. *Harvard Business Review*.

Chang, Y.-L., & Ke, J. (2023). Socially Responsible Artificial Intelligence Empowered People Analytics: A Novel Framework Towards Sustainability. *Human Resource Development Review*, *23*(1), 88–120. DOI: 10.1177/15344843231200930

Cowgill, B., Dell'Acqua, F., Deng, S., Hsu, D., Verma, N., & Chaintreau, A. (2020). *Biased programmers? Or biased data? A field experiment in operationalizing AI ethics*. DOI: /arXiv.2012.02394DOI: 10.1145/3391403.3399545

Dastin, J. (2018). *Amazon scrapped 'AI' recruiting tool that showed bias against women*. Reuters. https://www.reuters.com/article/us-amazon-com-jobs-automation -insight-idUSKCN1MK08G

Dordunoo, L. (2025). Integrating organizational and social network theories to mitigate racial bias in facial recognition technology. In Burrell, D. (Ed.), *Organizational Readiness and Research: Security, Management, and Decision Making* (pp. 283–348). IGI Global Scientific Publishing., DOI: 10.4018/979-8-3693-8562-3.ch009

Doshi-Velez, F., & Kim, B. (2017). *Towards a rigorous science of interpretable machine learning. arXiv preprint*. https://arxiv.org/abs/1702.08608

Dwork, C., Hardt, M., Pitassi, T., Reingold, O., & Zemel, R. (2011). *Fairness through awareness*. https://doi.org/DOI: 10.1145/2090236.2090255

Gaebler, J. D., Goel, S., Huq, A., & Tambe, P. (2025). Auditing large language models for race & gender disparities: Implications for artificial intelligence-based hiring. *Behavioral Science & Policy, 10*(2), 46–55. DOI: 10.1177/23794607251320229

Geden, M., & Andrews, J. (2021). Fair and interpretable algorithmic hiring using evolutionary many-objective optimization. *The Thirty-Fifth AAAI Conference on Artificial Intelligence (AAAI-21)* 14795-14803. DOI: 10.1609/aaai.v35i17.17737

Glikson, E., & Woolley, A. W. (2020). Human trust in artificial intelligence: Review of empirical research. *The Academy of Management Annals, 14*(2), 627–660. DOI: 10.5465/annals.2018.0057

Kaplan, R. S., & Norton, D. P. (1992). The balanced scorecard: Measures that drive performance. *Harvard Business Review*. PMID: 10119714

Kaplan, R. S., & Norton, D. P. (1996). *The balanced scorecard: Translating strategy into action*. Harvard Business School Press.

Kotter, J. P. (1996). *Leading change*. Harvard Business School Press.

Kubiak, E., Efremova, M. I., Baron, S., & Frasca, K. J. (2023). Gender equity in hiring: Examining the effectiveness of a personality-based algorithm. *Frontiers in Psychology, 14*, 1219865. DOI: 10.3389/fpsyg.2023.1219865 PMID: 37655204

Mullin, A. E., Coe, I. R., Gooden, E. A., Tunde-Byass, M., & Wiley, R. E. (2021). Inclusion, diversity, equity, and accessibility: From organizational responsibility to leadership competency. *Healthcare Management Forum, 34*(6), 311–315. DOI: 10.1177/08404704211038232 PMID: 34535064

O'Neil, C. (2016). *Weapons of math destruction: How big data increases inequality and threatens democracy*. Crown Publishing Group.

Pierce, E. (2022). A Balanced Scorecard for Maximizing Data Performance. *Frontiers in Big Data, 5*, 821103. DOI: 10.3389/fdata.2022.821103 PMID: 35434610

Radanliev, P. (2025). AI ethics: Integrating transparency, fairness, and privacy in AI development. *Applied Artificial Intelligence, 39*(1), 2463722. Advance online publication. DOI: 10.1080/08839514.2025.2463722

Raghavan, M., Barocas, S., Kleinberg, J., & Levy, K. (2020). Mitigating bias in algorithmic hiring: Evaluating claims and practices. *Proceedings of the 2020 Conference on Fairness, Accountability, and Transparency*, 469–481. https://doi.org/ DOI: 10.1145/3351095.3372828

Raisch, S., & Krakowski, S. (2021). Artificial intelligence and management: The automation augmentation paradox. *Academy of Management Review*, *46*(1), 192–210. DOI: 10.5465/amr.2018.0072

Raji, I. D., & Buolamwini, J. (2019). Actionable auditing: Investigating the impact of publicly naming biased performance results of commercial AI products. *Proceedings of the 2019 AAAI/ACM Conference on AI, Ethics, and Society*, 429–435. https://doi.org/DOI: 10.1145/3306618.3314244

Raji, I. D., Gebru, T., Mitchell, M., Boulamwini, J., Lee, J., & Denton, E. (2020). *Saving face: Investigating the ethical concerns of facial recognition auditing*. Proceedings of the 2020 AAAI/ACM Conference on AI, Ethics, and Society. DOI:DOI: 10.1145/3375627.3375820

Sambasivan, N., Kapania, S., Highfill, H., Akrong, D., Paritosh, P., & Aroyo, L. (2021). Everyone wants to do the model work, not the data work: Data cascades in high-stakes AI. *Proceedings of the 2021 CHI Conference on Human Factors in Computing Systems*, 1–15. https://doi.org/DOI: 10.1145/3411764.3445518

Sartor, G. 2020. *The impact of the general data protection regulation (GDPR) on artificial intelligence*. European Parliament. European Parliamentary Research Service.

Tambe, P., Cappelli, P., & Yakubovich, V. (2019). Artificial intelligence in human resources management: Challenges and a path forward. *California Management Review*, *61*(4), 15–42. DOI: 10.1177/0008125619867910

Turner Lee, N., Resnick, P., & Barton, G. (2019). *Algorithmic bias detection and mitigation: Best practices and policies to reduce consumer harms*. Brooking Institute. https://www.brookings.edu/articles/algorithmic-bias-detection-and-mitigation-best-practices-and-policies-to-reduce-consumer-harms/

U.S. Equal Employment Opportunity Commission. (n.d.). *Title VII of the Civil Rights Act of 1964*. Retrieved from https://www.eeoc.gov/statutes/title-vii-civil-rights-act-1964

Veale, M., & Binns, R. (2017). Fairer machine learning in the real world: Mitigating discrimination without collecting sensitive data. *Big Data & Society*, *4*(2), 1–17. DOI: 10.1177/2053951717743530

Wachter, S., Mittelstadt, B., & Floridi, L. (2017). Transparent, explainable, and accountable AI for robotics. *Science Robotics*, *2*(6), eaan6080. Advance online publication. DOI: 10.1126/scirobotics.aan6080 PMID: 33157874

Yin, R. K. (2017). *Case study research and applications: Design and methods* (6th ed.). Sage Publications.

Chapter 2

Ethical Frameworks for the Responsible Deployment of Artificial Intelligence (AI)

Amalisha Sabie Aridi
http://orcid.org/0000-0002-7869-5530
Capitol Technology University, USA

ABSTRACT

This perspective style article proposes a comprehensive ethical framework for the responsible deployment of artificial intelligence (AI) in healthcare, grounded in a synthesis of philosophical ethics and practical governance principles. As AI technologies, particularly generative systems, become integral to healthcare operations, their implementation raises complex moral challenges related to bias, equity, transparency, and trust. The paper introduces Ethical AI Deployment Framework, which integrates deontology, utilitarianism, virtue ethics, the ethics of care, practical wisdom, moral particularism, social contract theory, stakeholder theory, and corporate social responsibility. The framework emphasizes inclusive design, lifecycle-oriented impact assessments, ethical leadership training, and continuous feedback mechanisms to ensure that AI-driven innovations serve all patient populations equitably and humanely. This multidisciplinary approach advances a vision of healthcare AI that is not only technologically effective but also morally legitimate and socially just.

DOI: 10.4018/979-8-2600-1016-7.ch002

INTRODUCTION

Artificial intelligence (AI) and other healthcare technologies continue to transform industries across the global economy, from healthcare to finance to public administration. As AI tools, particularly generative AI systems, are rapidly adopted for their efficiency, scalability, and analytical power, the need for ethical oversight becomes increasingly critical (Haley & Burrell, 2025). The allure of automation and predictive insight has led many organizations to implement AI technologies into essential business functions (Burrell, 2023). However, without principled leadership, these innovations risk reinforcing structural inequalities, producing misleading outputs, and eroding public trust (Haley & Burrell, 2025). In this context, ethical project management leadership plays a pivotal role in guiding the responsible development, deployment, and application of AI tools.

The expansion of telehealth exemplifies the dual nature of technological innovation in healthcare, its capacity to both democratize access and unintentionally exacerbate inequity (Burrell, 2023). On one hand, digital health platforms offer firms new markets, scalability, and operational efficiency by decentralizing care delivery. As Sharma, Saha, and Goldsack (2024) suggest, telehealth has the potential to enhance patient engagement and reduce infrastructure costs. However, the business case for telehealth remains complicated by disparities in digital access and literacy. Companies offering virtual care solutions face challenges penetrating markets where broadband coverage is sparse or where cultural and linguistic mismatches hinder adoption. For example, a telehealth startup expanding into rural Latinx communities in the U.S. Southwest may encounter low uptake rates unless they localize their interfaces and support services. From a business strategy perspective, failure to align product design with user realities can lead to low ROI, customer attrition, and regulatory scrutiny. Therefore, firms must develop context-sensitive deployment strategies that include investment in user education, mobile-optimized interfaces, and partnerships with local health organizations to ensure equitable and profitable scaling (Burrell, 2023).

A critical and often underappreciated business challenge in healthcare IT implementation lies in the racial and demographic biases embedded in diagnostic technologies, issues that directly affect project viability, organizational credibility, and regulatory compliance. Pulse oximeters and infrared thermometers, which are standard tools in clinical environments, have been found to produce inconsistent results across racial groups. These failures, such as the under-detection of fevers in Black patients by forehead thermometers (Hartnett, 2022), reflect not only technological deficiencies but systemic blind spots in the design and validation phases of product development. For IT project and organizational consultants, these discrepancies present significant risks during implementation phases, particularly in enterprise-scale rollouts for hospital systems or integrated care networks. A flawed technology solution, once deployed, can compromise clinical workflows, increase patient safety incidents, and erode trust among both clinicians and patients, requiring expensive remediation and damaging vendor-client relationships. Consultants must therefore advocate for inclusive design audits, demographic data validation, and cross-functional testing frameworks as standard components of digital health solution deployment strategies (Burrell, 2023).

The expansion of telehealth and remote monitoring platforms introduces another set of complex business dynamics. While these technologies offer attractive value propositions, such as operational scalability, reduced infrastructure costs, and broader patient reach, their successful adoption depends heavily on equitable infrastructure and user-centric design (Burrell, 2023). From a consultancy perspective, advising healthcare organizations on telehealth initiatives demands not only technical implementation skills but also a strategic understanding of digital equity barriers. Markets with poor broadband penetration, low digital literacy, or fragmented device ecosystems can significantly hinder user adoption and undermine business outcomes. For example, a health system investing in remote monitoring for chronic disease management in underserved regions may face low utilization rates if patients lack access to stable internet or compatible devices. Organizational development consultants must anticipate such barriers in the planning phase and integrate mitigative strategies, such as mobile-first design, offline functionality, or community-based digital education initiatives, into the technology adoption roadmap (Haley & Burrell, 2025). Ignoring these realities leads to inflated implementation costs, prolonged timelines, and unmet performance metrics.

Furthermore, the reliance on AI-powered platforms in healthcare business processes, ranging from automated triage systems to predictive analytics, presents both strategic opportunities and ethical hazards. While AI tools can streamline operations, reduce administrative burdens, and enhance decision-making precision, they also risk perpetuating biases that erode stakeholder confidence and compliance alignment (Haley & Burrell, 2025). Unsupervised machine learning models, if trained on non-representative datasets, may yield skewed outputs that disadvantage certain populations or generate inaccurate clinical risk scores. For consultants driving IT transformation efforts, this requires more than just technical integration; it necessitates governance frameworks that include continuous model auditing, explainability protocols, and stakeholder transparency. Consider the example of a large healthcare network deploying an AI-based patient prioritization system. Without bias mitigation strategies in place, the algorithm could inadvertently deprioritize high-need patients, prompting legal action or reputational damage (Haley & Burrell, 2025). Strategic consultants must therefore embed ethical AI oversight mechanisms into their delivery models and educate client leadership on the long-term business implications of algorithmic bias.

The implementation of advanced healthcare technologies presents a complex interplay of innovation potential and systemic risk. For IT project and organizational development consultants, success depends not merely on the technical execution of these systems, but on a deep and anticipatory understanding of the social, ethical, and operational realities that shape technology adoption. Firms that recognize and proactively address these multidimensional challenges will not only enhance their client outcomes but position themselves as trusted partners in a rapidly evolving digital healthcare ecosystem (Burrell, 2023).

One of the most pressing and complex risks in contemporary healthcare and enterprise technology implementation is the persistence of algorithmic bias in artificial intelligence (AI) systems. These concerns predate generative AI, as evidenced by the findings of the Gender Shades project, in which Buolamwini (2017) demonstrated that commercial gender classification systems performed significantly better on lighter-skinned male faces than on darker-skinned female faces. For IT project managers and healthcare administrators, these disparities are not merely technical anomalies, they represent strategic liabilities. A healthcare organization that deploys such flawed systems could inadvertently embed discrimination into diagnostic tools, patient-facing applications, or administrative workflows. Similarly, strategic planners must assess the long-term reputational and regulatory risks of adopting AI systems that have not been adequately tested for demographic accuracy. Embedding equity-focused audits into procurement and system validation processes is not optional; it is essential to ethical and sustainable technology governance (Haley & Burrell, 2025).

The development phase of AI systems is where many of the most critical decisions about data sourcing, model architecture, and algorithmic objectives are made. These decisions, though often technical, are fundamentally ethical. For instance, the Gender Shades project (Buolamwini, 2017) exposed significant racial and gender disparities in commercial facial recognition systems, where algorithms performed accurately on light-skinned male faces but had high error rates for darker-skinned females. These outcomes are not incidental; they reflect biases embedded in training datasets and the lack of diverse representation in system testing (Haley & Burrell, 2025).

Ethical project management leadership ensures that these foundational issues are addressed early in the lifecycle. Project managers must go beyond scope, budget, and schedule to champion inclusive design principles and equitable data practices. This includes advocating for diverse training datasets, consulting multidisciplinary stakeholders, and instituting ethics reviews as part of the development process. Without such interventions, organizations risk releasing products that are not only flawed but also socially harmful, jeopardizing both consumer trust and brand integrity (Haley & Burrell, 2025).

PROBLEM STATEMENT

As artificial intelligence (AI) and digital health technologies become increasingly embedded in the core operations of healthcare organizations, the rush to capitalize on their efficiency, predictive capabilities, and scalability often outpaces the establishment of ethical oversight structures (Burrell, 2023). This misalignment poses significant risks, particularly in the form of algorithmic bias, inequitable access to telehealth services, and the marginalization of vulnerable populations. Evidence shows that AI systems, such as diagnostic tools and facial recognition software, can yield inaccurate or discriminatory results when trained on non-representative data (Buolamwini, 2017; Hartnett, 2022), undermining clinical accuracy, stakeholder trust, and regulatory compliance. Despite their transformative potential, the ethical pitfalls of poorly governed technologies remain a critical, underexplored challenge for healthcare IT project managers and strategic consultants.

THE NATURE OF THE INQUIRY

This inquiry adopts a perspective-driven commentary approach to critically examine the ethical, strategic, and operational challenges associated with the integration of artificial intelligence (AI) into healthcare organizations. Central to this exploration is the pivotal role of ethical project management leadership in navigating risks such as algorithmic bias, inequitable access, and erosion of stakeholder trust. The inquiry aims to articulate how principled leadership can meaningfully embed values like fairness, transparency, demographic accountability, and stakeholder engagement across the entire AI lifecycle, from data sourcing and system design to deployment and post-implementation governance. By offering theoretically informed and practically grounded insights, this work seeks to equip healthcare consultants, organizational leaders, and technology developers with actionable strategies for fostering equity-driven, socially responsive AI systems.

Perspective academic papers such as this are essential to scholarly dialogue because they illuminate emerging ethical tensions before they are codified by empirical research or regulatory frameworks. In fast-moving domains like AI and digital health, where technologies evolve faster than institutions can adapt, commentary papers offer timely, critical reflections that can guide responsible innovation. Rather than simply cataloging data, these papers synthesize cross-disciplinary insights, provoke thoughtful debate, and bridge theory with application. Their value lies in catalyzing conversations that shape academic research agendas, inform policy decisions, and provide moral clarity in complex, high-stakes environments. As such, this inquiry contributes to the academic and professional discourse by asserting that ethical leadership is not a peripheral concern but a strategic imperative in the governance of intelligent healthcare technologies.

SIGNIFICANCE OF THE INQUIRY

The significance of this inquiry lies in its capacity to illuminate the often-overlooked intersection of ethical governance, social justice, and business performance in healthcare technology implementation. By examining case-specific risks such as biased diagnostic outputs, inequitable telehealth adoption, and the exclusion of marginalized voices in system design, this study underscores the importance of ethical foresight as a strategic advantage. For healthcare organizations, the inquiry offers a framework for avoiding reputational damage, legal liability, and operational inefficiencies caused by ethical blind spots. For project managers and consultants, it provides practical guidance on cultivating inclusive, value-driven leadership that can respond to the evolving demands of a digital healthcare ecosystem.

DEONTOLOGICAL ETHICS

Deontological ethics focuses on adherence to moral duties, rules, and principles, regardless of outcomes (Steerling et al, 2022; Gibelli et al., 2024; Hofmannn et al., 2015). In human-technology integration, it obligates organizations to uphold ethical principles like privacy, autonomy, and fairness, even when violating them could improve efficiency or reduce costs. In healthcare strategy, applying deontological ethics means that organizational leaders must center their AI initiatives on the moral imperative to uphold patient dignity and equality, principles that transcend mere profitability or operational efficiency. For instance, a hospital system considering the integration of AI-driven diagnostic tools must begin with the question: *Are we ethically obligated to ensure this tool works equally well for all patients, regardless of race, gender, or socioeconomic status?* A strategic plan guided by this duty-based ethic would require that fairness and inclusivity be foundational, not supplemental, criteria in vendor selection, model procurement, and long-term technology planning. Even if a tool promises to reduce costs or increase speed, its use would be morally indefensible if it fails marginalized populations. A deontological strategy framework mandates that healthcare executives refuse to implement systems that compromise these ethical duties, much like a physician is expected to prioritize patient welfare above institutional convenience.

When it comes to project management, deontological ethics demands a disciplined commitment to procedural integrity and universal rights throughout the development and deployment process. Imagine a project team rolling out a machine learning algorithm intended to predict hospital readmissions. If the team discovers during testing that the model underperforms for older Black women due to historical data bias, a deontological project manager would not justify pushing the system live for the majority population while working on improvements later. Instead, this leader would halt deployment until all patient groups are treated with equal concern and respect. This duty-oriented decision, perhaps unpopular with executives focused on launch timelines, reflects a commitment to the categorical imperative: never treat any group as merely a means to a broader institutional goal. In practice, this might involve expanding the testing sample, conducting ethical reviews with community advisors, or reallocating resources to enhance demographic accuracy, steps taken not for their expediency, but for their moral necessity.

In business applications, deontological ethics challenges healthcare organizations to resist the utilitarian temptation to accept AI tools that benefit the majority while disadvantaging a few. Consider a case where an AI-powered triage chatbot is deployed to handle patient intake via a digital portal. If this system is optimized primarily for English-speaking users and lacks cultural or linguistic flexibility, it may inadvertently exclude non-native speakers or patients from immigrant communities. A deontologically guided health IT leader would argue that such exclusion is ethically indefensible, even if data shows a net gain in efficiency or throughput. Instead of accepting this imbalance, the business must be redesigned to honor each individual's intrinsic dignity, perhaps by integrating multilingual capabilities, testing with ethnically diverse users, or including community health workers in the design phase. These decisions may require greater investment or longer timelines, but they reflect a principled commitment to respect and fairness that defines ethical leadership in healthcare innovation (Burrell, 2023).

UTILITARIAN ETHICS

Utilitarianism evaluates actions based on their consequences, aiming to maximize overall happiness or minimize suffering (Emdad et al., 2023; Hofmann et al., 2015; Mack, 2004). This theory encourages organizations to deploy technologies that produce the greatest good for the greatest number, while ensuring that harmful impacts, especially on marginalized groups, are minimized. From a strategic standpoint, utilitarian ethics calls on healthcare executives and policymakers to evaluate AI adoption through the lens of population-level benefit. Consider a regional healthcare system evaluating two AI tools for diabetic retinopathy screening. One tool is highly accurate for middle-aged white male patients, the majority demographic in its suburban clinics. The second tool, though slightly less precise overall, has been validated across multiple racial and age groups, including underserved urban populations. A utilitarian framework would favor the latter, as it maximizes the overall well-being of the entire service population, not just the statistical majority. The ethical calculus here involves recognizing that even modest improvements in diagnostic equity can dramatically reduce suffering and improve outcomes for patients who are typically marginalized. Strategically, this approach aligns with long-term public health goals, reduces systemic health disparities, and promotes a reputation for inclusive excellence, a utilitarian win across operational, ethical, and social dimensions.

In the realm of project implementation, utilitarian ethics pushes project managers to prioritize inclusive practices that enhance overall benefit and reduce harm. Imagine a cross-functional team charged with deploying a natural language processing (NLP) tool to summarize patient-provider conversations and auto-generate visit notes. Early testing shows that the tool functions exceptionally well with standard American English but struggles with regional dialects, accents, and non-native speech patterns. A project manager guided by utilitarian reasoning would recognize the potential downstream harms: mis-documentation, delayed treatment, and patient alienation. Rather than proceeding with a premature launch that benefits only the majority, they might delay implementation to incorporate voice data from diverse linguistic communities, work with sociolinguists to refine model accuracy, and establish real-time human review for flagged conversations. While this path may extend timelines and increase upfront costs, it ultimately maximizes the quality of care for a broader swath of patients, thereby increasing collective utility.

In terms of business application, utilitarian ethics becomes especially relevant when balancing automation gains against the human consequences of those efficiencies. Consider a hospital network using AI to schedule staff and allocate nursing resources based on predicted patient volumes and acuity. While such automation might streamline workforce management and reduce operational costs, it could unintentionally deprioritize units serving lower-income or rural populations where data trends are less predictable. A utilitarian business leader would not merely look at operational efficiency but ask: *Does this AI system improve care delivery across the entire organization, or does it leave some units perpetually understaffed?* To maximize collective well-being, the leader might adjust the algorithm to account for social determinants of health, incorporate community-level data, or build in manual override options that allow nurse managers to make context-aware staffing decisions. These adaptations would ensure that the gains in efficiency do not come at the expense of equity, ultimately leading to a healthier, more satisfied, and more stable patient population.

VIRTUE ETHICS

Virtue ethics emphasizes the character and moral integrity of decision-makers rather than rules or results (Bolsin et al., 2005; Reijers, 2019; Tollon, 2024). It guides leaders to cultivate qualities like honesty, empathy, and courage when integrating technology, promoting ethically grounded organizational cultures. At the strategic level, virtue ethics challenges healthcare leaders to develop AI visions that reflect moral excellence, not just technological ambition. Imagine a health system's executive team deciding whether to invest in a predictive analytics platform designed to identify patients at high risk of hospitalization. A purely utilitarian approach might focus on ROI, reducing readmissions and lowering operational costs. But a leader grounded in virtue ethics would ask deeper questions: *Whom does this model serve? Whose health outcomes are prioritized? Whose data is missing?* Embodying foresight and justice, they might scrutinize whether the algorithm accounts for social determinants of health, such as housing instability or language barriers, and insist on the inclusion of data from underrepresented communities. This approach does not just protect the brand or minimize liability, it expresses a commitment to moral leadership, where strategic choices advance equity and demonstrate compassion toward the most vulnerable patients.

In project management, virtue ethics is evident when leaders foster cultures of integrity, humility, and ethical accountability throughout the AI development lifecycle. Consider a project manager overseeing the deployment of an AI-powered triage chatbot in emergency departments. The team discovers during user testing that the system responds inconsistently to queries from elderly patients with cognitive impairments or those using non-standard grammar. Rather than rushing to meet a launch deadline, a virtue-driven project manager exercises responsibility and empathy by halting rollout. They engage patient advocates, bring in geriatric specialists, and modify the system's language model to better accommodate linguistic diversity. This decision may incur short-term costs, but it reflects moral courage, the willingness to protect dignity over expedience. Within this framework, ethical action arises not from obligation but from *who the leader chooses to be*, shaping a culture where doing what's right is not extraordinary but expected.

From a business application perspective, virtue ethics insists that AI systems reflect the values of the organization and serve the holistic well-being of all stakeholders. Picture a healthcare startup that develops a generative AI tool for patient education materials. The early version of the tool creates highly technical content that excludes patients with low health literacy. A business leader shaped by virtue ethics does not merely adjust the tool for better market reach; they act from compassion and a sense of justice, ensuring the content is accessible, culturally sensitive, and available in multiple languages. They collaborate with community health workers and patient advisory boards to guide refinement, not because the market demands it, but because *ethical excellence* demands it. Over time, this commitment to virtue builds brand loyalty, enhances patient trust, and attracts partnerships with like-minded institutions. Thus, business success is achieved not in spite of moral integrity, but because of it.

ETHICS OF CARE

The ethics of care prioritizes relational responsibility, emotional attentiveness, and support for the vulnerable (Stokes & Palmer, 2020; Villegas-Galaviz & Martin, 2024; Tavory, 2024; Smallman, 2022). It urges organizations to design and implement technologies that consider the lived experiences of those most affected, especially patients, low-wage workers, or digitally marginalized communities. At the strategic level, the ethics of care demands that healthcare leaders adopt a values-driven approach to AI planning, one that places the needs of vulnerable patients at the center of design and deployment decisions. Imagine a public hospital system considering an AI-based patient risk stratification tool to prioritize follow-up care. A traditional model might rely heavily on insurance data and prior visit history, inadvertently sidelining uninsured or transient populations. However, a strategic leader informed by the ethics of care would recognize that such an approach neglects the realities of low-income patients, those with unstable housing, or undocumented individuals. Rather than accepting this blind spot as a data limitation, they would proactively engage community organizations, case managers, and social workers to understand care gaps and modify risk algorithms accordingly. The result is not just a more ethically robust tool, but a strategy that embodies relational accountability and actively repairs historical exclusions in the healthcare system.

In project management, the ethics of care translates into day-to-day decisions that humanize AI development and implementation. Consider a project team tasked with deploying a natural language chatbot to support mental health screening in primary care settings. During early testing, the team observes that the bot fails to respond empathetically to trauma survivors, often offering generic or impersonal prompts. A care-focused project manager, instead of dismissing the issue as a coding oversight, sees it as a critical moment to recalibrate the system's purpose. They consult psychologists, patients with lived experience, and trauma-informed care specialists to refine the algorithm's response protocols. The revised tool learns to detect emotional cues, offers validation, and direct patients to appropriate resources. More than just improving functionality, this approach reinforces the project's ethical foundation, one built on respect, listening, and a commitment to emotional safety for those most at risk (Haley & Burrell, 2025).

On the business application front, the ethics of care challenges organizations to move beyond transactional models and foster long-term, trust-based relationships with patients and communities. Picture a health tech firm launching an AI-driven mobile app to support prenatal care in underserved rural areas. While the algorithm efficiently delivers medical content and reminders, feedback reveals that many users feel the app lacks cultural relevance and doesn't address fears around maternity care, particularly among women of color with a history of obstetric mistreatment. A care-oriented business leader responds not with marketing spin, but with humility and accountability. They initiate listening sessions with affected users, adapt the app's voice and imagery to reflect users' communities, and add features that connect expectant mothers with midwives and doulas. By centering relational ethics over short-term ROI, the firm not only deepens user trust but demonstrates that AI can be a compassionate partner in care, not just a tool of efficiency.

PRACTICAL WISDOM (PHRONESIS)

Practical wisdom is the ability to apply moral judgment effectively in complex, context-sensitive situations (Eisikovits & Feldman, 2022; Zelny, 2025; Graves, 2024). It helps leaders make ethically sound decisions in gray areas of technology use, such as when balancing automation with human oversight in clinical or managerial workflows. At the strategic level, practical wisdom empowers healthcare executives to navigate ethical ambiguity with sound moral judgment rooted in lived experience and contextual understanding. Imagine a hospital consortium evaluating whether to scale an AI system designed to allocate ICU beds based on projected patient survival rates. The model appears to optimize resource use across the system, but deeper analysis reveals that it consistently deprioritizes patients with multiple chronic conditions, many of whom are from historically marginalized communities. While policy frameworks and cost-benefit analyses may support immediate deployment, a leader guided by phronesis would pause and reflect on the long-term ethical consequences. They would ask: *Are we inadvertently valuing some lives over others? What do our actions say about our commitment to health equity?* Rather than defaulting to procedural logic, they might convene an interdisciplinary ethics panel, engage with patient advocacy groups, and develop guidelines that safeguard vulnerable populations, balancing efficacy with moral integrity in strategy design.

During project implementation, phronesis becomes crucial when unexpected dilemmas arise that require discernment beyond technical or contractual obligations. Consider a scenario in which a project manager is rolling out an AI-powered diagnostic tool for dermatological conditions in community clinics. Halfway through deployment, clinical users report that the algorithm underperforms in identifying skin conditions on darker skin tones, a flaw that could lead to delayed or incorrect diagnoses. A rigid procedural manager might push forward to meet contractual timelines, citing later updates as a fix. A project manager guided by practical wisdom, however, would assess the ethical implications of deploying a biased tool in underserved areas. Recognizing the stakes, they might halt further deployment, secure emergency funding for more inclusive training data, and coordinate with dermatologists who specialize in diverse skin types. Here, phronesis guides a morally sound decision, not just in policy compliance, but in *doing what is right under pressure*, even when solutions are imperfect or politically inconvenient.

In business applications, practical wisdom offers a compass for reconciling the tensions between innovation, profitability, and ethical responsibility. Imagine a digital health company preparing to launch a generative AI platform that produces automated discharge instructions for patients. Market research suggests strong demand, and early prototypes show cost savings and improved workflow efficiency. However, pilot testing uncovers that the tool produces confusing instructions for patients with limited health literacy and fails to translate medical jargon appropriately into other languages. A purely metrics-driven executive might prioritize rollout and frame these issues as user-side problems. In contrast, a leader exercising practical wisdom would see this as a moment to recalibrate business goals with ethical accountability. They might delay the launch, invest in multilingual community advisors, and partner with local clinics to co-design clear, accessible templates. In doing so, they protect not only end users but the company's long-term reputation, demonstrating that wisdom in business is not about avoiding risk, but *choosing the right risks to take in pursuit of morally meaningful success*.

MORAL PARTICULARISM

Moral particularism argues that ethical decision-making depends on the specific context, not fixed rules or principles (Calo, 2024; Song & Yeung, 2024; Tanenbaum, 2014). It supports flexible, case-by-case evaluations in tech deployment, recognizing, for example, that transparency might be ethical in one instance but harmful in another (e.g., disclosing sensitive health data). At the strategic level, moral particularism challenges healthcare leaders to move beyond one-size-fits-all ethical frameworks when making decisions about AI adoption. Picture a large academic medical center preparing to partner with a third-party vendor to develop an AI-driven predictive model for suicide prevention. On paper, full transparency with the public might seem like an ethical ideal, disclosing which data will be used and how predictions are calculated. But in practice, publicly revealing that the model relies heavily on patients' electronic health records, including psychiatric notes, could lead to fear, stigma, and decreased patient disclosure in mental health encounters. A morally particularist strategist recognizes that while transparency is generally good, in this context, it could produce greater harm. Instead, they pursue a more nuanced approach that includes limited disclosure combined with robust internal safeguards, patient representation on ethics committees, and strict data governance policies. This contextual sensitivity is the hallmark of moral particularism, it asks leaders to weigh values dynamically, not rigidly, for the sake of ethical clarity in complexity.

In project implementation, moral particularism plays a critical role when ethical trade-offs arise in real time, especially in high-stakes environments like hospitals. Imagine a project manager leading the integration of an AI triage system in an emergency department. The tool is designed to prioritize patients based on real-time vitals and symptom descriptions. However, in early use, it becomes apparent that the algorithm under-prioritizes elderly patients who often underreport pain or present atypically. A universalist mindset might suggest treating all users equally under the model's parameters, but a morally particularist project manager understands that equality does not always equate to fairness. They adjust the model or its application to better reflect geriatric clinical realities, even if this means creating an exception to the standard algorithmic logic. This decision is not about breaking rules, it is about *responsibly adapting them* based on the specific moral features of the situation. Moral particularism thus guides the project leader to respond not with abstract principles, but with ethically attuned judgment tailored to patient context.

In business applications, moral particularism becomes crucial when leaders face decisions that pit standard ethical expectations against complex real-world consequences. Consider a digital health startup preparing to launch an AI-powered chatbot for post-discharge patient monitoring. During beta testing, the chatbot performs well overall, but performs poorly when interacting with patients experiencing acute grief or trauma, failing to pick up on distress signals that a human might notice. From a compliance standpoint, the company has met regulatory thresholds, and pushing the product to market could position it as a cost-saving innovation. However, a morally particularist business leader pauses and recognizes that in this particular context, dealing with emotionally fragile individuals, standard deployment practices fall short of ethical responsibility. Rather than rushing the release, they partner with mental health experts to refine the tool's language, build escalation pathways, and co-design safeguards with patients who've had traumatic medical experiences. Their leadership reflects not just legal defensibility, but *context-aware moral integrity*, showing that ethical excellence often means *discerning exceptions, not enforcing absolutes.*

SOCIAL CONTRACT THEORY

Social contract theory posits that individuals consent to systems that protect their rights and interests in exchange for social order and cooperation (Ashrafian, 2023; Kleiner, 2025; Monlezun, 2022). It requires organizations to maintain public trust by integrating technology transparently and fairly, honoring the implicit agreement to serve stakeholders equitably.

At the strategic level, Social Contract Theory reminds healthcare leaders that adopting AI technologies is not just a technical or financial decision, it is a moral agreement with the public to uphold fairness, transparency, and patient dignity. Imagine a major hospital system considering a strategic partnership with a private AI vendor to implement a predictive model for emergency department utilization. The model is designed to forecast which patients are likely to return to the ER within 30 days, with the goal of reducing congestion. While the technology is promising, the training data includes patterns that inadvertently link race and zip code to repeat visits, effectively flagging patients from underserved communities as "high-risk" without context. A strategist grounded in Social Contract Theory recognizes that blindly deploying this model would violate the implicit agreement between the institution and its community: that patients will be treated equitably, not algorithmically profiled. Instead, the hospital pauses implementation, publicly discloses the concerns, and engages community health advocates in re-evaluating the algorithm, thereby honoring the mutual trust on which healthcare legitimacy is built.

In project implementation, Social Contract Theory guides project managers to act as ethical intermediaries between institutional goals and public interest. Take, for example, a project team deploying an AI-driven diagnostic assistant within a primary care network. During the pilot phase, clinicians begin to raise concerns that the assistant disproportionately flags male patients for cardiovascular risk assessments, potentially due to historical bias in the training data. A manager solely focused on performance metrics might dismiss these anomalies as statistical noise. However, a project manager operating with an understanding of social contract obligations takes such concerns seriously, recognizing that continuing deployment without investigation could erode physician trust and patient confidence. They convene a review board, publish interim findings transparently, and revise the model's criteria before full rollout. This proactive accountability doesn't just improve system performance; it affirms that the organization takes its ethical contract with patients and professionals seriously.

In business applications, Social Contract Theory serves as a compass for balancing innovation with ethical accountability, especially in commercial ventures involving sensitive health data. Imagine a healthcare AI startup marketing a wearable device that monitors patient symptoms and shares data with providers for real-time intervention. The product is successful in trials, but media reports begin to surface questioning whether patients were adequately informed about how their data would be used and monetized. Rather than issuing a generic PR statement or burying terms in an update, a CEO committed to the social contract understands that informed consent is not just a checkbox, it is a pillar of public legitimacy. They launch a campaign to educate users, simplify consent processes, and offer opt-out features for data sharing. By doing so, they preserve trust, sustain long-term user engagement, and demonstrate that business growth in healthcare must be rooted in social responsibility. In this way, Social Contract Theory helps ensure that technological progress doesn't outpace the ethical foundations on which it depends.

STAKEHOLDER THEORY

Stakeholder theory holds that ethical decisions must consider the impact on all affected parties, not just shareholders (Figueiredo, 2024; Lebcir, 2021; Sujan, 2022). This theory guides technology integration efforts that respect the concerns of patients, employees, regulators, and underrepresented populations, rather than prioritizing only profit or technical efficiency. At the strategic level, Stakeholder Theory challenges healthcare leaders to look beyond conventional financial or operational benchmarks and instead design AI initiatives with the interests of a broad and diverse network of stakeholders in mind. Consider a regional health system planning to adopt an AI-driven patient engagement platform aimed at reducing no-show rates for follow-up appointments. From an efficiency standpoint, the system shows promise, automated reminders, behavior-based scheduling, and data-driven communication strategies. However, during strategic assessment, leaders realize that the tool was trained on datasets excluding non-English-speaking patients and those with limited access to smartphones. A stakeholder-informed strategy, grounded in this theory, would require leaders to engage with community health workers, patient advocacy groups, and even language justice experts before finalizing the deployment. Rather than retrofitting accessibility after rollout, the system would be designed with multilingual, low-tech engagement options from the outset. In doing so, the organization demonstrates not only ethical foresight but strategic alignment with the real-world conditions of its service population.

In the implementation phase, Stakeholder Theory directs project managers to conduct continuous stakeholder mapping and engagement, not as a bureaucratic exercise, but as a moral imperative. Imagine a team rolling out a machine learning tool to assist radiologists in diagnosing breast cancer. Early testing reveals the model performs exceptionally on data from urban academic hospitals but has significantly lower accuracy for images sourced from smaller, rural clinics with different imaging equipment and patient demographics. A project manager operating from a stakeholder-centered ethic doesn't push forward to meet a timeline; instead, they broaden stakeholder involvement by bringing in rural clinicians, patients, and data scientists familiar with low-resource settings. They initiate a cross-institutional feedback loop to refine the model and incorporate diverse imaging inputs. This not only enhances the system's robustness but fosters trust, equity, and cross-site collaboration, critical success factors in healthcare innovation that a narrow, shareholder-focused mindset would easily overlook.

In the realm of business applications, Stakeholder Theory is especially vital when AI solutions intersect with sensitive domains like health data, workforce dynamics, and patient-provider relationships. Picture a healthcare AI company developing a platform to optimize staffing schedules in large hospital systems. While the algorithm reduces labor costs and improves shift coverage, it begins to generate resistance from nurses who report that the system ignores caregiving continuity and personal preferences, factors crucial to burnout prevention and patient care quality. A stakeholder-driven executive would recognize that nurses are not just employees but critical knowledge bearers and end users whose lived experience must inform algorithmic logic. Rather than treating their concerns as fringe feedback, the company pauses to co-create a version of the tool that incorporates nurse input, balances efficiency with well-being, and is field-tested in partnership with labor unions and HR departments. This results in a more sustainable product, increased staff morale, and long-term client retention, demonstrating that value creation in healthcare AI depends not just on innovation, but on inclusive, stakeholder-aligned design.

CORPORATE SOCIAL RESPONSIBILITY (CSR)

Corporate Social Responsibility (CSR) refers to an organization's obligation to act in ways that benefit society and the environment beyond legal requirements (Gagliardi & Tomaselli, 2025; Khan et al., 2024; Monroe, 2024). In technology integration, CSR encourages ethical data governance, digital equity, and responsible innovation to ensure that tech advances do not harm societal well-being or exacerbate inequalities. At the strategic level, Corporate Social Responsibility (CSR) guides healthcare executives to make technology decisions that benefit society, not just shareholders or patients with purchasing power. For example, imagine a national health network deciding whether to implement a new AI-powered diagnostic imaging tool that improves cancer detection rates. While the technology is state-of-the-art, its high licensing costs and hardware requirements would likely exclude small, rural hospitals from adoption. A CSR-focused strategy would not stop at internal ROI projections but ask: *How can this innovation be extended to underserved com-*

munities? Leadership might negotiate tiered pricing models with the vendor, fund mobile imaging units for low-access areas, or partner with public health agencies to ensure equitable rollout. By framing strategic planning through a CSR lens, the organization demonstrates that ethical innovation in healthcare means delivering cutting-edge care *without deepening the digital divide.*

In project implementation, CSR manifests in the ethical treatment of data and inclusive design practices that reflect real-world diversity. Consider a project team deploying a machine learning model for predicting postpartum complications. The initial model is trained primarily on data from urban, privately insured patients, leading to lower prediction accuracy for Medicaid recipients and women in rural or immigrant communities. A project manager operating under a CSR ethic doesn't treat this as a technical bug to patch later, they recognize it as a social obligation to correct now. The team expands its data partnerships, including community clinics and public health departments, to retrain the algorithm on a more representative dataset. They also embed culturally competent health educators into the development cycle to guide messaging and deployment. This approach not only improves the algorithm's performance, it fulfills the CSR mandate to ensure technology works *for all patients, not just those with a voice in the system.*

In terms of business applications, CSR encourages healthcare AI companies to develop products and practices that promote long-term societal trust and value, not just short-term market success. Imagine a startup offering a conversational AI tool for post-operative recovery support. The company collects sensitive patient feedback to fine-tune its algorithms, but some of this data includes information about undocumented status, mental health, or domestic violence, topics patients shared without knowing their responses were used for commercial training purposes. A company guided by CSR principles responds not with legal defensiveness, but with proactive transparency: they revise consent protocols, anonymize historical datasets, and form an independent ethics board to oversee data governance. They even create open-access resources that help patients understand how their data supports public health research. As a result, the company earns not just users, but *trust*, transforming CSR from a branding exercise into a core business value that fuels innovation with integrity.

PRACTICAL RECOMMENDATIONS

1. **Conduct inclusive, lifecycle-oriented AI impact assessments prior to deployment.**

Why it matters: Evaluating the social, legal, and ethical risks at each phase of development helps prevent the entrenchment of algorithmic bias, identifies equity gaps, and ensures AI applications align with organizational and societal values.

2. **Establish mandatory human-in-the-loop oversight protocols for all critical decision-making AI systems.**

Why it matters: Keeping a human agent involved ensures accountability and mitigates the risks of erroneous or discriminatory outputs, especially in high-stakes domains like clinical triage, finance, or legal processing.

3. **Create multidisciplinary AI review boards with representation from clinicians, ethicists, technologists, and affected community members.**

Why it matters: Involving diverse expertise and lived experiences leads to more nuanced evaluations of AI systems and counters the tunnel vision that can emerge in purely technical teams.

4. **Integrate stakeholder voice, particularly from historically marginalized populations, into design, testing, and post-deployment evaluation.**

Why it matters: AI systems often fail to perform equitably across racial, gender, and socioeconomic lines; amplifying stakeholder voices helps prevent exclusion and builds community legitimacy.

5. **Promote digital health literacy initiatives that inform patients and users about how AI technologies function and affect their lives.**

Why it matters: Informed users are empowered users; transparency and education reduce fear, foster trust, and enhance the ethical legitimacy of AI deployment in public-facing services.

6. **Develop partnerships with community organizations to contextualize data ethics and technology acceptance in local cultural and social norms.**

Why it matters: Ethical AI is not universally defined—understanding the social context improves system usability, fairness, and public buy-in, particularly in diverse or under-resourced communities.

7. **Institutionalize ethical AI leadership training for all project managers and executives involved in AI-driven initiatives.**

Why it matters: Ethical oversight must be embedded in leadership, not outsourced; cultivating ethical literacy at the top ensures consistent moral reasoning in strategic and operational decisions.

8. **Mandate ongoing algorithmic audits and public reporting mechanisms for bias, fairness, and outcome disparities.**

Why it matters: Transparency and accountability are cornerstones of ethical governance, regular audits help detect emergent harms, while public disclosure maintains trust and regulatory alignment.

9. **Adopt a formal organizational AI ethics charter that defines guiding values, boundaries, and responsibilities.**

Why it matters: A clearly articulated ethics framework anchors AI innovation within organizational integrity, guiding future use cases and preventing value drift over time.

10. **Ensure AI procurement policies include criteria for vendor ethics, data transparency, and compliance with equity standards.**

Why it matters: Many ethical risks are embedded upstream in vendor relationships; responsible sourcing ensures third-party technologies align with the organization's social mission and legal duties.

AMALISHA SABIE-ARIDI ETHICAL AI DEPLOYMENT FRAMEWORK

This framework integrates key ethical theories into a practical model for the development, deployment, and business application of AI technologies. It is designed to guide healthcare executives, IT project managers, and organizational consultants in aligning innovation with ethical integrity and societal value.

1. Ethical Grounding (Foundational Stage)
    - **Deontological Commitment**: Prioritize universal ethical principles such as fairness, autonomy, and privacy. Ensure every AI tool or system

treats individuals as ends in themselves, not merely as data points or efficiency metrics.

- **Virtue-Oriented Leadership**: Cultivate leaders who embody justice, responsibility, and empathy. Encourage ethical reflection in leadership decisions from strategy through implementation.
- **Ethics of Care Focus**: Center the lived experiences of marginalized and vulnerable populations. Identify whose voices are missing and actively seek their input before any technical decision is finalized.

2. Strategic Planning
   - **Utilitarian Benefit Assessment**: Evaluate whether AI applications maximize collective benefit while minimizing harm. Prioritize tools that improve access, health equity, and quality of care across populations.
   - **Social Contract Alignment**: Ensure that strategic goals reflect a shared societal agreement that healthcare innovation upholds dignity, transparency, and fairness. Include communities in strategic planning.
   - **CSR Integration**: Use Corporate Social Responsibility (CSR) principles to broaden strategic impact. Develop tiered rollout strategies to prevent digital exclusion and commit to environmental and social stewardship in vendor partnerships.
3. Inclusive Design and Development
   - **Stakeholder Theory Application**: Identify all stakeholders (patients, clinicians, regulators, underserved populations) and embed their concerns into the design process. Conduct stakeholder mapping early and often.
   - **Practical Wisdom in Design**: Apply ethical judgment when universal rules fall short. Adjust plans based on context-specific needs such as cultural variance or clinical realities.
   - **Moral Particularism in Practice**: Recognize that ethical solutions are not one-size-fits-all. Build flexible development cycles that adapt based on localized challenges, such as health disparities or rural infrastructure gaps.
4. Implementation Oversight
   - **Bias Auditing and Data Justice**: Audit datasets for demographic biases before deployment. Incorporate intersectional representation in testing groups.
   - **Ethics Review and Accountability Structures**: Establish standing ethics review boards composed of clinicians, ethicists, community advocates, and data scientists. Conduct ongoing reviews of algorithmic behavior.

- **Care-Based Deployment**: Avoid systems that alienate or exclude users due to language, disability, digital literacy, or trauma. Build for emotional intelligence and relational integrity.

5. Business and Operational Governance
   - **Transparent Consent and Data Use**: Build clear, accessible, and opt-in informed consent protocols for data collection and usage.
   - **Equity Metrics and ROI**: Include metrics for health equity, patient satisfaction, and stakeholder trust in performance KPIs. Don't just measure efficiency and profit.
   - **CSR-Driven Business Practices**: Engage in ethical data governance, open communication, and social value creation as core business strategies, not peripheral programs.
6. Feedback, Learning, and Continuous Improvement
   - **Stakeholder Feedback Loops**: Maintain continuous engagement with affected communities through surveys, focus groups, and advisory panels.
   - **Ethical Adaptability**: Regularly review ethical assumptions and revise tools as new challenges emerge. Encourage an organizational culture that normalizes learning from ethical missteps.
   - **Public Trust and Transparency**: Proactively share findings, bias discoveries, and system updates with the public. Reinforce the institution's commitment to ethical responsibility.

CONCLUSION

This framework is not prescriptive but aspirational. It provides a roadmap for embedding ethical responsibility at every stage of AI adoption. Through the integration of these philosophical foundations and practical mechanisms, healthcare organizations can lead with integrity, promote equity, and ensure that innovation truly serves the common good.

REFERENCES

Ashrafian, H. (2023). Engineering a social contract: Rawlsian distributive justice through algorithmic game theory and artificial intelligence. *AI and Ethics, 3*(4), 1447–1454. DOI: 10.1007/s43681-022-00253-6

Bolsin, S., Faunce, T., & Oakley, J. (2005). Practical virtue ethics: Healthcare whistleblowing and portable digital technology. *Journal of Medical Ethics, 31*(10), 612–618. DOI: 10.1136/jme.2004.010603 PMID: 16199607

Burrell, D. N. (2023). Dynamic evaluation approaches to telehealth technologies and artificial intelligence (AI) telemedicine applications in healthcare and biotechnology organizations. *Merits, 3*(4), 700–721. DOI: 10.3390/merits3040042

Calo, Z. R. (2024). AI, medicine and Christian ethics. *Research Handbook on Health, AI and the Law*, 219-233.

Eisikovits, N., & Feldman, D. (2022). AI and phronesis. *Moral Philosophy and Politics, 9*(2), 181–199. DOI: 10.1515/mopp-2021-0026

Emdad, F. B., Ho, S. M., Ravuri, B., & Hussain, S. (2023). Towards a unified utilitarian ethics framework for healthcare artificial intelligence. *arXiv preprint arXiv:2309.14617.*

Figueiredo, J. M. P. C. (2024). *The Impact of Artificial Intelligence on the Stakeholder Theory: A Bibliometric Review Analysis*. PQDT-Global.

Gagliardi, A. R., & Tomaselli, G. (2025). Aligning corporate social responsibility with artificial intelligence in healthcare in the context of the post-COVID-19 recovery: A viewpoint. *Journal of Health Organization and Management*. Advance online publication. DOI: 10.1108/JHOM-06-2024-0244 PMID: 39763013

Gibelli, F., Maio, G., & Ricci, G. (2024). Healthcare in the age of sapient machines: Physician decision-making autonomy faced with artificial intelligence. Ethical, deontological and compensatory aspects. *Frontiers in Medicine, 11*, 1477371. DOI: 10.3389/fmed.2024.1477371 PMID: 39267961

Graves, M. (2024). Apprehending AI moral purpose in practical wisdom. *AI & Society, 39*(3), 1335–1348. DOI: 10.1007/s00146-022-01597-7

Haley, P., & Burrell, D. N. (2025). Using Artificial Intelligence in Law Enforcement and Policing to Improve Public Health and Safety. *Law. Economics and Society, 1*(1), 46–p46. DOI: 10.30560/les.v1n1p46

Hartnett, K. (2022). Racially biased medical device results raise patient safety concerns. Modern Healthcare. Retrieved from: https://www.modernhealthcare.com/providers/bias-medical-device-results-raises-patient-safety-concerns

Hofmannn, B., Oortwijn, W., Lysdahl, K. B., Refolo, P., Sacchini, D., Van Der Wilt, G. J., & Gerhardus, A. (2015). Integrating ethics in health technology assessment: Many ways to Rome. *International Journal of Technology Assessment in Health Care, 31*(3), 131–137. DOI: 10.1017/S0266462315000276 PMID: 26063128

Hofmannn, B., Oortwijn, W., Lysdahl, K. B., Refolo, P., Sacchini, D., Van Der Wilt, G. J., & Gerhardus, A. (2015). Integrating ethics in health technology assessment: Many ways to Rome. *International Journal of Technology Assessment in Health Care, 31*(3), 131–137. DOI: 10.1017/S0266462315000276 PMID: 26063128

Khan, H., Pandey, S., Kumar, B. V., Akram, S. V., & Pal, P. (2024, March). Artificial Intelligence (AI) in the Field of Corporate Social Responsibility. In *2024 3rd International Conference on Sentiment Analysis and Deep Learning (ICSADL)* (pp. 164-168). IEEE.

Kleiner, J. (2025). The social contract theory meets cybersecurity: Systematic literature review. *Digital Policy. Regulation & Governance, 27*(4), 446–465.

Lebcir, R., Hill, T., Atun, R., & Cubric, M. (2021). Stakeholders' views on the organisational factors affecting application of artificial intelligence in healthcare: A scoping review protocol. *BMJ Open, 11*(3), e044074. DOI: 10.1136/bmjopen-2020-044074 PMID: 33753441

Mack, P. (2004). Utilitarian ethics in healthcare. *International journal of the computer, the internet and management, 12*(3), 63-72.

Monlezun, D. J., Sotomayor, C., Peters, N. J., Steigner, L., Gallagher, C. M., & García, A. (2022). The global AI ethics of COVID-19 recovery: Narrative review and Personalist Social Contract ethical analysis of AI-driven optimization of public health effectiveness and social equities. *Medicina y Etica : Revista Internacional de Bioetica, Deontologia y Etica Medica, 33*(2), 357–394. DOI: 10.36105/mye.2022v33n2.02

Monroe, J. (2024). Corporate Social Responsibility in the MedTech Industry, the Emergence of Artificial Intelligence in the ERA of COVID-19. *American Journal of Artificial Intelligence, 8*(1), 1–4. DOI: 10.11648/j.ajai.20240801.11

Reijers, W. (2019). *Practicing narrative virtue ethics of technology in research and innovation* (Doctoral dissertation, Dublin City University).

Sharma, Y., Saha, A., & Goldsack, J. (2024). Defining the Dimensions of Diversity to Promote Inclusion in the Digital Era of Health Care: A Lexicon. *JMIR Public Health and Surveillance*, *10*, e51980. https://publichealth.jmir.org/2024/1/e51980. DOI: 10.2196/51980 PMID: 38335013

Smallman, M. (2022). Multi scale ethics—Why we need to consider the ethics of AI in Healthcare at different scales. *Science and Engineering Ethics*, *28*(6), 63. DOI: 10.1007/s11948-022-00396-z PMID: 36441282

Song, F., & Yeung, S. H. F. (2024). A pluralist hybrid model for moral AIs. *AI & Society*, *39*(3), 891–900. DOI: 10.1007/s00146-022-01601-0

Steerling, E., Houston, R., Gietzen, L. J., Ogilvie, S. J., de Ruiter, H. P., & Nygren, J. M. (2022). Examining how ethics in relation to health technology is described in the research literature: Scoping review. *Interactive Journal of Medical Research*, *11*(2), e38745. DOI: 10.2196/38745 PMID: 35969434

Stokes, F., & Palmer, A. (2020). Artificial intelligence and robotics in nursing: Ethics of caring as a guide to dividing tasks between AI and humans. *Nursing Philosophy*, *21*(4), e12306. DOI: 10.1111/nup.12306 PMID: 32609420

Sujan, M. A., White, S., Habli, I., & Reynolds, N. (2022). Stakeholder perceptions of the safety and assurance of artificial intelligence in healthcare. *Safety Science*, *155*, 105870. DOI: 10.1016/j.ssci.2022.105870

Tanenbaum, S. J. (2014). Particularism in health care: Challenging the authority of the aggregate. *Journal of Evaluation in Clinical Practice*, *20*(6), 934–941. DOI: 10.1111/jep.12249 PMID: 25406384

Tavory, T. (2024). Regulating AI in mental health: Ethics of care perspective. *JMIR Mental Health*, *11*(1), e58493. DOI: 10.2196/58493 PMID: 39298759

Tollon, F. (2024). Technology and the situationist challenge to virtue ethics. *Science and Engineering Ethics*, *30*(2), 10. DOI: 10.1007/s11948-024-00474-4 PMID: 38536486

Villegas-Galaviz, C., & Martin, K. (2024). Moral distance, AI, and the ethics of care. *AI & Society*, *39*(4), 1695–1706. DOI: 10.1007/s00146-023-01642-z PMID: 37358944

Zelny, A. (2025). Offloading Wisdom: Four Technological Relations that Mediate Phronesis. *Philosophy & Technology*, *38*(2), 56. DOI: 10.1007/s13347-025-00889-2

Chapter 3
An Industrial and Organizational Psychology (I-O) Perspective of the Discrimination Risks of Using AI in Hiring

Darrell Norman Burrell
http://orcid.org/0000-0002-4675-9544
Marymount University, USA

Adina Lundy
http://orcid.org/0000-0001-7564-2110
University of Rhode Island, USA

Quatavia McLester
http://orcid.org/0000-0003-1596-0517
Columbus State University, USA

Calvin Nobles
http://orcid.org/0000-0003-4002-1108
University of Maryland Global Campus, USA

Natasha Harris
http://orcid.org/0009-0002-1745-7966
Marymount University, USA

Hilda Eke
http://orcid.org/0009-0006-2021-178X
Marymount University, USA

Samantha Thibodeau
http://orcid.org/0009-0000-4639-9166
Marymount University, USA

KerriLaine Prunella
http://orcid.org/0009-0001-0177-3545
Marymount University, USA

Phillip Reed
http://orcid.org/0009-0000-1266-0151
Marymount University, USA

Teresa Manfreda-Foley
http://orcid.org/0009-0002-9136-9673
Brookdale Community College, USA

DOI: 10.4018/979-8-2600-1016-7.ch003

Garrett Hart
http://orcid.org/0009-0008-8003-2032
Marymount University, USA

Chitra Perera
http://orcid.org/0009-0005-3431-4969
Marymount University, USA

Maria R. Mondala-Duncan
http://orcid.org/0009-0000-4586-8434
Marymount University, USA

Sharon L. Burton
http://orcid.org/0000-0003-1653-9783
Embry-Riddle Aeronautical University, USA

Maurice Dawson
http://orcid.org/0000-0003-4609-3444
Illinois Institute of Technology, USA

ABSTRACT

This qualitative study examines the organizational and behavioral implications of artificial intelligence (AI) use in hiring through an industrial and organizational (I-O) psychology lens, informed by a discrimination case involving JKU Global. Using a rigorous three-phase, consensus-based focus group design, data were collected from ten doctoral-level experts: five I-O psychology researchers and five AI policy researchers. Participants independently responded to structured questions, developed discipline-specific consensus lists, and collaboratively generated final interdisciplinary conclusions. Findings indicate that AI-based hiring systems can disadvantage applicants and perpetuate discrimination when over-relied upon, insufficiently audited, or embedded within organizational cultures that prioritize efficiency over fairness. Results emphasize that biased algorithms amplify systemic inequities through opaque decision-making and weakened accountability.

INTRODUCTION

A recent class action lawsuit brought by minority job applicants against JKU Global (A fictitious name used to protect the privacy of the actual organization), a multinational healthcare organization, underscores the growing intersection between artificial intelligence (AI), employment decision-making, and organizational justice. A former employee became a whistleblower and disclosed problems concerning discrimination with the use of the AI technology tools in hiring. The lawsuit, which resulted in a 20-million-dollar settlement during arbitration, alleged that the organization's AI-based recruitment system systematically excluded qualified minority applicants and internal employees from advancement opportunities. Evidence presented during arbitration demonstrated that the algorithm embedded biased assumptions within its programming logic, producing adverse employment outcomes for protected groups.

From an industrial and organizational psychology perspective (I-O), this case illustrates a critical failure in personnel selection systems as it relates to fairness. Selection tools, whether human- or algorithm-driven, are expected to predict job performance while minimizing bias and ensuring equitable access to employment opportunities (Omar & Burrell, 2024). When AI systems replicate historical inequities embedded in training data or developer assumptions, they function not as neutral decision aids but as amplifiers of systemic bias, shaping organizational culture in exclusionary ways (Omar & Burrell, 2024).

The increasing reliance on AI in recruitment has been widely promoted as a mechanism for efficiency, consistency, and objectivity (Omar & Burrell, 2024). However, as demonstrated in the JKU Global case, technological sophistication does not inherently translate into psychological or ethical soundness. In this instance, the AI tool screened applicants using programmed linguistic markers and historical hiring patterns that disadvantaged minority candidates, thereby restricting workforce diversity and reinforcing inequitable organizational norms. Such outcomes directly undermine inclusive organizational climates and erode trust in organizational decision-making processes (Burton, 2025; Omar & Burrell, 2024).

Discrimination in hiring remains one of the most persistent barriers to building equitable organizational cultures. I-O psychology research emphasizes that perceived fairness in hiring practices strongly influences applicant attraction, employee engagement, and long-term organizational commitment. Legal frameworks serve as structural safeguards against discriminatory practices, establishing boundaries within which organizations must design and implement selection systems (Huff et al., 2023; McLester et al., 2021).

In the United States, Title VII of the Civil Rights Act of 1964 serves as the foundational legal mechanism prohibiting employment discrimination based on race, color, religion, sex, or national origin. Complementary statutes such as the Age Discrimination in Employment Act (ADEA), the Americans with Disabilities Act (ADA), and the Genetic Information Nondiscrimination Act (GINA) further delineate protected characteristics within employment contexts (Cheung et al., 2016; Huff et al., 2023; McLester et al., 2021). From an organizational psychology standpoint, these laws operationalize principles of distributive and procedural justice by mandating equal access to employment opportunities and transparent decision-making criteria (Omar & Burrell, 2024; Lundy et al., 2025).

State-level anti-discrimination statutes frequently extend beyond federal protections by covering additional demographic categories or applying to smaller organizations. These layered legal frameworks reflect an evolving understanding of how structural inequities manifest within organizational systems and emphasize the importance of contextual sensitivity when implementing standardized hiring technologies (McLester et al., 2021).

The Equal Employment Opportunity Commission (EEOC) plays a central role in enforcing compliance with federal anti-discrimination laws and shaping organizational behavior through guidance, investigation, and litigation (Lundy et al., 2025). From an I-O psychology lens, EEOC enforcement mechanisms function as external accountability systems that influence organizational policies, leadership decision-making, and ethical climates (Huff et al., 2023; McLester et al., 2021).

Two legal doctrines are particularly relevant when evaluating AI-based hiring systems: disparate treatment and disparate impact. Disparate treatment refers to intentional discrimination against individuals based on protected characteristics, while disparate impact addresses employment practices that appear neutral yet disproportionately disadvantage protected groups. AI-driven selection tools frequently fall into the latter category, as biased outcomes may emerge without explicit discriminatory intent. I-O psychology research highlights that organizations remain responsible for outcomes regardless of whether bias originates from human judgment or automated systems (Huff et al., 2023; McLester et al., 2021).

PROBLEM STATEMENT

Recent scholarship has increasingly examined AI-mediated employment processes, including algorithmic resume screening, job recommendation systems, and automated applicant tracking platforms (Zapata, 2021). Empirical findings reveal concerning patterns: approximately 40% of job seekers reported receiving recommendations shaped by personal identity characteristics rather than objective qualifications, while 30% received job alerts misaligned with their skill levels (Zapata, 2021). Moreover, nearly 63% of respondents indicated that academic or professional recommendations failed to reflect their actual achievements (Zapata, 2021). These findings are particularly striking given that Black women represent the most highly educated demographic group in the United States, suggesting a disconnect between human capital and algorithmic recognition (Zapata, 2021).

From an organizational behavior perspective, these mismatches contribute to perceptions of systemic unfairness, diminished organizational legitimacy, and disengagement among marginalized professionals (Omar & Burrell, 2024). When AI systems inaccurately assess competence, they weaken meritocratic norms and distort talent pipelines, ultimately constraining organizational effectiveness (Omar & Burrell, 2024).

A structural contributor to these outcomes lies in the persistent lack of diversity within the technology sector, particularly in Silicon Valley, where predominantly white, male professionals continue to dominate leadership and AI development roles. I-O psychology emphasizes that homogenous decision-making teams are more likely to overlook bias, underestimate contextual variability, and normalize inequitable assumptions. Consequently, AI systems developed within such environments may unintentionally encode exclusionary values into organizational processes (Zapata, 2021).

A well-documented real-world example is Amazon's discontinuation of an AI recruiting tool in 2018 after internal audits revealed that the system penalized resumes associated with women and underrepresented groups. This case parallels the JKU Global lawsuit, illustrating how algorithmic tools trained on historically biased data sets can perpetuate discriminatory hiring patterns rather than disrupt them (Zapata, 2021).

If AI systems are developed without deliberate psychological oversight, diversity-informed design, and continuous validation, they risk institutionalizing bias at scale. For Black professionals, these systemic failures manifest in persistent disparities, including 30% to 50% fewer job callbacks when racial or ethnic identifiers are present on resumes (Zapata, 2021). From an I-O psychology standpoint, such outcomes are not merely technical flaws but indicators of deeper organizational and cultural dysfunctions that demand intervention at the levels of leadership, system design, and ethical governance. This inquiry uses the case study JKU to drive the discussion of the complexities of using AI tools in recruiting and hiring.

PURPOSE STATEMENT

The purpose of this qualitative focus group study is to examine how artificial intelligence researchers and industrial and organizational psychology researchers conceptualize, interpret, and evaluate bias, fairness, and accountability in AI-driven hiring systems. Specifically, this study seeks to explore how disciplinary perspectives shape understandings of algorithmic decision-making, validation practices, and ethical responsibility within organizational recruitment and selection contexts. By engaging experts from technical and behavioral science domains, the study aims to surface convergences and divergences in how bias is identified, mitigated, and addressed across the AI development lifecycle.

A secondary purpose of the study is to explore how interdisciplinary collaboration, or the absence of it, affects the design, implementation, and governance of AI-based hiring tools within organizations. Through structured focus group discussions, the study intends to generate insight into how organizational culture, professional norms, and epistemological assumptions influence the integration of psychological principles into AI systems. The findings are intended to inform more psychologically grounded, ethically responsible, and legally compliant approaches to AI-supported personnel selection.

SIGNIFICANCE STATEMENT

This study is significant because it addresses a critical gap at the intersection of artificial intelligence, industrial and organizational psychology, and organizational justice. While AI-driven hiring technologies are increasingly adopted to improve efficiency and scalability, research demonstrates that these systems frequently reproduce systemic biases when psychological principles of validity, fairness, and contextual sensitivity are insufficiently incorporated. By centering the perspectives of both AI researchers and I-O psychologists, this study contributes to a deeper understanding of how disciplinary silos may inadvertently sustain inequitable hiring outcomes.

The findings of this study have practical significance for organizations, policymakers, and technology developers seeking to implement AI hiring tools responsibly. Insights derived from expert focus group dialogue may inform best practices for interdisciplinary collaboration, ethical AI governance, and evidence-based validation frameworks. From an organizational behavior perspective, the study also has implications for cultivating inclusive organizational cultures, enhancing trust in automated decision-making systems, and reducing legal and reputational risks associated with discriminatory hiring practices.

NATURE OF THE STUDY

This study employs a qualitative research design using a focus group methodology to explore expert perspectives on AI bias in employment decision-making. A purposive sample of ten participants, five AI researchers and five industrial and organizational psychology researchers, will be recruited based on their professional expertise in algorithm development, personnel selection, organizational behavior, or related areas. Focus groups are well suited for this inquiry because they facilitate interactive dialogue, allow participants to challenge and refine one another's perspectives, and surface collective meaning-making processes across disciplinary boundaries.

Data will be collected through facilitated focus group sessions guided by semi-structured questions addressing AI design assumptions, bias mitigation strategies, validation practices, and organizational responsibility. This qualitative approach is appropriate because the study seeks to understand complex social, ethical, and organizational dynamics rather than to test hypotheses or measure variables. The design prioritizes depth, context, and interpretive richness to illuminate how expert knowledge informs the development and use of AI in organizational hiring systems.

CULTURAL ICEBERG MODEL AND ORGANIZATIONAL BIAS

The cultural iceberg model offers a useful lens for understanding how organizations experience and respond to visible crises while overlooking deeper cultural dynamics that shape behavior and decision-making. From an I-O psychology perspective, the "above-the-surface" elements of culture include observable outcomes such as legal action, financial losses, public scrutiny, and employee turnover. In the context of an AI-related discrimination lawsuit, these visible indicators, such as multimillion-dollar settlements or damaged employer branding, represent only a fraction of the cultural conditions influencing organizational behavior (Cuevas & Boen, 2021).

Beneath these visible manifestations lie less observable yet more influential cultural elements, including shared assumptions, implicit biases, norms surrounding accountability, and leadership beliefs about merit and objectivity. These unconscious and semi-conscious factors often guide how technologies are selected, implemented, and evaluated within organizations. For example, an organization may publicly endorse diversity and inclusion while simultaneously relying on AI tools trained on historically biased data, reflecting a misalignment between espoused values and enacted practices. A comprehensive, top-down meta-analysis of organizational culture can help surface these hidden assumptions, enabling leaders to address inequities embedded both in human judgment and automated systems (Wazed, 2018).

UNCERTAINTY, CULTURE, AND ORGANIZATIONAL BEHAVIOR

Uncertainty plays a central role in shaping organizational culture, particularly during periods of technological change and social accountability. The iceberg framework has long been used to explain how values, belief systems, and informal norms influence behavior beneath formal policies and procedures. In contemporary organizations, this model has gained renewed relevance as issues related to gender identity, socioeconomic inequality, and systemic racism challenge traditional assumptions about neutrality and fairness in organizational systems (Vaudrin, 2019).

From an I-O psychology standpoint, uncertainty heightens employees' reliance on cultural cues to guide behavior. When leadership responses to uncertainty are ambiguous or inconsistent, employees may default to ingrained habits or implicit biases, reinforcing inequitable outcomes. For instance, during rapid AI adoption, organizations that fail to clarify ethical standards and decision-making accountability may inadvertently normalize biased outcomes as "technical errors" rather than cultural failures. Addressing these hidden cultural layers requires updating organizational processes to reflect evolving social standards and explicitly rejecting biased practices, even when they are technologically mediated (Vaudrin, 2019).

DENISON ORGANIZATIONAL CULTURE MODEL AND BEHAVIORAL ALIGNMENT

The Denison Organizational Culture Model offers a behaviorally grounded framework for understanding how shared values, norms, and practices influence organizational effectiveness. Rooted in industrial and organizational psychology, the model emphasizes that culture operates as a system of learned behaviors rather than a collection of individual personality traits. It identifies four interdependent cultural dimensions including employee involvement, consistency of core values, adaptability, and mission clarity, that collectively shape how organizations interpret challenges, make decisions, and coordinate action (Ahmady et al., 2016). These dimensions are especially useful for diagnosing systemic issues because they illuminate how organizational behavior emerges from collective patterns rather than isolated individual choices.

From an I-O psychology perspective, the strength of the Denison model lies in its ability to link culture directly to performance outcomes and ethical behavior. For example, organizations with high involvement scores tend to empower employees through participative decision-making, skill development, and shared ownership of outcomes. In contrast, low involvement may signal psychological disengagement, reduced voice, and limited upward communication; conditions under which biased or flawed systems, such as AI-driven hiring tools, may persist unchallenged. When employees do not feel authorized to question decisions or raise ethical concerns, organizational silence becomes a behavioral norm rather than an exception.

CULTURAL CONSISTENCY, ADAPTABILITY, AND ETHICAL DECISION-MAKING

The consistency dimension of the Denison model reflects the extent to which organizations maintain coherent values, agreement, and coordination across units. While consistency can promote stability and predictability, I-O psychology research cautions that excessive emphasis on uniformity may suppress critical thinking and reinforce outdated practices. For instance, organizations that prioritize procedural consistency without revisiting underlying assumptions may continue using biased technologies simply because they align with "how things have always been done." In such cases, consistency functions less as a strength and more as a mechanism for preserving systemic inequities.

Adaptability, by contrast, captures an organization's capacity to respond to environmental change, learn from feedback, and revise ineffective practices. This dimension is particularly salient in contexts involving rapid technological advancement and heightened scrutiny of fairness and accountability. Low adaptability scores may indicate resistance to revising AI algorithms despite evidence of disparate impact, reflecting cognitive rigidity or fear of disruption. Conversely, organizations with strong adaptability cultures are more likely to engage in iterative testing, bias audits, and cross-functional collaboration. A real-world example can be seen in organizations that paused AI deployment after early warning signs of inequitable outcomes and restructured their systems through multidisciplinary oversight, demonstrating learning-oriented behavior rather than defensive inertia (Ahmady et al., 2016).

MISSION CLARITY AND LEADERSHIP INFLUENCE ON CULTURE

The mission dimension of the Denison model refers to the clarity of an organization's strategic direction, goals, and purpose. From an I-O psychology standpoint, a well-articulated mission serves as a cognitive anchor that guides behavior, prioritization, and ethical judgment. When mission statements explicitly emphasize equity, integrity, and evidence-based practice, they provide a psychological reference point against which employees evaluate organizational actions. However, when mission rhetoric is disconnected from daily operations, employees may perceive hypocrisy, leading to cynicism and reduced organizational commitment.

Leadership plays a central role in translating mission into practice. Ahmady et al. (2016) emphasize that managers are not merely transmitters of culture but active agents who shape, reinforce, and model cultural norms. Leaders who leverage the Denison model as a diagnostic tool can identify misalignments between espoused values and enacted behaviors, such as proclaiming a commitment to diversity while minimizing reports of algorithmic bias. In practice, effective leaders use cultural assessments to inform targeted interventions; such as revising governance structures, redefining accountability metrics, and embedding ethical review processes into decision-making workflows.

IMPLICATIONS FOR ORGANIZATIONAL CULTURE AND BEHAVIOR

When applied holistically, the Denison Organizational Culture Model enables organizations to move beyond surface-level compliance toward deeper cultural alignment. By examining involvement, consistency, adaptability, and mission simultaneously, leaders can better understand how organizational systems either support or undermine ethical behavior and effective performance. From an I-O psychology perspective, culture change is most sustainable when it is behaviorally reinforced through leadership actions, feedback systems, and shared learning experiences.

In environments increasingly shaped by AI and data-driven decision-making, the Denison model offers a valuable lens for ensuring that technological tools align with human values and organizational purpose. Organizations that actively assess and recalibrate their culture are better positioned to prevent the normalization of biased practices and to cultivate climates of accountability, psychological safety, and continuous improvement. In this way, the model functions not only as a diagnostic instrument but also as a strategic guide for shaping organizational behavior in complex and evolving contexts.

DIFFUSION OF INNOVATIONS THEORY AND ORGANIZATIONAL ADOPTION DYNAMICS

The Diffusion of Innovations theory provides a robust framework for understanding how new technologies are adopted, contested, and normalized within organizations. From an industrial and organizational psychology perspective, the theory is particularly useful because it situates innovation adoption as a social and behavioral process rather than a purely technical one. Individuals and groups within organizations do not adopt innovations uniformly; instead, they progress through distinct stages of awareness, evaluation, experimentation, and acceptance. In complex organizational systems, misalignment across these stages often produces resistance, misunderstanding, or unintended consequences, especially when innovations such as AI-driven hiring tools directly affect identity, opportunity, and perceived fairness (Alsheibani et al., 2018).

The theory conceptualizes adoption as unfolding over time in a non-linear pattern, often represented as an S-shaped curve, reflecting how innovations gain momentum as social validation increases (Alsheibani et al., 2018). Individuals are categorized along a continuum of innovativeness, ranging from innovators and early adopters to early majority, late majority, and laggards. In organizational settings, these categories often map onto functional roles and power structures. For example, AI engineers and senior executives may function as innovators or early adopters due to their technical expertise or strategic authority, while frontline employees or compliance personnel may fall into later adoption categories because they bear the operational or ethical consequences of the technology. Recognizing these differences allows organizations to anticipate behavioral responses and design adoption strategies that are psychologically informed rather than coercive.

RESISTANCE, PERCEPTION, AND ORGANIZATIONAL BEHAVIOR

A central contribution of the Diffusion of Innovations theory is its emphasis on perceived attributes of an innovation, relative advantage, compatibility, complexity, trialability, and observability, as determinants of adoption behavior (Alsheibani et al., 2018). From an I-O psychology lens, these perceptions are shaped by prior experiences, organizational culture, and trust in leadership rather than by objective technical features alone. For instance, an AI hiring system may be perceived by executives as offering efficiency and cost savings (relative advantage), while employees may perceive the same system as incompatible with organizational values of fairness and inclusion (Omar & Burrell, 2024). These divergent interpretations can produce resistance that is often mislabeled as irrational or anti-innovation, when in fact it reflects legitimate concerns about equity and accountability.

Real-world examples illustrate this dynamic clearly. When Amazon discontinued its AI recruiting tool after discovering gender bias in resume screening, resistance from internal stakeholders was not rooted in opposition to innovation itself, but in concerns about reputational harm and ethical misalignment. Diffusion theory helps explain why early adopters may initially champion AI systems, while later adopters raise critical questions once observable outcomes, such as skewed hiring data, become apparent. Addressing resistance, therefore, requires reframing AI adoption as an iterative learning process rather than a one-time implementation, reinforcing psychological safety and encouraging critical evaluation across adoption stages (Haley, 2025; Haley & Burrell, 2025; Omar & Burrell, 2024).

COMMUNICATION CHANNELS AND SOCIAL SYSTEMS

Communication channels play a pivotal role in shaping how innovations are interpreted and accepted within organizations (Omar & Burrell, 2024). Diffusion theory emphasizes the influence of opinion leaders and trusted social networks in legitimizing new technologies (Alsheibani et al., 2018). In organizational contexts, these opinion leaders are often middle managers, HR professionals, or respected technical experts who translate abstract innovations into meaningful workplace implications. From an I-O psychology standpoint, these individuals function as sensemakers, influencing how employees cognitively and emotionally process change.

Social systems, including organizational culture, hierarchy, and informal power structures, further shape diffusion outcomes (Huff et al., 2023; Omar & Burrell, 2024). Organizations with strong cultures of transparency and participation are more likely to surface concerns about AI bias early, enabling corrective action before harm occurs (Haley & Burrell, 2025; Haley, 2025). Conversely, cultures that prioritize speed, control, or unquestioned authority may suppress dissent, allowing flawed technologies to diffuse unchecked (Omar & Burrell, 2024; Haley & Burrell, 2025). Understanding these social dynamics enables leaders to design communication strategies that foster dialogue rather than compliance, aligning innovation adoption with collective values and ethical standards (Alsheibani et al., 2018).

TIME, LEARNING, AND ETHICAL INTEGRATION

Time is a critical yet often underestimated dimension of innovation diffusion. Adoption does not occur instantaneously, nor should it be forced prematurely. Diffusion theory emphasizes the importance of allowing individuals and groups sufficient time to experiment, evaluate outcomes, and adjust behaviors (Alsheibani et al., 2018). From an I-O psychology perspective, this temporal dimension aligns with learning theory and behavior change principles, which stress reinforcement, feedback, and reflection as prerequisites for sustainable change.

In the context of AI integration, organizations that provide pilot programs, human-in-the-loop review processes, and structured feedback mechanisms are better positioned to detect bias and refine systems over time (Omar & Burrell, 2024; Haley & Burrell, 2025). For example, organizations that pause large-scale deployment of AI tools to conduct bias audits and employee focus groups demonstrate a commitment to ethical learning rather than technological determinism. Such practices enhance trust, reduce resistance, and support the gradual institutionalization of innovation.

APPLICATION TO AI-DRIVEN RECRUITMENT SYSTEMS

The Diffusion of Innovations theory offers a comprehensive framework for understanding the organizational challenges associated with integrating AI into recruitment processes. AI-based hiring tools represent a high-stakes innovation because they directly influence access to employment, career advancement, and organizational diversity (Omar & Burrell, 2024). Applying diffusion theory allows organizations to systematically assess how perceptions of fairness, communication practices, and social influence shape adoption trajectories. Importantly, the theory aligns with calls for transparency, accountability, and ethical oversight by emphasizing that successful diffusion depends not only on technical effectiveness but also on social legitimacy (Haley, 2025; Haley & Burrell, 2025; Omar & Burrell, 2024).

In sum, the Diffusion of Innovations theory underscores that the successful adoption of AI in organizational settings requires more than technical readiness; it demands psychological insight, cultural alignment, and ethical stewardship. By attending to individual differences in adoption readiness, leveraging trusted communication channels, and allowing time for learning and adaptation, organizations can mitigate resistance and prevent the institutionalization of biased systems (Haley, 2025; Haley & Burrell, 2025; Omar & Burrell, 2024). This approach positions innovation not as an imposed solution, but as a collectively negotiated process that shapes, and is shaped by, organizational culture and behavior.

CULTURE OF CHANGE AND ORGANIZATIONAL ADAPTABILITY

Organizational culture is not static; it evolves in response to leadership actions, environmental pressures, and collective learning. Denison's research highlights adaptability as a core cultural capability, particularly in organizations facing technological disruption. In I-O psychology, adaptability reflects an organization's ability to learn from feedback, revise ineffective practices, and align behavior with strategic goals. When organizations lack a coherent culture, employees often exhibit disengagement, resistance, and counterproductive work behaviors, which can ultimately result in financial and reputational losses (Abdavi et al., 2018).

Empirical studies suggest that strong organizational cultures are sustained through shared commitments among stakeholders and continuous investment in development processes (Omar & Burrell, 2024; Haley & Burrell, 2025; Haley, 2025). However, findings across industries are mixed. For example, while some sectors demonstrate strong links between cultural adaptability and performance, others, such as construction, have shown lower compliance and weaker cultural integration (Abdavi et al., 2018). These inconsistencies underscore the importance of context-sensitive cultural interventions rather than one-size-fits-all solutions.

KOTTER'S CHANGE MANAGEMENT THEORY

Kotter's eight-step change management model offers a comprehensive framework for understanding how organizations can initiate, implement, and sustain large-scale change. From an industrial and organizational psychology perspective, the model is particularly valuable because it recognizes that change is fundamentally a behavioral and social process rather than a purely technical one. The first step, establishing a sense of urgency, involves helping organizational members recognize the psychological and operational consequences of maintaining the status quo (Kotter, 2017). Urgency is most effective when it is grounded in credible data and emotionally resonant narratives. For example, in response to an AI-related discrimination lawsuit, leadership may present evidence of legal risk, reputational damage, and employee disengagement while also sharing firsthand accounts from affected employees to foster empathy and moral accountability (Kotter, 2017; Sarayreh et al., 2013).

The second and third steps, forming a guiding coalition and developing a clear vision, address the social dynamics of influence and alignment (Kotter, 2017). A guiding coalition should consist of individuals with formal authority, technical expertise, and informal influence across organizational levels. In organizations adopting AI-driven hiring systems, this coalition might include executives, human resources leaders, AI developers, legal advisors, and industrial psychologists. The vision created by this group must articulate not only what will change but why the change aligns with organizational values such as fairness, inclusion, and evidence-based decision-making. From an I-O psychology standpoint, a compelling vision reduces ambiguity, increases psychological safety, and serves as a shared cognitive framework that guides behavior during periods of uncertainty.

Communicating the vision and empowering others to act represent the fourth and fifth steps of Kotter's model and are critical for translating intention into action. Effective communication extends beyond formal announcements; it requires consistent messaging through multiple channels and visible reinforcement by leaders' behavior (Kotter, 2017). For instance, leaders who advocate for ethical AI practices must demonstrate their commitment by reallocating resources, revising performance metrics, and removing structural barriers that prevent employees from questioning biased systems. Empowerment also involves enhancing employees' self-efficacy by providing training, decision authority, and access to feedback mechanisms, enabling individuals to contribute meaningfully to the change process (Kotter, 2017).

The sixth step, generating short-term wins, addresses motivation and reinforcement. Short-term wins provide tangible evidence that change efforts are producing desired outcomes and help counteract change fatigue. In the context of AI reform, early wins might include the successful audit of an algorithm for bias, the implementation of human-in-the-loop review processes, or measurable improvements in hiring diversity metrics. These outcomes reinforce adaptive behaviors and strengthen employees' belief that their efforts matter. The seventh step, sustaining momentum, requires organizations to avoid complacency by continuously identifying opportunities for improvement and embedding learning into routine practices (Kotter, 2017). Finally, anchoring change in organizational culture ensures that new behaviors become normative rather than episodic (Kotter, 2017). This involves integrating ethical and inclusive practices into leadership development, performance evaluation, and organizational storytelling so that the change is perceived as "the way we do things here" rather than a temporary initiative (Kotter, 2017).

BEHAVIORAL ANALYSIS AND COLLECTIVE LEADERSHIP

Addressing deeply rooted organizational problems often requires collective leadership approaches that extend beyond traditional hierarchical models. Research examining collective leadership in socially complex environments demonstrates its effectiveness in mobilizing diverse stakeholders toward shared goals. For instance, Caulfield and Brenner (2020) analyzed a decade-long initiative that successfully reduced teen birth rates through coordinated leadership, strategic communication, and sustained community engagement.

Although the context differs from organizational settings, the behavioral principles are transferable. The initiative leveraged Kotter's change framework to align stakeholders, maintain momentum, and institutionalize change. From an I-O psychology standpoint, this case illustrates how bold leadership, creative messaging, and shared ownership can overcome resistance and foster large-scale behavioral change. These insights are particularly relevant for organizations attempting to reform entrenched systems, such as biased hiring technologies, that affect multiple stakeholder groups (Caulfield & Brenner, 2020).

BRIDGES' TRANSITION MODEL AND THE PSYCHOLOGY OF ORGANIZATIONAL CHANGE

Unlike traditional change management frameworks that prioritize structural redesign, timelines, and process implementation, the Bridges' Transition Model centers on the psychological journey individuals experience as they adapt to change. From an industrial and organizational psychology perspective, this distinction is critical because organizational outcomes are ultimately shaped by how employees interpret, emotionally respond to, and behaviorally adjust to change initiatives. The model conceptualizes transition as a three-phase process, ending, neutral zone, and new beginning, each of which represents a distinct set of cognitive, emotional, and motivational challenges that must be managed deliberately (Miller, 2017).

The first phase, often referred to as "ending" or "letting go," involves the psychological disengagement from familiar roles, routines, identities, or competencies. Employees may experience loss, anxiety, or resistance as they confront the erosion of established expertise or status. In technology-driven change, such as the introduction of AI-supported decision systems, this phase is especially pronounced among employees whose professional identity has been closely tied to human judgment or legacy systems. If leaders fail to acknowledge these emotional responses, resistance may manifest as withdrawal, skepticism, or passive noncompliance. I-O psychology research emphasizes that validation of employee experiences during this phase enhances trust and reduces defensive behavior, laying the groundwork for adaptive change.

THE NEUTRAL ZONE AND BEHAVIORAL UNCERTAINTY

The second phase, the neutral zone, represents a psychologically ambiguous period in which old practices have been disrupted, but new ones have not yet been fully internalized. From a behavioral standpoint, this phase is characterized by role ambiguity, reduced performance consistency, and heightened cognitive load as employees attempt to reconcile competing expectations. Although often perceived as unproductive or risky, the neutral zone also presents opportunities for learning, innovation, and redefinition of work processes (Miller, 2017).

In organizational contexts involving AI implementation, the neutral zone may involve employees experimenting with new systems while questioning their reliability, fairness, or ethical implications. For example, recruiters transitioning to AI-assisted screening tools may oscillate between reliance on algorithmic recommendations and reassertion of human judgment. I-O psychology suggests that without structured support, such as training, feedback loops, and psychological safety, this phase can lead to frustration and disengagement. However, when leaders intentionally frame the neutral zone as a learning period rather than a performance failure, organizations can harness it as a developmental space where employees co-create new norms and competencies.

NEW BEGINNINGS AND IDENTITY RECONSTRUCTION

The final phase, the new beginning, occurs when individuals cognitively and emotionally commit to new roles, behaviors, and identities. This phase is not simply marked by the completion of technical implementation but by internalized acceptance and renewed purpose. From an I-O psychology perspective, successful new beginnings are associated with increased self-efficacy, clarity of expectations, and alignment between individual values and organizational goals. Employees begin to see themselves as capable contributors within the new system, reinforcing motivation and engagement (Miller, 2017).

In practice, new beginnings are strengthened through symbolic and structural reinforcement. For instance, organizations adopting AI tools responsibly may integrate ethical AI competencies into performance evaluations, promotion criteria, and leadership development programs. Celebrating milestones, such as successful bias audits or improved hiring equity metrics, helps employees associate the change with positive outcomes. These reinforcement mechanisms anchor new behaviors into organizational culture, reducing the likelihood of regression to outdated practices.

PRACTICAL APPLICATIONS AND LEADERSHIP IMPLICATIONS

Effective application of the Bridges' Transition Model requires leaders to actively manage psychological transitions alongside operational change. Structured communication strategies, such as regular town halls, transparent updates, and two-way feedback mechanisms, help employees make sense of where they are in the transition process. Visual tools, including transition maps or dashboards, can further enhance understanding by making progress visible and normalizing temporary uncertainty (Miller, 2017).

In AI system migrations, transition mapping allows leaders to anticipate emotional responses, identify skill gaps, and allocate resources accordingly. For example, organizations that schedule biweekly reflection sessions during AI rollout phases enable employees to voice concerns, share learning experiences, and recalibrate expectations. From an I-O psychology standpoint, such practices reduce turnover risk, foster resilience, and promote sustained behavioral adaptation. By attending to the human experience of change rather than assuming automatic compliance, leaders can transform disruption into an opportunity for cultural learning and long-term organizational effectiveness.

METHODS AND RESEARCH DESIGN

This study employed a qualitative focus group methodology designed to capture expert-level perspectives on the organizational and behavioral implications of artificial intelligence (AI) in hiring and recruitment. A qualitative approach was selected to allow for in-depth exploration of complex, value-laden issues such as bias, fairness, accountability, and organizational decision-making; phenomena that are not easily reducible to quantitative measures. The study was conducted entirely via Zoom and unfolded across three structured phases to promote individual reflection, disciplinary consensus, and interdisciplinary integration.

The design was informed by industrial and organizational (I-O) psychology principles emphasizing collective sensemaking, social influence, and the co-construction of meaning within expert communities. This multi-phase approach enhanced analytical rigor by reducing dominance effects, encouraging reflexivity, and allowing ideas to evolve through structured dialogue.

The ten responses reported for each research question represent the final, consensus-based outcomes of the full interdisciplinary group of ten participants, rather than preliminary or individual-level findings. Following the three-phase data collection process, all responses were iteratively refined and validated through structured dialogue. In the final phase, the combined group of five industrial and organizational psychology researchers and five AI policy researchers jointly reviewed the consolidated response lists generated during the discipline-specific focus groups. Through facilitated discussion, participants evaluated each response for relevance, explanatory strength, applicability across organizational contexts, and alignment with ethical and behavioral considerations. Only those responses that achieved collective agreement among all ten participants were retained as final results.

This final integration phase ensured that the reported responses reflect shared expert judgment across disciplinary boundaries, rather than isolated perspectives. Responses that overlapped conceptually were merged, while those deemed redundant, insufficiently substantiated, or overly discipline-specific were removed. The resulting lists therefore represent the most salient, defensible, and interdisciplinary insights regarding AI use in hiring, grounded in both behavioral science and AI governance expertise.

Rigor and Advantages of the Multi-Phase Consensus Approach

The rigor of this study is strengthened by its three-phase qualitative design, which deliberately separates individual cognition, intra-disciplinary consensus, and interdisciplinary integration. Phase One minimized conformity bias by capturing independent expert responses prior to any group interaction. Phase Two enhanced depth and internal validity by allowing each disciplinary group to negotiate meaning, clarify assumptions, and resolve internal disagreements, producing discipline-specific master lists grounded in shared expertise. Phase Three further elevated rigor by subjecting these lists to cross-disciplinary scrutiny, requiring participants to reconcile technical, ethical, and organizational perspectives.

This consensus-driven approach offers several methodological advantages. First, it reduces the influence of dominant voices by structuring participation and requiring agreement at multiple stages. Second, it enhances credibility by ensuring that findings are not the product of a single analytical lens, but rather the outcome of interdisciplinary deliberation. Third, it increases transferability by focusing on responses that were judged to be broadly applicable across organizational contexts rather than context-specific anecdotes. Finally, the process aligns with industrial and organizational psychology principles of collective sensemaking and social validation, reinforcing the study's emphasis on how expert knowledge is constructed, negotiated, and stabilized within complex organizational systems. Together, these design features ensure that the final ten responses for each research question represent methodologically rigorous, expert-validated results that capture the most critical organizational, behavioral, and ethical implications of AI use in hiring and recruitment.

Participants

The purposive sample consisted of ten doctoral-level experts divided evenly into two disciplinary groups:

- Five PhD-level industrial and organizational psychology researchers with expertise in personnel selection, organizational culture, and workplace equity.
- Five PhD-level AI policy researchers with backgrounds in algorithmic governance, ethical AI, and regulatory frameworks.

All participants had prior research or applied experience related to AI systems in organizational contexts. This composition allowed for both depth within disciplines and breadth across socio-technical perspectives.

Data Collection Procedure

Data collection occurred in three sequential phases.

Phase One: Individual Response Collection

Participants received four open-ended questions electronically and were asked to submit written responses independently. This phase minimized groupthink and ensured that initial perspectives reflected individual expertise rather than social influence.

Phase Two: Disciplinary Focus Groups

Two separate Zoom focus groups were conducted; one with the five I-O psychology researchers and one with the five AI policy researchers. During these sessions, participants shared their individual responses, discussed points of convergence and divergence, and collaboratively generated a master list of responses for each question within their respective disciplines. Duplicate or redundant responses were removed through group consensus.

Phase Three: Interdisciplinary Integration Focus Group

A final Zoom session included all ten participants. The two disciplinary master lists were reviewed collectively, refined, and consolidated. Through structured discussion and consensus-building, participants identified the ten most critical and salient responses to each question, reflecting interdisciplinary agreement on organizational, behavioral, and ethical implications.

Data Analysis

Data analysis followed a consensus-based qualitative reduction process rather than thematic coding. Responses were evaluated based on prominence, explanatory power, relevance to organizational behavior, and applicability across contexts. The final results represent the most critical responses as determined by collective expert judgment, consistent with qualitative expert-panel methodologies.

Data Results

Research Question 1

In what ways can the use of AI in hiring be a disadvantage for applicants?

1. AI systems may replicate historical hiring biases embedded in training data, disadvantaging applicants from marginalized groups.
2. Automated screening tools often prioritize proxy variables (e.g., school attended, employment gaps) that systematically exclude qualified candidates.
3. Applicants are frequently denied transparency regarding how decisions are made, limiting their ability to contest outcomes.
4. AI tools may fail to account for contextual or non-linear career paths, penalizing career changers or caregivers.

5. Over-standardization in AI screening reduces opportunities for applicants to demonstrate unique competencies or potential.
6. Linguistic and cultural bias in resume-parsing algorithms can disadvantage non-dominant communication styles.
7. Applicants experience reduced perceptions of fairness and procedural justice when human judgment is absent.
8. Algorithmic errors disproportionately affect applicants who lack social capital or internal referrals.
9. AI systems may prematurely eliminate candidates before meaningful human review occurs.
10. The absence of feedback mechanisms limits applicant learning and future employability.

Research Question 2

What are the potential problems of overreliance on AI in recruiting and hiring processes?

1. Overreliance on AI can erode human accountability for hiring decisions.
2. Organizations may develop false confidence in algorithmic objectivity and overlook discriminatory outcomes.
3. Excessive automation weakens recruiters' critical evaluation skills over time.
4. AI systems may be treated as decision-makers rather than decision-support tools.
5. Organizational learning is reduced when human judgment is removed from evaluative processes.
6. Ethical concerns may be deferred to technical teams rather than addressed at leadership levels.
7. Bias detection becomes reactive rather than proactive.
8. Organizational culture may shift toward efficiency over fairness.
9. Legal and reputational risks increase when AI outputs are insufficiently monitored.
10. Employees may disengage if they perceive hiring practices as impersonal or unjust.

Research Question 3

How can AI tools with biased algorithms lead to discrimination?

1. Biased training data can produce systematically unequal outcomes across demographic groups.

2. Algorithmic proxies may indirectly encode race, gender, or socioeconomic status.
3. Feedback loops can amplify existing disparities over time.
4. Disparate impact may occur without intentional discrimination.
5. Bias may remain undetected due to lack of transparency or auditing.
6. Developers' assumptions can shape model priorities and exclusions.
7. Organizational silence may prevent reporting of biased outcomes.
8. AI tools may legitimize discriminatory outcomes under the guise of neutrality.
9. Discriminatory outputs can scale rapidly across large applicant pools.
10. Lack of interdisciplinary oversight increases the likelihood of ethical blind spots.

Research Question 4

What are best-practice recommendations for using AI tools in hiring while avoiding discrimination?

1. Treat AI as a decision-support system rather than a replacement for human judgment.
2. Conduct regular bias audits using interdisciplinary review teams.
3. Incorporate industrial and organizational psychology principles into model design and validation.
4. Ensure transparency in algorithmic decision criteria and outcomes.
5. Maintain human-in-the-loop review for all high-stakes hiring decisions.
6. Align AI tools with organizational values and mission statements.
7. Train recruiters and leaders to interpret and question AI outputs critically.
8. Establish clear accountability structures for AI-related decisions.
9. Pilot AI tools before full-scale implementation to assess unintended consequences.
10. Continuously evaluate outcomes using equity-focused performance metrics.

CONCLUSIONS

This qualitative focus group study examined expert perspectives on the use of artificial intelligence in hiring through a structured, three-phase consensus process involving five industrial and organizational psychology researchers and five AI policy researchers. The findings demonstrate that AI-driven hiring systems, while offering efficiency and scalability, pose significant behavioral, ethical, and organizational risks when implemented without adequate psychological oversight and governance. The final results, ten consensus-based responses for each research question, reflect interdisciplinary agreement that AI in hiring is not inherently neutral and that its impact is shaped by organizational culture, leadership decisions, and accountability structures.

A central conclusion of this study is that the disadvantages and risks associated with AI in hiring are not primarily technical failures, but organizational and behavioral ones. Bias, discrimination, and overreliance on automation emerge when organizations substitute algorithmic outputs for human judgment rather than integrating AI as a decision-support tool. The findings further indicate that transparency, continuous evaluation, and interdisciplinary collaboration are essential for preventing AI systems from institutionalizing inequitable practices. By grounding AI adoption within principles of organizational justice, psychological safety, and evidence-based decision-making, organizations can mitigate harm and enhance both fairness and effectiveness in hiring.

Leadership Implications

The findings of this study underscore the pivotal role of leadership in shaping how AI tools influence organizational behavior and culture. Leaders are ultimately responsible for how hiring decisions are made, regardless of whether those decisions are supported by algorithms or human judgment. From an I-O psychology perspective, delegating decision authority to AI without maintaining human accountability reflects a leadership failure rather than a technological inevitability. Leaders must therefore model critical engagement with AI outputs, demonstrating that efficiency does not supersede ethical responsibility.

Effective leadership in AI-enabled organizations requires fostering cultures where questioning, auditing, and challenging algorithmic decisions are normalized rather than discouraged. Leaders should ensure that managers and recruiters are trained not only in how to use AI tools, but in how to interpret, contextualize, and override them when necessary. The consensus findings suggest that leadership credibility is enhanced when executives visibly align AI use with organizational values, reinforce ethical standards through action, and establish clear accountability for outcomes. In doing so, leaders signal that AI adoption is a strategic and moral choice, not merely a technical upgrade.

Organizational Implications

At the organizational level, the results indicate that AI hiring systems have profound implications for culture, trust, and employee perceptions of fairness. Organizations that rely heavily on automated decision-making risk eroding procedural justice if applicants and employees perceive hiring outcomes as opaque or unchallengeable.

Such perceptions can weaken employer branding, reduce engagement, and contribute to organizational silence, particularly among marginalized groups.

The findings suggest that organizations must treat AI integration as a cultural change initiative rather than a discrete technological implementation. This includes embedding human-in-the-loop processes, establishing formal bias audit mechanisms, and creating feedback channels for applicants and employees. Organizations that successfully align AI tools with participatory decision-making and learning-oriented cultures are more likely to prevent discriminatory outcomes and sustain long-term effectiveness. From an I-O psychology standpoint, organizations that fail to address these cultural dynamics risk normalizing inequity and undermining the legitimacy of their talent management systems.

Policy Implications

The consensus-based findings of this study also carry important implications for organizational policy and external governance. At the organizational level, policies governing AI use in hiring must move beyond compliance checklists to explicitly define accountability, transparency, and ethical standards. Clear policies should specify who is responsible for AI-related decisions, how bias is monitored, and under what conditions human judgment must override algorithmic recommendations.

At a broader level, the findings support the need for policy frameworks that recognize AI hiring systems as socio-technical systems rather than neutral tools. Policymakers and regulators should encourage interdisciplinary oversight, documentation of algorithmic decision processes, and routine impact assessments focused on equity and discrimination. Importantly, policy approaches should not assume that technical fixes alone can resolve bias; instead, they must incentivize organizational practices that integrate behavioral science expertise into AI design and deployment. Such policy alignment reinforces the conclusion that ethical AI in hiring is as much an organizational and leadership challenge as it is a technological one.

RECOMMENDATIONS FOR FUTURE RESEARCH

Future research should make benchmarking a central methodological and governance priority in the study and deployment of AI-driven hiring systems. Benchmarking, in this context, refers to the systematic process of evaluating AI-based selection tools against clearly defined, theory-driven, and equity-centered standards in order to assess their performance, fairness, and validity relative to accepted best practices and legally defensible outcomes. Unlike ad hoc audits or post hoc compliance checks, benchmarking is a continuous and comparative process that situates AI tools within a broader evidentiary framework grounded in industrial and organizational psychology, organizational justice theory, and employment law. As the findings of this study suggest, many of the failures associated with AI in hiring stem not from a lack of technical sophistication, but from the absence of structured reference points against which algorithmic decisions can be evaluated for disparate impact, predictive accuracy, and alignment with organizational values.

The benefits of benchmarking are both scientific and practical. From a research perspective, benchmarking enables cumulative knowledge development by allowing scholars to compare AI systems across organizations, industries, and demographic contexts using shared metrics and assumptions. This comparability is essential for distinguishing isolated implementation problems from systemic patterns of bias and for identifying which design features, validation practices, or governance structures are associated with more equitable outcomes. From an organizational perspective, benchmarking functions as an early-warning system that can surface inequities before they escalate into legal, reputational, or cultural crises. By systematically comparing algorithmic outcomes across protected groups, job categories, and time periods, organizations can move from reactive compliance to proactive ethical stewardship of AI-enabled decision-making. Importantly, benchmarking reinforces accountability by underscoring that AI tools are organizational instruments subject to the same standards of evaluation and responsibility as traditional human-driven selection systems.

Future research should therefore prioritize the development and empirical testing of benchmarking frameworks that integrate technical performance metrics with psychological, ethical, and legal criteria. An effective benchmarking process should begin with the explicit articulation of normative standards, including job-related validity, procedural and distributive justice, transparency, and equity. These standards should be derived from established industrial and organizational psychology principles rather than narrowly defined efficiency or optimization goals. Researchers should then evaluate AI systems against multiple reference points, such as human-based selection methods, alternative algorithms trained on different data sets, and longitudinal workforce outcomes that capture changes over time. Critically, benchmarking should be iterative rather than static, with repeated assessments conducted as algorithms are retrained, organizational contexts evolve, and labor markets shift. Incorporating interdisciplinary review and oversight into this process can further enhance rigor by ensuring that technical findings are interpreted alongside behavioral, cultural, and legal implications.

By embedding benchmarking into future research designs, scholars can help shift the discourse on AI in hiring away from abstract claims of objectivity and innovation toward empirically grounded evaluations of real-world impact. Such an approach directly addresses the central risks identified in this study by providing a structured mechanism for detecting bias, validating fairness, and aligning AI-driven hiring practices with principles of organizational justice, scientific rigor, and ethical responsibility.

REFERENCES

Abdavi, F., Fateh, H., & Pashaie, S. (2018). The Effects of Denison's Model of Organizational Culture on Customer Relationship Management (CRM): Case Study of Ministry of Sports and Youth in Iran. *International Journal of Management, Accounting & Economics, 5*(6), 461–472. https://www.researchgate.net/profile/Sajjad-Pashaie/publication/360791392_The_Effects_of_Denison's_Model_of_Organizational_Culture_on_Customer_Relationship_Management_CRM_Case_Study_of_Ministry_of_Sports_and_Youth_in_Iran/links/628ba1d739fa217031682af0/The-Effects-of-Denisons-Model-of-Organizational-Culture-on-Customer-Relationship-Management-CRM-Case-Study-of-Ministry-of-Sports-and-Youth-in-Iran.pdf

Ahmady, G. A., Nikooravesh, A., & Mehrpour, M. (2016). Effect of organizational culture on knowledge management based on Denison Model. *Procedia: Social and Behavioral Sciences, 230*, 387–395. https://www.sciencedirect.com/science/article/pii/S1877042816311508. DOI: 10.1016/j.sbspro.2016.09.049

Alsheibani, S., Cheung, Y., & Messom, C. (2018). Artificial Intelligence Adoption: AI-readiness at Firm-Level. *PACIS, 4*, 231-245. https://research.monash.edu/en/publications/artificial-intelligence-adoption-ai-readiness-at-firm-level/

Bridges, S. (2020, March 12). *Bridges transition model.* William Bridges Associates. Retrieved March 21, 2023, from https://wmbridges.com/about/what-is-transition/

Burton, S. L. (2025). Integrating Cybersecurity and Artificial Intelligence: Adaptive Frameworks for Future-Ready Education. https://doi.org/10.5281/zenodo.16333218

Caulfield, J. L., & Brenner, E. F. (2020). Resolving complex community problems: Applying collective leadership and Kotter's change model to wicked problems within social system networks. *Nonprofit Management & Leadership, 30*(3), 509–524. https://onlinelibrary.wiley.com/doi/abs/10.1002/nml.21399?casa_token=SE49ZSKJpHUAAAAA%3AIx7MEpsN-No4ZQq24qjdlnajh3MB3vvPwz2Vqw8yPI7kfcEcRPvW1fi8kVByVvrP0OPsp7vVIFyRsva5. DOI: 10.1002/nml.21399

Cheung, H. K., King, E., Lindsey, A., Membere, A., Markell, H. M., & Kilcullen, M. (2016). Understanding and reducing workplace discrimination. *Research in Personnel and Human Resources Management*, •••, 101–152. https://www.emerald.com/books/edited-volume/12777/chapter-abstract/83108905/Understanding-and-Reducing-Workplace?redirectedFrom=fulltext

Collins, R. (2010). *A graphical method for exploring the business environment.* Henley Business School., http://dl1.icdst.org/pdfs/files/3debe72112ec5b1d1abd4f83ced389a8.pdf

Cuevas, A. G., & Boen, C. (2021). Tip of the iceberg: Measuring racial discrimination in studies of health. *Stress and Health, 37*(5), 1043–1050. https://pmc.ncbi.nlm.nih.gov/articles/PMC8449795/. DOI: 10.1002/smi.3047 PMID: 33739613

Haley, P. (2025). Artificial intelligence and ethical dimensions of automated traffic enforcement: Implications for public health, healthcare equity, and social justice. *Health Economics and Management Review, 6*(2), 32-49. https://armgpublishing.com/wp-content/uploads/2025/07/HEM_2_2025_3.pdf

Haley, P., & Burrell, D. N. (2025). Integrating Artificial Intelligence into Law Enforcement: Socioeconomic and Ethical Challenges. *SocioEconomic Challenges, 9*(2), 60-77. https://armgpublishing.com/wp-content/uploads/2025/07/SEC_2_2025_4.pdf

Huff, A., Burrell, D. N., Richardson, K., Springs, D., Aridi, A. S., Crowe, M. M., & Lewis, E. (2023). Illegal Pregnancy Discrimination Is a Severe Business, Legal, and Public Health Issue. In Burrell, D. (Ed.), *Real-World Solutions for Diversity, Strategic Change, and Organizational Development: Perspectives in Healthcare, Education, Business, and Technology* (pp. 119–129). IGI Global., DOI: 10.4018/978-1-6684-8691-7.ch008

Kotter, J. P. (2017). What leaders really do. In *Leadership perspectives* (pp. 7–15). Routledge. DOI: 10.4324/9781315250601-2

Lundy, D., Burrell, D. N., McCargo, T., Lima, F. M., Harris, N., Eke, H., & Prunella, K. 2025, November. Understanding the Psychology of Pregnancy Discrimination as a Challenging Womanâ€™ s Mental Health Workplace Dynamic. In *RAIS Conference Proceedings 2022-2025* (No. 0608). Research Association for Interdisciplinary Studies. https://ideas.repec.org/p/smo/raiswp/0608.html

McLester, Q., Burrell, D. N., Nobles, C., & Castillo, I. (2021). Advancing Knowledge About Sexual Harassment Is a Critical Aspect of Organizational Development for All Employees. [IJKBO]. *International Journal of Knowledge-Based Organizations, 11*(4), 48–60. DOI: 10.4018/IJKBO.2021100104

Miller, J. L. (2017). Managing transitions: Using William Bridges' transition model and a change style assessment instrument to inform strategies and measure progress in organizational change management. In *The 12th International Conference on Performance Measurement in Libraries Proceedings* (p. 357). https://digitalcommons.butler.edu/librarian_papers/74/

Omar, M., & Burrell, D. N. (2024). Organizational Dynamics and Bias in Artificial Intelligence (AI) Recruitment Algorithms. In E. Lewis (Ed.), Evolution of Cross-Sector Cyber Intelligent Markets (pp. 269-290). IGI Global Scientific Publishing. DOI: 10.4018/979-8-3693-1970-3.ch015

Sarayreh, B. H., Khudair, H., & Barakat, E. A. (2013). Comparative study: The Kurt Lewin of change management. *International Journal of Computer and Information Technology*, *2*(4), 626–629. https://d1wqtxts1xzle7.cloudfront.net/33293215/Paper020413-libre.pdf?1395622098=&response-content-disposition=inline%3B+filename%3DComparative_Study_The_Kurt_Lewin_of_Chan.pdf&Expires=1770182492&Signature=P0VtSo-TcWR92-ie039dtlfSb56JOoOwNeIUa0YWE5sM-jsQA9rTK2kYWJedz9kK7HFvRQnpLPXI8mFHFvvE-4kO8f4jXZF7aU5rVC8Uw0pPgoeWyOwE9-b4SI3OI6tYWNxN2NnCkdREtv4caktFeu4mHIx8qS14LQD0l-JxNwzZBvheE7Sr6BaPjO1ZHu6S0ZNteVX3NEFbio~yaTBNEz-EGhMLufzyyF72TUyIkqNDQzLktgHCaNd6tjoW1QuRJNq-eJ40yGxCoGOf8o-pi5lHgQslIHazfQATW30RmQuxGCFsoqwjz-QbCxnnX6~--1CFZNIziAXusCxaR1nRXQ__&Key-Pair-Id=APKAJLOHF5GGSLRBV4ZA

Vaudrin, C. J. (2019). Melting the Cultural Iceberg in Indigenizing Higher Education: Shifts to Accountability in Times of Reconciliation. *New Directions for Teaching and Learning*, *2019*(157), 105–118. DOI: 10.1002/tl.20333

Wazed, S. (2018, August 2). *Council post: Grow your organization with top talent using the iceberg interview model.* Forbes. Retrieved March 21, 2023, from https://www.forbes.com/sites/forbeshumanresourcescouncil/2018/08/02/grow-your-organization-with-top-talent-using-the-iceberg-interview-model/?sh=41d17c2175b8

Zapata, D. (2021, June). New study finds AI-enabled anti-Black bias in recruiting. Thomson Reuters. Retrieved from: https://www.thomsonreuters.com/en-us/posts/legal/ai-enabled-anti-black-bias/

Zoričić, D., Knežević, G., Miletić, M., Dolinar, D., & Sprčić, D. M. (2022). Integrated Risk Analysis of Aggregators: Policy Implications for the Development of the Competitive Aggregator Industry. *Energies (19961073), 15*(14), N.PAG. DOI: 10.3390/en15145076

Chapter 4
Bridging the Gender Gap in AI:
A Conceptual Framework for Assessing and Addressing AI's Impact on Women

Annamaria Szakonyi
http://orcid.org/0000-0002-1958-2042
Embry-Riddle Aeronautical University, USA

Constantine Michael Koursaris
Embry-Riddle Aeronautical University, USA

ABSTRACT

The chapter introduces a conceptual framework for understanding and mitigating the negative impacts of artificial intelligence (AI) on women. Through a qualitative, interpretive synthesis of peer-reviewed research, it investigates AI's negative impacts centered around bias, workforce transformation, and health and wellbeing. Proposed solutions involve increasing gender equity in the AI workforce, transforming organizational culture, adopting human-centered approaches, ensuring procedural fairness and transparency, and prioritizing security, privacy, and ethics. The socio-cultural context is identified with a focus on societal expectations and the role of education in shaping our future. The framework links gender-inclusive AI practices to organizational agility, arguing that gender equity in AI design and governance improves firms' adaptive capacity, innovation potential, and resilience in rapidly changing technological environments. It aims to reverse negative impacts, fostering inclusivity and breaking traditional cultural norms for a positive organizational and societal impact.

DOI: 10.4018/979-8-2600-1016-7.ch004

INTRODUCTION

In recent years, the field of artificial intelligence (AI) has experienced unprecedented growth, revolutionizing various industries and aspects of daily life. AI has demonstrated remarkable potential in areas such as healthcare, finance, education, entertainment, supply chain, service operations, product and service development, hiring, and risk modeling (Buolamwini & Gebru, 2018; Lloyd's Register Foundation, 2022; Manyika et al., 2019; Maslej et al., 2023; McKinsey & Company, 2023; World Economic Forum, 2023). The ability of AI systems to analyze complex datasets, recognize patterns, and make informed decisions has led to breakthroughs in medical diagnostics, personalized recommendations, autonomous vehicles, process automations, among many other applications. The benefits of AI are multifaceted, contributing to reduced costs, increased productivity, improved decision-making, enhanced overall user experiences, and the development of innovative solutions to complex problems (Manyika et al., 2019; McKinsey & Company, 2023; Yoldemir, 2020; World Economic Forum, 2023).

However, alongside these advancements, concerns and risks have emerged, particularly in the realm of equity. One of the major apprehensions revolves around the potential for AI-driven algorithms, employed for decisions impacting individuals' lives (such as evaluating job qualifications or creditworthiness) to generate or magnify discriminatory outcomes. Unfortunately, AI technologies still have significant shortcomings when it comes to handling and mitigating the influence of human bias in AI technology designs (Buolamwini & Gebru, 2018; Lloyd's Register Foundation, 2022; Manyika et al., 2019; McKinsey & Company, 2023).

The risks associated with AI impact women disproportionately, emphasizing the urgency to address these issues and promote inclusivity. Biases embedded in AI algorithms can perpetuate gender-based discrimination, affecting women's opportunities in areas such as hiring, finance, and healthcare. Research suggests that organizations with diverse teams, including a significant representation of women, tend to outperform their counterparts in terms of productivity and innovation (Deloitte AI Institute, 2021; Simonite, 2018). Therefore, it is imperative to examine the impacts of AI on women, namely, understanding and addressing the complex interplay between women in the AI workplace, biases against women embedded in AI systems, negative impacts on women, and the broader influence of socio-cultural contexts on these dynamics.

The chapter frames the challenges and opportunities of AI through the twin lenses of gender equity and organizational agility. It argues that the social design of AI (who builds systems, whose data are represented, and what evaluation metrics are prioritized) directly influences organizations' capacity to adapt, innovate, and manage risk. By centering gender in both analysis and intervention design, organizations can strengthen decision-making diversity, reduce algorithmic harms, and enhance adaptive capabilities required for resilient technological adoption.

To guide this analysis, the chapter introduces a three-part conceptual framework, organized into three interacting dimensions that together provide a diagnostic and prescriptive schema for assessing AI's impact on women:

(1) Negative impacts include the pathways through which AI systems produce gendered harms, including dataset and model bias, disparate workforce effects, and domain-specific harms (e.g., healthcare misdiagnoses) that disproportionately affect women.
(2) The organizational and technical solutions serve as levers organizations can deploy to mitigate these harms, such as gender-diverse teams, participatory human-centered design, fairness-aware model development, continuous auditing, and governance structures that embed transparency and accountability into lifecycle processes.
(3) Finally, the socio-cultural context applies to the external and internal cultural, legal, and structural forces that shape both the manifestation of harms and the feasibility of interventions.

The framework is intentionally socio-technical and dynamic, and is linked to organizational agility, arguing that embedding gender-equity practices into AI governance increases adaptive capacity, improves decision diversity, and reduces systemic risk in organizations facing rapid technological change. In practice, the framework functions as a diagnostic tool (to map current vulnerabilities) and a planning instrument (to prioritize interventions and assign responsibilities) for progress across technical, organizational, and cultural dimensions.

PROBLEM STATEMENT

Despite advances in artificial intelligence (AI) and its growing integration into global industries, the gender gap in AI creation, access, and benefit remains a persistent and systemic issue. Women continue to be underrepresented in AI-related professions, comprising only 26% of the global AI workforce (UNESCO, 2024). At the same time, gender disparities are reflected in the use of AI: women are 7–12% less likely than men to use generative AI tools at work, limiting their exposure to digital upskilling opportunities (AI Literacy Institute, 2024). This imbalance reinforces a feedback loop: when women are excluded from AI design, the resulting technologies often fail to meet women's needs or reflect their lived experiences.

Evidence also shows that algorithmic systems frequently reproduce and amplify gender bias (Hall & Ellis, 2023; O'Connor & Liu, 2023; Shrestha & Das, 2022). Moreover, an estimated 4.7% of women's jobs are highly vulnerable to displacement by AI worldwide, compared to 2.4% of men's positions (Tamayo & Petrelli, 2025). This disparity widens sharply in high-income countries, where almost 9.6% of female employment faces high automation risk, while the figure for men is around 3.5% (Tamayo & Petrelli, 2025). These inequities threaten to deepen socio-economic divides unless addressed through inclusive, ethical, and transparent AI design and governance frameworks.

This chapter addresses this problem by proposing a conceptual framework for assessing and mitigating AI's impact on women. Using an interpretive, qualitative approach, it synthesizes current evidence to identify how gender bias manifests in AI systems and proposes organizational and cultural interventions to promote gender equity in AI adoption. By articulating both diagnostic and prescriptive elements, this framework aims to support organizations, researchers, technologists and policymakers in developing the agility, foresight, and ethical grounding required to ensure AI serves as a tool of empowerment rather than exclusion for women in the digital era.

SIGNIFICANCE

Understanding and addressing the gendered impacts of artificial intelligence (AI) is essential for ensuring that technological progress contributes to equity rather than reinforcing existing disparities. As automation and AI reshape the global labor market, women face a disproportionate risk of job displacement and exclusion from emerging digital roles (Tamayo & Petrelli, 2025). If left unaddressed, these inequities could deepen gender gaps in economic participation, leadership, and technological literacy.

From an organizational perspective, addressing gender disparities in AI is essential for cultivating agility to adapt, innovate, and respond effectively to technological change. Research shows that gender-diverse and inclusive teams enhance problem-solving, reduce blind spots, and improve organizational responsiveness in rapidly evolving environments (Díaz-García et al., 2013; World Economic Forum, 2023). When gender inequities persist in AI development and governance, organizations risk embedding biased assumptions into automated systems, weakening decision quality and undermining trust among employees, consumers, and regulators. Conversely, gender-inclusive AI practices strengthen innovation pipelines, improve risk management, and enhance organizational resilience in the face of uncertainty

(UNESCO, n.d.).. Failure to address these disparities not only perpetuates systemic inequities but also constrains an organization's ability to leverage AI strategically and sustainably.

This chapter delves into the societal impacts of artificial intelligence, specifically focusing on the experiences and contributions of women. It sheds light on AI's challenges for women and proposes solutions related to these problems. The chapter goes beyond the technical lens, examining AI within a broader social context, particularly focusing on women's roles, experiences, and the intersections of gender, inclusivity, and broader societal impact.

This study is significant because it offers a holistic framework for identifying and mitigating the systemic and structural factors through which AI affects women. By linking gender representation, algorithmic fairness, and socio-cultural dynamics, the research provides organizations and policymakers with a roadmap for inclusive AI development and governance. By addressing gender bias in AI, organizations not only advance equity but also cultivate true organizational agility; the capacity to adapt, innovate, and respond effectively to technological disruption. Inclusive AI practices foster diverse perspectives and equitable participation, which research consistently links to greater creativity, resilience, and responsiveness in technology adoption and implementation, aligning directly with the book's vision of agility as both a technical and cultural capability.

METHODOLOGY

This chapter adopts a conceptual and integrative methodology consistent with contemporary approaches to perspective and commentary research. Conceptual synthesis is a rigorous method for developing theoretical frameworks, particularly in emerging domains where empirical evidence is still fragmented (Jaakkola, 2020). Rather than collecting original empirical data, the study synthesizes peer-reviewed scholarship, institutional reports, and interdisciplinary research to explore the intersection of gender, artificial intelligence (AI), and organizational agility. By identifying patterns, gaps, and converging themes related to gender disparities in AI, the chapter critically examined how AI systems shape women's participation and representation in the digital economy. The interpretive lens allows for a nuanced understanding of the social, cultural, and organizational contexts that influence both the design and outcomes of AI technologies.

The literature informing this chapter was identified through a structured search of peer-reviewed journals, major institutional publications, and interdisciplinary research reflecting the rapidly evolving nature of AI technologies and gender equity discourse. Priority was given to empirical studies, systematic reviews, and high-credibility institutional and governmental analyses that examine gendered impacts of AI within organizations, sociotechnical contexts, and global development systems.

Using a thematic analytic approach, the chapter is grounded in socio-technical systems (STS) theory, which emphasizes the interdependence between people, technology, and organizational structures (Bostrom & Heinen, 1977; Cherns, 1976, 1987; Trist & Bamforth, 1951). From this perspective, AI is not viewed solely as a technical innovation but as a system embedded within, and shaped by, social norms, institutional practices, and human values. Applying this framework enables the study to assess how organizational and policy decisions around AI adoption and implementation can either reinforce or mitigate gender inequities. By integrating socio-technical insights with this analysis, the paper aims to inform more agile, inclusive, and ethically grounded approaches to technology-driven transformation.

In addition to sociotechnical systems theory, this chapter draws on Critical Data Studies (CDS) to examine how data practices and algorithmic design choices embed power relations and historical inequalities into AI systems. CDS provides a normative lens for interrogating how gendered assumptions shape data collection, model training, and deployment, revealing how AI systems can reproduce or amplify structural inequities unless organizational safeguards are intentionally designed (Boyd & Crawford, 2012; Crawford et al., 2014; Dalton & Thatcher, 2014; Ekbia et al., 2015; Iliadis & Russo, 2016). Incorporating CDS into the methodological foundation strengthens the chapter's argument that organizational agility must be paired with critical digital responsibility, ensuring that innovation does not perpetuate harm for marginalized groups of women. This combined method enables a holistic understanding of AI's gendered impacts and supports theory-building that can guide future empirical research.

THEORIES FROM THE LITERATURE

The literature examining gender, AI, and organizational practice increasingly demonstrates that the ability of institutions to adapt to technological transformation depends on their capacity to integrate diverse perspectives, establish inclusive governance structures, and respond to emerging risks with flexibility and speed. Organizational agility (i.e. the dynamic capability to sense technological change, interpret its implications, and respond through iterative learning, collaboration, and adaptive decision-making) is particularly critical in AI adoption, where complex sociotechnical risks, such as algorithmic bias, inequitable data practices, and workforce exclusion, require organizations to coordinate technical expertise with ethical and social considerations (Muduli & Choudhury, 2025; Nguyen et al., 2025). Studies show that inclusivity and gender-diverse teams strengthen innovation performance, expand cognitive range, reduce blind spots in system design, and enable responsible and adaptive AI implementation (Alakaş, 2024; Díaz-García et al., 2013; World Economic Forum, 2023).

Together, these organizational perspectives highlight that agility in AI-intensive environments depends not only on adaptive leadership and diverse teams, but also on a clear understanding of the sociotechnical risks embedded in algorithmic systems. A core component of organizational agility is the ability to anticipate, identify, and mitigate sources of bias that emerge from data practices that shape how AI systems affect women. Accordingly, the next section examines algorithmic bias to establish the technical foundations of gender disparities in AI and to clarify why addressing these risks is essential for building responsive, equitable, and resilient organizations.

Artificial Intelligence and Machine Bias

AI systems acquire decision-making capabilities by learning from training data, which might include biased human decisions or mirror historical and social inequities, even when sensitive variables such as gender, race, or sexual orientation are excluded. AI and machine learning uses examples from the real world to learn and to generate outputs. This is why historical and representation bias can creep into the process due to existing social and cultural standards and stereotypes (Barocas & Selbst, 2016; Lee et al., 2019; Mehrabi et al., 2021; Suresh & Guttag, 2019). As an example, certain words may represent certain genders due to historically influenced circumstances, such as nurse versus engineer (Barocas & Selbst, 2016; Suresh & Guttag, 2019). Selection and sample bias, as well as exclusion bias may be present during the data collection phase of AI development. This can happen when the sample is not random and therefore the results are not generalizable, or when certain subgroups are more likely to be included than others (Lee et al., 2019; Mehrabi et al., 2021).

Data is then cleaned and various features are identified to be used in the process. At this phase, we may experience measurement bias, because the features we select to predict the problem may actually be proxies to the real problem (Mehrabi et al., 2021; Suresh & Guttag, 2019). For example, GPA may not always be an accurate representation of academic success. In the next phase, the model is selected and trained on the training data. During model training, aggregation bias may appear when a one-size-fits-all approach is applied to various subsets of groups (Mehrabi et al., 2021; Suresh & Guttag, 2019).

Finally, the model is tested on the test data for its functionality and performance, and it is evaluated on other benchmark datasets to compare its effectiveness to other existing models and to implement any improvements necessary, before applying it in a real-world setting. At these phases, evaluation and confirmation bias may creep in, since when the benchmark is just as faulty as the original model, the bad result will be confirmed and accepted as a positive outcome (Mehrabi et al., 2021; Suresh & Guttag, 2019). If this model is then deployed in a real-world setting, it will just reinforce the existing issues and feed the newer models with these biased results (Mehrabi et al., 2021). This process and the integrated bias components are described in Figure 1.

Figure 1. Simplified diagram of bias in the machine learning process

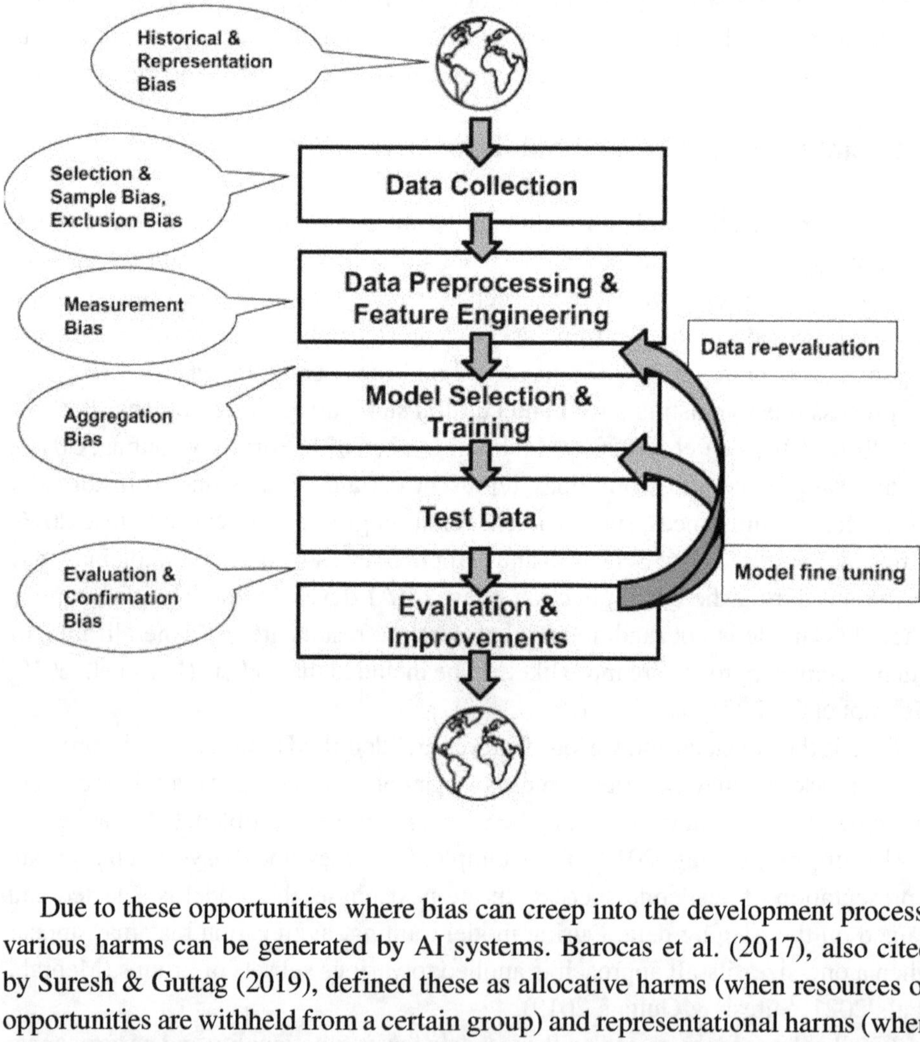

Due to these opportunities where bias can creep into the development process, various harms can be generated by AI systems. Barocas et al. (2017), also cited by Suresh & Guttag (2019), defined these as allocative harms (when resources or opportunities are withheld from a certain group) and representational harms (when a system reinforces certain stereotypes for a group). If AI is trained on real-life data, which is inherently biased, these issues will also be represented in the output of AI technologies, creating various harms for women (Scotti, 2023).

Gender Issues with AI

Gender Bias in AI

Having established the presence of biases in artificial intelligence systems and the resulting harms, we now turn to examine how these biases specifically manifest in the context of women. According to a Pew Research Center study, there is a 15 percentage point difference in people's perceptions of AI developers positively considering the experiences and views of men over women in the design of AI systems (Rainie et al., 2022). Clearly, these results reflect some serious concerns related to how AI may impact women. Are these concerns warranted?

Due to the inherent difficulties with AI systems, there have been various examples that resulted in both allocative and representational harms against women. Facial recognition technologies have historically had higher error rates for women, performing better on men's faces compared to faces of women (Gendered Innovations, n.d.; Manyika et al., 2019). Image recognition and labeling tools often misclassify men as women when depicted in traditionally female roles, such as in the kitchen (Gendered Innovations, n.d.; Simonite, 2018; Zhao et al., 2017). Considering this in significant gender-based social issues such as human trafficking or gender-based violence, AI tools attempting to fix these problems must account for these complexities.

Another example is Amazon's discontinued, AI-powered hiring tool that made gender-biased selections in the hiring process (Lee et al., 2019; Manyika et al., 2019; Scotti, 2023). The algorithm favored applicants who used words like "executed" or "captured", which are more typically used in men's resumes (Lee et al., 2019; Manyika et al., 2019). This outcome stemmed from the historical predominance of men in that particular role, because of which the AI systems devalued resumes containing references to women (Scotti, 2023).

Reviewing performance of AI systems that rely on language models, the results are also in favor of men. When analyzing machine translation outcomes, language models translating to English often perform 2–9% worse when the output requires gender pronouns of "she" compared to "he" (Maslej et al., 2023). Some of these issues, of course, are a result of the unrepresentative training data used when training the model.

In general, Stanford's 2023 AI Index Report found that AI models that are more accurate are generally more fair, but there is no clear correlation between accuracy and gender bias (Maslej et al., 2023). Models that perform better on fairness metrics often showcase heightened gender bias, while less gender-biased models tend to display increased toxicity (Maslej et al., 2023). This implies the existence of trade-offs between fairness and bias that should be investigated further.

The evidence demonstrates that gender bias in artificial intelligence (AI) systems is both pervasive and multifaceted, producing tangible harms for women across social and professional domains. These biases are not isolated errors but systemic outcomes of data imbalances, cultural stereotypes, and the underrepresentation of women in AI development. The negative outcomes reveal the dual nature of bias in AI: allocative harms, where opportunities and resources are denied, and representational harms, where women are mischaracterized or rendered invisible. The persistence of these issues highlights the urgent need for deeper inquiry into how fairness, accuracy, and inclusion can coexist within AI design. Without intentional efforts to correct these biases, AI technologies risk perpetuating structural gender disparities under the guise of objectivity and innovation.

AI and Women's Health and Wellbeing

AI has been used in healthcare in diverse ways from risk assessments for diseases to automating diagnosis determination from medical images (Yoldemir, 2020). Healthcare research, however, has been historically lagging for women compared to studies conducted on men (Epker, 2023; Yoldemir, 2020). Considering that successful AI tools rely on significant amounts of training data, we must consider the risks this can pose for these products when applied to female versus male populations (Yoldemir, 2020). As an example, there exists a significant gender gap in pain assessment data, which can have serious negative consequences on treatment related predictions in women's health (Calderone, 1990).

In addition, AI and machine learning algorithms are often trained on real-world data such as electronic health records and insurance claim data, which also raises the concerns of privacy (Yoldemir, 2020). How can women be secure and safe when all of their health data is digitized and shared across providers? In a post Roe v. Wade era in the US, this can have even more significant impacts on women's health, and can pose additional risks considering that abortion access in some states is criminalized. AI tools can be exploited to further marginalize women in already vulnerable situations if their electronic health records can be used against them to prosecute them in abortion cases. Therefore, privacy and security should be a crucial component in how AI developers deploy these tools (Raji et al., 2020).

In addition to clinical and diagnostic disparities, emerging research highlights that generative AI technologies, including deepfakes, sexualized synthetic imagery, and digitally mediated harassment, have become significant mental health threats for women. Studies show that non-consensual deepfake pornography disproportionately victimizes women and is strongly associated with psychological distress, reputational harm, coercion, and ongoing trauma responses, particularly among those from marginalized communities who already face heightened digital vulnerability

(Flynn et al., 2022; Henry et al., 2020; Martin, 2022; Okolie, 2023). Because these harms are fueled by misogynistic and transphobic patterns embedded in training data and platform ecosystems, they illustrate how sociotechnical dynamics can directly impact women's mental health, safety, and sense of agency online. These findings reinforce the health dimension of the conceptual framework by showing that AI-enabled harms extend well beyond technical misclassification, shaping emotional and psychological well-being in ways that organizations must anticipate when developing risk management practices and employee support systems. These risks require dedicated research to understand how organizations can develop protective, gender-responsive safeguards against AI-driven harassment and abuse.

Artificial intelligence (AI) has the potential to revolutionize healthcare and well-being, yet persistent gender disparities in research and data collection still limit its equitable impact. The additional mental health and abuse-related risks women face due to emerging AI-enabled technologies make the wellbeing perspective even more pressing. Collectively, these issues highlight that technological advancement in AI related to healthcare and wellbeing must be accompanied by gender-aware design, data inclusivity, and robust ethical oversight to ensure that AI enhances rather than endangers women's health and autonomy.

Women in the AI Workforce and The Future of Work

We can observe a significant disparity between the demographic composition of AI developers and users (Maslej et al., 2023). In North America, AI practitioners are predominantly white males (Maslej et al., 2023). According to the World Economic Forum, women are still significantly underrepresented in the STEM fields (2024). Women constitute nearly half (42%) of the global workforce, yet they represent only 28.2% of all STEM workers (World Economic Forum, 2024). Despite a significant surge in overall AI talent, only 26% of the global AI workforce is female (UNESCO, 2024). In fact, female representation in AI talent is lower than that of men across all major industries (World Economic Forum, 2023).

This lack of representation and diversity can lead to the reinforcement of existing societal inequalities and biases (Maslej et al., 2023). However, AI teams with higher female representation can better challenge assumptions, flag problems and identify unconscious biases to assure its benefits to diverse populations (Deloitte AI Institute, 2021; Lee et al., 2019; Simonite, 2018). Therefore, to reap these benefits, it is crucial to instill an inclusive culture in AI as well as to improve access and opportunity for growth and advancement for women in the field (Deloitte AI Institute, 2021). It is evident that the participation of women in Artificial Intelligence design and development must be increased to benefit society.

It is also interesting to mention gender representation in chatbots currently on the market. In an analysis of 100 open-domain conversational AI systems, it was found that 37% of those products had a female gender, while 20% was male, and 40% genderless (Maslej et al., 2023). In commercial conversational AI systems, this number was even higher, with 62.5% of them being female (Maslej et al., 2023). This seems to reinforce a gender-based assumption; that administrative roles, such as personal assistants, are female.

Even when in the AI workforce, women face various challenges that are different from those faced by men. Women are more often faced with situations where they have to prove themselves credible when interacting with male colleagues, while the expertise of their male counterparts' are generally assumed (Deloitte AI Institute, 2021). In addition, women working in AI and data science jobs have higher turnover (i.e. changing roles) and attrition rates (i.e. leaving the industry) than men (Deloitte AI Institute, 2021; Simonite, 2018; Young et al., 2021). This is likely due to gender discrimination and the lack of recognition compared to men (Deloitte AI Institute, 2021). Furthermore, women in these fields often face sexual harassment that steer them away from the industry after these bad experiences (Simonite, 2018).

Another area to study when considering the impacts of AI on the workforce is related to the transformation of occupations due to automation and robotics. Considering that AI will likely result in significant job losses across industries, concerns should be raised how this may impact women further. Women are expected to lose jobs at a higher rate than their male counterparts due to automation, because female-dominated professions will be impacted at a higher rate than those dominated by men (Idemudia & Onoshakpor, 2023; Roopaei et al., 2021). Since women often bear a disproportionate responsibility for caring for children and elderly parents, reskilling for a new occupation will be a challenge for many (Idemudia & Onoshakpor, 2023; Roopaei et al., 2021).

With the changing workforce landscape due to the prevalence of AI and automation, we must create more avenues for women to get retrained from historically female-dominated professions that will be replaced by these technologies. For this, we must create a social environment where women can choose to learn new skills that can help them transition into the new era of shifting workplace dynamics driven by artificial intelligence.

Mitigating Gender Issues in AI

There are various ways to improve these negative outcomes of AI systems. First, using a human-centered design approach is crucial when building any type of technology to build the best outcomes for our target users (Google AI, n.d.). Relying on data that appropriately represents users and the real world ensures that the solutions designed consider the experiences and realities of all groups involved (Google AI, n.d.). Human-centered design means cross-functional experts and representatives must be involved in the process (Lee et al., 2019). This can be important already in the very first step when AI teams frame the problem, as that can result in assumptions made already before the appropriate data is collected.

This also means the involvement of women at all phases of AI. Deloitte's survey conducted with the AI workforce determined that the presence of women would be beneficial for the design of AI tools (Deloitte AI Institute, 2021). 71% of respondents said that women bring unique perspectives to AI, 66% said that AI solutions would benefit having women in developer positions, and 63% said AI tools will never be without bias unless there's increased representation in the industry (Deloitte AI Institute, 2021).

Women bring unique insights, creativity, and problem-solving skills to the table, leading to more robust and well-rounded decision-making processes. If women were included in the AI development process, they could be influential in the original problem definition and data collection, to avoid bias related to different issues. More women in the AI workforce could assure that their differing perspectives are present in the AI development pipeline, mitigating potential bias during data curation, model building and training, testing, and interpretation.

To assure these benefits are present, we must increase the representation of women in AI. To do so, we must reimagine organizations to treat women the same way as men: with opportunities, promotions, pay, recognition and expectations to be comparable irrespective of one's gender identity. This, however, does not only mean the creation of formal initiatives such as women-only training and mentorship programs. Rather, this should mean an all-encompassing, gender inclusive culture (Deloitte AI Institute, 2021). The goals should be to change the environment, and not to change women. Scotti echoes this sentiment in her paper, where she stresses the importance of shifting our culture, rather than the intervention of the industry, to eliminate built-in biases against women (2023). She mentions the importance of social, cultural, and political ways to encourage and grow the representation of women in AI (Scotti, 2023). This will not only fix the problem related to the lack of women in AI, but will also automatically patch the biased training data problem.

Evidently, education plays a pivotal role in advancing women's circumstances in AI. As the workforce undergoes transformations due to automation, continuous education becomes essential in retraining women who may be adversely affected by job displacement. This retraining not only helps them adapt to emerging technologies but also empowers them to pursue new opportunities in growing sectors such as AI, narrowing the current AI workforce gap. Moreover, cultural awareness and education can contribute significantly to fostering inclusive cultures within industries that can assure that women pursuing STEM careers stay in their chosen specialties due to equal opportunities and treatment.

Additionally, an emphasis on education for women has the potential to reshape societal roles by challenging traditional norms and expectations. As women acquire education and skills across various fields, they can break free from predefined roles, contributing to a more equitable distribution of responsibilities and opportunities within families and communities. This shift not only benefits individual women but also fosters a broader societal transformation towards recognizing and valuing the diverse contributions and capabilities of women.

In addition, auditing not just fairness outcomes, but procedural fairness should be a requirement in how organizations develop and deploy AI solutions (Raji et al., 2020). Formal, regular audits of both algorithms and related processes should result in better outcomes and less negative consequences for select populations (Lee et al., 2019; Selbst et al, 2019). This will assure transparency and accountability from AI creators and developers to assure positive outcomes for all, and the ability to rectify issues when they happen. Therefore, mandating procedural fairness as a policy should be a priority around the controls and governance of AI programs.

Finally, privacy and security requirements are a must when designing and building AI tools to safeguard the well-being of women in various contexts. As AI technologies become more ingrained in daily life, there is a growing concern regarding the potential misuse of personal data. Ensuring robust security measures helps protect women from unauthorized access, data breaches, and potential exploitation. By prioritizing security and privacy in AI frameworks, we can create a more inclusive and equitable technological landscape, fostering trust and confidence among women who interact with AI systems. This approach not only safeguards individual privacy but also contributes to the overall ethical development and deployment of AI technologies.

Socio-Cultural Influences of Gender in AI

The gendered impacts of AI are shaped not only by technical design choices but also by deeply rooted socio-cultural and regional dynamics that influence digital access, representation, labor participation, and algorithmic vulnerability. While gendered AI disparities are often documented in North American and European contexts, global evidence shows that women's experiences with AI vary significantly across regional, economic, and cultural settings. In many low- and middle-income countries, women face limited connectivity, lower mobile phone ownership, reduced digital literacy, and restricted access to STEM and AI-related education, all of which constrain their participation in and benefit from emerging AI ecosystems (UNESCO, n.d., 2024; GSMA, 2025). These structural disparities also heighten their vulnerability to algorithmic exclusion, surveillance harms, and labor displacement in sectors undergoing rapid automation.

From a socio-technical systems perspective, such inequalities reflect the interdependence between technological systems and the broader social, economic, and cultural contexts in which they operate (Cherns, 1976). Thus, understanding AI's gendered effects requires grappling with the ways societal norms, global development disparities, and institutional structures co-produce the conditions that allow algorithmic harms to emerge and unevenly affect women across social structures, cultures and regions. This evidence directly informs the socio-cultural dimension of the conceptual framework developed in this chapter, emphasizing that gender-inclusive AI strategies must account for contextual variations in social norms, infrastructure, and institutional environments to meaningfully support organizational agility and equitable AI adoption.

RESULTS AND RECOMMENDATIONS: A CONCEPTUAL FRAMEWORK FOR AI'S IMPACT ON WOMEN

Based on this analysis, this chapter proposes a conceptual framework for AI's impact on women to establish the various areas of study required to address this problem in a holistic manner, depicted in Figure 2. This conceptual framework sets the foundation for future research, policy, and technical considerations as organizations embark on their AI development and adoption journeys.

Figure 2. A Conceptual Framework for AI's Impact on Women

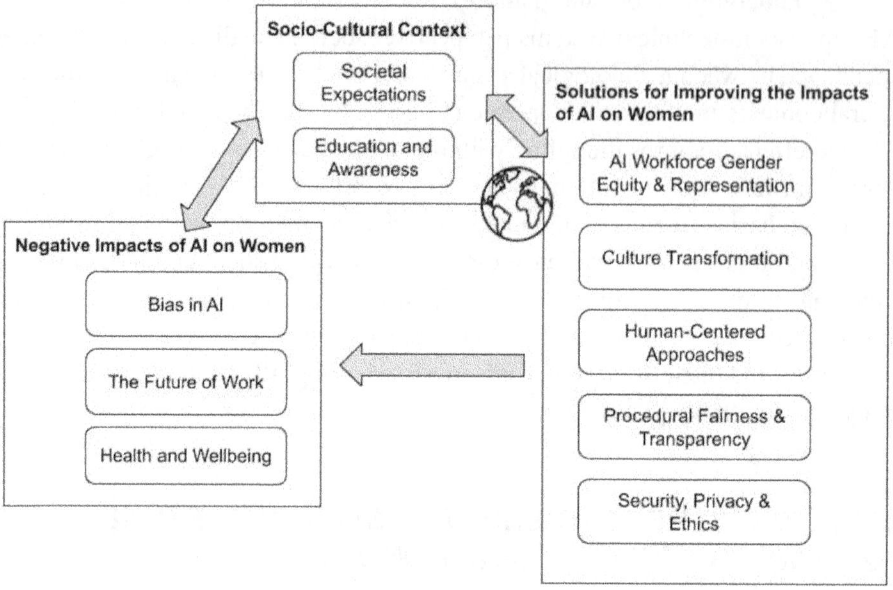

Negative Impacts of AI on Women

- **Bias in AI:** Bias plays a crucial role in the negative aspects of AI. Emphasis must be placed on investigating how bias in data and algorithms can lead to gender-discriminatory outcomes and perpetuate or exacerbate existing gender disparities.
- **The Future of Work:** Organizations must investigate how AI technologies may reinforce or challenge traditional workplace structures and norms, including potential job displacement and the impact on job satisfaction for women.
- **Health and Wellbeing:** It is imperative to assess the implications of AI in healthcare on women's well-being, considering issues such as biased medical diagnoses, the impact on reproductive health, and mental health implications.

Solutions for Improving the Impacts of AI on Women

- **Representation and Gender Equity in the AI Workforce:** Organizations must increase the current representation of women in AI-related roles to reap the benefits of their diverse perspectives.

- **Culture Transformation**: Organizational culture must be adjusted to address the challenges that hinder equal participation and opportunities for career growth for women, with the ultimate goal of assuring women will stay in these occupations.
- **Human-Centered Approaches:** Problems addressed by AI solutions must promote the collaboration among cross-disciplinary teams and apply a human-centered problem-solving approach.
- **Procedural Fairness & Transparency:** Policies must be reviewed and new frameworks must be developed that address challenges in the AI pipeline, and encourage AI developers and organizations to be transparent about their development practices.
- **Security, Privacy & Ethics:** Security and privacy must be mandated in AI solutions to protect sensitive information about women and vulnerable populations. Open discussions must be encouraged around the ethics of AI and how it impacts society as a whole.

Socio-Cultural Context

- **Societal Expectations:** Understanding how societal expectations and cultural norms and behaviors shape perceptions of gender roles, and exploring how these expectations may influence career choices and opportunities for women is a must for the listed solutions.
- **Education and Awareness:** Investigating the role of education and training programs in shaping women's entry into AI fields is more pressing than ever, as traditionally female occupations will be on the decline due to the presence of AI technologies.

Overall, the socio-cultural context influences the negative results of AI: current socio-cultural patterns influence how AI exists today (i.e. the data AI relies on), resulting in its negative consequences on women. In turn, those negative impacts will reinforce these cultural traditions, exacerbating the gender gap. With the help of the solutions listed, we can reverse those negative impacts into positive ones, which in turn can help break traditional cultural norms and reinforce improved cultural norms and awareness. Better cultural context and understanding can lead to faster implementation of these solutions, as those original cultural biases will gradually dissipate from the AI development pipeline.

This conceptual framework provides a holistic perspective on the multifaceted issues surrounding women in AI, acknowledging the interplay between workplace dynamics, biases in AI systems, negative impacts on women, and the broader socio-cultural context. Addressing these components collectively is crucial for fostering a diverse, fair, and thriving AI ecosystem that benefits everyone.

CONCLUSIONS

It is evident that, despite its transformative potential, artificial intelligence continues to produce gendered inequities that disadvantage women as both users and contributors. While AI has revolutionized decision-making, efficiency, and productivity across industries, it has also reinforced pre-existing societal and structural biases. The limited representation of women in AI development and leadership, coupled with algorithmic bias and inequitable access to technology, highlights the need for a multi-disciplinary, systems-level approach. Addressing this challenge requires perspectives not only from technologists and data scientists, but also from ethicists, social scientists, policymakers, and organizational leaders who understand the human dimensions of technological change.

To fully capitalize on the benefits of AI and foster innovation, organizations must cultivate organizational agility, a dynamic capability that integrates inclusion, adaptability, and foresight into every stage of AI adoption and implementation. True agility demands not only technical competence but also cultural responsiveness, where gender equity becomes a core principle of AI strategy. To achieve this, several actionable recommendations emerge from this study:

1. **Increase Women's Representation in AI Leadership and Design:** Organizations should actively recruit, retain, and promote women in AI-related roles, ensuring diverse perspectives inform data collection, model development, and ethical governance. Representation strengthens agility by improving innovation, creativity, and decision-making quality.
2. **Implement Bias Audits and Procedural Fairness Checks:** Regular auditing of algorithms for bias, transparency, and fairness must become a standard organizational practice. Embedding procedural fairness into governance systems enhances trust and adaptability in AI-driven operations.
3. **Adopt Human-Centered and Socio-Technical Design Principles:** Drawing from socio-technical systems theory, AI initiatives should balance technical performance with social outcomes. Incorporating user diversity in problem framing and solution design fosters agility by making systems more inclusive and sustainable.
4. **Invest in Education and Reskilling Programs for Women:** Policymakers and organizations should collaborate to provide training in digital literacy, data eth-

ics, and AI development. Empowering women to transition into emerging roles enhances workforce agility and reduces the risk of gendered job displacement.

5. **Create Inclusive Organizational Cultures:** Beyond formal diversity programs, companies must address cultural barriers that marginalize women. Psychological and physical safety, equitable pay, and transparent career advancement pathways are critical to retaining female talent in technology.
6. **Establish Ethical and Regulatory Frameworks for Responsible AI:** Policymakers should mandate transparency and accountability standards that require organizations to document how AI systems are trained, validated, and monitored. These frameworks strengthen societal agility by ensuring that innovation evolves responsibly.
7. **Integrate Gender Impact Assessments into AI Projects:** Prior to implementation, organizations should evaluate how AI systems affect different genders, particularly in hiring, healthcare, and financial services. Such assessments can prevent harm and guide equitable innovation.
8. **Encourage Multi-Stakeholder Collaboration:** Effective solutions require cooperation among academia, government, industry, and civil society. Cross-sector partnerships can accelerate the design of equitable AI ecosystems and ensure that agility remains aligned with ethical progress.

In summary, bridging the gender gap in AI is not only a moral imperative but a strategic necessity for cultivating organizational agility. Inclusive AI practices strengthen resilience, responsiveness, and innovation, key attributes for thriving amid technological disruption. To fully capitalize on the benefits of AI and foster innovation, it is imperative to cultivate a diverse and inclusive environment that acknowledges and addresses the specific challenges faced by women in the field of artificial intelligence. By embedding gender equity into the design, governance, and deployment of AI, organizations can lead digital transformation that is both adaptive and just, ensuring that the future of AI improves outcomes not only for organizations but also society at large.

LIMITATIONS AND FUTURE RESEARCH

As artificial intelligence continues to reshape global systems, further research is essential to deepen understanding of its gendered impacts and to inform equitable technology governance. The Conceptual Framework for AI's Impact on Women proposed in this chapter identifies several areas where future inquiry can expand both theoretical and practical knowledge across the 3 dimensions of issues, solutions, and the socio-cultural context.

A key limitation of this chapter is its treatment of "women" as a broad analytical category, which does not fully capture the intersectional variations in how AI systems affect different groups of women. Research shows that gender rarely operates alone; instead, women's experiences with AI systems are shaped by overlapping identities, including race, socioeconomic status, disability, age, and geographic location (Crenshaw, 1989; Noble, 2018). These intersecting factors can intensify algorithmic harms for women who occupy marginalized social positions, such as women of color, disabled women, and women from low-income regions, revealing the need for analytical approaches that move beyond categorical gender assessments. Future research should therefore test and refine the conceptual framework presented in this chapter using intersectional methodologies that can account for heterogeneity within groups of women and produce more contextually responsive organizational strategies.

A further limitation of this chapter is its predominant focus on women as a binary gender category, which does not fully represent the experiences of gender-diverse and non-binary individuals in AI systems and organizational environments. Emerging research shows that AI systems frequently misclassify, erase, or pathologize gender-diverse identities due to binary assumptions embedded in training data, resulting in organizational harms such as misgendering, exclusion in HR technologies, and heightened surveillance risks for non-binary and transgender individuals (Keyes, 2018; Scheuerman et al., 2020). Because this conceptual framework was not designed to fully interrogate these distinct forms of harm, future research should explicitly examine how gender-diverse individuals experience AI-mediated systems and how organizations can build inclusive governance, design practices, and evaluation metrics that account for more expansive gender identities.

In addition, future studies should move beyond qualitative analysis to empirical measurement of gender bias in AI systems by developing standardized metrics that quantify gender bias across AI models, datasets, and decision outputs. Comparative studies across industries could reveal sector-specific patterns of inequity. As generative AI tools proliferate, research should also examine how these technologies influence representation, creativity, and visibility of women across digital and professional spaces.

Furthermore, while current data indicate disproportionate automation risks for women, longitudinal research is needed to track how these trends evolve over time and how reskilling initiatives affect women's economic mobility. Since gendered impacts of AI can also vary by region and socio-cultural context, comparative research across low-, middle-, and high-income countries can illuminate how local norms, education systems, and labor markets shape women's participation in the AI economy.

Researchers should also assess the effectiveness of current AI ethics and policy interventions (such as bias audits, transparency laws, and data protection regulations) in mitigating gender disparities. Expanding this scholarship through the use of socio-technical systems theory to model interactions between policy, organizational culture, technology design, and social inclusion can also enhance understanding of how structural and cultural factors jointly influence AI adoption and organizational agility.

By advancing research across these domains, scholars can help build a more comprehensive evidence base to guide ethical AI innovation. Continued interdisciplinary study, spanning technology, policy, sociology, and organizational behavior, will be critical to ensuring that the next generation of AI systems enhances equity, resilience, and agility for all.

REFERENCES

AI Literacy Institute. (2024). Gender and age gaps in generative AI. https://ailiteracy.institute/gender-and-age-gaps-in-generative-ai

Alakaş, E. Ö. (2024). Digital transformational leadership and organizational agility in digital transformation: Structural equation modelling of the moderating effects of digital culture and digital strategy. *The Journal of High Technology Management Research, 35*(2), 100517. Advance online publication. DOI: 10.1016/j.hitech.2024.100517

Barocas, S., Crawford, K., Shapiro, A., & Wallach, H. (2017). The problem with bias: Allocative versus representational harms in machine learning. In *Proceedings of the 9th Annual Conference of the Special Interest Group For Computing, Information And Society. [SIGCIS].* Philadelphia, PA.

Barocas, S., & Selbst, A. D. (2016). Big data's disparate impact. *California Law Review, 104*(3), 671–732. DOI: 10.15779/Z38BG31

Bostrom, R. P., & Heinen, J. S. (1977). MIS problems and failures: A socio-technical perspective, Part I: The causes. *Management Information Systems Quarterly, 1*(3), 17–32. DOI: 10.2307/248710

Boyd, D., & Crawford, K. (2012). Critical questions for Big Data: Provocations for a cultural, technological, and scholarly phenomenon. *Information Communication and Society, 15*(5), 662–679. DOI: 10.1080/1369118X.2012.678878

Buolamwini, J., & Gebru, T. (2018). Gender shades: Intersectional accuracy disparities in commercial gender classification. *Proceedings of the 1st Conference on Fairness, Accountability and Transparency, 81*, 77-91. https://proceedings.mlr.press/v81/buolamwini18a/buolamwini18a.pdf

Calderone, K. L. (1990). The influence of gender on the frequency of pain and sedative medication administered to postoperative patients. *Sex Roles, 23*(11-12), 713–725. DOI: 10.1007/BF00289259

Cherns, A. (1976). The principles of sociotechnical design. *Human Relations, 29*(8), 783–792. DOI: 10.1177/001872677602900806

Cherns, A. (1987). Principles of sociotechnical design revisited. *Human Relations, 40*(3), 153–161. DOI: 10.1177/001872678704000303

Crawford, K., Miltner, K., & Gray, M. L. (2014). Critiquing Big Data: Politics, ethics, epistemology. *International Journal of Communication*, *8*, 1663–1672. https://ijoc.org/index.php/ijoc/article/view/2167/1164

Crenshaw, K. (1989). Demarginalizing the intersection of race and sex: A black feminist critique of antidiscrimination doctrine, feminist theory and antiracist politics. *University of Chicago Legal Forum*, *1989*(1), 139–167. https://chicagounbound.uchicago.edu/uclf/vol1989/iss1/8

Dalton, C., & Thatcher, J. (2014). What does a Critical Data Studies look like, and why do we care? Seven points for a critical approach to 'big data.' *Environment and Planning D: Society and Space. Online journal companion.* https://societyandspace.com/material/commentaries/craig-dalton-and-jim-thatcher-what-does-a-critical-data-studies-look-like-and-why-do-we-care-seven-points-for-a-critical-approach-to-big-data/

Deloitte, A. I. Institute. (2021). *Women in AI.* https://www2.deloitte.com/content/dam/Deloitte/us/Documents/deloitte-analytics/us-consulting-women-in-ai.pdf

Díaz-García, C., González-Moreno, A., & Sáez-Martínez, F. J. (2013). Gender diversity within R&D teams: Its impact on radicalness of innovation. *Innovation (North Sydney, N.S.W.)*, *15*(2), 149–160. DOI: 10.5172/impp.2013.15.2.149

Ekbia, H., Mattioli, M., Kouper, I., Arave, G., Ghazinejad, A., Bowman, T., Suri, V.R., Tsou, A., Weingart, S. & Sugimoto, C.R. (2015), Big data, bigger dilemmas: A critical review. *Journal of The Association for Information Science & Technology, 66*(8), 1523-1545. (First published in 2014)DOI: 10.1002/asi.23294

Epker, E. (2023, August 1). Artificial intelligence in women's health: The pros, the cons, and the guardrails needed to improve care. *Forbes*. https://www.forbes.com/sites/evaepker/2023/08/01/artificial-intelligence-in-womens-health-the-pros-the-cons-and-the-guardrails-needed-to-improve-care/?sh=3ecb29d34c87

Flynn, A., Powell, A., Scott, A. J., & Cama, E. (2022). Deepfakes and digitally altered imagery abuse: A cross-country exploration of an emerging form of image-based sexual abuse. *British Journal of Criminology*, *62*(6), 1341–1358. DOI: 10.1093/bjc/azab111

Google, A. I. (n.d.). *Responsible AI practices.* https://ai.google/responsibility/responsible-ai-practices/

GSMA. (2025). The mobile gender gap report 2025. https://www.gsma.com/r/gender-gap/

Hall, P., & Ellis, D. (2023). A systematic review of socio-technical gender bias in AI algorithms. *Online Information Review*, *47*(7), 1264–1279. DOI: 10.1108/OIR-08-2021-0452

Henry, N., Flynn, A., & Powell, A. (2020). Technology-facilitated sexual violence: A review of the literature. *Violence Against Women*, *26*(15–16), 1828–1854. DOI: 10.1177/1077801219875821

Idemudia, I., & Onoshakpor, C. (2023). Gender, workforce and artificial intelligence. *2023 IEEE AFRICON*, 1-3. DOI: . https://ieeexplore.ieee.org/document/10293367DOI: 10.1109/AFRICON55910.2023.10293367

Iliadis, A., & Russo, F. (2016). Critical data studies: An introduction. *Big Data & Society, 3*(2). (Original work published 2016)DOI: 10.1177/2053951716674238

Innovations, G. Stanford University. (n.d.) *Facial recognition: Analyzing gender and intersectionality in machine learning*. https://genderedinnovations.stanford.edu/case-studies/facial.html#tabs-2

Jaakkola, E. (2020). Designing conceptual articles: Four approaches. *AMS Review, 10*), 18–26. DOI: 10.1007/s13162-020-00161-0

Keyes, O. (2018). The misgendering machines: Trans/HCI implications of automatic gender recognition. *Proceedings of the ACM on Human-Computer Interaction, 2*(CSCW), 1–22. DOI: 10.1145/3274357

Lee, N. T., Resnick, P., & Barton, G. (2019). Algorithmic bias detection and mitigation: Best practices and policies to reduce consumer harms. https://www.brookings.edu/articles/algorithmic-bias-detection-and-mitigation-best-practices-and-policies-to-reduce-consumer-harms/

Lloyd's Register Foundation & Gallup. (2022). *World risk poll 2021: A digital world perceptions of risk from AI and misuse of personal data*. https://wrp.lrfoundation.org.uk/LRF_2021_report_a-digtial-world-ai-and-personal-data_online_version.pdf

Manyika, J., Silberg, J., & Presten, B. (2019, October 25). What do we do about the biases in AI? *Harvard Business Review*. https://hbr.org/2019/10/what-do-we-do-about-the-biases-in-ai

Martin, N. (2022). Image-based sexual abuse and deepfakes: A survivor turned activist's perspective. In *The Palgrave handbook of gendered violence and technology* (pp. 55–72). Springer., DOI: 10.1007/978-3-030-83734-1_4

Maslej, N., Fattorini, L., Brynjolfsson, E., Etchemendy, J., Ligett, K., Lyons, T., Manyika, J., Ngo, H., Niebles, J. C., Parli, V., Shoham, Y., Wald, R., Clark, J., & Perrault, R. (2023). *Artificial Intelligence Index Report 2023.* Stanford University, Human-Centered Artificial Intelligence. https://aiindex.stanford.edu/wp-content/uploads/2023/04/HAI_AI-Index-Report_2023.pdf

McKinsey & Company. (2023). *The state of AI in 2023: Generative AI's breakout year.* https://www.mckinsey.com/capabilities/quantumblack/our-insights/the-state-of-ai-in-2023-generative-ais-breakout-year

Mehrabi, N., Morstatter, F., Saxena, N., Lerman, K., & Galstyan, A. (2021). A survey on bias and fairness in machine learning. *ACM Computing Surveys, 54*(6), 1–35. DOI: 10.1145/3457607

Muduli, A., & Choudhury, A. (2025). Exploring the role of workforce agility on digital transformation: A systematic literature review. *Benchmarking, 32*(2), 492–512. DOI: 10.1108/BIJ-02-2023-0108

Nguyen, T. N., Le, C. V., Nguyen, M., Nguyen, G., Lien, T. T. H., & Nguyen, O. (2025). The organisational impact of agility: A systematic literature review. *Management Review Quarterly, 75*(3), 2709–2757. DOI: 10.1007/s11301-024-00446-9

Noble, S. U. (2018). *Algorithms of oppression: How search engines reinforce racism.* NYU Press. DOI: 10.18574/nyu/9781479833641.001.0001

O'Connor, S., & Liu, H. (2023). Gender bias perpetuation and mitigation in AI technologies: Case studies and lessons learned. *AI & Society, 29*, 2045–2057. DOI: 10.1007/s00146-023-01675-4

Okolie, C. (2023). Artificial intelligence-altered videos (deepfakes), image-based sexual abuse, and data privacy concerns. *Journal of International Women's Studies, 25*(2), 11. https://vc.bridgew.edu/jiws/vol25/iss2/11

Rainie, L., Funk, C., Anderson, M., & Tyson, A. (2022). AI and human enhancement: Americans' openness is tempered by a range of concerns. *Pew Research Center.* https://www.pewresearch.org/internet/2022/03/17/how-americans-think-about-artificial-intelligence/

Raji, I. D., Gebru, T., Mitchell, M., Buolamwini, J., Lee, J., & Denton, E. (2020). Saving face: Investigating the ethical concerns of facial recognition auditing. *Proceedings of the AAAI/ACM Conference on AI, Ethics, and Society*, 145-151. https://dl.acm.org/doi/pdf/10.1145/3375627.3375820

Roopaei, M., Horst, J., Klaas, E., Foster, G., Salmon-Stephens, T. J., & Grunow, J. (2021). Women in AI: Barriers and solutions. *2021 IEEE World AI IoT Congress (AIIoT)*, 0497-0503. . https://ieeexplore.ieee.org/document/9454202DOI: 10.1109/AIIoT52608.2021.9454202

Scheuerman, M. K., Wade, K., Lustig, C., & Brubaker, J. R. (2020). How we've taught algorithms to see identity: Constructing race and gender in image databases for facial analysis. *Proceedings of the ACM on Human-Computer Interaction, 4*(CSCW1), 1–35. DOI: 10.1145/3392866

Scotti, V. (2023). Women in engineering: AI and the empowerment of gender equality. *IEEE Instrumentation & Measurement Magazine, 26*(9), 32–37. https://ieeexplore.ieee.org/document/10328674. DOI: 10.1109/MIM.2023.10328674

Selbst, A. D., Boyd, D., Friedler, S. A., Venkatasubramanian, S., & Vertesi, J. (2019). Fairness and abstraction in sociotechnical systems. *FAT '19: Conference on Fairness, Accountability, and Transparency,* 59–68. https://dl.acm.org/doi/10.1145/3287560.3287598

Shrestha, S., & Das, S. (2022). Exploring gender biases in ML and AI academic research through systematic literature review. *Frontiers in Artificial Intelligence, 5,* 976838. Advance online publication. DOI: 10.3389/frai.2022.976838

Simonite, T. (2018, August 17). AI Is the future — but where are the women? Wired. https://www.wired.com/story/artificial-intelligence-researchers-gender-imbalance/

Suresh, H., & Guttag, J. (2019). A framework for understanding unintended consequences of machine learning. *Proceedings of EAAMO '21: 1st ACM Conference on Equity and Access in Algorithms, Mechanisms, and Optimization, 1–9.* https://dl.acm.org/doi/10.1145/3465416.3483305

Tamayo, S. G., & Petrelli, A. (2025). Work transformed: The promise and peril of artificial intelligence. ILO. https://www.ilo.org/sites/default/files/2025-07/ilo%20brief%20work%20transformed%20promise%20and%20peril%20of%20ai.pdf

Trist, E. L., & Bamforth, K. W. (1951). Some social and psychological consequences of the Longwall Method of coal-getting: An examination of the psychological situation and defences of a work group in relation to the social structure and technological content of the work system. *Human Relations, 4*(1), 3-38. (Original work published 1951)DOI: 10.1177/001872675100400101

UNESCO. (2024). *Global education monitoring report 2024. Gender report: Technology on her terms.* DOI: 10.54676/WVCF2762

UNESCO. (n.d.). *HerAtlas: Monitoring the right to education for girls and women.* https://www.unesco.org/en/heratlas

World Economic Forum. (2023). Global Gender Gap Report 2023. https://www3.weforum.org/docs/WEF_GGGR_2023.pdf

World Economic Forum. (2024). Global Gender Gap Report 2024. https://www3.weforum.org/docs/WEF_GGGR_2024.pdf

Yoldemir, T. (2020). Artificial intelligence and women's health. *Climacteric, 23*(1), 1–2. DOI: 10.1080/13697137.2019.1682804

Young, E., Wajcman, J., & Sprejer, L. (2021). *Where are the women? Mapping the gender job gap in AI.* The Alan Turing Institute. https://www.turing.ac.uk/sites/default/files/2021-03/where-are-the-women_public-policy_summary-report.pdf

Zhao, J., Wang, T., Yatskar, M., Ordonez, V., & Chang, K. W. (2017). Men also like shopping: Reducing gender bias amplification using corpus-level constraints. *arXiv preprint arXiv:1707.09457.* https://arxiv.org/abs/1707.09457 DOI: 10.18653/v1/D17-1323

UNICEF (n.d.). [illegible]

World Economic Forum. (2020). The Global Gender Gap Report 2020. [illegible] weforum.org/docs/WEF_GGGR_2020.pdf

World Economic Forum. (2024). [illegible] Gender Gap Report 2024. [illegible] weforum.org/docs/WEF_GGGR_2024.pdf

[illegible]

[illegible]

[illegible]

Chapter 5
Exploring Gender Inequity for Women in Artificial Intelligence Technology Job Roles in Healthcare

Amalisha Sabie Aridi
http://orcid.org/0000-0002-7869-5530
Washington University of Science and Technology, USA

ABSTRACT

As artificial intelligence (AI) becomes increasingly embedded in healthcare systems, a critical paradox emerges. Although women represent the majority of the healthcare workforce, they remain significantly underrepresented in AI-specific job roles and responsibilities. Within healthcare institutions, between 66% and 80% of female healthcare workers report having experienced some form of gender discrimination, including sexual harassment, wage disparities, and limited access to leadership pathways. These inequities are not only interpersonal but deeply embedded in institutional structures, regulatory frameworks, and organizational cultures that marginalize women from emerging domains such as AI. This inquiry examines how the underrepresentation of women in AI-related healthcare roles has far-reaching implications for the ethical development, governance, and implementation of healthcare technologies.

DOI: 10.4018/979-8-2600-1016-7.ch005

INTRODUCTION

The emergence of artificial intelligence as a transformative force in healthcare introduces new job roles and professional responsibilities that, if designed inclusively, could disrupt entrenched gender and racial inequities within the health workforce. However, if these technologies are embedded in existing hierarchies without deliberate equity-focused intervention, they risk reinforcing the very disparities they have the potential to dismantle (Haley & Burrell, 2025).

Persistent systemic inequities continue to plague the healthcare sector, with women, particularly Black and minority women, overrepresented in underpaid, high-risk roles and disproportionately affected by occupational stress and discrimination (Burrell, 2022). During the COVID-19 pandemic, for instance, female healthcare workers reported markedly higher rates of anxiety, depression, and post-traumatic stress symptoms compared to their male peers, with such outcomes closely linked to gendered caregiving burdens, professional undervaluation, and lack of institutional support (Hennein et al., 2023). Black women, who comprise 23% of their demographic labor force in healthcare, are heavily concentrated in the most vulnerable positions, 42% in licensed practical nurse or aide roles and 37% in long-term care, earning wages that barely exceed subsistence levels (Dill & Duffy, 2022). These workers face elevated exposure to workplace violence, viral contagions, and psychological trauma (Burrell et al., 2021). Additionally, gendered power imbalances manifest as wage gaps, harassment, and exclusion from decision-making: 43% of female nurses have experienced sexual harassment, often from patients or physicians (Kahsay et al., 2020), and 24% of the average global gender pay gap in the health sector disproportionately affects women during their reproductive years, especially among Black and Hispanic care workers (ILO & WHO, 2022). Even in academic settings, nearly 37% of female medical students report sexual harassment from faculty or peers, highlighting the systemic nature of gender-based marginalization (McClain et al., 2021).

As healthcare organizations increasingly adopt AI, they must ensure that the creation and implementation of AI systems do not perpetuate these inequities. The rise of specialized roles, such as clinical AI ethicists, data governance analysts, algorithmic fairness auditors, and health informatics engineers, presents an opportunity to embed equity into the architecture of AI-driven healthcare. For example, natural language processing (NLP) tools used to analyze clinical notes can identify linguistic markers of burnout among nursing staff and prompt early organizational interventions. Predictive algorithms can project workforce strain based on historical scheduling data and highlight where overtime burdens are disproportionately falling on women, enabling equitable staffing adjustments. Sentiment analysis tools embedded in internal communication platforms can detect subtle cues of workplace hostility or harassment, offering HR departments a proactive lens into employee well-being, particularly for historically marginalized workers. Moreover, AI-assisted compensation audit systems can assess salary progression across gender and racial lines, flagging anomalies in pay equity that might otherwise remain obscured. However, these tools are only as fair as the data and perspectives that shape them. If development teams remain homogeneous and blind to structural bias, AI outputs will simply replicate past injustices under the guise of objectivity.

To truly reconfigure the healthcare workforce landscape, AI job roles must be conceptualized with an explicit mandate to advance equity, not just efficiency. This necessitates diversifying AI teams, embedding ethical oversight in algorithm design, and empowering historically excluded voices, particularly women of color, to influence how these technologies are imagined, deployed, and governed. When AI development is steered by principles of inclusion and justice, it holds the potential not merely to optimize health systems but to reconstruct them in ways that honor the dignity, safety, and aspirations of all workers. Such an approach aligns with the broader objectives of the Sustainable Development Goals, which call for systemic transformation to eliminate disparities and promote well-being for all (Dhatt et al., 2017; Burrell et al., 2021; McLester et al., 2021).

PROBLEM AND SIGNIFICANCE STATEMENT

Despite the growing integration of artificial intelligence (AI) into healthcare systems, there remains a profound gender disparity in AI-specific job roles and responsibilities, reflecting systemic inequities that continue to marginalize women, particularly within healthcare organizations where they constitute the majority of the workforce. Data reveals that a mere 29% of AI-skilled workers globally are women, while men dominate the remaining 71% of the workforce, revealing a striking 42-percentage point gender gap (Constantino, 2024). This inequity is further entrenched at the research level, where women comprise less than one-third of AI professionals and only 18% of AI researchers worldwide (Grau & Klien, 2025). The gender imbalance in AI is particularly paradoxical in the healthcare sector, where women hold approximately 76% of all jobs (Hennein et al., 2023). However, even within this female-majority field, gender-based discrimination is endemic. According to Hennein et al. (2023), between 66% and 80% of female healthcare workers report having experienced gender discrimination in some form, including sexual harassment, wage disparities, restricted access to leadership roles, and frequent mischaracterizations of their professional responsibilities. Such discrimination is not only interpersonal but also embedded in institutional structures and regulatory frameworks that systemically disadvantage women (Hennein et al., 2023).

This dual-layered inequity, where women are marginalized both in healthcare leadership and in the evolving field of healthcare AI, has significant implications for the ethical development, implementation, and governance of AI technologies. The underrepresentation of women in AI roles undermines the diversity of perspectives essential to designing equitable algorithms for patient care, workforce management, and clinical decision support. For instance, AI systems used to predict staffing needs or patient risk scores may inadvertently encode gender bias if developed without diverse input. A hospital deploying an AI-powered triage tool might unknowingly deprioritize symptoms commonly presented by women, simply because historical data used for model training reflected male-dominant clinical baselines. Furthermore, women in healthcare, despite their frontline expertise, are frequently excluded from AI governance structures, which limits their ability to influence the trajectory of technological change and fosters tools misaligned with on-the-ground realities. This disconnect perpetuates a feedback loop of exclusion, wherein male-dominated AI teams design systems that reflect and reinforce the same institutional biases women face in their daily work.

To rectify these intersecting disparities, healthcare systems must not only prioritize gender equity in workforce policies but also ensure equitable representation of women in AI-specific roles, from data scientists and clinical informaticians to governance board members overseeing algorithmic ethics. Doing so will enable the development of AI technologies that are both socially responsive and clinically effective, while simultaneously addressing the root causes of gender inequity within healthcare environments. As AI continues to redefine job responsibilities and reshape the clinical landscape, inclusive participation in its development is not merely aspirational, it is imperative.

METHOD

An integrative review of literature serves as a powerful methodological tool to evaluate the evolving roles and responsibilities of artificial intelligence (AI) professionals in healthcare, particularly as these roles intersect with issues of gender inequity, discrimination, and systemic bias in the clinical environment. Defined by Torraco (2016) as a rigorous and systematic approach to synthesizing a wide range of empirical, theoretical, and methodological sources, the integrative review is uniquely suited to explore the complex interplay between AI implementation and socio-professional disparities in healthcare settings. This method accommodates the breadth and diversity of literature spanning clinical informatics, organizational behavior, gender studies, and health technology ethics. Its strength lies in its ability to weave together multiple strands of evidence into a coherent narrative, enabling scholars to trace patterns of exclusion, power asymmetry, and innovation across disciplines. In the context of AI in healthcare, this methodology allows for a comprehensive mapping of the field, from technical skill requirements and workforce demographics to the ethical responsibilities tied to data stewardship, algorithmic transparency, and clinical accountability.

As AI becomes increasingly embedded in healthcare operations, job roles are evolving beyond traditional clinical or IT functions into hybrid positions such as algorithmic bias auditors, AI clinical liaison officers, and equity-centered data engineers. An integrative review enables scholars to assess not only the technical specifications of these roles but also the structural and cultural conditions under which they emerge. For instance, while AI has the potential to reduce clinician burnout by automating time-intensive tasks such as documentation or diagnostic imaging analysis, it also opens the door to new forms of occupational exclusion if recruitment and training pipelines do not prioritize gender diversity. Moreover, the literature reveals a persistent underrepresentation of women (Constantino, 2024), particularly women of color, in AI leadership and development roles, perpetuating gendered knowledge gaps in system design and implementation. Through the synthesis of these findings, the integrative review method surfaces critical knowledge deficits, such as the limited availability of case studies involving women-led AI projects or the paucity of metrics evaluating gender-sensitive outcomes in algorithm deployment.

The insights gleaned from an integrative review have substantial implications for both policy and practice. They offer a foundation for formulating inclusive workforce development strategies, guiding curriculum design for AI in health education, and crafting regulatory frameworks that embed equity and ethical accountability into AI governance. By identifying where the literature converges, and more importantly, where it remains silent, this method equips stakeholders with the evidence necessary to reimagine AI job roles not merely as technical functions but as socially embedded positions with the power to advance or inhibit gender equity in healthcare.

The literature search was conducted across multiple academic databases, including PubMed, Scopus, Web of Science, Google Scholar, Research Gate, IEEE Xplore, and PsycINFO, to capture interdisciplinary research from healthcare, technology, and social sciences. Keywords and Boolean operators included combinations of:

"artificial intelligence" AND "healthcare" AND "gender equity"

"AI workforce" AND "healthcare leadership" AND "women in STEM"

"Gender equity" AND "healthcare" AND "organizational culture"

"AI roles in health" AND "diversity" AND "decision-making"

The search core focus was on peer-reviewed articles published in English between 2010 and 2025 to ensure both recency and relevance given the rapid evolution of AI technologies.

INCLUSION CRITERIA

Studies were included if they:

- Addressed artificial intelligence applications within healthcare or public health contexts
- Examined gender disparities in professional roles, leadership, training, or governance of AI systems
- Provided empirical, theoretical, or policy-oriented insights into ethical AI implementation or workforce development
- Focused on institutional or structural barriers related to gender inclusion in health technology roles.
- Focused on gender inequity in healthcare.
- Focused on unhealthy workplace cultures for women.

ADDRESSING GENDER INEQUITY

The emergence of artificial intelligence (AI) in healthcare presents a critical inflection point at which long-standing gender inequities, institutional discrimination, and systemic sexism can either be perpetuated through technological inertia or dismantled through ethically designed AI job functions and responsibilities. As AI transforms the structure of healthcare delivery and administration, its workforce implications demand a proactive, equity-oriented framework (Burrell, 2023). Gender inequity within healthcare institutions has deeply embedded consequences that extend beyond individual harm and manifest in organizational dysfunction and cultural deterioration (Burrell et al., 2021; McLester et al., 2021). Women, who comprise the majority of the healthcare workforce, remain systematically marginalized from leadership pipelines and decision-making roles. Research has shown that such exclusion leads to professional stagnation, emotional exhaustion, and reduced workplace engagement (Burrell et al. 2021). Discriminatory environments catalyze experiences of chronic stress, burnout, imposter syndrome, and work-life imbalance, particularly for women who are burdened with dual expectations of professional output and caregiving obligations (Burrell et al., 2021). These conditions often result in decreased job satisfaction and eventual resignation, eroding institutional knowledge and destabilizing team dynamics (Burrell et al., 2021). On an organizational level, the repercussions are equally severe. Failure to retain and advance talented women leads to attrition of high-potential employees, stifles innovation, and incurs reputational and legal risks. A workplace culture that tolerates inequity becomes toxic, resistant to innovation, and devoid of diverse leadership, diminishing its relevance in an evolving healthcare landscape (McLester et al., 2021).

Artificial intelligence has the capacity to reconfigure this status quo, provided that the job roles associated with its development, deployment, and governance are deliberately structured to confront and correct systemic biases. The creation of roles such as gender equity algorithm auditors, AI ethics compliance officers, and inclusive data governance leads not only to technological accuracy but also to institutional accountability. For example, an AI fairness specialist embedded in a hospital system can monitor how machine learning models triage patients or allocate resources, ensuring that these systems do not replicate discriminatory decision-making patterns. Similarly, an AI integration strategist might analyze workforce scheduling algorithms to detect gendered patterns in task assignments or overtime distribution, enabling data-driven corrections to labor inequity. These professionals can work cross-functionally with human resources, compliance teams, and clinical operations to embed equity metrics into every phase of AI lifecycle management. Furthermore, these AI roles can champion transparency by designing algorithms that explain their decision-making logic, critical in cases where career advancement decisions or patient outcomes are affected. However, these transformations are contingent upon inclusive hiring and training practices that prioritize intersectional expertise and the lived experiences of marginalized groups (Omar & Burrell, 2024).

In order for AI to become a catalyst for gender equity in healthcare, its job roles must evolve beyond technical competencies to encompass ethical stewardship, cultural literacy, and social accountability. AI professionals must not only build functional systems but also dismantle the discriminatory frameworks that have historically governed healthcare institutions. By integrating equity-focused AI roles into healthcare infrastructures, organizations can mitigate talent loss, foster innovation, and cultivate a work environment grounded in inclusion, psychological safety, and shared purpose (Haley & Burrell, 2025). As Burrell et al. (2021) and McLester et al. (2021) argue, eliminating gender inequity is not simply a matter of social justice but a strategic imperative for sustainable institutional success in a digitized healthcare future.

SOCIAL CONSTRUCTION OF AI JOB ROLES IN HEALTHCARE

Symbolic interactionism, a sociological framework grounded in the interpretation of meaning through human interaction, provides a compelling lens for examining how emerging AI job roles and responsibilities are socially constructed within healthcare environments. This perspective is particularly useful in understanding how power, identity, and gender expectations are inscribed into and reproduced through technological roles, impacting who is seen as legitimate or capable in the rapidly evolving AI-healthcare interface.

At its core, symbolic interactionism contends that individuals act based on the meanings things have for them, and these meanings arise through social interactions and are constantly interpreted and reinterpreted in dynamic contexts (Basson & Botha, 2012; Chomczyński, 2020). Within healthcare institutions, roles such as AI data analysts, machine learning ethicists, and clinical algorithm developers are not merely technical designations but symbolic positions imbued with social expectations and cultural meanings. Titles like "AI engineer" or "informatics lead" often carry gendered connotations, subtly communicating authority, innovation, and expertise, attributes traditionally aligned with masculine-coded professional identities (Ueno et al., 2020; Mik-Meyer et al., 2020). As such, women entering these roles often find themselves negotiating not only the technical demands of their positions but also the symbolic baggage that accompanies them. For example, a female AI implementation lead in a hospital may need to repeatedly assert her authority in meetings where male counterparts are automatically presumed to be more technically competent, despite comparable or superior expertise.

Symbolic interactionism illuminates how women in AI-related healthcare roles engage in "identity work" to challenge stereotypes and reshape expectations. These professionals must continually navigate micro-interactions that either affirm or undermine their credibility. Everyday interactions, such as the language used to describe their contributions, the way colleagues react to their decisions, or the visibility afforded to their successes, play a critical role in shaping both their self-concept and others' perceptions. This dynamic aligns with the "looking-glass self," wherein individuals come to see themselves as they believe others see them (Basson & Botha, 2012). Women who consistently receive dismissive feedback or who are overlooked in algorithm design discussions may internalize these messages, leading to diminished self-efficacy and reluctance to pursue advancement. Conversely, organizational cultures that validate women's input in AI innovation, offer meaningful mentorship, and normalize female leadership in data science can construct new symbolic meanings that empower participation and redefine success.

By applying symbolic interactionism to the development of AI job roles in healthcare, it becomes evident that equity is not solely a matter of hiring more women or eliminating overt discrimination. Rather, it requires a deliberate reengineering of the symbolic architecture that defines roles, communicates value, and constructs professional identities. Institutions must be vigilant in how they name roles, recognize contributions, and structure interactions to dismantle the implicit hierarchies encoded in language, symbols, and feedback loops. As healthcare systems increasingly rely on AI to make critical decisions, from patient triage to staffing algorithms, the social meanings attached to the architects of these technologies will shape not only institutional culture but also the fairness and inclusivity of care itself (Burrell, 2023).

STRUGGLE FOR EQUITY IN AI ROLES WITHIN HEALTHCARE

Conflict theory, with its emphasis on structural inequality and power dynamics, offers a powerful lens for analyzing the gendered and hierarchical formation of artificial intelligence (AI) job roles in the healthcare sector. As AI continues to reshape healthcare delivery and decision-making, the distribution of these high-status, technologically advanced roles reveals persistent disparities rooted in gendered exploitation and occupational segregation. The healthcare workforce remains stratified along both gender and power lines, with men disproportionately occupying high-paying, high-prestige positions such as physician-leaders, C-suite executives, and, increasingly, AI-focused roles such as clinical data scientists and algorithm developers. In contrast, women continue to be clustered in undervalued and labor-intensive occupations such as bedside nursing, medical assisting, and administrative support (Barkan, 2018; Campbell, 2011). Conflict theory emphasizes that such unequal distributions are not incidental but are actively maintained by dominant groups, typically men in positions of institutional control, who seek to preserve access to economic and cultural capital. The proliferation of AI in healthcare has only amplified these divides (Haley & Burrell, 2025). Emerging positions in AI implementation, data governance, and machine learning ethics are rapidly becoming new centers of influence and compensation, yet they remain largely inaccessible to women due to exclusionary hiring practices, gender-biased perceptions of technical competence, and unequal access to training pipelines.

Ideology plays a critical role in perpetuating this inequity. Deeply embedded cultural narratives associate women with caregiving and emotional labor, while valorizing men as logical, analytical, and technologically adept. These gendered stereotypes subtly inform how AI roles are advertised, how applicants are evaluated, and how performance is recognized within healthcare systems (Barkan, 2018; Campbell, 2011). A male informatics officer proposing an AI-driven triage tool might be lauded as a visionary, whereas a female colleague suggesting similar innovations could be perceived as stepping outside her domain. Conflict theory helps explain how such symbolic power consolidates the dominance of certain groups while marginalizing others. Furthermore, this unequal structure is often masked by the neutral language of "merit" and "objectivity" in technology hiring, which fails to acknowledge how access to technical education, mentorship, and institutional support is itself unequally distributed.

Despite these challenges, conflict theory also foregrounds the potential for disruption and resistance. Women and marginalized groups in healthcare have increasingly begun to contest the gendered boundaries of AI work by creating inclusive research collaboratives, advocating for algorithmic accountability, and demanding gender-equitable recruitment practices in digital health roles. These movements represent not just demands for representation, but challenges to the very ideological and economic structures that have historically excluded women from technological authority in healthcare. As AI becomes central to healthcare's future, recognizing and redressing these inequities is essential, not only for workforce justice but also to ensure that the technologies shaping clinical care reflect the values and realities of all those who deliver and receive it (Burrell, 2023).

SOCIAL DIMENSIONS OF AI WORKFORCE INTEGRATION IN HEALTHCARE

Human Relations Theory, a foundational paradigm in organizational sociology and management, underscores the primacy of interpersonal dynamics, communication, and relational structures in shaping workplace behavior and culture (Nicotera, 2019). When applied to the integration of artificial intelligence (AI) roles in healthcare, this theory illuminates how social environments, not merely technical expertise, fundamentally determine who succeeds, who is included, and how equitably AI-related responsibilities are distributed within healthcare institutions.

Central to Human Relations Theory is the belief that productive organizations rely on strong interpersonal relationships and effective communication (Nicotera, 2019). Within the context of AI's expanding role in healthcare, these human elements often go underappreciated, yet they play a decisive role in how new job roles, such as AI implementation strategists, algorithmic fairness officers, and clinical machine learning coordinators, are conceptualized and allocated. In many cases, women entering technology leadership roles must navigate not only the technical expectations of the position but also the gendered nature of informal networks, collaborative dynamics, and mentorship pipelines (Burrell, 2022). For instance, a female data scientist tasked with developing predictive models for patient risk stratification may find her contributions undervalued in leadership discussions if her interpersonal access to key decision-makers is limited or if she is excluded from informal channels of influence. Conversely, when healthcare teams cultivate inclusive and supportive working relationships, women in AI roles are more likely to gain visibility, secure resources, and be promoted into decision-making positions (Nicotera, 2019).

Motivation and job satisfaction, also central pillars of Human Relations Theory, are deeply affected by relational equity in AI team structures. Women in AI-centric roles often report lower job satisfaction when their labor is rendered invisible or when their ideas are adopted without attribution. These dynamics can erode intrinsic motivation, foster disengagement, and contribute to attrition, particularly in high-stakes environments where technical innovation and interpersonal collaboration are tightly intertwined (Burrell et al., 2021). In contrast, inclusive environments that prioritize open communication, equitable recognition, and transparent feedback cultivate higher levels of motivation, creativity, and retention among women in AI positions. The influence of leadership is equally consequential (Burrell, 2022). Leaders who prioritize relational equity, model inclusive language in technical discussions, and actively support gender-diverse teams not only create healthier organizational cultures but also improve the ethical and clinical outcomes of AI deployment. Without intentional leadership, AI integration risks becoming another domain where structural inequity is merely translated into digital form (Haley & Burrell, 2025).

Human Relations Theory provides a vital framework for understanding how AI job roles in healthcare are shaped not only by technological change but by the quality of social interaction, leadership commitment, and cultural inclusion within organizations. As hospitals and health systems accelerate their adoption of AI technologies, they must ensure that the design and distribution of these roles are informed by principles of relational equity and social justice. By embedding human-centered values into the management of AI-focused teams, healthcare institutions can foster environments where women are not only included in the technological future but are empowered to shape it.

EMPLOYEE ENGAGEMENT

Zinger's Employee Engagement Model, which emphasizes the interrelated elements of Meaning, Competence, Impact, and Connection (MCIC), provides a critical framework for fostering engagement and gender equity in the evolving landscape of artificial intelligence (AI) roles within healthcare institutions (Krause, 2015; Kusuma & Madasu, 2015). As AI technologies increasingly reshape clinical decision-making, diagnostics, and operational logistics, healthcare organizations must ensure that women are not merely included in these emerging roles but are actively supported and empowered within them.

The first pillar of the model, Meaning, relates to how employees interpret the significance of their work. For women in AI healthcare roles, such as clinical data scientists, AI compliance officers, or algorithmic governance leads, meaning is cultivated when their labor is recognized as essential to patient safety, ethical technology use, and systemic equity. When a female AI analyst develops a bias-detection algorithm that prevents misdiagnosis in minority patients, her work not only exemplifies technical competence but also reinforces the moral architecture of healthcare. Yet without explicit institutional reinforcement of this meaning, such contributions risk being rendered invisible within male-dominated AI teams (Krause, 2015).

The second component, Competence, focuses on perceived capability. For women entering AI job tracks in healthcare, often transitioning from clinical, administrative, or informatics backgrounds, structured training opportunities, access to certifications in data science, and pathways to advanced technical education are vital. Without these, women may be excluded from the most influential AI roles despite possessing deep domain knowledge critical to responsible algorithmic development (Kusuma & Madasu, 2015).

The third element, Impact, pertains to whether employees believe their work makes a tangible difference. Within the AI ecosystem of healthcare, impact is often measured through operational efficiency, accuracy, or cost-savings. However, when women in AI roles are not credited for their innovations or are relegated to supportive rather than leadership tasks, the perceived and actual impact of their labor is diminished. Celebrating women's contributions to projects like AI-assisted diagnostic systems, patient stratification tools, or workforce scheduling algorithms is necessary not only for retention but for correcting longstanding patterns of under-recognition. Finally, the fourth pillar, Connection, underscores the importance of professional relationships and inclusion. In AI healthcare environments, where interdisciplinary collaboration is key, exclusion from informal networks or mentorship channels can isolate women and stunt their professional development. Implementing mentorship structures that pair women in AI roles with senior leaders or creating peer forums for cross-disciplinary collaboration helps reinforce a culture where gender diversity is seen as an asset rather than an exception (Krause, 2015; Kusuma & Madasu, 2015).

By applying Zinger's MCIC model to AI job roles in healthcare, institutions can cultivate a more inclusive and resilient workforce that supports the equitable participation of women in shaping the future of healthcare technology. Creating environments where AI professionals, particularly women, find deep purpose in their work, are given the tools to excel, see the impact of their efforts, and feel connected to a broader professional community is essential for both gender equity and the ethical advancement of AI in health systems. Zinger's model thus serves as both a diagnostic and prescriptive framework for transforming AI from a tool of efficiency into a platform for empowerment and organizational justice.

CHANGE MANAGEMENT

The Satir Change Model, a five-stage framework for understanding human responses to transformation, provides an incisive roadmap for managing cultural and structural shifts as healthcare organizations integrate artificial intelligence (AI) into their workforce. Applied to the development of equitable AI job roles and responsibilities, the model offers a powerful lens through which to examine how institutions move from resistance to renewal, especially in addressing persistent gender inequities within the technological domains of healthcare (El-Amin, 2022; Hillebrand, 2019).

The journey begins at the Late Status Quo, where existing organizational norms remain unchallenged and gender disparities in AI-related roles are entrenched. In this phase, women are often underrepresented in emerging positions such as AI systems architects, machine learning engineers, and algorithmic ethics consultants. These roles are typically occupied by men due to longstanding gender biases in both tech and healthcare spheres, and their exclusion is often normalized within institutional structures. Recognition of this imbalance is the necessary first step toward change. As awareness builds, organizations often enter the Resistance phase. Here, discomfort arises, not necessarily from hostility but from the fear of disrupting established hierarchies or questioning who holds technical authority. For example, introducing a female-led AI governance task force might meet subtle opposition in meetings where decision-making power has historically skewed male. Resistance can manifest through skepticism about qualifications or passive dismissal of contributions, requiring targeted interventions such as gender-equity training, strategic mentorship initiatives, and visible support from leadership (El-Amin, 2022).

Progress into the Chaos stage represents the organizational turbulence that follows as traditional norms begin to unravel. This is the moment when healthcare systems attempt to reconfigure their AI workforce pipelines to be more inclusive, recalibrate recruitment and advancement practices, and dismantle informal networks that have historically excluded women. Chaos, while disorienting, is productive, it is the creative tension that allows for redefinition. During this phase, hospitals might restructure data science teams to include diverse expertise or revise hiring protocols to ensure AI job descriptions are inclusive in both language and accessibility. As the turbulence subsides, the Integration phase begins. At this point, AI roles evolve into spaces where women's contributions are not only visible but foundational to innovation. Institutions may institutionalize sponsorship programs, elevate women into AI leadership roles, and embed fairness audits into every algorithm developed.

Integration means these practices become part of the organizational DNA, no longer seen as exceptional but essential. Finally, the New Status Quo is achieved when the presence of women in technical, strategic, and ethical AI positions is both normalized and sustained through continuous investment. AI becomes a shared domain, no longer siloed or symbolically masculine, but shaped collaboratively by all who build, govern, and apply it (Hillebrand, 2019).

By adopting the Satir Change Model, healthcare organizations can move beyond performative gestures and toward transformative equity in AI job design and distribution. Each phase of the model offers a structured pathway for confronting resistance, fostering inclusive innovation, and embedding lasting cultural change. As AI becomes a permanent fixture of healthcare systems, ensuring that its workforce reflects the full spectrum of talent and experience, especially that of women, is not only a matter of social justice but a prerequisite for ethical, effective, and human-centered technological advancement.

PRACTICAL RECOMMENDATIONS

Leadership and Executive Accountability

1. Tie executive compensation and performance evaluations to measurable gender equity outcomes in AI hiring, promotion, and retention within healthcare organizations, including disaggregated metrics by race and role type.
2. Mandate gender-diverse leadership representation on all AI governance, ethics, and steering committees, with explicit inclusion of women clinicians and women of color who possess domain expertise but are historically excluded from technical decision-making.
3. Create a Chief Equity and AI Accountability Officer role with authority to audit algorithmic design, workforce impact, and leadership practices, reporting directly to the CEO or board.
4. Require senior leaders to undergo advanced training in gender bias, symbolic power, and AI ethics, emphasizing how leadership behaviors shape inclusion in emerging technical roles.

Organizational Structures and Systems

5. Institutionalize AI equity audits that examine how AI systems affect workforce scheduling, promotion pathways, compensation, and burnout—specifically identifying gendered and racialized patterns.

6. Develop transparent AI career lattices that define pathways from clinical, administrative, or informatics roles into AI leadership positions, reducing reliance on informal sponsorship networks that disadvantage women.
7. Implement anonymized screening for AI and informatics roles, removing gender-coded language and credentials that privilege traditional STEM trajectories over applied healthcare expertise.
8. Publish annual internal equity dashboards that track gender representation, pay equity, and advancement in AI-related roles to normalize transparency and accountability.

Mentorship, Sponsorship, and Professional Networks

9. Shift from mentorship-only models to structured sponsorship programs, requiring senior leaders to actively advocate for women's placement on high-visibility AI projects and leadership tracks.
10. Create cross-disciplinary AI mentorship cohorts pairing women clinicians, data scientists, ethicists, and administrators to reduce silos and strengthen social capital.
11. Recognize mentorship and sponsorship as formal leadership responsibilities, embedding them into workload models and promotion criteria to avoid invisible labor burdens.
12. Fund protected time for women to participate in AI innovation initiatives, preventing mentorship and development opportunities from becoming unpaid or extracurricular labor.

Training, Education, and Leadership Development

13. Provide organization-funded AI upskilling pathways for women, including certifications in data science, informatics, and algorithmic ethics that do not require prior computer science degrees.
14. Integrate leadership development with technical training, ensuring women in AI roles receive preparation for decision-making authority, budget control, and strategic influence.
15. Embed equity-centered AI competencies into continuing professional education, reframing AI literacy as a core leadership skill rather than a niche technical function.

Recruitment Reform and Talent Pipelines

16. Ensure women comprise at least 50% of AI hiring committees, with decision-making authority rather than symbolic participation.
17. Establish formal recruiting partnerships with historically women's colleges, historically Black Colleges and Universities (HBCUs), and minority-serving institutions, focused specifically on healthcare AI fellowships, residencies, and apprenticeships.
18. Create paid AI transition fellowships for women already employed in healthcare, leveraging their clinical expertise rather than privileging external tech hires.

Cultural Change and Innovation

19. Redesign AI role titles, job descriptions, and success metrics to avoid masculine-coded language that symbolically excludes women and reinforces technical gatekeeping.
20. Use AI itself as a tool for cultural accountability, deploying sentiment analysis and organizational analytics to detect patterns of exclusion, harassment, or inequitable recognition in real time, followed by leadership intervention.

CONCLUSIONS

As artificial intelligence becomes an increasingly integral component of healthcare delivery, the emergence of AI-specific job roles necessitates a parallel reimagining of organizational leadership practices to ensure gender equity. Drawing on insights from Morgenroth and Ryan (2018), a comprehensive understanding of the stages of institutional bias and gender-based harm is essential not only to prevent discrimination but also to promote equity through systemic change. Leadership plays a critical role in creating an ecosystem where women can thrive in the highly specialized and influential spaces of AI innovation in healthcare.

At the heart of effective leadership in this context is the cultivation of structures that protect against harm, foster participation, and amplify underrepresented voices. In the AI domain—where roles such as clinical machine learning strategist, algorithmic ethics lead, and health data scientist are rapidly proliferating, women remain disproportionately underrepresented. This underrepresentation is not solely a pipeline issue but a reflection of persistent organizational blind spots. Leadership committed to equity must distinguish between reactive measures, such as addressing instances of gender-based exclusion, and proactive strategies that build inclusive systems from the outset (Morgenroth & Ryan, 2018). For example, when hospital administrators establish AI hiring panels without women or fail to consult women clinicians in the design of decision-support algorithms, they not only risk embedding bias into technological tools but also perpetuate structural inequity in influence and recognition.

To address these disparities meaningfully, leadership must embed equity into the fabric of AI workforce development. This involves institutionalizing mentorship programs tailored to women entering AI healthcare careers, where guidance is paired with sponsorship—an intentional advocacy for advancement into strategic roles. Equally critical is the implementation of gender-neutral recruitment strategies, such as anonymized application reviews for data science positions and inclusive language in job postings for AI engineers. Leadership must also champion transparency in role expectations and evaluation metrics. In one example, a hospital system that published disaggregated salary data for its digital health division was able to identify and correct a gender pay gap affecting women in informatics and analytics roles. Such actions illustrate how leadership practices grounded in transparency, accountability, and responsiveness can move beyond performative allyship to structural transformation. Furthermore, equity in AI healthcare cannot exist without psychological safety. Leaders must enforce a zero-tolerance policy toward discrimination, ensure mechanisms for anonymous reporting, and actively protect those who challenge inequitable norms, all while modeling inclusive behavior themselves.

Ultimately, advancing gender equity in AI healthcare roles demands more than policy statements; it requires leadership that consistently translates principles into practice. Through intentional mentorship, equitable recruitment, continuous training, and transparent evaluation, healthcare organizations can create a new standard, one in which AI is not merely a tool for innovation but a domain where equity, inclusion, and diversity are intentionally engineered into both the technology and the workforce that creates it. As Morgenroth and Ryan (2018) emphasize, true progress begins not with reactive interventions but with the foresight and courage to lead cultural change from within.

Social Implications

The underrepresentation of women in artificial intelligence (AI) job roles within healthcare carries profound social consequences that extend beyond organizational boundaries and into broader systems of care, equity, and public trust. Healthcare technologies are not value-neutral tools; they are socially constructed artifacts shaped by the norms, power relations, and institutional histories of the environments in which they are developed. When women—particularly women of color who comprise a substantial portion of the healthcare workforce—are excluded from AI development and governance, the resulting technologies risk embedding and legitimizing gendered inequities under the guise of objectivity.

At the societal level, inequitable participation in AI workforces undermines the ethical credibility of healthcare innovation. AI systems increasingly influence clinical prioritization, diagnostic pathways, workforce allocation, and risk assessment. If these systems are designed without inclusive representation from those with lived clinical experience and historical exposure to workplace inequities, they may reproduce biased assumptions about caregiving labor, professional authority, and clinical competence. Such outcomes reinforce long-standing societal narratives that devalue women's expertise and normalize their exclusion from technologically powerful domains.

The social implications also extend directly to patient populations. Algorithmic systems trained on historically biased data can exacerbate disparities in diagnosis, treatment access, and health outcomes, particularly for women and marginalized groups. Excluding women from AI design roles diminishes opportunities to identify and mitigate these biases before they are operationalized at scale. Over time, this erosion of equity threatens public trust in AI-enabled healthcare systems and deepens skepticism among communities already affected by systemic injustice. As such, gender inequity in healthcare AI roles is not merely a workforce issue but a broader social justice concern with implications for health equity, democratic accountability, and the legitimacy of digital medicine.

Policy Implications

The persistence of gender inequity in healthcare AI roles highlights significant gaps in existing policy and regulatory frameworks. While current AI governance structures prioritize technical performance, data security, and patient safety, they largely overlook workforce composition, leadership diversity, and the social consequences of exclusion. This omission allows inequities in AI job roles to persist unchecked, even as these technologies exert increasing influence over healthcare delivery and labor management.

Policy responses must therefore expand beyond technical compliance to include equity-centered workforce mandates. Regulatory agencies and accrediting bodies should require healthcare organizations to report gender-disaggregated data on AI-related hiring, promotion, compensation, and leadership representation. Such transparency would establish accountability mechanisms that discourage performative inclusion and incentivize structural change.

Additionally, public funding for healthcare AI research and innovation should be contingent upon demonstrable commitments to gender equity. Granting agencies and policymakers can play a catalytic role by requiring inclusive leadership plans, equitable training pipelines, and governance structures that embed ethical oversight into AI development. Without these policy interventions, AI adoption risks reinforcing existing power asymmetries, privileging institutions and actors who already dominate technological spaces while marginalizing those most affected by healthcare inequities.

Organizational Implications

For healthcare organizations, the integration of AI presents both an opportunity for transformation and a risk of institutional harm. Organizations that neglect gender equity in AI job roles expose themselves to operational inefficiencies, ethical failures, and reputational damage. Homogeneous AI teams are more likely to overlook contextual realities of clinical work, misinterpret workforce data, and deploy systems that exacerbate burnout, inequitable scheduling, and biased performance evaluation. These outcomes contribute to employee disengagement, increased turnover, and the loss of institutional knowledge, particularly among women who already face disproportionate workplace stress.

In contrast, organizations that intentionally embed gender equity into AI workforce design can leverage technology as a driver of cultural renewal. Diverse AI teams bring broader perspectives to data interpretation, algorithm design, and governance decision-making, resulting in systems that are more accurate, fair, and aligned with frontline realities. Such inclusivity strengthens innovation capacity, enhances organizational resilience, and improves employee engagement across disciplines.

Importantly, organizational change cannot be achieved through surface-level diversity initiatives alone. Healthcare institutions must interrogate the informal networks, symbolic hierarchies, and promotion pathways that define who is perceived as a legitimate technical expert. Without structural reforms, such as transparent AI career ladders, equity audits, and executive accountability, organizational cultures will continue to reproduce exclusion, even as they adopt increasingly advanced technologies.

Leadership Implications

Leadership plays a decisive role in determining whether AI becomes a tool for equity or an amplifier of existing injustice within healthcare systems. Leaders shape not only resource allocation and hiring practices but also the symbolic meanings attached to AI expertise, authority, and innovation. When leadership fails to challenge gendered assumptions about technical competence, women are systematically excluded from AI governance and strategic influence, regardless of their qualifications or clinical insight.

Equity-centered leadership requires a shift from passive neutrality to intentional action. Leaders must recognize that inaction perpetuates existing power hierarchies and that inclusive AI workforce development demands deliberate intervention. This includes sponsoring women into high-impact AI roles, legitimizing nontraditional pathways into technical leadership, and embedding ethical accountability into executive performance expectations.

Furthermore, leaders must cultivate psychological safety and visibly protect individuals who challenge biased systems or raise concerns about algorithmic harm. Without such protections, women in AI roles face heightened risks of marginalization, retaliation, and burnout. Ultimately, leadership commitment to gender equity in healthcare AI is not ancillary to organizational success; it is foundational to ethical legitimacy, workforce sustainability, and the responsible advancement of AI in healthcare.

RECOMMENDATIONS FOR FUTURE RESEARCH

To build upon the current understanding of gender equity in AI job roles within healthcare, future research should adopt empirical approaches that can illuminate the lived experiences, organizational dynamics, and sociocultural mechanisms that shape inclusion and exclusion in this evolving domain. Specifically, two qualitative methodologies, focus group research and grounded theory, are well-suited to advance this area of inquiry and should be prioritized in subsequent studies.

Qualitative Focus Group Approach

Given the interpersonal and institutional complexity surrounding gender equity in AI roles, a qualitative focus group approach would offer a valuable avenue for capturing collective perceptions, shared challenges, and dialogic insights among key stakeholders. Facilitated discussions with women occupying or aspiring to AI-related positions, such as clinical data scientists, AI implementation leads, or algorithm governance officers, could uncover nuanced perspectives on barriers to inclusion, mentorship experiences, psychological safety, and perceptions of leadership responsiveness.

These group interactions would allow researchers to probe how women interpret leadership behaviors, evaluate organizational equity practices, and navigate implicit biases in AI design and governance. Moreover, focus groups could bring to light the informal cultures and unspoken norms that shape hiring, promotion, and innovation processes, particularly in male-dominated technical teams within healthcare institutions. Such insights would not only inform more responsive leadership training and equity audits but also guide the development of inclusive frameworks for structuring AI work environments that are psychologically safe and socially just.

Grounded Theory Approach

To conceptualize a deeper theoretical understanding of how gender equity can be structurally embedded within AI workforce development in healthcare, a grounded theory approach is recommended. Grounded theory allows for the generation of an inductively derived framework that is rooted in the experiences and processes described by participants themselves. Through iterative coding and constant comparison, researchers could develop a theoretical model that explains how women in healthcare AI roles navigate institutional constraints, access or are denied leadership opportunities, and negotiate recognition within algorithm-driven ecosystems.

This approach would be particularly useful in uncovering latent processes, such as how organizational policies are interpreted at different levels, how allyship is enacted or withheld, or how psychological safety emerges or erodes in AI project teams. It would also facilitate the identification of critical turning points or "equity catalysts" that shift organizational cultures from performative inclusion to genuine transformation. The resultant theory could serve as a foundation for designing institutional change models tailored to AI contexts, with specific implications for recruitment practices, leadership accountability, and the ethical implementation of emerging technologies in healthcare.

REFERENCES

Barkan, S. E. (2018). The Conflict Approach. *The Cambridge Handbook of Social Problems, 1*, 241. https://books.google.com/books?hl=en&lr=&id=g9tPDwAAQBAJ&oi=fnd&pg=PA241&dq=1.%09Barkan,+S.+E.+(2018).+The+Conflict+Approach.++The+Cambridge+Handbook+of+Social+Problems,+1,+241.&ots=Y3o2m68ZIU&sig=PGW9NqLpmOg7hTevn1Ynajy7Ag0#v=onepage&q&f=false

Basson, M., & Botha, C. (2012). Towards meaning: Symbolic interactionism and workplace bullying. In *BULLYING: An assault on human dignity* (pp. 77–91). Brill., https://www.researchgate.net/publication/341240876_Towards_Meaning_Symbolic_Interactionism_and_Workplace_Bullying DOI: 10.1163/9781848881020_010

Burrell, D. N. (2022). Creating inclusive, diverse, and psychologically safe workplaces for African-American women working in public health response supply chain and logistics. *Land Forces Academy Review, 27*(2), 134-140. https://www.armyacademy.ro/reviste/rev2_2022/Art_Burrell_Raft_2_2022.pdf

Burrell, D. N. (2023). Dynamic evaluation approaches to telehealth technologies and artificial intelligence (AI) telemedicine applications in healthcare and biotechnology organizations. *Merits, 3*(4), 700–721. https://www.mdpi.com/2673-8104/3/4/42. DOI: 10.3390/merits3040042

Burrell, D. N., Barrett, S. J., Lewis, E. J., Dawson, M., Bovell, K., & Crowe, M. (2021). Creating Inclusive Workplaces for Women in Health Organizations Engaging in Digital Economy-Driven Innovations. [IJIDE]. *International Journal of Innovation in the Digital Economy, 12*(2), 18–31. https://www.igi-global.com/article/creating-inclusive-workplaces-for-women-in-health-organizations-engaging-in-digital-economy-driven-innovations/273608. DOI: 10.4018/IJIDE.2021040102

Burrell, D. N., Shufutinsky, A., Duncan, T. D., Springs, D., McLester, Q., & Mozes, R. (2021). Organizational Dynamics Around Sexual Harassment Interventions and Occurrences in Clinical Training Healthcare Environments. In Johnson, R. (Ed.), *Handbook of Research on Multidisciplinary Perspectives on Managerial and Leadership Psychology* (pp. 300–319). IGI Global., DOI: 10.4018/978-1-7998-3811-1.ch015

Campbell, D. (2011). Diversity and job satisfaction: Reconciling conflicting theories and findings. *International Journal of Applied Management and Technology, 10*(1), 1. https://scholarworks.waldenu.edu/ijamt/vol10/iss1/1/

Chomczyński, P. (2020). Mobbing from the standpoint of symbolic interactionism. *Qualitative Sociology Review, 16*(4), 52-62. https://www.ceeol.com/search/article-detail?id=909745

Constantino, T. (2024, November 12) Women Make Up 29% Of The AI Workforce; Here's How To Fix It. Forbes. Retrieved from: https://www.forbes.com/sites/torconstantino/2024/11/12/women-make-up-29-of-the-ai-workforce---heres-how-to-fix-it/

Dhatt, R., Theobald, S., Buzuzi, S., Ros, B., Vong, S., Muraya, K., Molyneux, S., Hawkins, K., González-Beiras, C., Ronsin, K., Lichtenstein, D., Wilkins, K., Thompson, K., Davis, K., & Jackson, C. (2017). The role of women's leadership and gender equity in leadership and health system strengthening. *Global Health, Epidemiology and Genomics, 2*, e8. https://www.cambridge.org/core/journals/global-health-epidemiology-and-genomics/article/role-ofwomens-leadership-and-gender-equity-in-leadership-and-health-systemstrengthening/A6AEB63AFE17295E0EF9E40741A2EC5B. DOI: 10.1017/gheg.2016.22 PMID: 29868219

Dill, J., & Duffy, M. (2022). Structural Racism And Black Women's Employment In The US Health Care Sector: Study examines structural racism and black women's employment in the US healthcare sector. *Health Affairs, 41*(2), 265–272. https://www.healthaffairs.org/doi/full/10.1377/hlthaff.2021.01400. DOI: 10.1377/hlthaff.2021.01400 PMID: 35130061

El-Amin, A. (2022). Organizational climate change: diversity, equity, inclusion, and belonging. In *Implementing Diversity, Equity, Inclusion, and Belonging Management in Organizational Change Initiatives* (pp. 1–23). IGI Global. https://www.igi-global.com/chapter/organizational-climate-change/304638

Grau, E., & Klien, K. (2025, January 29). Why We Need More Women In The AI Revolution. Time. Retrieved from: https://time.com/7210973/women-in-the-ai-revolution/

Haley, P., & Burrell, D. (2025, February 14). Using Artificial Intelligence in Law Enforcement and Policing to Improve Public Health and Safety. *Law. Economics and Society, 1*(1), 46. DOI: 10.30560/les.v1n1p46

Hennein, R., Gorman, H., Chung, V., & Lowe, S. R. (2023). Gender discrimination among women healthcare workers during the COVID-19 pandemic: Findings from a mixed methods study. *PLoS One, 18*(2), e0281367. https://journals.plos.org/plosone/article?id=10.1371/journal.pone.0281367. DOI: 10.1371/journal.pone.0281367 PMID: 36745623

Hillebrand, T. M. (2019). *The critical role of leadership in implementing the adequate change management model for effective organizational change* (Doctoral dissertation). https://opus.hs-furtwangen.de/frontdoor/index/index/docId/5958

International Labour Organization (ILO). the World Health Organization (WHO). (2022, July 13). Women in the health and care sector earn 24 percent less than men. Retrieved from: https://www.who.int/news/item/13-07-2022-women-in-the-health-and-care-sector-earn-24-percent-less-than-men

Kahsay, W. G., Negarandeh, R., Dehghan Nayeri, N., & Hasanpour, M. (2020). Sexual harassment against female nurses: A systematic review. *BMC Nursing, 19*(1), 1–12. https://link.springer.com/article/10.1186/s12912-020-00450-w. DOI: 10.1186/s12912-020-00450-w

Krause, M. E. (2015). *The role of personal values in shaping leaders' experiences with employee engagement: A qualitative phenomenological study* (Doctoral dissertation, University of Phoenix). https://www.proquest.com/openview/18c17edefb1935f4a07a2ca309ce11f5/1?pq-origsite=gscholar&cbl=18750

Kusuma, P. G., & Madasu, S. (2015). 'A Great Place to Work': A comparison of Employee Engagement Practices of select companies with David Zinger Engagement Pyramid. *Aweshkar Research Journal, 19*(1). https://www.semanticscholar.org/paper/%27A-Great-Place-to-Work%27-%3A-A-comparison-of-Employee-Kusuma-Madasu/dca59a224130758224dc04e66711fc00ec0d3fad

McClain, T. S., Kammer-Kerwick, M., Wood, L., Temple, J. R., & Busch-Armendariz, N. (2021). Sexual harassment among medical students: Prevalence, prediction, and correlated outcomes. *Workplace Health & Safety*, *69*(6), 257–267. https://journals.sagepub.com/doi/full/10.1177/2165079920969402. DOI: 10.1177/2165079920969402 PMID: 33331247

McLester, Q., Burrell, D. N., Nobles, C., & Castillo, I. (2021). Advancing Knowledge About Sexual Harassment Is a Critical Aspect of Organizational Development for All Employees. [IJKBO]. *International Journal of Knowledge-Based Organizations, 11*(4), 48–60. https://www.igi-global.com/article/advancing-knowledge-about-sexual-harassment-is-a-critical-aspect-of-organizational-development-for-all-employees/287776. DOI: 10.4018/IJKBO.2021100104

Mik-Meyer, N., Mik-Meyer, N., & Järvinen, M. (2020). Symbolic interactionism, stigma, and othering. *Qualitative analysis: Eight approaches for the social sciences*, 51-72. https://www.researchgate.net/publication/348677705_Symbolic_interactionism_stigma_and_othering

Morgenroth, T., & Ryan, M. K. (2018). Addressing gender inequality: Stumbling blocks and roads ahead. *Group Processes & Intergroup Relations, 21*(5), 671–677. https://journals.sagepub.com/doi/full/10.1177/1368430218786079?casa_token=9ZRbr3InQZ4AAAAA%3Ahze0HaTkvuFWSh9R9MN1x0OiRDKnEHY3lirKO2A_zYJ2AN22jEPwCmKjlbDHR190n0i1mAFb_VF3mw. DOI: 10.1177/1368430218786079

Nicotera, A. M. (2019). Human relations theory. In *Origins and Traditions of Organizational Communication* (pp. 106–127). Routledge. DOI: 10.4324/9780203703625-8

Omar, M., & Burrell, D. N. (2024). Organizational Dynamics and Bias in Artificial Intelligence (AI) Recruitment Algorithms. In E. Lewis (Ed.), *Evolution of Cross-Sector Cyber Intelligent Markets* (pp. 269-290). IGI Global Scientific Publishing. DOI: 10.4018/979-8-3693-1970-3.ch015

Torraco, R. J. (2016). Writing integrative literature reviews: Using the past and present to explore the future. *Human Resource Development Review, 15*(4), 404–428. https://journals.sagepub.com/doi/full/10.1177/1534484316671606?casa_token=QEKxwTdnxCoAAAAA%3ARowmT1h-GhD4p7Am6FffLJFOTm-IjNPDoQHiSifn3tiRXpTp2DOtBvW2EonEIRQeNFZq_-3pIlHwbQ. DOI: 10.1177/1534484316671606

Ueno, K., Jackson, T. M., Ingram, R., Grace, J., & Šaras, E. D. (2020). Sexual minority young adults' construction of workplace acceptance in the era of diversity and inclusion. *Social Currents, 7*(2), 91–108. https://journals.sagepub.com/doi/full/10.1177/2329496519888539?casa_token=SCmK8Sj-nI0AAAAA%3AaRVG1lUQJuoIMpisBGXSZEC4DOStjWvxbZM2kcTz4NT-bPJPbCuZn_TpMCj0ueAojUApl8oKZOUCqg. DOI: 10.1177/2329496519888539

Chapter 6
Ethical and Psychological Signals Embedded Within Organizations Where AI Tools Can Address Financial Misconduct

Stacey L. Morin
http://orcid.org/0000-0003-2935-8332
Marymount University, USA

Darrell Norman Burrell
http://orcid.org/0000-0002-4675-9544
Marymount University, USA

Natasha Harris
http://orcid.org/0009-0002-1745-7966
Marymount University, USA

Garrett Hart
http://orcid.org/0009-0008-8003-2032
Marymount University, USA

Adina Lundy
http://orcid.org/0000-0001-7564-2110
University of Rhode Island, USA

KerriLaine Prunella
http://orcid.org/0009-0001-0177-3545
Marymount University, USA

Samantha Thibodeau
http://orcid.org/0009-0000-4639-9166
Marymount University, USA

William Quisenberry
Purdue Global University, USA

Arthur D. Bradford
http://orcid.org/0009-0009-7276-2825
Marymount University, USA

Jason D. West
http://orcid.org/0009-0003-0439-8626
Marymount University, USA

Phillip Reed
http://orcid.org/0009-0000-1266-0151
Marymount University, USA

Laura A. Jones
http://orcid.org/0000-0002-0299-370X
Capitol Technology University, USA

DOI: 10.4018/979-8-2600-1016-7.ch006

Kylei L. Conti
http://orcid.org/0009-0009-0495-6601
Marymount University, USA

Julia DeFrance
http://orcid.org/0009-0005-8105-2594
Marymount University, USA

ABSTRACT

This management consulting case study examines how organizational culture and employee behavior contributed to prolonged misuse of corporate purchase cards at Quest Wellness Consortium (QWC) and how artificial intelligence (AI) can be leveraged to detect fraud and reshape ethical conduct. Drawing on a qualitative, three-phase focus group methodology involving auditors, organizational development specialists, and AI implementation experts, the study translates expert recommendations into actionable consulting deliverables. Findings demonstrate that unethical behavior among skilled employees emerged from normalized deviance, moral licensing, and low perceived accountability, exacerbated by reliance on manual controls. Results show that AI-enabled anomaly detection, behavioral nudges, and transparency dashboards function not only as fraud detection mechanisms but as behavioral interventions that increase ethical salience and accountability.

INTRODUCTION

The proliferation of corporate purchase cards (PCards) represents more than an operational convenience; it is a psychological signal embedded within organizational culture that communicates trust, autonomy, and expectations of ethical self-regulation. Once reserved almost exclusively for senior executives, PCards have gradually been distributed across hierarchical levels to support agility, decentralized decision-making, and uninterrupted workflow execution. While this expansion reflects modern organizational demands for speed and flexibility, it simultaneously increases exposure to behavioral risk, particularly when cultural norms, monitoring systems, and ethical reinforcement mechanisms fail to evolve in parallel.

At Quest Wellness Consortium (QWC), a mission-driven enterprise that formally espouses ethical integrity and regulatory compliance, the misuse of PCards exposes a deeper cultural contradiction. The issue is not merely transactional impropriety but a misalignment between espoused values and enacted behaviors. Organizational psychology suggests that when employees perceive weak accountability structures or inconsistent enforcement, ethical boundaries become psychologically negotiable rather than fixed. In this context, PCard misuse becomes less an isolated violation and more a behavioral artifact of cultural drift, one that signals the erosion of ethical salience within everyday decision-making. As a management consulting case, this scenario underscores the urgency of addressing not only policy deficiencies but also the underlying cultural and psychological conditions that enable sustained misconduct.

QWC's internal review uncovered a persistent and troubling pattern of PCard misuse, concentrated primarily among mid-level managers and extending uninterrupted for more than five years. This duration is not incidental; from a behavioral psychology perspective, prolonged misconduct without consequence reinforces normalization through habituation. When employees repeatedly engage in minor violations that go unchallenged, cognitive dissonance diminishes, ethical fading intensifies, and the behavior becomes psychologically reframed as acceptable or inconsequential. Over time, the organization inadvertently trains its workforce to deprioritize compliance in favor of personal convenience or perceived entitlement.

While individual cardholders bear responsibility for misuse, a consulting analysis reveals that the more consequential failure resides within the organizational system itself. Multiple control breakdowns point to systemic cultural weaknesses: transactions were approved within the enterprise resource planning framework, supervisory oversight failed to detect anomalies, and policy enforcement mechanisms lacked both visibility and consequence. These failures suggest a culture in which accountability is diffused, ethical vigilance is assumed rather than reinforced, and compliance functions operate reactively instead of proactively.

From an organizational culture standpoint, unanswered questions become diagnostic indicators. Why were abnormal purchasing patterns not escalated? Why did supervisors remain unaware or disengaged? What implicit norms governed PCard usage beyond formal policy language? These questions reveal a psychological environment where rule adherence is perceived as secondary to performance outcomes, and where managerial silence functions as tacit approval. In such cultures, employees often engage in moral licensing; justifying unethical behavior by offsetting it against perceived contributions or workload intensity.

Real-world parallels are evident across industries. High-profile cases in healthcare systems and financial institutions demonstrate that fraud and misuse rarely originate from malicious intent alone; rather, they emerge from cultures that reward results while neglecting ethical process. When organizations fail to integrate behavioral analytics and AI-driven anomaly detection into financial controls, they rely excessively on human vigilance; an approach proven to be both cognitively limited and culturally fragile. AI tools capable of identifying spending deviations, temporal patterns, and peer-based outliers could have flagged QWC's misuse within weeks rather than years, transforming oversight from passive detection to active behavioral correction.

Ultimately, the prolonged undetected misuse at QWC reflects a cultural equilibrium where unethical behavior persisted because it was psychologically safe to do so. For management consultants, the implication is clear: remediation must extend beyond policy revision and disciplinary action. Effective intervention requires recalibrating organizational culture through transparent accountability, psychologically informed leadership practices, and AI-enabled systems that both detect misconduct and reshape employee behavior by making ethical compliance visible, measurable, and unavoidable.

PROBLEM STATEMENT

Quest Wellness Consortium (QWC) is experiencing a demonstrable breakdown in ethical governance evidenced by the sustained misuse of corporate purchase cards by mid-level managers over a period exceeding five years without detection or corrective intervention. The duration, consistency, and managerial concentration of this misuse constitute empirical proof of a systemic failure rather than isolated misconduct. From a behavioral and cultural standpoint, the organization's existing controls did not merely fail to prevent fraud; they unintentionally enabled it by allowing improper financial behavior to persist unchallenged, thereby reinforcing psychological normalization and perceived permissibility.

This problem is fundamentally rooted in the interaction between human behavior and inadequate monitoring systems. Research indicates that organizational cash and cash-equivalent assets represent the most accessible and therefore most vulnerable targets for employee misuse due to routine access and discretionary control (Association of Certified Fraud Examiners [ACFE], 2020). In 2020 alone, documented fraud cases in the United States and Canada, including PCard misuse, totaled 895 incidents, with a median loss of $568,000 per case, underscoring the material consequences of weak financial oversight (ACFE, 2020). QWC's prolonged failure to detect anomalous purchasing patterns signals not only a lack of effective controls but also an overreliance on manual review processes that are psychologically prone to fatigue, bias, and omission.

Compounding this issue is the absence of advanced, AI-enabled analytics capable of identifying behavioral deviations, transaction anomalies, and longitudinal spending patterns that exceed normative thresholds. Without such tools, unethical behavior remained cognitively invisible to supervisors and psychologically safe for employees. The lack of timely detection eroded ethical salience, encouraged moral disengagement, and fostered an implicit organizational narrative that policy violations carried minimal risk. In this environment, misconduct evolved from a conscious ethical breach into an embedded routine.

The problem confronting QWC is therefore twofold. At the general level, the organization lacks technologically sophisticated mechanisms to detect, predict, and interrupt financial misuse before it escalates. At the specific level, QWC must address how its organizational culture, leadership practices, and control infrastructure failed to leverage AI technologies not only as fraud detection instruments but as behavioral signals that shape employee decision-making. Without integrating AI-driven oversight into the cultural fabric of accountability, QWC remains exposed to recurring fraud, diminished trust, and continued erosion of its ethical identity.

PURPOSE STATEMENT

The purpose of this management consulting case study is to examine how organizational culture and employee behavior psychology contributed to sustained PCard misuse at Quest Wellness Consortium and to evaluate how artificial intelligence–enabled controls can be leveraged to both detect financial misconduct and reshape ethical behavior. This inquiry seeks to move beyond transactional explanations of fraud by analyzing the psychological mechanisms, such as ethical fading, normalization of deviance, and perceived behavioral safety, that allowed misconduct to persist within a values-driven organization.

Additionally, the case aims to provide evidence-based consulting recommendations that integrate AI technologies with culturally informed leadership and governance practices. By reframing AI not merely as a surveillance tool but as a behavioral feedback mechanism, the study illustrates how organizations can reinforce ethical norms, restore accountability, and realign employee behavior with organizational values. The ultimate intent is to support QWC's leadership in implementing sustainable, psychologically grounded interventions that strengthen ethical culture while reducing fraud risk.

NATURE OF THE INQUIRY

This inquiry is a management consulting case study that applies principles from organizational psychology, behavioral ethics, and technology-enabled governance to analyze a real-world ethical control breakdown. The case study approach is appropriate given the complexity of the problem, which spans individual behavior, managerial oversight, organizational culture, and technological infrastructure. Rather than isolating misconduct as an individual failure, the inquiry examines the dynamic interaction between employee cognition, cultural norms, and systemic control mechanisms.

The analysis adopts a diagnostic and prescriptive orientation consistent with management consulting practice. Diagnostic inquiry focuses on identifying cultural signals, leadership behaviors, and control gaps that contributed to the normalization of unethical PCard usage. Prescriptive inquiry evaluates the role of AI-driven analytics, such as anomaly detection, behavioral pattern recognition, and predictive risk modeling, in enhancing fraud detection while simultaneously influencing employee decision-making through increased transparency and perceived accountability.

By integrating psychological theory with applied AI governance strategies, this case study advances a holistic understanding of how organizations can intervene effectively when ethical failures are culturally embedded rather than episodic. The inquiry positions AI as both a technical and behavioral instrument, capable of disrupting unethical routines and catalyzing cultural recalibration when aligned with leadership intent and organizational values.

Occupational Fraud as a Behavioral and Cultural Phenomenon

Occupational fraud, the misuse of organizational resources for personal gain, remains one of the most persistent and psychologically intricate threats within modern enterprises. Empirical evidence confirms its prevalence when it is considered that only 15 percent of surveyed organizations reported no fraud losses in a given year, while 31 percent of fraud incidents originated internally (KPMG, 2022). These figures suggest that fraud is not an episodic anomaly but an expected organizational risk shaped by access, opportunity, and behavioral rationalization.

At Quest Wellness Consortium (QWC), the prolonged misuse of corporate purchase cards (PCards) by mid-level managers over more than five years demonstrates a systemic failure of ethical governance. From an organizational psychology standpoint, the duration and consistency of the misconduct are more revealing than the financial losses themselves. Sustained unethical behavior indicates that the organizational environment inadvertently rewarded or tolerated deviations, allowing employees to cognitively reframe misconduct as acceptable, justified, or inconsequential.

The Psychology of Skilled Employees and Ethical Drift

One of the most challenging dynamics in cases such as QWC's involves talented, experienced employees who possess both organizational expertise and positional trust. Research in behavioral ethics consistently shows that high-performing or highly specialized employees are particularly susceptible to moral licensing; the belief that prior contributions, long hours, or exceptional performance justify rule-bending (Omar et al., 2016). In practice, a mid-level manager who consistently delivers results may view minor PCard misuse as a deserved perk rather than an ethical violation.

Real-world corporate investigations frequently reveal that fraud is not driven by ignorance of policy but by confidence in one's indispensability. In healthcare systems, for example, senior clinicians have been found to bypass procurement rules under the belief that their expertise supersedes administrative oversight. Similarly, in financial services firms, top-performing traders have rationalized policy violations as necessary for maintaining competitive advantage. At QWC, the misuse of PCards by managers suggests a comparable psychological dynamic: expertise and trust created a sense of behavioral immunity.

Cultural Signals, Silence, and the Normalization of Deviance

Organizational culture is shaped less by formal policy than by observed behavior and institutional response. When improper actions go undetected or unaddressed, silence functions as a powerful cultural signal. Over time, this silence fosters normalization of deviance, a process by which unethical actions gradually become routine and socially acceptable within a group.

At QWC, PCards were approved through existing financial systems, yet anomalous patterns were not escalated. This failure did not merely reflect process inefficiency; it conveyed to employees that compliance was aspirational rather than enforced. As ethical salience diminished, moral disengagement increased, enabling employees to separate their professional identity from the ethical implications of their actions. The longer this pattern persisted, the more difficult it became to reassert ethical boundaries without triggering resistance, defensiveness, or perceived injustice.

Human Limitations and the Case for AI-Enabled Detection

Traditional control mechanisms rely heavily on human judgment, manual reviews, supervisory approvals, and periodic audits. Cognitive psychology explains why these methods are insufficient in high-volume transactional environments: humans are prone to fatigue, confirmation bias, and attentional blind spots. Subtle but consistent misuse patterns often evade detection when reviewers focus on individual transactions rather than behavioral trends.

AI-enabled fraud detection tools address these limitations by identifying anomalies across time, individuals, and peer groups. Machine learning algorithms can flag deviations from normative spending behavior, detect unusual vendor patterns, or identify transaction timing inconsistencies that suggest misuse. In organizations that have adopted AI-driven expense analytics, irregularities are often detected within weeks rather than years, significantly reducing financial exposure.

More importantly, AI tools influence behavior. When employees are aware that transactions are continuously monitored and benchmarked against objective standards, perceived accountability increases. Behavioral research indicates that transparency alone can reduce unethical behavior, even in the absence of punitive action. In this sense, AI functions not merely as a detection mechanism but as a behavioral intervention that reshapes decision-making environments.

Organizational Impact: Beyond Financial Loss

The consequences of prolonged occupational fraud extend well beyond financial metrics. Internally, unchecked misuse erodes trust among employees who adhere to rules, contributing to disengagement, burnout, and cynicism (Omar et al., 2016). Employees may question why compliance is expected of them when violations appear tolerated among influential peers.

Externally, organizational reputation and stakeholder confidence are placed at risk. Financial health depends on disciplined expense management, governance credibility, and transparent controls (Sullivan, 2015). In large enterprises such as QWC, public disclosure of fraud often triggers regulatory scrutiny, tighter lending conditions, and reputational damage that compounds financial losses. Historical cases across regulated industries illustrate that the reputational fallout from fraud frequently exceeds the original monetary impact.

Cultural Misalignment and Ethical Identity

QWC's situation reveals a critical misalignment between espoused ethical values and enacted organizational practices. According to organizational culture theory, ethical identity is sustained only when values are reinforced through visible systems and consistent leadership behavior (Schein, 1995). At QWC, the absence of effective monitoring undermined the credibility of ethical commitments, allowing employees to infer that results mattered more than process.

Ethical decision making within organizations such as Quest Wellness Consortium (QWC) is not governed by static moral rules but by dynamic psychological interpretations of context, consequence, and perceived accountability. McMahon and Harvey (2007) argue that ethical judgment is inherently situational, shaped by how individuals cognitively appraise their circumstances rather than by formal policy alone. In practice, this means that employees, particularly those with expertise and institutional trust, do not ask whether an action violates policy in the abstract, but whether it *feels* unethical given the surrounding conditions.

At QWC, prolonged misuse of purchase cards illustrates how ethical erosion occurs incrementally. The perceived scale of consequences plays a decisive role in this process. Minor, recurring misuse of organizational funds is psychologically reframed as inconsequential when contrasted with large-scale fraud, making rationalization easier and moral resistance weaker (McMahon & Harvey, 2007). Real-world investigations across healthcare systems and technology firms reveal similar patterns, where employees justify repeated small violations under the belief that "no real harm" is being done. AI-enabled monitoring systems fundamentally disrupt this reasoning by making even minor deviations visible, aggregated, and measurable, thereby recalibrating employees' perception of consequence magnitude.

SOCIAL CONSEQUENCES, VISIBILITY, AND THE POWER OF PERCEIVED NORMS

Social consequences exert a powerful influence on ethical behavior, often outweighing formal penalties. McMahon and Harvey (2007) emphasize that individuals assess how their actions may affect social standing, peer relationships, and professional reputation. In organizational cultures where unethical behavior is silently tolerated, especially among high performers, employees infer that social risk is low. At QWC, the absence of detection mechanisms allowed misuse to persist without reputational damage, reinforcing a norm of permissibility rather than accountability.

AI tools alter this dynamic by increasing behavioral visibility. For example, peer-comparison algorithms that flag anomalous spending patterns subtly introduce reputational accountability without immediate punitive action. In multinational corporations that have implemented such systems, employees report heightened ethical awareness simply because their behavior is no longer socially invisible. Thus, AI functions not only as a control mechanism but as a cultural signal that reshapes informal norms governing behavior.

PROBABILITY, TEMPORAL IMMEDIACY, AND THE PSYCHOLOGY OF DELAYED CONSEQUENCES

Ethical judgment is further shaped by perceptions of detection likelihood and temporal distance between misconduct and consequences. When employees believe the probability of effect is low and penalties are delayed, unethical behavior becomes cognitively easier to justify (McMahon & Harvey, 2007). At QWC, the lack of real-time analytics meant that misuse was unlikely to be detected promptly, if at all, creating a psychological buffer that insulated employees from ethical discomfort.

AI-enabled systems collapse this buffer. Continuous transaction monitoring reduces the temporal gap between action and response, increasing psychological immediacy. In financial institutions that have adopted AI-driven fraud detection, employees demonstrate lower risk tolerance not because sanctions increase, but because uncertainty about detection decreases. This shift highlights a critical behavioral insight: certainty of oversight is often more influential than severity of punishment in shaping ethical conduct.

PROXIMITY, CONCENTRATION OF EFFECT, AND ORGANIZATIONAL DIFFUSION

Employees are more likely to engage in unethical behavior when the perceived victims are abstract or distant. McMahon and Harvey (2007) describe proximity and concentration of effect as key determinants of moral concern. At QWC, misuse of corporate funds likely felt victimless; losses were diffused across the organization rather than concentrated on identifiable individuals. This diffusion weakens moral restraint, particularly among technically skilled employees who view organizational resources as impersonal and abundant.

AI analytics counteract this diffusion by translating abstract losses into concrete organizational impact. Dashboards that quantify cumulative misuse in financial terms, operational disruptions, or downstream workforce consequences restore psychological proximity to harm. In organizations where such tools are used, employees report greater awareness of how individual actions affect collective outcomes, reinforcing ethical responsibility.

WITNESSED MISCONDUCT, WHISTLEBLOWING, AND PSYCHOLOGICAL SAFETY

Ethical complexity intensifies when employees observe misconduct and must decide whether to report it. Without protective systems, witnessing unethical behavior often leads to moral silence rather than whistleblowing. Lussier and Achua (2012) emphasize that individual characteristics, situational pressures, and perceived organizational response interact to shape ethical outcomes. At QWC, the absence of trusted reporting mechanisms likely discouraged intervention, allowing misconduct to persist unchecked.

AI-enabled reporting and detection systems partially alleviate this burden by reducing reliance on individual courage. Automated anomaly detection shifts responsibility from witnesses to systems, lowering social risk and fear of retaliation. In public-sector agencies that have adopted such tools, whistleblower reports have decreased while fraud detection rates have increased; suggesting that ethical systems, not heroic individuals, are more effective safeguards.

MORAL REASONING, COGNITIVE LOAD, AND TECHNOLOGICAL SUPPORT

Rest's (1979) four-component model of moral reasoning underscores the cognitive demands placed on individuals to recognize, evaluate, commit to, and act upon ethical choices. In high-pressure environments such as QWC, cognitive load, time constraints, and role conflict often undermine these processes. Ethical failure is therefore not always intentional but emerges from decision fatigue and competing priorities.

AI systems support moral reasoning by reducing ambiguity and cognitive strain. Automated alerts, contextual explanations, and decision-support tools enhance moral sensitivity and judgment by clarifying risks and consequences at the point of action. This aligns with findings by Greenfield and Jensen (2010) and Swisher and Davis (2005), who caution that ethical models must account for hidden biases and emotional complexity. AI does not replace moral agency; rather, it scaffolds ethical decision making within complex organizational systems.

TRUST, VULNERABILITY, AND ETHICAL INFRASTRUCTURE

Trust is foundational to ethical culture, particularly in environments where vulnerability is inherent. Robbins and Judge (2017) argue that trust emerges when individuals feel safe exposing themselves to scrutiny without fear of disproportionate consequences. At QWC, restoring trust requires visible commitment to ethical conduct, inclusive consideration of stakeholder interests, and demonstrated competence in ethical governance.

AI-enabled controls contribute to trust when framed as protective rather than punitive. Transparent communication about how data is used, how alerts are interpreted, and how fairness is ensured is essential. Organizations that fail to manage this narrative risk resistance, especially from high-status employees who may perceive monitoring as an erosion of autonomy. Effective consulting interventions therefore integrate AI implementation with cultural dialogue, leadership modeling, and ethical education.

Implications for Management Consulting Intervention

From a management consulting perspective, QWC's case demonstrates that effective fraud prevention requires simultaneous attention to technology, culture, and human behavior. AI tools must be embedded within a broader change strategy that addresses psychological resistance, redefines accountability norms, and recalibrates leadership expectations. Continuous assessment methodologies such as the Plan–Do–Study–Act cycle allow organizations to evaluate whether AI-enabled interventions are producing intended behavioral and cultural outcomes (Popescu & Popescu, 2015).

Ultimately, the urgency of intervention lies not only in preventing future misuse but in restoring ethical coherence. When talented employees engage in unethical behavior without consequence, the organization risks institutionalizing misconduct. By leveraging AI as both a detection system and a behavioral signal, QWC can disrupt unethical routines, reinforce ethical identity, and establish a culture where expertise and integrity coexist rather than conflict.

METHODS

Research Design and Methodological Approach

This study employed a qualitative focus group methodology to support a management consulting intervention examining the intersection of organizational culture, employee behavior, and artificial intelligence–enabled fraud detection at Quest Wellness Consortium (QWC). A qualitative design was selected due to the psychologically complex and context-dependent nature of ethical decision-making, fraud rationalization, and cultural normalization processes described in the case. Consistent with organizational psychology research, qualitative inquiry allows for the exploration of expert judgment, professional interpretation, and applied recommendations that cannot be meaningfully captured through purely quantitative instruments.

The focus group approach was deliberately structured to generate actionable recommendations rather than thematic abstraction. The intent was not to inductively code perceptions, but to elicit expert-driven guidance that could inform consulting solutions related to AI adoption, behavioral controls, and ethical culture reinforcement.

Participants and Expert Composition

The study consisted of twelve subject-matter experts selected through purposive sampling based on professional experience relevant to fraud detection, organizational behavior, and AI implementation. Participants were divided into three expert sub-groups:

- **Four auditors** with direct responsibility for fraud oversight, financial controls, and regulatory compliance

- **Four organizational development specialists** with expertise in organizational culture, leadership behavior, and change management
- **Four AI implementation specialists** with experience deploying analytics, machine learning, and automated monitoring systems in enterprise environments

This multidisciplinary composition ensured that recommendations reflected technical feasibility, behavioral realism, and cultural sensitivity, an essential requirement given the behavioral and systemic nature of PCard misuse at QWC.

Three-Phase Focus Group Procedure

The data collection process unfolded across three sequential phases designed to balance independent reflection, peer calibration, and cross-functional integration.

Phase One: Pre-Session Question Distribution

In the first phase, participants received three open-ended data collection questions via email one week prior to any live discussion. This step was intended to reduce social desirability bias, allow for deliberate cognitive processing, and ensure that participants grounded their responses in professional experience rather than real-time group influence. Participants were instructed to focus exclusively on providing recommendations applicable to QWC's context rather than describing problems or theoretical constructs.

Phase Two: Sub-Group Consensus Development

In the second phase, participants met in discipline-specific focus groups via ZOOM. Auditors, organizational development specialists, and AI implementation specialists met separately to discuss their preliminary responses and develop consensus within their professional cohort. This step allowed each group to reconcile internal differences, challenge assumptions, and refine recommendations through shared professional norms and expertise.

Phase Three: Integrated Full-Group Focus Session

The final phase consisted of a ZOOM-based session involving all twelve participants. During this session, each sub-group presented its consolidated recommendations to the full group. Cross-disciplinary dialogue was facilitated to test coherence, feasibility, and behavioral implications. Final recommendations reflected convergence across auditing, organizational psychology, and AI implementation perspectives, consistent with the systems-oriented nature of the consulting case.

Data Collection Questions

The following three questions guided data collection. The questions were intentionally framed to elicit practical, implementation-oriented recommendations, rather than perceptions or thematic narratives.

1. **What specific AI-enabled mechanisms should QWC implement to detect PCard misuse early and consistently?**
2. **How can AI tools be designed and implemented to influence employee behavior and reduce ethical rationalization?**
3. **What organizational and leadership practices must accompany AI adoption to ensure cultural acceptance, trust, and sustained ethical behavior?**

Focus Group Recommendations

Question 1: AI-Enabled Mechanisms for Fraud Detection

1. Implement machine learning–based anomaly detection to flag deviations from individual and peer spending baselines
2. Use real-time transaction monitoring with automated alerts for high-risk vendors and categories
3. Apply longitudinal pattern analysis to identify repeated low-value misuse that aggregates into material risk
4. Integrate AI with enterprise resource planning systems to prevent post-approval blind spots
5. Deploy risk scoring models that assign behavioral risk profiles to PCard usage
6. Utilize natural language processing to analyze transaction descriptions for policy inconsistencies
7. Establish automated escalation protocols for unresolved anomalies
8. Implement continuous auditing dashboards accessible to compliance leadership
9. Leverage AI to detect approval reciprocity or collusion patterns among managers
10. Use predictive analytics to identify employees at elevated risk of future misuse

Question 2: AI as a Behavioral and Ethical Influence Tool

1. Design AI systems to provide immediate feedback at the point of transaction

2. Use transparency dashboards to show employees how their behavior compares to organizational norms
3. Incorporate behavioral nudges that remind users of policy and ethical expectations in real time
4. Frame AI alerts as protective safeguards rather than punitive surveillance
5. Provide explanatory feedback that links flagged behavior to organizational impact
6. Use AI-generated reports in ethics training to reinforce behavioral awareness
7. Reduce moral licensing by applying consistent monitoring across hierarchical levels
8. Increase perceived accountability through visible, predictable system responses
9. Use AI insights to support coaching conversations rather than discipline alone
10. Reinforce ethical salience by integrating AI feedback into performance discussions

Question 3: Organizational and Leadership Practices Supporting AI Adoption

1. Clearly communicate the ethical purpose of AI implementation to all employees
2. Train leaders to interpret AI outputs responsibly and consistently
3. Align AI governance with existing ethical codes and cultural values
4. Establish psychological safety by protecting employees from retaliatory misuse of data
5. Involve employees in the design and rollout of AI-enabled controls
6. Ensure leadership modeling of compliance and ethical use of PCards
7. Pair AI adoption with updated policies and consequences applied uniformly
8. Use change management strategies to address resistance among high-status employees
9. Create cross-functional oversight committees for AI ethics and governance
10. Continuously evaluate cultural impact alongside technical effectiveness

Analytic Orientation

Data analysis emphasized synthesis rather than thematic coding. Recommendations were consolidated through expert consensus and evaluated for alignment with behavioral science principles, organizational culture theory, and practical feasibility within QWC's operational context. This approach ensured that findings directly supported consulting intervention design rather than abstract theorization.

Overview of Results and Consulting Orientation

The qualitative focus group process yielded a set of integrated, implementation-ready results that translate expert recommendations into concrete consulting deliverables for Quest Wellness Consortium (QWC). Rather than producing abstract themes, the results are structured as operational outputs that can be directly embedded into QWC's fraud prevention, ethical governance, and AI deployment strategy. The findings demonstrate convergence across auditing, organizational development, and AI implementation perspectives, reinforcing the necessity of a systems-based intervention that simultaneously addresses detection capability, behavioral influence, and cultural legitimacy.

Three categories of results emerged corresponding to the data collection questions: (a) AI-enabled fraud detection architecture, (b) AI-driven behavioral influence mechanisms, and (c) governance and leadership structures required to sustain ethical and cultural alignment. Together, these results form an integrated consulting solution rather than discrete technical or cultural fixes.

Result Set One: AI-Enabled Fraud Detection as a Control Infrastructure

Consulting Deliverable: Intelligent PCard Risk Detection Architecture

Participants reached strong consensus that QWC requires a shift from episodic, human-dependent controls to a continuous, AI-enabled fraud detection infrastructure. The resulting deliverable is a multilayered AI system architecture designed to identify misuse early, consistently, and without reliance on whistleblowing or managerial intuition.

At the foundational level, transaction ingestion layers integrate real-time PCard data from enterprise resource planning systems. Above this layer, machine learning models establish individual and peer-group spending baselines, enabling anomaly detection that identifies deviations across amount, frequency, vendor type, timing, and approval patterns. Longitudinal analytics aggregate low-value but repetitive misuse into material risk indicators, addressing the behavioral reality that fraud often occurs incrementally rather than dramatically.

Risk scoring engines synthesize these signals into dynamic behavioral risk profiles, which trigger automated escalation protocols based on severity and persistence. Dashboards designed for compliance leadership provide continuous auditing visibility, replacing retrospective reviews with proactive oversight. Importantly, this architecture aligns with enterprise risk management principles while compensating for known human cognitive limitations in detecting subtle behavioral drift.

Result Set Two: AI as a Behavioral and Ethical Influence System

Consulting Deliverable: Behavioral Ethics Enablement Layer

Beyond detection, the focus group results emphasize that AI must function as a behavioral intervention that reshapes employee decision-making environments. The second consulting deliverable is a behavioral ethics enablement layer embedded within the AI architecture.

This layer introduces real-time feedback mechanisms at the point of transaction, such as policy reminders, ethical nudges, and contextual warnings triggered by risk indicators. Transparency dashboards allow employees to view anonymized comparisons between their spending behavior and organizational norms, increasing perceived accountability without immediate punitive action. These mechanisms directly address moral licensing and ethical fading by making ethical boundaries cognitively salient during decision moments.

AI-generated insights are also designed to support developmental rather than exclusively disciplinary responses. For example, flagged patterns inform coaching conversations, ethics training scenarios, and performance discussions, reframing AI outputs as tools for growth and alignment. This approach reflects behavioral research demonstrating that predictability and visibility of oversight exert stronger deterrent effects than severity of punishment alone.

Result Set Three: Governance and Cultural Integration Mechanisms

Consulting Deliverable: AI Ethics and Governance Framework

The third result set highlights that AI adoption without governance legitimacy risks resistance, particularly from high-status or highly skilled employees. Accordingly, the focus group results translate into a comprehensive AI ethics and governance framework that anchors technology within QWC's organizational culture.

This framework establishes clear ownership structures for AI oversight, including cross-functional governance committees responsible for ethical use, data integrity, and fairness. Policies explicitly define acceptable use, escalation thresholds, and protections against retaliatory misuse of AI outputs. Leadership training ensures managers interpret AI insights consistently and responsibly, preventing selective enforcement that could undermine trust.

Change management strategies are embedded into the rollout plan, including employee involvement in system design, transparent communication of purpose, and alignment with existing ethical codes. These practices position AI as a protective organizational asset rather than a surveillance mechanism, thereby preserving psychological safety while reinforcing accountability.

Table 1. Mapping Recommendations to AI System Architecture and Governance Models

Recommendation Focus	AI System Architecture Component	Governance Model Alignment
Fraud Detection	Anomaly Detection Engines	Enterprise Risk Governance
Behavioral Influence	Ethical Nudges and Transparency Dashboards	Ethical Decision Governance
Accountability	Peer Benchmarking Analytics	Procedural Justice Framework
Whistleblower Protection	Automated Escalation and Alerting Mechanisms	Psychological Safety Controls
Leadership Alignment	Executive Analytics Interfaces	Leadership Governance Standards

CONCLUSION

This management consulting case study demonstrates that prolonged misuse of corporate purchase cards at Quest Wellness Consortium (QWC) cannot be understood or resolved through a narrow compliance lens. Instead, the findings reveal that unethical behavior emerged from a complex interaction among organizational culture, psychological rationalization, and inadequate systems of oversight. When skilled and trusted employees operate within environments characterized by weak behavioral visibility and delayed consequences, ethical boundaries become negotiable rather than fixed. Over time, this dynamic allowed misconduct to normalize and persist without triggering corrective action.

The qualitative focus group methodology employed in this study provided a critical lens through which multidisciplinary expertise converged. Auditors, organizational development specialists, and AI implementation professionals collectively reinforced the conclusion that fraud prevention is most effective when detection mechanisms, behavioral influence strategies, and governance structures operate as an integrated system. The resulting consulting deliverables illustrate that artificial intelligence is not merely a technical enhancement but a cultural instrument capable of reshaping how employees interpret accountability, consequence, and ethical responsibility.

The Results section further underscores that AI-enabled fraud detection must extend beyond retrospective auditing toward continuous, real-time monitoring architectures. Anomaly detection engines, risk-scoring models, and automated escalation protocols reduce reliance on human vigilance and eliminate the psychological safety that often enables unethical conduct. Importantly, these tools also alter employee behavior by increasing perceived certainty of oversight, a factor shown to be more influential than punitive severity in ethical decision making.

Equally significant is the role of AI as a behavioral feedback mechanism. Ethical nudges, transparency dashboards, and peer benchmarking systems make ethical expectations cognitively salient at the moment decisions are made. By embedding ethical reinforcement into everyday workflows, AI reduces moral licensing and ethical fading, particularly among high-performing employees who may otherwise rationalize minor violations as deserved or harmless. This reframing transforms ethics from an abstract organizational value into an operational reality.

The governance mapping further demonstrates that technological effectiveness alone is insufficient without cultural legitimacy. AI systems must be embedded within governance models that emphasize procedural justice, psychological safety, and leadership accountability. Without these safeguards, AI adoption risks resistance, distrust, or selective enforcement—outcomes that would undermine both ethical culture and organizational trust. The alignment of AI architecture with enterprise risk governance, ethical decision frameworks, and leadership standards ensures that accountability is applied consistently and transparently across hierarchical levels.

Collectively, this case study affirms that ethical resilience in modern organizations requires intentional design of both systems and culture. QWC's experience illustrates that when organizations fail to integrate behavioral science with advanced analytics, they inadvertently create conditions in which unethical behavior can thrive, even among talented and well-intentioned employees. By leveraging AI as both a detection mechanism and a cultural signal, QWC has the opportunity to disrupt entrenched patterns of misconduct, restore trust, and reinforce an ethical identity aligned with its mission and values.

From a management consulting perspective, the urgency of intervention lies not solely in preventing future financial loss, but in safeguarding the psychological and cultural foundations of the organization. The integration of AI-enabled controls, behaviorally informed governance, and leadership commitment offers QWC a sustainable pathway toward ethical accountability, organizational integrity, and long-term operational resilience.

Recommendations for Future Research

Future research building on the findings of this study would benefit substantially from the application of organizational ethnography as a primary research method. While the current inquiry effectively surfaces expert-driven insights through qualitative focus groups, it remains limited in its ability to capture the lived, everyday enactment of ethical decision making, cultural signals, and informal norms that shape behavior over time. Organizational ethnography is particularly well suited to examining the gap between espoused values and enacted practices identified in this case, as it allows researchers to observe how ethical boundaries, accountability expectations, and AI-enabled controls are interpreted and negotiated in situ rather than retrospectively or abstractly.

Organizational ethnography is a qualitative research method grounded in sustained, immersive engagement within an organizational setting. Rather than relying solely on self-reported perceptions or expert reflection, the method emphasizes direct observation of daily work practices, informal interactions, decision routines, and symbolic behaviors that collectively constitute organizational culture. In the context of financial misconduct and AI-enabled governance, ethnography enables researchers to examine how employees actually interact with purchase card systems, how managers respond to anomalies, how AI alerts are discussed or disregarded, and how ethical norms are reinforced or undermined through routine leadership behavior. This approach is particularly valuable in environments where misconduct persists not because of policy absence, but because of cultural normalization and psychological safety surrounding unethical actions.

The ethnographic method typically unfolds through a series of interrelated steps that prioritize depth, reflexivity, and longitudinal insight. First, the researcher gains negotiated access to the organization and establishes trust with participants, a critical prerequisite when studying sensitive topics such as fraud, ethics, and monitoring technologies. Second, prolonged participant observation is conducted across multiple organizational levels, allowing the researcher to witness routine transactions, approval processes, meetings, and informal conversations that shape ethical sensemaking. Third, observational data are complemented with in-depth interviews and document analysis to triangulate observed behavior with formal policies and stated intentions. Finally, iterative analysis is employed to identify patterns of normalization, resistance, adaptation, and ethical recalibration as employees respond to both organizational expectations and AI-enabled oversight mechanisms over time.

The primary advantage of organizational ethnography in future research lies in its capacity to surface latent cultural dynamics that are often invisible to audits, surveys, or short-term qualitative methods. Ethnography captures how silence, managerial inattention, peer influence, and informal workarounds function as powerful behavioral signals that either reinforce or erode ethical conduct. In the specific domain of AI-enabled fraud detection, ethnography can illuminate how employees interpret monitoring as either protective or punitive, how trust is negotiated in response to algorithmic oversight, and how ethical behavior evolves as visibility and accountability increase. By revealing these micro-level processes, organizational ethnography provides a richer empirical foundation for designing AI governance systems that are not only technically effective but also culturally legitimate and psychologically sustainable.

Collectively, the use of organizational ethnography in future research would extend the present study by moving from expert-informed diagnosis to embedded cultural understanding. Such an approach would enable scholars and practitioners to more precisely explain why ethical drift persists, how AI systems reshape behavioral norms in everyday practice, and under what conditions technological controls succeed or fail as instruments of ethical governance.

REFERENCES

Association of Certified Fraud Examiners. (2020). *Report to the nations: 2020 global study on occupational fraud and abuse.* https://acfepublic.s3-us-west-2.amazonaws.com/2020-Report-to-the-Nations.pdf

Greenfield, B., & Jensen, G. M. (2010). Beyond a code of ethics: Phenomenological ethics for everyday practice. *Physiotherapy Research International, 15*(2), 88–95. https://onlinelibrary.wiley.com/doi/abs/10.1002/pri.481?casa_token=1Q_foO-riuQAAAAA%3APHkMu5tnhGDQK03SiV9mlDFSlihwNac0UtYcxD8aGyKPwsK8AXU9vMLvs2Y2IX8nsh5PbQ-Vlm3Y4Kc2. DOI: 10.1002/pri.481 PMID: 20564757

KPMG. (2022). *A triple threat across the Americas: 2022 KPMG fraud outlook.* https://assets.kpmg.com/content/dam/kpmg/xx/pdf/2022/01/fraud-survey.pdf

Lussier, R. N., & Achua, C. F. (2012). *LEADERSHIP Theory, Application, & Skill Development.* Cengage Learning.

McMahon, J. M., & Harvey, R. J. (2007). The effect of moral intensity on ethical judgment. *Journal of Business Ethics, 72*(4), 335-357. Retrieved from ABI/INFORM Global database. (Document ID: 1247251681). https://link.springer.com/article/10.1007/s10551-006-9174-6

Omar, M., Nawawi, A., & Salin, A. (2016). The causes, impact and prevention of employee fraud: A case study of an automotive company. *Journal of Financial Crime, 23*(4), 1012–1027. https://www.emerald.com/jfc/article-abstract/23/4/1012/446872/The-causes-impact-and-prevention-of-employee?redirectedFrom=fulltext. DOI: 10.1108/JFC-04-2015-0020

Popescu, C. R., & Popescu, V. A. (2015). The assessment methodology PDCA/PDSA – A methodology for coordinating the efforts to improve the organizational processes to achieve excellence. *Challenges of the Knowledge Society,* 693-696. https://www.proquest.com/openview/645eef907f691293b2009e53424df806/1?pq-origsite=gscholar&cbl=2036059&casa_token=MkyH-_I3fnIAAAAA:qanFrg_pA8NbSOrrSqH5zEK5gJBAJ5NsJe-0pXAihFa78gnoJKx5wCoyNSNf_PuRRTFPvIEWTUs

Rest, J. (1979). *Development in judging moral issues.* University of Minnesota Press., https://www.amazon.com/Development-Judging-Moral-Issues-James/dp/0816608911

Robbins, S., & Judge, T. (2017). *Organizational Behavior.* Person.

Schein, E. H. (1995). The role of the founder in creating organizational culture. *Family Business Review*, *8*(3), 221–238. DOI: 10.1111/j.1741-6248.1995.00221.x

Swisher, L. L., & Davis, C. M. (2005). The realm-individual-process-situation (RIPS) model of ethical decision-making. HPA Resource, 5(3), 1-8.). https://www.semanticscholar.org/paper/The-Realm-Individual-Process-Situation-(-RIPS-)-of-Lee-Swisher/a83a548c3c59e7c7945ca3f0d4b42207dc46e1a4

Chapter 7
AI and Cybersecurity Revisited:
Leadership, Ethics, Human Capital, and Workforce Evolution in the Post-Pandemic Era

Sharon L. Burton
http://orcid.org/0000-0003-1653-9783
Embry-Riddle Aeronautical University, USA

ABSTRACT

The rapid evolution of artificial intelligence (AI) is reshaping workforce dynamics, organizational culture, and ethical norms, demanding new models of human-AI collaboration. This work examines the intersection of AI and human capital, emphasizing trust, bias, and workforce readiness. Special focus is given to aviation, aerospace, and infotainment systems, where AI drives safety, efficiency, and user experience but still requires adaptive human oversight. Integrating human talent and AI necessitates actionable frameworks, building trust, mitigating algorithmic bias, and fostering continuous learning for adaptability. About 70% of this discussion addresses practical solutions: education, training, and ethical safeguards, while also exploring legal and cultural challenges. Drawing on current case studies and industry views, this chapter guides leaders in aligning human capital strategies with the evolving demands of an AI-driven workplace, emphasizing workforce resilience and equitable access.

DOI: 10.4018/979-8-2600-1016-7.ch007

INTRODUCTION

AI is no longer a peripheral technology but a central force transforming workplaces, redefining leadership, and reshaping the social contract between organizations and their people (Demir et al., 2023; Budhwar et al., 2022). The intersection of AI and human capital has become especially salient since 2021, as organizations across sectors have experienced rapid digitalization due to pandemic-related disruptions. These changes have driven organizations to confront new realities: remote work as a norm, the democratization of digital tools, and the emergence of AI-driven decision support systems that are increasingly central to talent management and organizational strategy (Chalmers et al., 2021; Seeber et al., 2020).

Considering these profound developments, the relevance and urgency of this subject span theoretical, practical, and policy domains. From a theoretical standpoint, the co-evolution of humans and AI within an organization demands fresh interpretations of leadership, agency, skill acquisition, and organizational change (Bankins, Ocampo et al., 2024a). Practically, leaders must integrate AI into operational workflows, and also foster trust, ethical use, and shared value creation amidst ambiguity and public skepticism (Basu et al., 2023; Salifu et al., 2025). At a policy level, the rise of algorithmic management and automated systems necessitates new frameworks to ensure fairness, social sustainability, and regulatory compliance (UNESCO, 2024). The following research questions guide this chapter, each question reflecting ongoing scholarly debate and practice-oriented concern:

> **RSQ1:** How are organizations and leaders experiencing the integration of AI into human capital management?
> **RSQ2:** What ethical and organizational dilemmas arise in the pursuit of AI-enabled change, and how are these addressed?
> **RSQ3:** Which strategies support the development of trust, inclusion, and resilience as AI reshapes work?

The rationale for a qualitative-only approach is anchored in a recognition that numbers alone cannot capture the complexity or lived reality of digital transformation. Rich, context-sensitive understanding is required to uncover nuanced experiences, local meanings, and emergent interpretation in organizations navigating the AI transition (Behrend et al., 2024). Nonetheless, this chapter is bound by several practical constraints, including limited direct access to highly proprietary organizational contexts and a research focus oriented towards English-language, peer-reviewed sources published from 2021 onward. Furthermore, the dynamic pace of AI evolution introduces challenges for research currency and generalizability, which are critically reflected upon throughout the chapter.

Figure 1 depicts "AI, Cybersecurity, and Human Capital: The Workforce Evolution Model (2025)" as a comprehensive conceptual framework presented through a visually striking infographic design. The diagram utilizes a concentric circle structure set against a deep blue background, symbolizing the layered and interconnected nature of modern workforce transformation in the post-pandemic era. At the center of this model, three interlocking symbols serve as the foundational pillars: a neural network or brain icon representing artificial intelligence, a cybersecurity shield symbolizing digital security infrastructure, and human silhouettes depicting the workforce and human capital elements.

The outer ring of the model establishes the strategic framework through key organizational principles positioned at cardinal points around the circle. "Leadership & Ethics" appears prominently at the top, emphasizing the critical role of governance and moral guidance in workforce evolution. "Trust & Resilience" is positioned on the left side, highlighting the importance of organizational stability and adaptability. At the bottom, "Risk & Compliance" addresses the essential regulatory and security requirements that organizations must navigate. The middle ring contains operational elements, including "Workforce Readiness," "Upskilling," "Accumulation Adaptation," and "Organizational Adaptation," which represent the practical mechanisms through which transformation occurs.

Dynamic arrows throughout the design connect all elements, illustrating the cyclical and interdependent relationships between these components. This visual representation emphasizes that AI integration, cybersecurity considerations, and human capital development cannot function in isolation but must work synergistically. The model's caption reinforces this concept, explaining that organizations must foster adaptive leadership, robust cybersecurity measures, and continuous workforce development to remain resilient in an increasingly AI-driven and digitally secure business environment. The overall design effectively communicates the complexity and interconnectedness of modern workforce evolution while maintaining visual clarity and professional presentation standards.

The following primary sections are included in this book chapter: Background, Assumptions, Limitations, and Delimitations, Statement of The Problem and The Research Gap, Research Methodology and Design, Literature Review, Conceptual Framework, Critique: Conceptual Framework, Originality of the Text, plus Presentation and Analysis of Interview Findings, Conclusion and Future Studies.

Figure 1. AI, Cybersecurity, and Human Capital: The Convergent Workforce Ecosystem (2025)

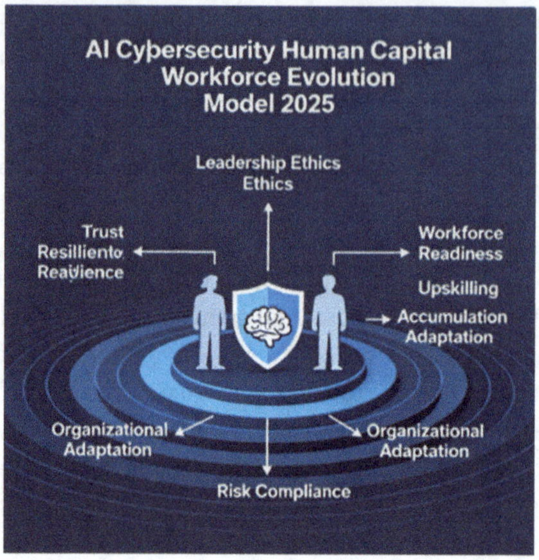

The integration of AI and cybersecurity within organizational strategy drives continuous workforce evolution, requiring adaptive leadership, ethical innovation, and resilient, upskilled teams for a sustainable future.

BACKGROUND

This chapter employs a qualitative research orientation designed to generate nuanced insights into the interplay of AI and human capital in contemporary organizations. The approach is inspired by constructivist paradigms, which prioritize the formation of meaning through lived experiences, social interaction, and reflective interpretation (Bankins, Ocampo et al., 2024a). Qualitative research is especially appropriate when the research aims are to uncover how individuals and organizations perceive, interpret, and adapt to innovation, rather than to test hypotheses or generalize probabilities (Cunningham & Carmichael, 2017).

The backbone of the research is a systematic qualitative literature review, enriched through the integration of semi-structured interviews and multi-case study syntheses drawn from recent scholarship. The literature review targets peer-reviewed articles, academic books, and industry documents published from 2019 to 2025. Particular attention is paid to themes of leadership adaptation, ethical governance, and organizational learning in the age of AI (Chalmers et al., 2021). To extend beyond the secondary literature, the chapter draws on published interview data and illustrative case studies, focusing on leader narratives, employee perspectives, and thematic case exemplars where organizations have confronted significant AI-related transformation (Benabou & Touhami, 2025).

Instruments utilized include comprehensive document analysis protocols, qualitative coding frameworks, and qualitative analysis software to support systematic categorization and interpretation of themes (Jia et al., 2024). Where available, expert interview transcripts and organizational documents were coded using thematic analysis, enabling the emergence of higher-order patterns and cross-case comparisons (Donald et al., 2024). Validity is strengthened by the triangulation of multiple data types (i.e., literature, interview, and case evidence), thereby allowing for the corroboration and deepening of findings (Behrend et al., 2024; Donald et al., 2024).

Credibility and reliability in this study were reinforced through a rigorous and transparent coding process, with each text or transcript independently coded by two scholars and discrepancies resolved through consensus discussions to foster stronger inter-coder agreement (Donald et al., 2024). Triangulation was systematically applied by integrating insights across literature reviews, semi-structured interviews, and exploratory case studies, which strengthened the robustness of findings and helped mitigate single-source bias (Saldaña, 2025; Donald et al., 2024). An audit trail of coding decisions, analytic memos, and defined themes was maintained to ensure transparency and facilitate replication (Jia et al., 2024). Reflexivity was incorporated throughout the process by regularly reviewing positionality and researcher assumptions, with analytic memoing undertaken to consider the influence of context, power dynamics, and blind spots (Madanchian & Taherdoost, 2025). The selection of case and interview sources adhered to recognized criteria for trustworthiness in qualitative research, namely, source authenticity, relevance, and saturation of categories (Cunningham & Carmichael, 2017). Additionally, thick description was used in reporting cases and interviews to support transferability of findings and help readers judge applicability to their own settings (Behrend et al., 2024). Member checking was conducted in relevant studies, further validating interpretations where participant feedback was available (Bankins, Formosa et al., 2024b).

The design is inherently iterative, allowing for the refinement of codes and analytic focus in light of new insights and the fast-moving developments in AI applications (Behrend et al., 2024). Reflexivity is applied throughout, with regular review of researcher assumptions, context-specific influences, and potential deficiencies in the interpretation of organizational behavior and leadership responses to technological change (Madanchian & Taherdoost, 2025). This methodology, while rigorous, recognizes the impossibility of complete neutrality in qualitative inquiry and openly incorporates critical reflection as an integral component of research design.

The central contribution of this approach lies in its capacity to illuminate the lived dynamics of AI–human capital integration as they unfold in multiple contexts, providing texture and depth that would be unattainable through quantitative survey methods alone (Behrend et al., 2024). The chapter remains attentive to the contextual variables, such as organizational culture, regional digital maturity, and sectoral regulatory pressures, that mediate the experiences observed in the cases and interviews analyzed (Behrend et al., 2024). Next are the assumptions, limitations, and delimitations.

ASSUMPTIONS, LIMITATIONS, AND DELIMITATIONS

A rigorous examination of any research endeavor requires explicit acknowledgment of its underlying assumptions, inherent limitations, and the boundaries that define its scope (Saldaña, 2025). Clarifying these elements is essential for contextualizing the findings, guiding the interpretation of results, and identifying avenues for future inquiry. In this chapter, the integration of technical, psychological, and governance perspectives in the analysis of malvertising defense necessitates a transparent articulation of the foundational premises, potential constraints, and deliberate exclusions that shape the research design and its conclusions.

Assumptions

This research operates on several foundational assumptions. First, it assumes that integrating interdisciplinary perspectives, including technical, psychological, and policy-oriented frameworks, yields a richer, more actionable understanding of the relationship between AI and human capital than any single-discipline approach (Saldaña, 2025). This researcher presumes that the data sources, peer-reviewed articles, industry reports, case studies, and interview data from 2019 to 2025, are accurate reflections of current trends, challenges, and strategies relevant to workforce transformation in the age of AI (Benabou & Touhami, 2025). Additionally, the researcher assumes that the thematic patterns identified through qualitative analysis can be reasonably extended to inform organizational practices and policy formation across diverse sectors, given the breadth of cases and perspectives included (Saldaña, 2025). Finally, it is assumed that the rapidly evolving nature of technology and organizational context requires flexible, continuously updated frameworks for assessment and decision-making (Saldaña, 2025).

Assumptions are essential in research because they clarify the foundational premises on which the chapter is built. Clearly articulating assumptions allows readers and scholars to comprehend the underlying logic, contextual scope, and the interpretive lens that shape the inquiry and its conclusions. By explicitly stating what is presumed (e.g., the reliability of data sources or the applicability of analytical frameworks), researchers equip readers to better assess the appropriateness, scope, and transferability of the findings (Saldaña, 2025).

Limitations

Limitations are significant because they openly acknowledge the boundaries, weaknesses, and potential sources of bias that could affect the validity or generalizability of results. Transparently stating limitations demonstrates scholarly rigor and equips readers to interpret findings with a balanced understanding of their strengths and constraints. This openness not only helps future researchers identify areas for further investigation but also builds trust in the research process by emphasizing humility and honesty about what can or cannot be known from the study (Saldaña, 2025).

This study is subject to several notable limitations that the reader should consider in the interpretation of its findings. The exclusive reliance on qualitative methods, centered on in-depth organizational cases and interview-based data, restricted the capacity to incorporate quantitative or longitudinal metrics to track AI's socio-economic effects over an extended period (Saldaña, 2025). Additionally, by drawing primarily from English-language, peer-reviewed scholarship and accessible organizational contexts, this research may have limited generalizability to different linguistic, regional, or cultural environments and may not fully capture global diversity perspectives in AI and human capital integration (Hong et al., 2023; Irmatova et al., 2024). The absence of empirical measurement of psychological well-being or emotional intelligence as outcomes also represents a constraint, as does potential selection bias inherent in sampling organizations and participants who were available and willing to participate (Bankins, Formosa et al., 2024b). These limitations point to the need for future research to employ broader, comparative, and quantitative approaches to enrich the evidence base and deepen insight into the socio-economic and psychological impacts of AI across different cultural, linguistic, and sectoral settings (Behrend et al., 2024; Demir et al., 2023).

Delimitations

Delimitations in this chapter are explicitly acknowledged to sharpen focus and analytic clarity. By design, the chapter is restricted to qualitative explorations of AI integration in formal, structured organizational contexts, thus excluding gig, freelance, or informal work environments (Bankins, Ocampo et al., 2024a). The chapter is temporally bounded, concentrating on developments and scholarly sources published or produced since 2021. This ensures that the findings are current and reflective of the accelerated wave of AI adoption and digital workplace transformation catalyzed by the COVID-19 pandemic and subsequent technological advances (World Economic Forum, 2023).

The scope of this study was deliberately delimited in several ways to promote analytical depth and maintain methodological coherence. The research focused exclusively on qualitative inquiry within formal, structured organizational environments, intentionally excluding the gig economy, freelance, and informal labor sectors, as well as larger macroeconomic or national policy analyses (Bankins, Ocampo et al., 2024a). Analysis and discussion were anchored in post-2021, English-language, peer-reviewed literature and contemporary organizational cases primarily in the aviation, aerospace, and infotainment sectors, chosen for their relevance to rapid post-pandemic digital transformation (Chalmers et al., 2021). Quantitative, longitudinal, and multinational comparative methods were not included, with the decision made to privilege context-rich, qualitative findings specific to the integration of AI and human capital according to the SYNTHESIS conceptual framework (Behrend et al., 2024; Jia et al., 2024). Technical analysis of AI models or detailed cybersecurity risk modeling was confined strictly to organizational governance and workforce practice implications, and broader cross-cultural or policy-level diversity was not pursued beyond delineated case or interview evidence (Jia et al., 2024; Hong et al., 2023). These delimitations reflect strategic scholarly choices aligned to the research questions and are clearly presented as drivers for future avenues of research and expansion (Saldaña, 2025). The study purposefully excludes direct assessment of individual psychological well-being or emotional intelligence. This decision was made by design, aligns with the organizational/ intermediate layer of analysis research lens, and is not a methodological failure or oversight.

These delimitations represent strategic scholarly choices, intended to enable deep, context-rich analysis of the phenomena most salient to leaders, HR professionals, and organization scholars interested in the lived integration of AI and human capital. Future research would benefit from relaxing some boundaries to examine cross-sectoral, cross-cultural, or policy-level issues that are outside the reach of this chapter (Hong et al., 2023). Nonetheless, by maintaining focus on qualitative, organizational perspectives after 2021, this study targets a well-defined gap in the contemporary literature and delivers practical insights for the current moment. The existing ending states the research boundaries and future relevance, but moves quickly to the statement of the problem and the research gap.

STATEMENT OF THE PROBLEM AND THE RESEARCH GAP

The precise statement of the problem is as follows: Despite the rapid proliferation of artificial intelligence across industries, there remains a profound and persistent uncertainty regarding how organizations can effectively align human capital strategies with the evolving demands and risks of AI-driven transformation.

Although AI technologies increasingly reinforce core business operations and decision-making, the challenge of fostering trust, mitigating bias, and ensuring workforce adaptability has outpaced the development of actionable frameworks that reliably support human-AI collaboration (Bankins et al., 2024a; Salifu et al., 2025). Existing scholarship has principally focused on the technical efficacy and operational efficiencies of AI, often neglecting the nuanced organizational, ethical, and psychological dimensions necessary to realize sustainable value (Chen, 2024). As a result, there is a scarcity of research that critically examines the lived experiences of leaders and employees confronting AI-induced disruptions, particularly within the context of sector-specific regulatory pressures and rapidly changing labor markets.

Recent advances accentuate the urgent need for integrative approaches that situate human capital at the yoke of organizational strategy, technological adoption, and ethical governance (Demir et al., 2023). However, current literature remains fragmented, lacking robust, empirical analyses that synthesize qualitative insights from real-world cases with theoretical perspectives on adaptability, equity, and innovation (Bankins, Ocampo et al., 2024a). This failure to holistically address the interplay between AI systems, cultural adaptation, and workforce readiness perpetuates strategic blind spots and missed opportunities for organizational resilience (Bankins et al., 2024a).

Accordingly, this chapter addresses a critical research gap by systematically investigating how organizations are navigating the integration of AI technologies, with particular attention paid to leadership adaptation, human capital development, and the cultivation of ethical, context-sensitive frameworks. Through a synthesis of contemporary literature, expert testimony, and cross-sector case analysis, the study seeks to illuminate actionable pathways for building trust, equity, and adaptability in the contemporary workplace (Salifu et al., 2025). In doing so, the research offers fresh insights that advance both academic scholarship and practical guidance in the era of pervasive AI adoption. Next is the research methodology and design.

RESEARCH METHODOLOGY AND DESIGN

This chapter adopts a qualitative inquiry framework, a methodological approach that provides a robust foundation for exploring multifaceted human experiences within interdisciplinary contexts. Contemporary qualitative inquiry is recognized for its capacity to probe complex social realities, illuminate nuanced processes, and inspire adaptation to emergent research problems within human-centered disciplines (Madanchian & Taherdoost, 2025). Rather than being anchored solely to the content or outcomes of research, qualitative methodology interrogates how, why, and under what circumstances human phenomena unfold, offering a pathway for reframing established perspectives and initiating new avenues of scholarly dialogue (Jia et al., 2024; Saldaña, 2025).

This research design is structured around three integrative qualitative methods: systematic literature review, semi-structured in-depth interviews, and an intrinsic exploratory case study. The literature review component employs a transparent, rigorous protocol to synthesize recent peer-reviewed scholarship between 2021 and 2025, ensuring that the proposed study is grounded in up-to-date theoretical trends and knowledge gaps (Behrend et al., 2024). An objective and critical stance is maintained throughout the review process, situating the current inquiry within a larger tapestry of ongoing scholarly debate and empirical discovery (Donald et al., 2024).

Semi-structured interviews form the core of the primary data collection. This method offers a flexible but systematic approach to capturing participants' lived experiences, social constructs, and emergent meanings (Saldaña, 2025). Interviews are designed with a blend of open and closed-ended questions, which are further supplemented by real-time probing ("how" and "why" questions) to elicit deeper reflection and narrative detail (Bankins, Ocampo et al., 2024a; Saldaña, 2025). Each one-on-one interview session, lasting approximately one hour, is digitally recorded and transcribed verbatim to enhance data integrity. The sample is determined using purposive and theoretical sampling strategies, wherein participants are selected for their expertise and diversity in fields including information technology, risk management, healthcare, and digital education (Behrend et al., 2024). This targeted sampling cultivates a dataset rich in diverse perspectives while allowing for the emergence of grounded, transferable theoretical insights (Jia et al., 2024).

In addition to literature synthesis and interviews, this study employs an intrinsic exploratory case study approach to examine focal phenomena within their real-world context. The intrinsic case study method is chosen when researchers have a particular investment in comprehending a bounded case for its own sake, rather than for generalizing across populations (Hong et al., 2023). Data collection incorporates multiple informants, document analysis, and observational evidence, allowing the research question to be viewed through multiple conceptual lenses (Madanchian & Taherdoost, 2025). The exploratory nature of the case study is especially suited to contexts where anticipated outcomes are unknown or the intervention's effects are diffuse, supporting a holistic comprehension of organizational and technological dynamics (Behrend et al., 2024; Jia et al., 2024).

Throughout the research process, analytic rigor is maintained via iterative coding, reflective note-taking, and regular validity checks. Thematic analysis is conducted using qualitative analysis software to identify recurring patterns and themes, ensuring transparency and reproducibility (Jia et al., 2024). Credibility is further enhanced through member checking, where participants are invited to review key findings and interpretations for resonance and accuracy, and through investigator triangulation, which involves multiple researchers independently reviewing and discussing codes and categories (Donald et al., 2024).

Ethical considerations are foregrounded at all stages: informed consent is obtained for all interviews, participant confidentiality is strictly observed, and data security is maintained according to the latest institutional protocols and international standards. Reflexive practice is integrated into the methodological design, ensuring that researchers remain attentive to positionality, power dynamics, and the evolving contexts impacting data interpretation (Behrend et al., 2024).

This qualitative research design employs a triangulated, contextually responsive methodology that integrates systematic literature review for foundational theory, semi-structured interviews for capturing lived experiences, and an intrinsic case study for in-depth contextual insight. This synthesis aligns with contemporary imperatives for methodological innovation and inclusivity in the human sciences, ultimately yielding a comprehensive comprehension of the dynamic interplay between human capital and AI in the current cyber age. As the interplay between AI and workforce capabilities intensifies, a comprehensive, evidence-based approach to research and policy is urgently needed to close these gaps and foster responsible, inclusive technological progress. The following literature review synthesizes current research and real-world perspectives on the evolving relationship between AI and human capital in the context of 2025.

LITERATURE REVIEW

The following literature review synthesizes current research and real-world perspectives on the evolving relationship between AI and human capital in the context of 2025. Drawing from recent scholarly work and practitioner insights, this section examines the impact of AI on organizational culture, workforce adaptation, ethical frameworks, and technological innovation. Attention is given to the opportunities and challenges arising from AI integration, highlighting the roles of education, continuous learning, and proactive ethical governance. With this foundation established, the discussion transitions to a focused analysis of how these developments manifest in specific organizational settings and influence future strategic directions. Subheadings include the shifting paradigm: AI, human capital, and workforce evolution, rethinking skills: upskilling, adaptability, and the era of hybrid roles, organizational culture: from technology adoption to human-centric transformation, the imperative of equity, ethics, and regulatory innovation, strategic planning, future readiness, and the fifth industrial revolution, voice technology, inclusion, and persistent limitations, and the conclusions and future research directions.

The Shifting Paradigm: AI, Human Capital, and Workforce Evolution

The literature as of 2025 reflects a pronounced paradigm shift in organizational strategy, where AI is no longer regarded as a supplemental productivity tool but as a catalyst for holistic transformation (Bean, 2025; Ochis, 2024; World Economic Forum, 2025). Recent advances show AI is no longer a distant threat but an active force transforming the labor market, with implications for workforce readiness and skills development in nearly every sector (Deming & Summers, 2025). Also, research underscores the magnitude and rapidity of this change, particularly within complex, knowledge-intensive sectors such as aviation, infotainment, and advanced manufacturing (Burton, 2019). AI's integration necessitates a foundational reevaluation of human capital strategy, emphasizing trust-building, continuous learning, and ethical safeguards alongside technical adoption (Salifu et al., 2025; Gadimah Consulting, 2023). Authors contend that successful AI integration is grounded not just in technological prowess but in cultivating adaptability, empathy, and collaborative habits among employees (Demir et al., 2023). Critically, the literature cautions that organizations failing to align human capital with the dynamic demands of the AI-driven workplace risk irrelevance or even existential decline (Babina & Fedyk, 2025).

Rethinking Skills: Upskilling, Adaptability, and the Era of Hybrid Roles

The effects of AI on workforce competencies are widely documented, with a consistent call for continuous, adaptive upskilling to maintain professional resilience (Ersanlı et al., 2025; Deming & Summers, 2025). Rather than witnessing a precipitous decline in jobs, scholars describe a qualitative transformation of roles and the skills underpinning them, thereby prompting a blended workforce in which humans and machines co-create value (Fathi & MacKinnon, 2024; Burton, 2019). New positions (i.e., AI trainers, automation strategists, and data ethicists) are emerging in tandem with the obsolescence of repetitive roles, catalyzing an urgent need for ongoing educational and training interventions (Ersanlı et al., 2025). Higher education institutions and professional organizations now shoulder the responsibility of designing curricula that are nimble and responsive to rapid technological evolution (Babina & Fedyk, 2025). As such, the review critiques traditional static models of skill assessment and advocates for dynamic, lifelong learning frameworks that valorize adaptability and critical reasoning over narrow technical proficiency (Burton, 2019).

Organizational Culture: From Technology Adoption to Human-Centric Transformation

Within the literature, there is a growing consensus that the integration of AI is fundamentally altering organizational culture, shaping how employees interact and also how they align with evolving missions, values, and collaborative practices (Grasso, 2024). Researchers note that the successful adoption of AI hinges on a parallel investment in cultural agility, transparency, and trust, themes now regarded as central to competitive advantage rather than peripheral HR concerns (Salifu et al., 2025; Demir et al., 2023). Organizational structures are converging toward greater cross-functionality and hybridity, enabling rapid adoption of AI within both operational and strategic domains (Burton, 2019). The literature critiques organizations that relegate AI integration to IT departments, emphasizing that such an approach limits both employee buy-in and holistic performance gains (Noble et al., 2022). Support is given instead to systemic, leader-driven cultural changes where values alignment, communication, and the democratization of AI literacy are prioritized (Nahavandi, 2019; Deming & Summers, 2025). As organizational culture advances through the adoption of AI, these shifts inevitably amplify the need for robust ethical, equitable, and regulatory frameworks to safeguard that technology-driven change supports fairness and social responsibility rather than inadvertently exacerbating risks

The Imperative of Equity, Ethics, and Regulatory Innovation

As AI becomes woven into the fabric of society, urgent ethical challenges take center stage, chief among these, fairness, transparency, privacy, interpretability, and long-term environmental impact (Floridi, 2022; Salifu et al., 2025; Burton, 2019). Literature critiques the lag between technological deployment and robust ethical oversight, particularly regarding algorithmic bias, data integrity, and consent (Burrell, personal communication, 2025). Evidence persists that without intentional inclusion of underrepresented voices, particularly Black, Indigenous, and other marginalized populations, AI systems perpetuate and exacerbate longstanding inequities in recognition accuracy, hiring, and decision-making (Salifu et al., 2025). Strategies emerging in 2025 include systematic bias audits, fairness metrics, and inclusive data pipelines, but these interventions are presented as works in progress rather than panaceas (Burton, 2019; Kenytinc, 2024). The literature is increasingly critical of both organizational and legal frameworks that remain static, calling for agile regulation and proactive stakeholder engagement to safeguard justice, due process, and accessibility within AI-powered systems (Grasso, 2024).

Strategic Planning, Future Readiness, and the Fifth Industrial Revolution

Research acknowledges that organizational strategy in 2025 must grapple with a globally networked, rapidly changing, and AI-mediated business environment (Gadimah Consulting, 2023; Grasso, 2024). The Fifth Industrial Revolution, distinguished by its human-centric focus and pursuit of ethical, sustainable innovation, promotes an entirely new set of imperatives for leaders: adaptability, resilience, and learning agility (Burton, 2019; Demir et al., 2023). Competitive advantage is thus increasingly defined by the degree to which organizations combine AI adoption with ethical foresight, equitable access to upskilling, and a robust sense of psychological safety and trust (Nahavandi, 2019; Noble et al., 2022). Literature critiques both business and governmental strategies that prioritize short-term efficiency at the cost of long-term social and organizational health (Babina & Fedyk, 2025). Instead, leading organizations are those that intentionally integrate human-AI partnership, fostering a climate where technology enhances, rather than displaces, the full spectrum of human potential (Burton, 2019).

Voice Technology, Inclusion, and Persistent Limitations

Despite significant progress in voice technology and AI-powered assistants, the literature points to ongoing obstacles in achieving equitable, context-sensitive, and emotionally intelligent workplace interactions (Salifu et al., 2025; Caldarini et al., 2022). Studies highlight notable improvements in tasks such as speaker identification, meeting transcription, and information retrieval, but emphasize persistent shortcomings in handling diverse accents, dialects, and multiparty, hybrid communication environments (Kenytinc, 2024; Burrell, personal communication, July 19, 2025). Existing systems are still prone to errors that can have real-world repercussions for employee equity, trust, and even legal compliance, especially in global or multicultural contexts (Salifu et al., 2025; Caldarini et al., 2022). As such, researchers advocate for much more robust evaluation frameworks, bias mitigation protocols, and transparent auditing to ensure fair and trustworthy deployment of voice AI in enterprise settings (Burton, 2019). The literature consistently warns against complacency, arguing that without these safeguards, advancements in voice technology may reproduce or amplify workplace inequities instead of resolving them.

Conclusions and Future Research Directions

In summation, the 2025 literature marks a decisive turn toward a holistic, human-centered approach to AI in organizations, foregrounding equity, trust, and continual learning alongside technological advancement (Burton, 2019; Gadimah Consulting, 2023). Rather than fixating on job displacement or efficiency gains alone, scholars increasingly frame the challenge as nurturing adaptable, ethically aware workforces capable of thriving in partnership with intelligent machines (Ersanlı et al., 2025). The next frontier for research, mirroring the evolution of practice, is the rigorous development and testing of frameworks that unify governance, ethics, inclusion, and innovation amidst unceasing technological disruption (Salifu et al., 2025; Nahavandi, 2019). Ultimately, the literature insists that only through an integrated, values-driven approach can organizations harness the full potential of AI while safeguarding societal well-being and organizational legitimacy (Demir et al., 2023; Noble et al., 2022).

SEMI-STRUCTURED EXPLORATORY GROUNDED THEORY INTERVIEWS

The exponential advances in information technology from 2021 to 2025 have revolutionized the ways in which vast quantities of data are stored, accessed, and transmitted in real time (Demir et al., 2023; Kraus et al., 2021). This ongoing transformation is fueling hyperconnectivity across regions and sectors, enabling seamless global communication and collaboration unrivaled in previous decades (Demir et al., 2023; Hong et al., 2023). As a result, organizations are able to integrate distributed teams and leverage global talent pools more effectively, and are also compelled to adopt agile, data-driven decision-making processes to remain competitive in an interconnected digital landscape (Lane et al., 2024).

Digital entrepreneurship, liberated from the traditional confines of geographical and national boundaries, now drives economic and social impact at a global scale. Innovations in digital infrastructure and networked platforms facilitate cross-border collaboration, giving rise to new business models, international partnerships, and the scaling of entrepreneurial ventures across multiple markets (Fogaça et al., 2024). Meanwhile, the continued evolution of mobile learning technologies has accelerated the creation of worldwide knowledge networks, expanding access to education and training regardless of physical location, and contributing to greater equity and lifelong learning opportunities in the digital era (Pegalajar-Palomino, 2022).

INNOVATIVE CONCEPTUAL FRAMEWORK: THE SYNTHESIS MODEL FOR AI–HUMAN CAPITAL INTEGRATION

This chapter is anchored by the SYNTHESIS conceptual framework, an original, integrative model crafted to guide scholarly inquiry and organizational practice in the era of AI and evolving human capital. The SYNTHESIS framework responds directly to the chapter's qualitative, context-sensitive approach and the complexities documented in contemporary research on digital transformation, leadership adaptation, and ethical governance (Bankins, Ocampo et al., 2024a; Raisch & Krakowski, 2021).

Overview and Structure

At its foundation, the SYNTHESIS framework interweaves three central domains: socio-technical transformation, trust-building, and human-centric governance. These pillars correspond to the multi-level changes facing organizations: technical innovation; lived experience among leaders, teams, and employees; and the ethical, regulatory, and sustainability challenges surrounding AI deployment (Chalmers et al., 2021). Three dimensions are salient to this conceptual framework. Collectively, these domains establish a comprehensive lens through which organizations can critically assess how technology, trust, and governance interact to shape both daily practices and long-term outcomes in the age of AI.

Socio-Technical Transformation:

The first dimension examines the introduction and adaptation of AI technologies within organizational systems and culture. It prioritizes continuous comprehension of how leaders and staff interpret AI's roles, manage workforce transitions, and recalibrate job roles, not as linear or top-down processes but as ongoing negotiation between human agency and algorithmic logics. This information aligns with emerging theories on human–machine co-evolution, which reject deterministic narratives of displacement in favor of interactive, participative reinvention of work (Raisch & Krakowski, 2021; Demir et al., 2023).

Trust-Building and Adaptive Leadership:

The second dimension centers on the development of trust, psychological safety, and inclusive participation as AI reshapes the workplace. Drawing on leadership studies and qualitative insights, this pillar emphasizes strategies such as transparent communication, joint upskilling, and participatory governance to foster resilience and mitigate resistance (Bankins, Ocampo et al., 2024a; UNESCO, 2024). It recognizes that successful AI adoption depends as much on social-emotional infrastructure as on technical capability.

Human-Centric Governance:

The third dimension of the SYNTHESIS model highlights the ongoing negotiation of ethical, social, and legal norms. It incorporates dynamic feedback between ethical principles, organizational policy, and practical learning, mirroring the iterative processes by which ethical issues (such as bias or transparency) are identified, reviewed, and embedded within evolving governance structures (Corrêa et al., 2023; UNESCO, 2024). This element is designed to be self-correcting and reflective, ensuring that practices adapt with emerging risks and lessons learned.

Mechanisms and Adaptability

A distinguishing characteristic of the SYNTHESIS framework is its emphasis on interpretive flexibility and continuous feedback. Just as socio-technical change is never complete, trust and ethical comprehending evolve through direct engagement with new dilemmas, unexpected outcomes, and diverse perspectives (Jia et al., 2024; Madanchian & Taherdoost, 2025). The model, therefore, incorporates mechanisms for regular dialogue, collaborative reflection, and cross-functional learning, enabling practice to remain aligned with shifting realities and stakeholder needs.

SYNTHESIS is built for adaptability: it encourages iterative cycles of action and review, learning from near-misses and unexpected outcomes, and updating human processes and technological policy as organizational maturity deepens. Cross-disciplinary engagement is specified as a core requirement, bringing together HR professionals, technologists, ethicists, and frontline workers to co-create new frameworks of practice and meaning (Chalmers et al., 2021; Bankins, Formosa et al., 2024b).

Contribution and Value

The SYNTHESIS framework makes an original contribution by explicitly integrating social construction, ethical co-design, and adaptive leadership in one unified model for research and organizational application. Its layered structure, flexibility, and focus on participatory co-creation make it uniquely suited to the qualitative study of AI–human capital integration. Rather than imposing prescriptive solutions, SYNTHESIS supports learning organizations, those equipped to rapidly adapt, reflect, and engage the multiple dimensions of transformation reflected in the post-pandemic era (Raisch & Krakowski, 2021).

In sum, SYNTHESIS provides a dynamic, innovative scaffold for examining and guiding AI-enabled change, supporting deep qualitative exploration and actionable development in contemporary organizational life. Its application ensures that research and practice are attuned to real-time complexity, diversity of experience, and the imperative for ethical, sustainable transformation across human capital systems (UNESCO, 2024; Jia et al., 2024; Corrêa et al., 2023).

CRITIQUE: CONCEPTUAL FRAMEWORK

The SYNTHESIS Model advances the field's comprehension of AI–human capital integration by deliberately centering dynamic alignment, adaptive leadership, and iterative organizational learning as the scaffolding for qualitative inquiry. Its explicit attention to the construction and negotiation of meaning, as well as its prioritization of reflexive adaptation, reflects a sophisticated response to enduring critiques of rigid or technically deterministic models found in earlier work (Jia et al., 2024). The model's accommodation for context, temporality, and cross-disciplinary perspectives ensures that it is attuned to the lived realities and contingencies that define organizational life, characteristics often marginalized in more quantitative, outcome-oriented schemas (Chalmers et al., 2021).

Nevertheless, there are substantive limitations to the SYNTHESIS Model that warrant attention. First, while the framework's inclusivity and interpretive flexibility are assets for qualitative depth, they may also pose challenges for replicability and for establishing generalizable propositions across diverse organizational settings (Jia et al., 2024; Behrend et al., 2024). The lack of a prescriptive, stepwise architecture means that applying the model in empirical studies could yield analyses that are difficult to compare or synthesize into broader theory, especially in fields seeking causal or predictive clarity (Cunningham & Carmichael, 2017). Second, there is a risk that the framework's multidimensionality could introduce analytic ambiguity, as researchers may prioritize certain domains over others based on subjective interpretation or limited data availability, potentially reducing consistency and coherence across studies (Bankins, Ocampo et al., 2024a).

Further, while SYNTHESIS elevates the principles of ethical reflection and participatory governance, the practical mechanisms by which organizations enact and measure success in these domains remain under-theorized. The model presumes a degree of institutional capacity and openness to dialogic learning that may not be present in highly hierarchical, resource-constrained, or rapidly changing environments (Madanchian & Taherdoost, 2025; Corrêa et al., 2023). Consequently, further research is needed to operationalize key constructs such as trust-building and critical reflection, as well as to develop robust indicators for evaluating whether iterative learning cycles truly result in meaningful adaptation or merely rhetorical change (Raisch & Krakowski, 2021). This analysis lays a direct foundation for the development of the chapter's unique approach, highlighting the need for original contributions that address identified gaps by critically examining the strengths and limitations of the existing framework. These evaluative insights directly inform the chapter's unique approach and innovations, as detailed in the following section.

ORIGINALITY OF THE TEXT

This chapter asserts its originality by addressing the rapidly evolving convergence of AI and human capital in ways distinctly advanced from the foundational analysis presented in the original article, "Grasping the Cyber-world: AI and Human Capital Meet to Inform Leadership." While the original study established baseline definitions of AI, mapped perceived threats to human employment, and surveyed the changing social contract between technology and workforce, the present chapter moves decisively beyond those early themes, explicitly engaging developments catalyzed by the COVID-19 pandemic and the post-2021 explosion of generative AI, digital collaboration, and ethical governance debates (Bankins, Ocampo et al., 2024a; Chalmers et al., 2021).

One of the primary differences is the interpretive depth and qualitative originality in this chapter's approach. Whereas the 2019 article emphasized foundational concerns (i.e., job displacement, basic skill shifts, and initial ethical anxieties), this research incorporates recent qualitative evidence from industry leaders, technologists, and frontline employees navigating the accelerated digital transformation of the 2020s (Behrend et al., 2024; Raisch & Krakowski, 2021). The present work foregrounds emergent practices of human–AI collaboration, moving from a disruptive/augmentative binary toward the co-evolution of human-machine teams, trust-building in AI-enabled workplaces, and context-specific strategies for ethical decision-making and bias mitigation that were not addressed in detail previously (Raisch & Krakowski, 2021).

Methodologically, this chapter diverges from the broad literature synthesis and mixed-methods approach of the original paper by employing a rigorously qualitative research paradigm. It utilizes recent semi-structured interviews, case study syntheses, and advanced thematic analysis to extract new insights into leadership adaptation, participatory learning, and digital trust formation, elements inspired by, but more deeply developed than in, the earlier work (Bankins, Formosa et al., 2024b). The incorporation of post-pandemic research and up-to-date, peer-reviewed scholarship gives this chapter unique empirical grounding, especially in its focus on lived, context-sensitive experience, organizational reflexivity, and evolving employee sentiments toward AI (Demir et al., 2023).

Theoretical innovation is achieved through the introduction and critical evaluation of the SYNTHESIS conceptual framework, a departure from the less richly articulated models of the prior study. While the previous article outlined key research themes, the current framework is designed to integrate leadership agency, ethical reflexivity, and iterative organizational learning into a multidimensional lens suitable for contemporary qualitative inquiry (Corrêa et al., 2023). Furthermore, the chapter challenges Western-centric assumptions found in earlier literature, explicitly advocating for research that is attentive to regional diversity, sectoral variation, and the differential impacts of AI technologies across global contexts (Irmatova et al., 2024).

Another novel contribution is the chapter's expanded engagement with ethical and governance issues. It scrutinizes advances in explainable AI, organizational accountability, and participatory governance mechanisms, going beyond the high-level ethical commentary of the original paper to offer concrete examples and critique implementation gaps in contemporary practice (UNESCO, 2024; Jia et al., 2024). In doing so, it addresses regulatory shifts, new international frameworks, and the increasing importance of cross-disciplinary and cross-functional collaboration for effective AI–human capital integration.

To summarize, the chapter's distinctiveness lies in its post-pandemic lens, exclusive qualitative methodology, integration of frontline perspectives, and introduction of a novel, multi-layered conceptual framework. It moves the scholarly conversation from documenting disruption to theorizing how organizations, leaders, and employees collectively shape the trajectories of AI adoption, emphasizing the value of continuous learning, equity, and ethical resilience. This nuanced synthesis bridges well-documented knowledge gaps and establishes a forward-looking agenda for both research and practice in an era marked by accelerated digital transformation and ongoing uncertainty (Budhwar et al., 2022; Raisch & Krakowski, 202). Building on these theoretical innovations, the analysis now turns to the lived experiences and perspectives of organizational leaders captured through interview findings.

PRESENTATION AND ANALYSIS OF INTERVIEW FINDINGS

This section provides a systematic synthesis of participant responses for each interview question, drawing on the rich qualitative data gathered through semi-structured interviews. Central discussion topics emerged organically during interview sessions, reflecting the lived experiences, expectations, and insights articulated by participants across diverse professional fields (Skelton-Wilson et al., 2021). The data collection yielded a total of nine thematic tables, each corresponding to a distinct set of recurrent topics and patterns identified during the analysis. For every group of themes, a concise summary is presented alongside illustrative quotations from the respondents, thereby contextualizing key observations with authentic participant voices.

Following each thematic overview, the narrative details the identified themes and supporting data, linking qualitative evidence to broader research questions. This approach ensures both transparency and depth in reporting, allowing for nuanced interpretation of the social and organizational dynamics revealed by the interviews. In doing so, the section foregrounds the significance of participant perspectives as the foundation for evaluating the implications of artificial intelligence on human capital in the cyber age. Given these comprehensive findings, translating conceptual lessons into actionable strategies emerges as the next critical step for leaders aiming to build ethical, adaptive, and resilient organizations in the era of AI (Smith et al., 2025).

Narrative Accounts from Semi-Structured Interview Question 1

To address the first research question, semi-structured interview participants were prompted with the question: "In what ways has the use of AI enhance your business operations or processes?" Qualitative content analysis of the interview data revealed three principal themes reflecting the adoption of AI and its transformative impact on organizational operations.

These themes, summarized in Table 1, are expounded upon below with illustrative participant quotations. One participant, Dr. K. L. Brown-Jackson, Sr. Regulatory Advisor, QMS SME, ACTTP, & National Science Foundation Fellow (personal communication, July 22, 2025), stated, "By using AI, we have unravelled patterns and trends in medical data, a fundamental to addressing healthcare's most demanding problems regarding predictive and preventative care." This information highlights AI's capacity to bring forth actionable insights from complex datasets, permitting significant advancements in predictive analytics and proactive healthcare interventions. In a different context, Brenden E. Green, Educator (personal communication, July 22, 2025), emphasized AI's role in creative industries, noting, "Currently AI not only assists composers in creating compositions for the entertainment industry and providing the content in the formats needed for the industry. AI is creating music."

From the perspective of technological evolution and risk management, L. A. Jones, Cyber Security and Risk Management Executive, (personal communication, July 25, 2025), reflected: "Since 2019, the term 'AI' has evolved from a somewhat overstated label into a broad descriptor for technologies, particularly generative models, that carry tangible operational, reputational, and regulatory risks. While machine learning remains the technical backbone, risk assessments now focus more on model transparency, bias mitigation, and governance rather than on definitional precision." Furthermore, Jones noted, "Moreover, since 2019, AI has transitioned from a conceptual layer atop machine learning to a set of deployable models and frameworks capable of automating rule-based and pattern-driven processes across domains such as IT operations, HR workflows, and business support services. The operational value lies in reducing dependency on human intervention for high-volume, low-complexity tasks. However, this shift has introduced new technical risk vectors, particularly around model drift, interpretability, accountability, data lineage, and integration governance within enterprise environments" (Cyber Security and Risk Management Executive, (personal communication, July 25, 2025).

Review the three (3) analyzed themes in Table 1.

Table 1. Themes Identified from Responses to Question 1

Theme Numbers	Themes
1.1	In what ways does AI facilitate effective communication and problem-solving within business settings?
1.2	How has or does the integration of AI reshape organizational processes and influence the development and management of human capital?
1.3	In which areas or functions do organizations realize the greatest effectiveness and value through the implementation of AI technologies?

Theme 1.1: The Role of AI in Supporting Communication within Business Environments to Address Emerging Challenges

Research Question: In what ways does AI facilitate effective communication and problem-solving within business settings?

Since 2019, AI has increasingly permeated various facets of business communication, providing substantive support in resolving operational concerns. As articulated by one participant: "AI is already making an impact on our industry in the form of mixing software and sound analysis software. There are recent attempts at actual artificially composed music. Even though systems are being used to handle the mixing, people are needed in terms of the analysis." This perspective, though originally observed in 2018, has become more salient as AI technologies have evolved from supplementary tools to collaborative systems complementing human expertise.

Another participant noted AI's role in internal decision support processes: "It [AI] can also help employees determine the best benefits and resources for them." Such insights align with prior research suggesting that machine learning algorithms increasingly automate routine analyses, freeing personnel to focus on higher-order tasks requiring real-time adaptability and nuanced judgment (Xu, Zhou et al., 2024). Since 2019, this supportive dynamic has intensified as AI-driven platforms have become more sophisticated at guiding decision-making and customizing business processes to individual needs.

Recent studies indicate that AI-powered communication tools have significantly improved internal collaboration and issue resolution in business contexts, streamlining interactions between teams and accelerating decision-making processes (Zeng et al., 2023).

Theme 1.2: The Impact of AI on Business Operations and Human Capital

Research Question: How has or does the integration of AI reshape organizational processes and influence the development and management of human capital?

The influence of AI on organizational workflows and human capital management has markedly expanded in recent years. One participant shared: "AI could assist me in interpreting complex HR legal situations. Working through forms could take hours by an individual like me attempting to track the data." Here, AI emerges as a vital tool for streamlining and accelerating intricate administrative processes, thereby alleviating cognitive and operational burdens on staff (Przegalinska et al., 2025).

Another participant highlighted AI's dual-edged potential: "I appreciate its AI undeniable utility; to the extent that we will be able to contain its progressive learning and ability to take decisive action over human will. Human abilities will still be needed." This reflection underscores AI's practical contribution to business efficiency, but it is also increasingly essential to maintain governance over autonomous systems. Moreover, the assertion that "AI will function in communication to help with determining learning paths for employees" demonstrates the technology's expanding role in personalized workforce development.

These themes echo the findings of Chen (2024), who observed that algorithmic neural networks have become increasingly adept at absorbing organizational intelligence and disseminating actionable knowledge. Since 2019, this trend has accelerated, with AI underpinning strategic decisions that directly affect both organizational performance and human capital cultivation. The deployment of AI technologies has fundamentally transformed HR functions, including talent acquisition, performance management, and employee development, enhancing organizational outcomes and HR effectiveness (Basu et al., 2023).

Theme 1.3: Optimal Applications of AI for Maximum Organizational Effectiveness

Research Question: In which areas or functions do organizations realize the greatest effectiveness and value through the implementation of AI technologies?

The identification of domains where AI delivers the greatest benefit has been a central topic since 2019. "One participant expressed: "In electrical work, AI is most effective for tasks such as predictive maintenance and system diagnostics. For example, AI-powered tools help us quickly identify faults in complex wiring systems and anticipate equipment failures before they happen. While manual expertise remains essential for installation and troubleshooting, AI greatly enhances efficiency and safety when analyzing data from smart grids and building automation systems. This information emphasizes the efficacy of AI in domains characterized by well-defined, data-intensive problem sets, areas that have witnessed considerable automation and gains in precision through machine-driven diagnostics and navigation.

Additional responses highlight AI's supremacy in data-centric contexts: "Data analysis is where AI will serve industries the most. This action is because it takes too many people to mine data and get the most accurate results." Since 2019, organizations have increasingly harnessed AI-driven analytics to process and interpret vast quantities of information, transforming data mining, predictive maintenance, and logistics forecasting. These capabilities have enabled businesses to extract deeper insights with greater speed and accuracy than traditional human-driven approaches could afford.

Emerging evidence suggests that AI delivers maximal value in sectors involving large-scale data analysis, predictive modeling, and automation of complex repetitive tasks, such as logistics, finance, and healthcare (Gupta & Kim, 2022).

Narrative Accounts from Semi-Structured Interview Question 2

To address the second research question, "Reflecting on the years from 2019 to 2025, what changes have you observed in your workplace as a result of AI?" semi-structured interview participants were invited to share their direct observations and experiences. Qualitative content analysis of their responses revealed three key themes, which are presented in Table 2 and expanded upon in the discussion below through representative quotes.

Participant responses revealed a spectrum of attitudes ranging from cautious optimism to concern over long-term implications. This quote reflects a broader theme identified in recent scholarship: while AI increases creative productivity and lowers barriers for entry, it may also erode technical depth and skill mastery within some domains (Zhou & Lee, 2024). For example, B. E. Green, Educator (personal communication, July 25, 2025) shared, "It [AI] is definitely helping to make music composition and production easier and faster, but there are those who would argue that the quality of the music and production has declined due to the ease of access to music production software. Educators were forced to learn new ways to teach music during the pandemic. Learners were shown how to use online tools to produce and learn music." This observation exemplifies ongoing debates in fields such as music, visual arts, and writing, where AI-driven tools democratize creative processes but can sometimes lead to a reduction in traditional skills or mastery, echoing concerns found across the literature (Benjamin, 2019; Zhou & Lee, 2024).

Another insight emerged regarding interpersonal and social dynamics in the workplace. One participant noted that: "Even though the technology is good, it is driving change in terms of people interaction." This comment reflects growing concern about how automation tools are reducing human-to-human collaboration, especially in hybrid or remote environments (Tarafdar, 2025). A distinct concern also arose around inequity in AI access, particularly for self-employed individuals (Hui & Reshef, 2025). Contrary to earlier concerns that AI tools would be largely out of reach for gig and freelance workers (Tarafdar, 2025), recent research shows a significant shift. According to the 2023 OECD Future of Work Brief, "Self-employed workers have increasingly adopted AI tools to stay competitive, particularly in content creation, marketing, and administrative automation. However, disparities remain in access to enterprise-level AI platforms, especially among low-income or rural freelancers." This update suggests that while the self-employed are no longer categorically excluded from AI benefits, gaps persist in terms of tool accessibility, training, and cost barriers (Purohit, 2025).

Review the three (3) analyzed themes in Table 2.

Table 2. Themes Identified from Responses from Question 2

Theme Numbers	Themes
2.1	How has AI influenced the assessment, acquisition, and automation of skillsets in business roles since 2019, and what implications does this have for workforce development and upskilling?
2.2	In what ways are AI-driven tools currently shaping hiring practices, team composition, and talent allocation in organizations, and how are employers addressing potential algorithmic bias and fairness concerns?
2.3	How are organizations using AI to monitor, evaluate, or enhance human interactions—such as communication, collaboration, and engagement; and what are the limitations or risks of relying on these models?

Theme 2.1 is AI's impact on skill assessment and workforce upskilling

Research Question: *How has AI influenced the assessment, acquisition, and automation of skillsets in business roles since 2019, and what implications does this have for workforce development and upskilling?*

One participant replied, "There's definitely been a natural phasing out of certain jobs, especially those that are repetitive or administrative. But, I also see new roles emerging, AI trainers, automation strategists, data ethicists, that didn't even exist when I started working professionally. The primary challenge lies in remaining current with ongoing developments. The workforce now has to evolve continuously and this can be hard. It's not optional anymore. Our livelihood and careers depend on our ability to adapt." This individual discussed the evolving nature of skillsets prompted by new technological developments. Another different offered, "Using AI has led to some workforce reduction, yes, but it's not entirely negative. It's forced us to rethink what skills are essential. The company I work for is now looking for employees who can work with tech and ask the right questions and interpret the results critically." Yet another participant, "Job candidates today need a mix of technical literacy and adaptability. In some fields, it's expected you'll work alongside robotic systems or AI platforms. That wasn't the case seven years ago." Ersanlı et al. (2025) noted that AI has not eliminated jobs across the board; however, it continues to reshape our comprehension of competence. The workforce must acquire new knowledge, skills, and abilities tailored to evolving employment demands if they are to remain relevant (Ersanlı et al. 2025). As given by Budhwar et al. (2022), research shows that as AI adoption accelerates, the workforce faces significant job transitions that demand continuous upskilling and adaptability to new roles and competencies.

Theme 2.2 is AI-driven hiring practices and managing bias

Research Question: *In what ways are AI-driven tools currently shaping hiring practices, team composition, and talent allocation in organizations, and how are employers addressing potential algorithmic bias and fairness concerns?* "AI has definitely streamlined hiring, resume screening, candidate matching, even interview scheduling is now automated. But I've noticed that it can also overlook soft skills or cultural fit, which are harder to quantify. Employers are starting to audit these systems more carefully to avoid bias, but it's still a work in progress." Another respondent added, "I've seen AI tools help build more diverse teams by anonymizing applications and focusing on skills. That said, there's concern about how training data might reinforce old biases. Some companies are now using fairness metrics and third-party audits to monitor their algorithms." Look at this response. "It's not far-fetched to say that AI is reshaping the job landscape. Many roles today didn't exist five to seven years ago, and the same will be true for the next generation. Hiring is becoming more predictive, AI forecasts not just who's qualified, but who's likely to succeed long-term. That's powerful, but it also raises questions about transparency and human oversight." Recent research highlights the necessity for transparent and accountable AI in hiring, highlighting that organizations are increasingly implementing fairness audits and human-in-the-loop review processes to ensure equitable outcomes and mitigate algorithmic bias (Jia et al., 2024; UNESCO, 2024).

Theme 2.3 is AI's role in monitoring and enhancing workplace interactions

Research Question: *How are organizations using AI to monitor, evaluate, or enhance human interactions—such as communication, collaboration, and engagement; and what are the limitations or risks of relying on these models?* "While AI platforms claim to quantify things like collaboration or trustworthiness, I am not convinced these metrics can actually account for distinction or intent. I have read of instances where algorithmic monitoring of workplace interactions has led to misunderstandings or even worsened tensions, especially across culturally diverse teams." "Frankly, the reliance on AI to evaluate employee relationships sometimes undermines authentic human connection. I've seen situations where the pressure to conform to algorithmic norms made people less likely to express dissenting views, which ultimately harms psychological safety and innovation." Recent research highlights that while AI can enhance organizational insight into employee engagement and communication patterns, it also risks oversimplification, misinterpretation, and even dehumanization if not carefully monitored and grounded in ethical frameworks (Valenzuela et al., 2024)

Narrative Accounts from Semi-Structured Interview Question 3

To address the third research question, semi-structured interview participants were asked the following question: "*How are emerging AI technologies reshaping the core cultural dimensions of organizations (i.e., collaboration, inclusion, values alignment, transparency, and adaptability), and what innovative practices are leading companies implementing in 2025 to identify, address, and proactively mitigate the cultural risks and challenges introduced by widespread AI integration?*" One anonymous participant offered, "Initially, I don't think AI would influence the culture of my current organization, they would be very resistant to it." As given by William Bardge, Drywall Technician Contractor (personal communication, July 25, 2025), "AI is poised to transform the construction industry, especially in how contractors monitor structural integrity and equipment performance. Much of this change will stem from the integration of smart sensors embedded throughout building systems and heavy machinery." Also, according to Brenden E. Green, Educator (personal communication, July 22, 2025), "In recent years, I've noticed AI has fundamentally shifted the landscape for music professionals and educators. While I still see major advantages in accessibility (i.e., the ability to quickly craft and share music using AI-powered tools has made creative expression easier for both students and working musicians) there are significant cultural tradeoffs. On one hand, there's greater inclusion: students from diverse backgrounds can experiment with a broader range of sounds and genres, enabling collaboration that crosses geographic and traditional boundaries. However, the expectation to rapidly adapt to new technology has also introduced pressure and uncertainty for many musicians. Roles have grown more fluid. For example, producers are programming entire tracks solo, reducing the need for session players, and educators are increasingly asked to teach both creative performance and technical fluency with music software. This action can challenge long-held values about musicianship and teamwork. Additionally, issues of transparency and fairness have become more pronounced: AI-driven platforms sometimes obscure who contributes what to a collaborative work, complicating credit and compensation. Leading institutions are starting to address these challenges by adopting transparent workflows and providing all contributors with visibility into AI-generated content and edits. Ultimately, adaptability and ongoing learning now define success. Organizations that openly discuss the cultural implications of AI, and offer training and ethical guidelines, are best positioned to support artists while navigating the risks and opportunities that come with integrating intelligent technologies into creative communities." Review the three (3) analyzed themes in Table 3.

Table 3. Themes Identified from Responses from Question 3

Theme Numbers	Themes
3.1	In what ways is AI actively reshaping organizational culture by influencing how employees interact, collaborate, and align with their company's mission and values?
3.2	How is AI acting as a transformative disruptor in today's business landscape, and what are the most significant shifts in strategy, operations, and industry competitive advantage resulting from its adoption?
3.3	Which key cultural dimensions within organizations are most affected by the integration of AI, including collaboration, inclusion, values alignment, transparency, and adaptability, and how are companies mitigating the associated risks and challenges?

Theme 3.1 is AI's influence on employee interactions and company culture

Research Question: *In what ways is AI actively reshaping organizational culture by influencing how employees interact, collaborate, and align with their company's mission and values?*

One building industry contractor said, "As a building contractor, I've read the manner in that AI revolutionizes how teams approach construction projects. Now, workers can use AI-powered tools to quickly access building codes, safety regulations, and troubleshooting guides right from the job site. This action enhances efficiency and enables real-time collaboration across diverse crews. On complex builds, AI-driven project management software streamlines scheduling, resource allocation, and issue tracking, ensuring everyone works towards a unified vision. With AI, the building industry can identify best practices from past projects and apply them to new ones, fostering a culture of continuous improvement and shared learning. These advancements are helping us build safer, higher-quality structures while strengthening alignment with our company's values of innovation and excellence." An IT professional said, "In the IT sector, I believe AI can initially feel intimidating for employees, mainly due to a lack of understanding about its benefits for people, processes, and technology. If organizations don't invest in helping employees grasp the purpose and advantages of AI, this knowledge gap can lead to resistance and even fear, adversely impacting organizational culture. However, when teams are empowered through training and transparent communication, AI becomes a catalyst for cross-functional collaboration, adaptable workflows, and stronger alignment with the company's mission."

Theme 3.2 is AI as a disruptive force transforming business strategy and operations.

Research Question: *How is AI acting as a transformative disruptor in today's business landscape, and what are the most significant shifts in strategy, operations, and industry competitive advantage resulting from its adoption*?

A Sr. Regulatory Advisor, "AI is rapidly establishing itself as one of the most profound disruptors shaping the modern business environment. From a regulatory perspective, I observe organizations transitioning from viewing AI purely as a source of risk to recognizing its role as a catalyst for compliance innovation, operational resilience, and ethical business practices. The paradigm is shifting as companies proactively embrace AI-driven technologies, not just to mitigate threats but to unlock new value streams, streamline decision-making, and adapt organizational culture for continual advancement." A risk executive replied, "At higher education conferences, there is a growing recognition that colleges and universities are quickly evolving into technology-powered institutions, with AI driving innovations far beyond classroom learning. AI is reshaping everything from student recruitment and admissions analytics to personalized learning pathways, academic advising, and campus security operations. The introduction of AI brings out a wide range of emotions across campus communities, from excitement and elation about new possibilities to apprehension and fear about change, job roles, and ethical uncertainties. From a risk management perspective, this emotional complexity highlights the necessity of providing robust training and education at every level of the institution. By fostering digital literacy, ethical awareness, and skill development, comprehensive training ensures that faculty, staff, and students adapt to transformative technologies and contribute meaningfully to institutional growth and long-term development. Higher education leaders must maintain a continuous refinement of strategies, safeguard sensitive data, and remain vigilant in fostering a culture of agility, emotional intelligence, and responsible technology adoption as the boundaries between education and technology continue to cloud."

Theme 3.3 is AI's impact on collaboration, inclusion, alignment of values, transparency, and adaptability in organizations.

Research Question: *Which key cultural dimensions within organizations are most affected by the integration of AI, including collaboration, inclusion, values alignment, transparency, and adaptability, and how are companies mitigating the associated risks and challenges?*

A pilot answered as follows. "AI is empowering organizations to proactively cultivate their cultures by enabling comprehensive 'as-is' cultural assessments. By leveraging AI's unparalleled data-processing abilities, companies can analyze far more information about behavioral patterns than would ever be possible through traditional assessment methods. This deeper, data-driven understanding helps organizations clearly identify and reinforce their unique cultural strengths, while also strategically defining and pursuing their ideal target cultures. Moreover, AI's predictive insights, drawing on extensive internal and external data, equip organizations to set and achieve inspiring cultural goals that best align with business objectives and workforce aspirations." Another respondent added, "AI's remarkable influence on cultural dimensions will be greatest when algorithms are trained on diverse, representative data sources. When AI tools are developed to reflect the richness of all cultures, they have the potential to enhance inclusion and collaboration across the organization, enabling fairer, more adaptive, and genuinely global workplace environments." This section highlights how AI is enabling organizations to conduct in-depth cultural assessments, identify growth opportunities, and proactively advance inclusion, collaboration, and values alignment. When algorithms are trained on diverse data, AI becomes a strategic tool to foster fairer and more adaptive workplace cultures. Recent research confirms that integrating AI with ethical oversight enhances organizational culture and performance (Valenzuela et al., 2024).

Narrative Accounts from Semi-Structured Interview Question 4

To address the fourth research question, semi-structured interview participants were asked the following: "*In what ways do you think that the introduction of AI will impact or influence the structure of your organization?*" According to one anonymous respondent, "I do believe it will have to do with the ready identification of fraudulent activities, asset protection, cybersecurity, supply chain and other areas." An electrical contractor (personal communication, October 8, 2019) offered, "Impact will include needed in-depth investigative and research processes." Other input included, "Higher education needs to respond sooner rather than later. We - administrators and educators - are churning out students into a world where AI job have not been wholly defined, and these students are not completely prepared to operate within this evolving ubiquitous technology." Another participant added, "I believe implementing AI will have an impact regarding reductions of workforces of people onsite." Review the three (3) analyzed themes in Table 4.

Table 4. Themes Identified from Responses from Question 4

Theme Numbers	Themes
4.1	In what ways is AI fundamentally transforming business fields by automating core processes, optimizing decision-making, and enabling new opportunities for productivity, customer engagement, and innovation?
4.2	What forms of organizational restructuring are being driven by advances in AI, and how are companies adapting their workforce, management, and operational models to maximize the benefits of AI integration?
4.3	How is AI influencing strategic planning for organizations with diverse workforces, global operations, and varying market needs, and what approaches are leading companies using to ensure equity, innovation, and resilience in an AI-driven world?

Theme 4.1 is Automating processes and enabling new opportunities with AI.

Research Question: *In what ways is AI driving transformative change across business fields, and how are organizations leveraging AI to innovate, streamline operations, and achieve competitive advantage?* One answer was, "In 2025, AI is deeply integrated into our organizational operations, especially in areas like fraud detection, asset protection, and cybersecurity. With AI's advanced pattern recognition and real-time analytics, we now identify risks and threats faster than ever before. AI-driven tools also streamline our supply chain and logistical processes, fundamentally reshaping how teams are structured and how resources are allocated for maximum agility and protection." An electrical contractor remarked, "AI has transformed the way we approach system diagnostics and project planning. Beyond just enhancing investigative and research processes, AI-powered monitoring now proactively flags anomalies in electrical systems, allowing us to prevent issues before they arise. Technicians work alongside intelligent automation, focusing their expertise on complex problem-solving while routine assessments are handled by smart systems. The structure of our teams has shifted, there's more collaboration with IT and security specialists, reflecting the convergence of operational technology and cybersecurity."

A higher education leader commented, "Higher education's response to AI has accelerated dramatically. Universities are redesigning curricula, launching AI literacy programs, and partnering with industry to bridge the gap between classroom learning and the evolving technology job market. We're preparing students for roles that didn't exist a few years ago, while organizational structures within universities are becoming more cross-functional to support rapid adoption of AI in teaching, administration, and research. There's an urgent emphasis on lifelong learning and adaptability to ensure graduates thrive in a workforce shaped by ubiquitous AI. AI adoption is undeniably impacting workforce dynamics, especially when it comes to onsite staffing. While certain roles are being automated, we're also seeing new positions emerge focused on AI management, analytics, and digital ethics. The key shift is toward a more flexible, hybrid workforce, where human creativity complements automation and continuous upskilling becomes essential for career growth."

The pervasive integration of AI is catalyzing the emergence of more decentralized organizational structures, blurring traditional boundaries between technology and operational functions, and necessitating heightened workforce agility across domains such as security, infrastructure, skilled trades, and education. Institutions that invest in advancing employee digital competencies, foster ongoing upskilling, and adopt adaptive organizational frameworks are well-positioned to capitalize on the transformative opportunities presented by AI, thereby sustaining resilience and competitive differentiation in a landscape characterized by rapid technological evolution (Brynjolfsson & McAfee, 2021).

Theme 4.2 is Organizational restructuring and adapting models for AI integration.

Research Question: *What forms of organizational restructuring are being driven by advances in AI, and how are companies adapting their workforce, management, and operational models to maximize the benefits of AI integration?*

A pilot who wished to remain anonymous offered the following. "In aviation and aerospace, advances in AI are fundamentally reshaping organizational structures at every level. We're seeing operational teams and management increasingly collaborate with data scientists and AI specialists to improve fleet maintenance, flight operations, and safety protocols. Human Resources is evolving swiftly, and AI-powered analytics now help refine hiring practices, tailor pilot and crew training, and inform workforce planning using real-time data from simulations, performance reviews, and incident analysis. "What's particularly transformative is the way AI integrates information from diverse sources, logbooks, maintenance reports, simulator data, and operational feedback, to build a dynamic picture of team performance and organizational culture. This enables airlines and aerospace companies to proactively address skills gaps, adapt leadership frameworks, and continuously enhance collaboration. Further the pilot offered, "It's important to recognize that while AI is automating some repetitive, procedural tasks such as scheduling, compliance checks, and diagnostics, it's elevating the roles of pilots, technicians, and support staff, freeing them for critical decision-making and complex problem-solving. At the same time, entirely new job categories are emerging, such as AI system trainers, unmanned systems supervisors, and human-AI interface designers, making ongoing professional development and adaptability essential in the industry. "Last, allow me to add that the integration of AI has also brought an increase in threat vectors. More interconnected systems have expanded the attack surface for cyber threats, increasing the risk of data breaches, system manipulation, and disruptions to flight operations. As a result, there is a growing emphasis on robust cybersecurity practices, cross-functional risk assessments, and collaborative incident response strategies. Workforce training now includes digital security protocols and awareness to safeguard both operational integrity and passenger safety. The industry's rapid digital evolution demands not just innovation, but unwavering vigilance against emerging technological risks."

Theme 4.3 is AI's role in strategic planning for equity, innovation, and resilience in diverse organizations.

Research Question: *How is AI influencing strategic planning for organizations with diverse workforces, global operations, and varying market needs, and what* *approaches are leading companies using to ensure equity, innovation, and resilience in an AI-driven world?*

One explanation is, "In 2025, AI-driven insights are basically transforming how organizations design their global talent and market strategies. Instead of just searching for candidates with the strongest technical expertise, companies are prioritizing hires who demonstrate cultural intelligence and adaptability, qualities essential for thriving in distributed, multicultural teams collaborating through AI-powered platforms. Strategic planning now goes beyond skills and experience to emphasize an individual's capacity to flex their communication, motivational style, and management approach across borders and cultures." Another participant added, "Leading organizations are embedding equity and inclusion into their AI systems, continually monitoring for algorithmic bias and adjusting hiring and promotion strategies accordingly. As AI matures, employees are expected to adopt a growth mind set, embracing ongoing learning to stay current with both technological advances and evolving norms for collaboration and innovation." Yet, another offered, "Forward-thinking companies are investing in cross-cultural training, transparency in AI decision-making, and initiatives that empower diverse voices, seeing these as critical drivers of innovation and organizational resilience in the AI-accelerated landscape of 2025." Review the three (3) analyzed themes in Table 5.

Narrative Accounts from Semi-Structured Interview Question 5

To address the fifth research question, semi-structured interview participants were asked the following, "*With the widespread integration of AI in 2025, what do you consider to be the most significant ethical challenges, including issues related to fairness, transparency, privacy, accountability, and societal impact, that organizations and society must address to ensure responsible and equitable AI development and use*" Participant responses reflected a broad and thoughtful range of ethical perspectives, shaped by their professional roles and personal experiences with AI systems. These insights were grouped into key thematic areas: automation and human replacement, algorithmic bias and fairness, accountability and transparency, data privacy, economic equity, robotic rights, and cybersecurity. "An ongoing ethical concern is the replacement of live people with AI systems. Unlike humans, AI doesn't fatigue or forget. While that sounds like a strength, it also removes the natural imperfection that fosters creativity, adaptability, and learning" (Anonymous Cloud Sr. Manager, personal communication, July 23, 2025). Other AI and ethical considerations include but are not limited to the following. "As a healthcare operations director, I see the real risk of over-automation. Patients want empathy, not just efficiency. We can't let machines replace the human touch where compassion is essential" (personal communication, Director of Healthcare Systems, July 23, 2025). "As a diversity officer in a tech firm, I see how quickly AI can reinforce systemic bias. We've had to audit every algorithm we use in hiring for bias, racial, gender, and even geographic" (personal communication, DEI Officer, Tech Industry, July 26, 2025). "The biggest issue is that no one knows how AI makes decisions. I'm an IT systems auditor, and even I struggle to get clear explanations of outcomes. That's unacceptable for regulated industries" (personal communication, IT Compliance Auditor, July 27, 2025). "As a small business owner using AI-powered tools, I'm concerned that large corporations are gaining disproportionate profits from automation. Where does that leave everyone else? (personal communication, Entrepreneur, Creative Industries, July 26, 2025). Another response was, "Employee-owned companies using robotics still struggle with how to share profits generated by machines. Do the robots earn equity? It's not just theoretical, it's a current accounting problem." Yet another salient response was as follows. "AI tools have become targets themselves, especially in finance. You're not just protecting customer data; you're protecting the AI model from adversarial attacks." Frenette (2023) stresses that while AI systems provide transformative capabilities across industries, their deployment must be guided by multidisciplinary oversight, human-in-the-loop frameworks, and ethics-by-default principles to ensure responsible and equitable outcomes.

The development of machines with cognitive or decision-making capabilities raises a host of ethical concerns. These concerns focus on two major issues: ensuring that intelligent systems do not harm humans or other morally significant beings, and understanding whether such machines possess any moral standing themselves. As AI becomes more autonomous, the line between tool and moral agent grows increasingly complex, demanding careful ethical scrutiny. Review the three (3) analyzed themes in Table 5.

Table 5. Themes Identified from Responses from Question 5

Theme Numbers	Themes
5.1	What pressing ethical challenges does AI pose today (i.e., fairness, transparency, privacy, interpretability, and environmental impact) and how are organizations proactively embedding ethical frameworks into their AI design and deployment processes?
5.2	What are the leading concerns surrounding bias, assumptions, and data integrity in AI systems, and what strategies are being implemented in 2025 to identify, mitigate, and monitor discriminatory outcomes in AI decision-making?
5.3	How is AI being integrated into the legal system in 2025, and what new opportunities, risks, and regulatory adaptations are emerging to ensure that AI complies with legal standards, supports justice, and upholds due process?

Theme 5.1 is Ethical challenges and frameworks for responsible AI.

Research Question: *What pressing ethical challenges does AI pose today (i.e., fairness, transparency, privacy, interpretability, and environmental impact), and how are organizations proactively embedding ethical frameworks into their AI design and deployment processes?*

"There's now a whole conversation about AI-generated music and who actually owns the copyright. It's not just an artistic issue, it's a legal and ethical one too." "Privacy concerns are growing, especially during internal HR investigations. The ability to gather sensitive data faster with AI tools must be weighed against employees' rights to dignity and fairness." "Ironically, AI might eventually improve privacy in certain areas, like reducing how many people need to see personal files. But that depends on how secure and accountable the system design is." "In automotive work, AI helps ensure transparency. It can reduce unnecessary repairs by accurately diagnosing the issue, which builds trust and keeps costs fair for the customer."

Theme 5.2 is Addressing bias, data integrity, and fairness in AI systems.

Research Question: *What are the leading concerns surrounding bias, assumptions, and data integrity in AI systems, and what strategies are being implemented in 2025 to identify, mitigate, and monitor discriminatory outcomes in AI decision-making?*

"A top concern remains the lack of diversity in AI training data and the design teams building these systems. Without input from historically underrepresented communities, especially Black and Indigenous populations, AI tools often make inaccurate or harmful decisions. For example, facial recognition still shows lower accuracy for darker skin tones, and voice recognition systems often misinterpret certain dialects. In 2025, we're seeing more organizations implement bias audits, fairness metrics, and inclusive data protocols, but the work is far from over. Integrity starts at data collection and continues through every phase of deployment."

Theme 5.3 is AI's integration into law and emerging legal/regulatory adaptations.

Research Question: *How is AI being integrated into the legal system in 2025, and what new opportunities, risks, and regulatory adaptations are emerging to ensure that AI complies with legal standards, supports justice, and upholds due process?*

The U.S. Department of War (2025), emphasizes that integrating AI into national security operations is critical for processing vast data streams, enhancing decision-making, and maintaining strategic superiority in an evolving geopolitical landscape. An anonymous participant in the legal field offered, "In legal and regulatory institutions, the algorithms used for public decision-making must demonstrate a level of transparency and predictability that aligns with judicial standards. Think of it this way: judges rely on precedent to guide decisions, there's a built-in logic to that consistency. But AI developers may see that logic as outdated or restrictive. The real challenge is this: how do we align dynamic, evolving technologies with systems rooted in precedent and due process? If we don't resolve that tension, we risk creating legal tools that undermine the very principles they're supposed to uphold."

As given by Ahmed et al. (2025), legal reasoning about AI is no longer limited to courts or legal scholars, it is now embedded in corporate governance, compliance protocols, and algorithmic accountability systems. As AI increasingly drives decision-making in areas like hiring, lending, and public administration, legal frameworks must evolve to ensure due process, transparency, and fairness across sectors. Moreover, the law must account for how AI systems reshape institutional decision-making, not just individual rights (Ahmed, 2025).

Narrative Accounts from Semi-Structured Interview Question 6

To address the sixth research question, semi-structured interview participants were asked the following question: "*How is AI being used to assess, enhance, or influence employee performance, and what are the potential benefits and risks of these applications in today's workplace?* According to L. A. Jones (Cyber Security and Risk Management Executive, Executive, July 25, 2025), "AI systems must be carefully trained to deliver meaningful insights, not just process raw data. In performance management, it's not just about volume, it's about context. Without precision and thoughtful design, these tools risk producing feedback that lacks nuance or fairness." Gupta (2023) details how AI systems can track employee achievements in real time, deliver prompt feedback, and personalize recognition based on individual preferences and performance data. It also highlights how such systems contribute to employee motivation, retention, and strategic HR decision-making." "AI usage has helped to remove ambiguous language that help to communicate clearer job expectations. Also, AI-powered performance platforms have helped eliminate delays in reviews and reduce the anxiety that often comes with unclear expectations. Real-time feedback empowers employees to make improvements before small issues become major concerns, and it supports more transparent, fairer evaluations" (S. R. Thomas, Human Resources Leader, personal communication, July 25, 2025). Review the two (2) analyzed themes in Table 6.

Table 6. Themes Identified from Responses from Question 6

Theme Numbers	Themes
6.1	In what ways is AI reshaping individual workflows in 2025, including impacts on task automation, decision support, productivity, and employee well-being?
6.2	How are organizations leveraging AI to enhance overall performance, drive innovation, and optimize resource allocation while addressing ethical, operational, and cultural considerations?

Theme 6.1 is AI's transformation of individual workflows and employee experience.

Research Question: *In what ways is AI reshaping individual workflows in 2025, including impacts on task automation, decision support, productivity, and employee well-being?*

"As day-to-day tasks become more 'intelligent' through AI integration, there's a risk that employees may rely too heavily on systems and put less effort into deep thinking or creative problem-solving. It's similar to how we used to memorize phone numbers, but now rely on smart devices to store everything. The convenience is undeniable, but we're offloading a lot of mental engagement to machines." Another semi-structured interview participant offered the following, "With the rise of hyper-connected devices and AI-powered platforms, workflows are faster and more efficient, but they're also more dependent on predictive algorithms. It makes me wonder: will AI eventually replace human innovation, or can we build systems that still leave room for creativity, curiosity, and independent thinking?"

Theme 6.2 is Organizational performance and innovation through responsible AI integration.

Research Question: *How are organizations leveraging AI to enhance overall performance, drive innovation, and optimize resource allocation while addressing ethical, operational, and cultural considerations?*

"AI technologies are now handling data processing and analysis at a scale, humans simply can't match, freeing teams to focus on high-value, strategic tasks." "What we're seeing in 2025 is that AI isn't just replacing work, it's creating new kinds of jobs that require human insight, creativity, and emotional intelligence. It's shifting the nature of work, not eliminating it." "In the electrical field, AI has eliminated much of the trial-and-error in system diagnostics. By analyzing circuit data, load patterns, and maintenance logs, it helps electricians quickly pinpoint faults and recommend precise solutions, improving job efficiency and client confidence."

Additionally, "In the electrical field, AI has eliminated much of the trial-and-error in system diagnostics. By analyzing circuit data, load patterns, and maintenance logs, it helps electricians quickly pinpoint faults and recommend precise solutions, improving job efficiency and client confidence."

Narrative Accounts from Semi-Structured Interview Question 7

To address the seventh research question, semi-structured interview participants were asked the following, *"In 2025, smart AI-enabled devices—such as voice assistants (e.g., Siri, Alexa, Google Assistant), connected smartphones, smart TVs, security systems, and workplace IoT tools—are widely used in professional settings. How do you see these technologies being applied in the workplace, and how do they influence human behavior, collaboration, and task execution?"* Having AI devices in the workplace is changing the trajectory of office and water cooler language as it captures wording, resonance, and mawkishness (Levy & Barocas, 2018). During an interview L. A. Jones, Cyber Security and Risk Management Executive (personal communication, July 25, 2025) offered, "These devices can serve as instantaneous communications, and alert systems." Also, "The use of voice activated assistant devices are being introduced in some offices, and more research is being conducted in other offices regarding the best way to use the devices," (Ranlin Sanders, Network Professional, personal communication, July 28, 2025). Further, "Voice activated assistant devices have grown in popularity. "Another significant detail about voice-activated assistant devices is their contextual awareness has advanced, enabling them to comprehend multiple-step commands, remember previous conversations, and carry out tasks across different devices or locations for seamless continuity. Increasingly, organizations are leveraging voice assistants not just for basic scheduling or reminders, but also to streamline meeting management, automate IT helpdesk tasks, and support HR processes such as data entry, employee performance tracking, and recruitment database screening. These capabilities boost overall productivity, reduce operational costs, and improve employee focus on strategic goals. On the other hand, these voice-activated assistant devices must be used carefully. These devices should not be used in areas where there is sensitive information," (Ranlin Sanders, Network Professional, personal communication, July 28, 2025). "Another concern regarding voice activated assistant devices is risk.

A key risk of voice-activated assistant devices is the potential for unauthorized access or data breaches, as voice commands can sometimes be intercepted, misinterpreted, or executed without proper user verification, leading to privacy and security vulnerabilities," (L. A. Jones, Cyber Security and Risk Management Executive, personal communication, July 25, 2025).

Review the three (3) analyzed themes in Table 7.

Table 7. Themes Identified from Responses from Question 7

Theme Numbers	Themes
7.1	In 2025, how are improvements in voice recognition accuracy shaping the way people communicate, access information, and complete tasks in the workplace, especially in environments with diverse speech patterns and real-time collaboration needs?
7.2	What real-world benefits are organizations seeing from using AI assistants today, particularly when it comes to automating scheduling, retrieving information, or supporting employees through voice-activated tools?
7.3	Besides increasing productivity, what factors are driving adoption of AI assistants in the workplace—such as enhancing accessibility, improving user experience, or providing better support for decision-making and team collaboration?

Theme 7.1 is Voice recognition improving workplace communication and accessibility.

Research Question: *In 2025, how are improvements in voice recognition accuracy shaping the way people communicate, access information, and complete tasks in the workplace—especially in environments with diverse speech patterns and real-time collaboration needs?*

The office environment poses challenges for which intelligent assistants are not ready to handle, such as full voice recognition. "Today's voice systems can often identify who is speaking and attach their comments to meeting notes, which boosts clarity and accountability. But in fast-paced or hybrid meetings, the tech can still misattribute statements, which has HR and legal implications around transparency and consent." The concern here drifts back to human resources, as well as legal concerns regarding privacy. Another concern with intelligent assistants is Kenytinc (2024) highlight that despite major advancements in NLP, challenges persist in understanding context, ambiguity, and emotional nuance, making full comprehension of user intent difficult for intelligent assistants. Caldarini et al., (2022) identified persistent challenges in Chatbot systems, including contextual understanding, emotional nuance, and gender bias, which hinder full comprehension of user intent. Yet other concerns are, "Voice recognition has improved dramatically, especially in capturing and transcribing conversations. But when several people talk at once, or someone has a nonstandard accent, misinterpretations still happen, and those mistakes can affect how people's contributions are perceived." Another participant offered the following, "For global teams, voice recognition tools help reduce communication barriers across languages and time zones. Still, if systems repeatedly struggle to recognize certain speech styles or tones, that erodes trust and raises equity concerns—especially for employees from underrepresented groups." "We're now living in an era where voice has become a central method for interacting with workplace technology. This shift increases accessibility and convenience, but it also amplifies concerns about how voice data is collected, stored, and ethically managed" (D. N. Burrell, Faculty, Organizational Social Scientist & Leadership Development Consultant, and Certified Diversity professional, personal communication, July 25, 2025). "All voice assistants considered should go through a rigorous audit process. Risks include the potential for accidental activation or misinterpretation of voice commands, which could result in unauthorized actions or sensitive data exposure; furthermore, these devices may inadvertently record or transmit confidential conversations, creating significant privacy and compliance concerns" (L. A. Jones, Cyber Security and Risk Management Executive, personal communication, July 25, 2025).

Although voice recognition technology has significantly advanced by 2025, persistent challenges remain in accurately interpreting diverse voice tones, accents, and speech patterns (Salifu et al., 2025). Research highlights the need for more inclusive training data and robust evaluation frameworks to ensure equitable performance across global user populations. Without these improvements, voice AI systems risk reinforcing communication inequities in multilingual and multicultural workplace environments (Salifu et al., 2025).

Theme 7.2 is Real-world organizational benefits of AI assistants for automation and support.

Research Question: *What real-world benefits are organizations seeing from using AI assistants today, particularly when it comes to automating scheduling, retrieving information, or supporting employees through voice-activated tools?*

"AI assistants now offer real-time access to enterprise data, helping employees quickly retrieve files, look up policies, and even operate secure systems like elevators or building access points using voice authentication. These tools are saving valuable time and streamlining routine interactions."

Zhou & Lee (2024) demonstrate that AI-powered assistants have become integral to workplace communication, offering real-time transcription, sentiment analysis, and actionable insights, especially in hybrid and remote environments. Their findings highlight significant improvements in natural language understanding and dialogue summarization. Other examples of AI in action are as follows. According to Holley (2018), a team of MIT-trained robotics engineers, in collaboration with Michelin-starred chef Daniel Boulud, opened a high-tech restaurant in downtown Boston that uses seven automated cooking pots to prepare meals in under three minutes, blending culinary precision with automation. Also, Robot Captain Crabs Cajun Seafood & Bar in Newark, Delaware, integrated robotics into customer service by using five robots, two as hostesses and three as servers, each imported from China at $20,000 apiece, showcasing a novel dining experience since its 2019 debut (Holley, 2019).

The Holley examples illustrate how technological innovation is accelerating and reshaping the labor market by creating new roles that complement emerging systems. Significantly, human workers remain essential, with AI augmenting rather than replacing their contributions. Productivity continues to rise as AI takes over repetitive tasks, allowing employees to focus on strategic and creative work. Society for Human Resource Management [SHRM]. (2025) reports that as AI tools become more integrated into daily operations, organizations are reimagining workforce development strategies to align with evolving technological demands, emphasizing human-AI collaboration, productivity gains, and the creation of new roles that complement emerging systems.

Theme 7.3 is Driving adoption of AI assistants through enhanced accessibility and user experience.

Research Question: *Besides increasing productivity, what factors are driving adoption of AI assistants in the workplace (i.e., enhancing accessibility, improving user experience, or providing better support for decision-making and team collaboration?)*

According to Yoshino W. White, Sr. Director of Product Development Excellence (personal communication, July 27, 2025), "In regulated environments like healthcare and life sciences, the adoption of AI assistants goes far beyond productivity. These tools are increasingly valued for their ability to streamline documentation, reduce cognitive load, and support data-driven decision-making while maintaining compliance with evolving regulatory frameworks. In clinical settings, AI assistants improve accessibility by providing voice-to-text support during patient encounters, allowing practitioners to focus more on care and less on administrative burden. For cross-functional teams, especially in global regulatory affairs, they enable faster access to guidance documents, submission timelines, and real-time collaboration, ultimately supporting safer, more efficient outcomes for patients." "One factor that is fueling the adoption of AI assistants in the workplace today is the emergence of digitally mediated emotional connections, what some might consider a modern form of para-social interaction. Employees often develop a sense of familiarity or trust with voice-activated systems, even though they're fully aware the 'assistant' isn't a person. This human-like responsiveness can enhance comfort, reduce friction in task execution, and contribute to higher engagement, especially in remote or isolated work environments," (K. L., Brown-Jackson, Sr. Regulatory Advisor, QMS SME, ACTTP, & National Science Foundation Fellow, personal communication, July 22, 2025).

As given by Merrill et al., 2022, business leaders and decision-makers in 2025 recognize the appeal of AI assistants as rooted in their task capabilities, social presence, physical embodiment, and security assurances. Task attraction involves users' confidence in the AI assistant's reliability, responsiveness, and ability to complete complex tasks with minimal supervision. More recent research emphasizes that AI systems are increasingly evaluated based on their human-like social behavior, including emotional tone, contextual awareness, and the ability to engage in adaptive dialogue, all of which can enhance user trust and cooperation (Glikson & Woolley, 2023). As given by (ALSaidi et al., 2024) physical attraction, often associated with embodied AI or smart devices, increases engagement by making AI interactions more tangible and intuitive, especially in customer-facing environments. At the same time, security attraction refers to the expectation that AI systems can handle sensitive data, authenticate users, and support regulatory compliance, all of which are essential for enterprise adoption (ALSaidi et al., 2024). These four dimensions, together, inform how leaders assess the broader value and risks of implementing AI assistants across functions.

Narrative Accounts from Semi-Structured Interview Question 8

To address the eighth research question, semi-structured interview participants were asked the following, "*As AI continues to reshape the workplace, what are your thoughts on how it is influencing job roles, workforce dynamics, and future employment opportunities?* According to D. N. Burrell, Faculty, Organizational Social Scientist & Leadership Development Consultant, and Certified Diversity professional (personal communication, October 15, 2019), "In 2025, AI technologies are deeply embedded across every major industry (e.g., Healthcare, aviation, education, law, automotive, building, and engineering) fueling unprecedented advances in automation, decision intelligence, and data-driven innovation. Today, AI systems frequently collaborate with or replace human workers in roles such as sales, marketing, customer engagement, proofreading, and instructional support. This rapid integration is fundamentally redefining job roles, skill requirements, and the nature of human–machine partnerships, prompting organizations and their leaders to rethink workforce strategies to ensure adaptability, equity, and resilience in the era of intelligent automation." Data shows that the Fourth Industrial Revolution fundamentally transformed how the world operates through digitization and automation, while the emerging Fifth Industrial Revolution is now redefining this progress by integrating human-centric technologies (i.e., such as AI, robotics, and biotechnology) focused on ethical innovation, collaboration, and societal well-being (Grasso, 2024). The Fifth Industrial Revolution represents a shift from the purely technology-driven focus of the Fourth Industrial Revolution (4IR) toward a more human-centered, ethical, and collaborative approach to innovation (Burton, 2019; Gadimah Consulting, 2023). This current revolution focuses on Human-AI collaboration rather than AI replacement, sustainability and inclusion in technological development, integration of emotional intelligence, creativity, and ethics into advanced technologies (i.e., AI, robotics, and biotech), and technologies that serve people, not just productivity (Burton, 2019; Gadimah Consulting, 2023). In 2019, J. V. Noel Sr., SPHR, retired Human Resources Director, and now University Professor (personal communication, October 22, 2019) mentioned the following. "Now, the world is faced with future technological displacement of labor forecasted to be momentous" (J. V. Noel Sr., SPHR, retired Human Resources Director, and now University Professor (personal communication, October 22, 2019). Today, there is widespread agreement among economists, labor researchers, and technologists that technological displacement of labor, particularly due to AI, automation, and robotics, is already underway and will have significant, possibly momentous effects on the global workforce (Babina & Fedyk, 2025; Deming & Summers, 2025; Fathi & MacKinnon, 2024).

"In today's rapidly evolving technological landscape, it is essential to implement robust checks and balances that ensure individuals are continuously educated, upskilled, and prepared to thrive alongside AI-driven systems. To avoid widening socioeconomic gaps, businesses must take an active role in workforce development and safeguard against large-scale structural unemployment. Proactive collaboration between industry, government, and education sectors is now critical to building a resilient, future-ready labor force." (D. N. Burrell, Faculty, Organizational Social Scientist & Leadership Development Consultant, and Certified Diversity professional, personal communication, July 28, 2025). AI is already reshaping the workplace by enhancing productivity, streamlining decision-making, and reducing the likelihood of human error in data-driven processes (Shergill, 2025). Designed for speed, precision, and scalability, AI systems are now integral to optimizing operations across industries. As adoption continues to grow, the focus is shifting toward integrating AI in ways that complement human expertise and uphold accountability (Shergill, 2025). Review the three (3) analyzed themes in Table 8.

Table 8. Themes Identified from Responses from Question 8

Theme Numbers	Themes
8.1	In what ways is AI currently transforming job roles, workforce structures, and employment patterns across industries?
8.2	What strategies can organizations, educators, and policymakers implement to mitigate the disruptive effects of AI on job security, role relevance, and career progression?
8.3	What frameworks or methods can be used to assess the short- and long-term impacts of AI on labor markets, skill demands, and organizational structures?

Theme 8.1 is AI transforming job roles, workforce structures, and employment patterns.

Research Question: *In what ways is AI currently transforming job roles, workforce structures, and employment patterns across industries?*

"While human cognition has its limits, AI systems are pushing the boundaries of processing power and knowledge integration, making it possible to perform tasks far beyond our mental bandwidth," said a participant. With this said "That action creates immense opportunity, but also requires us to rethink how we define human contribution in the workplace." Another semi-structured interview participant offered the following. "For forward-thinking organizations, AI is already streamlining repetitive HR tasks like benefits administration, resume screening, and even elements of performance reviews. But there's still a strong need for emotional intelligence, cultural alignment, and interpersonal connection, things AI can't replicate. HR has always thrived on human interaction, and that high-touch culture still matters, even as we adopt high-tech solutions." Yet another participant said. "Job disruption is most evident in roles with predictable, task-based functions, like data entry or assembly-line work, where automation can take over efficiently. But that doesn't mean all jobs are disappearing. It means the skill mix is changing, and new roles are emerging that require more critical thinking, oversight, and adaptability."

Theme 8.2 is Strategies to mitigate AI's disruptive effects on job security and career progression.

Research Question: *What strategies can organizations, educators, and policymakers implement to mitigate the disruptive effects of AI on job security, role relevance, and career progression? A participant offered,*

"Reduction of the effects on AI on jobs stem in understanding the job functions and what is needed to move to the next level of productivity." "Business leaders and strategists must recognize that jobs across all sectors are being reshaped by the convergence of machine learning's speed and precision with human creativity and critical thinking" (Yoshino W. White, Sr. Director of Product Development Excellence, personal communication, July 27, 2025).

"In 2025, it's clear that greater productivity and output driven by AI innovation don't automatically equate to expanded job opportunities. To ensure the workforce remains future-ready, organizations and educators must engage in strategic, forward-looking planning, specifically, mapping emerging skill requirements and rapidly evolving industry needs to adaptive curricula and continuous reskilling initiatives" (S. R. Thomas, Human Resources Leader, personal communication, July 25, 2025). "Achieving this vision requires a commitment to ongoing research and active collaboration with workforce innovation labs and public-private think tanks, coupled with agile, evidence-based policy development to keep pace with AI's dynamic impact on labor markets" (S. R. Thomas, Human Resources Leader, personal communication, July 25, 2025).

Theme 8.3 is Frameworks to assess AI's short- and long-term impacts on labor markets and organizations.

Research Question: *What frameworks or methods can be used to assess the short- and long-term impacts of AI on labor markets, skill demands, and organizational structures?*

"In 2025, the assessment of AI's workforce impacts relies on an evolving set of analytical frameworks and dynamic modeling approaches. Organizations and policymakers now leverage advanced labor market analytics, including industry specific employment outcomes (i.e., projecting automation potential by dissecting granular job task data), and also conduct iterative research across hundreds of real-world AI use cases to estimate broader economic and employment effects. Critically, these impact assessments are designed to inform proactive strategies that can mitigate large-scale societal and political disruption, supporting a more equitable and resilient transition in the era of pervasive AI adoption" (S. R. Thomas, Human Resources Leader, personal communication, July 25, 2025).

Responses to Semi-structured Participant Question 9

To address the ninth research question, semi-structured interview participants were asked the following, "*What specific steps are you taking, or planning to take, to ensure you're prepared for the ongoing advancement of AI in your workplace?*" All of the semi-structured interview participants had similar response to this question. Review some of the given responses. An anonymous respondent stated, "In 2025, AI is deeply woven into every aspect of legal practice, from drafting briefs to conducting research and even advising clients. To remain at the forefront of this rapidly evolving field, I am proactively earning specialized continuing legal education credits in AI ethics, data science, and legal technology. Staying AI-literate isn't optional; it's a baseline expectation for delivering effective and ethical counsel in today's legal environment." Another anonymous respondent offered, "As AI becomes an indispensable tool in modern policing, powering everything from facial recognition and surveillance analytics to real-time incident monitoring, I regularly enroll in advanced, scenario-based AI training programs. These courses ensure I'm up-to-date with evolving uses, ethical guardrails, and the responsible application of AI in law enforcement. Ongoing education is critical to using these tools safely, transparently, and effectively." As given by Brenden. E. Green, Educator, (personal communication, July 22, 2025), "Because I am an educator, I have to remain current. I plan on learning the new software and becoming proficient in music programming and using this ASI technology. This new knowledge will help me teach students."

"Recognizing that AI will gravely affect the workforce, I am actively researching and analyzing AI media to expand my understanding. I believe it's essential to stay ahead so I can support my organization's workforce as roles evolve," (S. R. Thomas, Human Resources Leader, personal communication, July 25, 2025). Another participant offered the following. "As I observe the impact of Artificial Intelligence on society, I am committed to championing this technology in social, community, and corporate environments" (R. McClintock, M.Ed., MSIT, Information Security Professional, personal communication, July 29, 2025).

"Acknowledging the impacts of AI, I will prepare by becoming more knowledgeable about AI in the HR community. By becoming knowledgeable I can serve as a champion for this technology," (R. McClintock, M.Ed., MSIT, Information Security Professional, personal communication, July 29, 2025). According to L. A. Jones, Cyber Security and Risk Management Executive (personal communication, October 11, 2019), "Also, I will continue to stay abreast of some of the changes that are happening with machine learning and AI and how they apply to my profession of managing risk." "Also, I am developing training information for teaching the public regarding a better understanding AI." (R. McClintock, M.Ed., MSIT, Information Security Professional, personal communication, July 29, 2025)." "Recognizing that AI is affecting all industries, by reading about AI, I will be ready and prepared when the time comes," (William Bardge, Drywall Technician Contractor, personal communication, July 25, 2025).

These real-world risk scenarios, as described by organizational educators, leaders, and security professionals in the interviews, illustrate how the introduction of AI can intensify operational vulnerabilities. They also demonstrate that these increasing risks require organizations to adopt more adaptive and responsive approaches to AI governance, extending beyond traditional technical safeguards. Collectively, these examples reinforce the urgent need for integrated frameworks that address cybersecurity threats, ethical compliance, and organizational accountability alongside ongoing technological innovation and workforce adaptation.

"The healthcare is using AI; however, more understanding is required. I am attending seminars, reading white papers and trade journals, and speaking at conferences to remain abreast of the on-going changes," (K. L., Brown-Jackson, Sr. Regulatory Advisor, QMS SME, ACTTP, & National Science Foundation Fellow, personal communication, July 22, 2025).

Table 9. Themes Identified from Responses from Question 9

Theme Numbers	Themes
9.1	How to prepare to learn more about AI and remain abreast of this evolving technology?

Theme 9.1 is *How to prepare to learn more about AI and remain abreast of this evolving technology?* Replies to this question wrapped around some form of education. Semi-structured interview participants spoke to enhancing knowledge through attending courses and reading. Other responses were, "To stay competitive in the rapidly evolving AI landscape of 2025, I am proactively enrolling in specialized courses and routinely reading the latest research and industry publications. Upskilling and continual learning are essential for adapting to new AI-driven workplace realities." Another participant said the following, "I plan to participate in leading-edge conferences and interactive workshops focused on AI. These events offer critical networking opportunities and keep me informed on emerging best practices, new regulatory developments, and practical applications relevant to my field." Another answer was, "My goal is to become formally certified in AI by 2025. Earning a certification demonstrates rigorous, up-to-date technical knowledge and signals my commitment to leading responsible AI integration within my organization." Yet another participant offer, "Given the transformative impact of AI on cybersecurity, I am considering pursuing a Ph.D. specializing in AI and cyber security. Advanced research training will enable me to contribute to innovative solutions and prepare for the complex ethical and technical challenges we face."

While each theme offers unique insights into how AI integration is reshaping the workplace, understanding their interconnections is vital for appreciating the broader organizational and human capital implications revealed by participants' experiences. These themes often overlap in practice, with advances in automation, culture, and inclusion reinforcing or challenging one another in complex ways. Recognizing these cross-cutting dynamics is essential for leaders seeking to develop integrated strategies that reflect the lived realities of AI-enabled work environments.

CONCLUSION AND FUTURE STUDIES

The landscape of AI and human capital has entered an era distinguished by rapid transformation, hybridized intelligence, and profound organizational recalibration (Burton, 2019; Chalmers et al., 2021). As 2025 unfolds, it is apparent that the synergies between human capital and AI are not merely technical enhancements, but deeply intertwined evolutions in how societies, economies, and individuals define value, equity, and purpose in work (Stanford Institute for Human-Centered Artificial

Intelligence, 2025; World Economic Forum, 2025). This conclusion considers the major lessons gleaned from current research and emergent practice, and outlines critical pathways for scholarly and applied inquiry going forward.

Toward Authentic Intelligence: Symbiosis, Not Substitution

A central insight from contemporary inquiry is the essential shift from a substitutional lens, where AI replaces human tasks, to a symbiotic one, in which human expertise and machine intelligence co-evolve and mutually amplify outcomes (Babina & Fedky, 2025; Luperti, 2025; Marr, 2025). This perspective calls for recognition that sustainable organizational growth and workforce wellbeing arise from integrating AI as a partner in creativity, ethical judgment, and complex decision-making rather than purely a vehicle of automation (Bughin et al., 2023; Criado et al., 2025; Xu, Zhou et al., 2024). In this model, "authentic intelligence" denotes the synthesis of computational power and irreplaceable human qualities (i.e., empathy, conflict resolution, and ethical discernment) that underpin organizational flourishing (Workday, 2025). The urgency now lies in operationalizing this principle: organizations and researchers must collaborate to develop frameworks, tools, and policies that deliberately align AI deployment with the nurturing of human ingenuity, psychological safety, and collective efficacy (Stanford Institute for Human-Centered Artificial Intelligence, 2025; Society for Human Resource Management, 2025; Budhwar et al., 2022; Grasso, 2024).

Ethical AI as Foundational Imperative

The question of fairness, transparency, and interpretability has now assumed a foundational place in the discourse on AI and human capital (Burton, 2019; Caldarini et al., 2022). Regulatory momentum is visible, from evolving General Data Protection Regulation (GDPR) interpretations to the prominence of algorithmic audits and bias-mitigation protocols in multinational enterprises (Marr, 2025; World Economic Forum, 2025). Yet, research documents persistent gaps, algorithmic opacity, exclusionary data practices, and variable governance capacity, which, if unaddressed, could erode trust, reinforce inequity, and hinder the realization of AI's potential for human advancement (Salifu et al., 2025; Budhwar et al., 2022). Future studies must therefore prioritize the design and validation of actionable ethical frameworks that embed transparent monitoring mechanisms, participatory governance, and inclusive stakeholder consultation in the full AI lifecycle (Fathi & MacKinnon, 2024; Zysman & Nitzberg, 2020). Comparative analyses across jurisdictions and industries are especially vital, given the divergence in legal, cultural, and social norms (Audretsch et al., 2023; Dasgupta et al., 2021; Kenytinc, 2024).

Workforce Development: Continuous Learning and Adaptation

As AI adoption accelerates, the challenge of continuously aligning workforce capabilities with emergent demands has become central in academic and practitioner deliberations (Cave et al., 2019; Frenette, 2023; Kujala et al., 2022). Empirical evidence underscores the inadequacy of traditional, episodic training models in sustaining employability and organizational competitiveness (Babina & Fedyk, 2025; Thomas, 2025). Instead, there is a mounting call for lifelong learning ecosystems, ones that connect formal education, workplace learning, and alternative credentialing into dynamic, modular pathways responsive to shifting technologies and labor market needs (Babina & Fedyk, 2025; Ersanlı et al., 2025; Zhou & Lee, 2024). Notably, community colleges, industry-academic partnerships, and credentialing initiatives have demonstrated particular promise in bridging systemic gaps and democratizing AI skills development (Brynjolfsson & McAfee, 2021; Bughin et al., 2023; Deming & Summers, 2025; Gupta & Kim, 2022).

Looking to the future, research must rigorously investigate the efficacy, equity, and scalability of these new workforce development approaches, especially in underserved regions and sectors marked by persistent digital divides (Brynjolfsson & McAfee, 2014; Bughin et al., 2023; Criado et al., 2025; Gadimah Consulting, 2023). Moreover, the determinants of "AI readiness," including organizational culture, individual adaptability, and leadership vision, merit deeper examination through longitudinal, cross-sectoral analyses (Grasso, 2024; Demir et al., 2023). With these lessons in mind, the following recommendations outline concrete actions organizations can take to advance ethical governance and responsible AI integration.

Practical Implications for Ethical AI Governance

The research shows that actionable strategies should be adopted to move beyond abstraction and support leaders in implementing ethical governance. These actions could include instituting regular bias audits, developing fairness and transparency metrics tailored to specific AI applications, and creating feedback mechanisms to ensure ethical concerns are systematically voiced and addressed (Smith et al., 2025). Leadership teams should establish clear guidelines for stakeholder participation, employ auditing tools to monitor ethical compliance over time, and publish key performance indicators related to transparency and accountability (Kujala, 2022; Wachter et al.,2021). By adopting these practical approaches, drawn from regulatory best practices and real-world organizational case studies, and interviews, leaders can more effectively bridge the gap between ethical intent and measurable outcomes, advancing a culture of responsible AI use and governance.

Organizational Strategy and the New Social Contract

Scholarly and industry commentary has converged on the imperative for holistic organizational strategies that transcend efficiency-driven technology adoption (World Economic Forum, 2025). The leading organizations of 2025 are not those that automate the fastest, but those that construct robust, agile architectures for continuous workforce reinvention, prioritizing trust, adaptability, and sustainable growth over transactional cost-cutting (Forbes, 2025; Xu et al., 2024). Research also highlights that AI-enabled transformation implicates the deep fabric of the social contract at work, demanding attention to power, representation, and accountability in the workplace (Raisch & Krakowski, 2021; Workday, 2025). In particular, the co-design of AI systems by diverse and representative teams is increasingly recognized as a precondition for both technical excellence and social legitimacy (Salifu et al., 2025; Kenytinc, 2024; Caldarini et al., 2022).

The future research agenda must interrogate which organizational cultures, incentives, and leadership approaches most effectively foster psychological safety, resilient upskilling, and collaborative innovation (Nahavandi, 2019; Deming & Summers, 2025). The effects of blended intelligence on systemic trust, inclusion, and employee wellbeing are especially fertile ground for multidisciplinary inquiry (Gadimah Consulting, 2023; Grasso, 2024). Advancing this agenda will require longitudinal studies and cross-sector comparisons to understand how different organizational settings mediate the opportunities and challenges posed by human-AI collaboration, particularly as socio-technical systems continue to evolve.

Global Equity and the Imperative of Inclusive AI

A stark warning of the period is the global concentration of AI benefits and persistent digital inequities (United Nations [UN], 2025; World Bank, 2021; United Nations Conference on Trade and Development [UNCTAD], 2025). The risk of AI amplifying disparities, within and between countries, compels urgent scholarly and policy attention (Burrell, 2025; Raisch & Krakowski, 2021). Future research must build on comparative, cross-national studies that examine how infrastructure, policy, education, and investment shape the distribution of AI's workforce and social impacts (UNESCO, 2024). Innovative models of South-South cooperation, capacity building, and technology transfer are needed to ensure that the digital revolution does not remain the privilege of a few, but instead advances social justice and shared prosperity (UNESCO, 2024).

Transitioning from this premise, scholars should also interrogate the interplay between labor market policies, educational interventions, and governance structures in shaping inclusive AI futures, with special emphasis on marginalized and low-resource contexts (Dasgupta et al., 2021; Behrend et al., 2024).

Future Studies: Key Directions

As AI accelerates its impact on organizations, the call for future research becomes both more urgent and more nuanced, demanding approaches that can address the complex and evolving interface between AI and human capital (Burton, 2019; Chalmers et al., 2021). The integration of AI across sectors like aviation, infotainment, and education necessitates a forward-thinking research agenda that moves beyond static models, advocating for longitudinal, cross-context analysis and participatory governance systems (Behrend et al., 2024; Raisch & Krakowski, 2021; UNESCO, 2024). Future studies must be designed with methodological reflexivity, leveraging qualitative and quantitative tools, such as systematic case analyses and semi-structured interviews, to capture the lived reality of AI integration in organizational life (Jia et al., 2024; Behrend et al., 2024). Emerging evidence highlights the need to bridge the gap between rapid technological advancement and adaptive workforce development, ensuring that the design of AI and associated skill-building initiatives is equitable, context-sensitive, and informed by robust empirical analysis (Demir et al., 2023). Only by pursuing these directions can researchers, practitioners, and policymakers collectively anticipate and guide the socio-technical transformations that AI is catalyzing across industries and communities (Bankins, Ocampo et al., 2024a; Behrend et al., 2024).

Longitudinal analyses of workforce adaptation are urgently needed because the psychosocial, professional, and well-being impacts of sustained AI integration unfold over extended timeframes, revealing complex, cumulative effects that cross-sectional studies cannot capture (Ersanlı et al., 2025; Demir et al., 2023). Such research is essential to discern patterns of resilience and vulnerability among diverse worker populations, ensuring that the long-term consequences of AI on job satisfaction, skill utilization, and mental health are fully understood. Without this robust evidence, organizations risk adopting AI strategies that inadvertently undermine workforce stability or exacerbate inequities in well-being (Stanford Institute for Human-Centered Artificial Intelligence, 2025; Burton, 2019).

Comparative cross-sector studies are crucial because AI's operationalization, ethical considerations, and upskilling approaches vary significantly across industries, professions, and national contexts (AI Accelerator Institute, 2025; UNCTAD, 2025). By systematically examining these differences, researchers can identify best practices and context-specific challenges, facilitating the tailoring of interventions that are both culturally and functionally relevant. This body of research is vital for informing scalable, inclusive innovation strategies, preventing the replication of mistakes, and ensuring that ethical AI implementation is truly global in its scope and sensitivity.

Action research centered on co-design and participatory governance is necessary to correct historical power imbalances and ensure that AI systems genuinely reflect the needs and values of those most affected, particularly marginalized and at-risk worker groups (Salifu et al., 2025; Burton, 2019). Such research supports the development of organizational processes where all stakeholders contribute meaningfully to the shaping of AI technologies, fostering deeper trust and increased legitimacy. Its significance lies in generating actionable frameworks for democratic technology governance, addressing technical efficacy and also societal acceptance and equity.

Experimental and implementation science approaches to workforce development are needed to rigorously evaluate which interventions (i.e., micro-credentialing programs or AI literacy boot camps) produce tangible improvements in job relevance, professional mobility, and social equity (World Bank, 2021). This line of inquiry fills a critical void in current evidence, enabling stakeholders to allocate resources toward methods proven to drive inclusive human capital advancement. The significance of such studies is that they provide empirical foundations for the design and scaling of future-ready, equitable workforce development policies, crucial as job roles continue to transform in the AI era.

Policy studies examining regulatory innovation, from interpretability standards to data sovereignty, are indispensable as technological change frequently outpaces legislative and ethical oversight (HR Morning, 2025; People Managing People, 2025). There is a clear need to assess which policy frameworks are most adaptable, effective, and just in guiding responsible AI and human capital development in diverse legal and socio-economic landscapes. The significance of this work extends beyond risk mitigation; it lays the groundwork for harmonized global policy, enabling the responsible acceleration of AI while safeguarding rights, fairness, and societal well-being.

Collectively, these research directions are needed to illuminate the multi-layered effects of AI integration and are also foundational for developing the next generation of organizational, legal, and educational frameworks. Only through sustained, high-quality scholarship can societies leverage the promise of AI while mitigating its risks, ultimately constructing an equitable and inclusive social contract for the intelligent age (Gadimah Consulting, 2023; Workday, 2025; Grasso, 2024).

In summary, the conclusion for 2025 is clear: realizing AI's promise for human capital demands commitment to authentic intelligence, ethical integrity, adaptive learning, inclusive innovation, and sustained collaborative research. These pillars will define whether AI becomes a force for renewal or risk, shared prosperity or deepening division, a determination still very much in humanity's hands (Stanford Institute for Human-Centered Artificial Intelligence, 2025; World Economic Forum,

2025; Youssef, 2022). The extent to which organizations and societies engage with these guiding principles will shape the future of work, and the broader trajectory of social progress in an increasingly intelligent and interconnected world.

REFERENCES

Ahmed, F. A., Gul, S., & Shahzad, S. (2025). Ensuring accountability and transparency in AI-driven corporate governance. *International Journal of Social Sciences Bulletin*. DOI: 10.5281/zenodo.15378921

ALSaidi. K. S., AL'Abd AL-Busaidi, A., & Sundaravadivazhagan, B. (2024). Securing Embodied AI: Addressing Cybersecurity Challenges in Physical Systems. In: Raj, P., Rocha, A., Singh, S.P., Dutta, P.K., Sundaravadivazhagan, B. (eds) Building Embodied AI Systems: The Agents, the Architecture Principles, Challenges, and Application Domains. *Information Systems Engineering and Management, 14*. Springer, Cham. DOI: 10.1007/978-3-031-68256-8_21

Audretsch, D. B., Belitski, M., Caiazza, R., Drapeau, M. D., Menter, M., & Wales, W. J. (2023). Resilience and digitally-advanced entrepreneurship. *Entrepreneurship and Regional Development*, *36*(1–2), 1–9. DOI: 10.1080/08985626.2023.2275193

Babina, T., & Fedyk, A. (2025). The effects of AI on firms and workers. *Brookings Institution*. https://www.brookings.edu/articles/the-effects-of-ai-on-firms-and-workers/

Bankins, S., Formosa, B., & Donald, W. E. (2024b). Human–machine collaboration in contemporary work. *Human Resource Management Review*, *34*(1), 100824. DOI: 10.1016/j.hrmr.2023.100824

Bankins, S., Ocampo, A. C. G., Marrone, J. A., Restubog, S. L. D., & Woo, S. E. (2024a). A multilevel review of artificial intelligence in organizations: Implications for organizational behavior research and practice. *Journal of Organizational Behavior*, *45*(2), 159–182. DOI: 10.1002/job.2735

Basu, S., Majumdar, B., Mukherjee, K., Munjal, S., & Palaksha, C. (2023). Artificial intelligence–HRM interactions and outcomes: A systematic review and causal configurational explanation. *Human Resource Management Review*, *33*(1), 100893. DOI: 10.1016/j.hrmr.2022.100893

Bean, R. (2025, January 2). 6 Ways AI changed business in 2024, According to executives. *Harvard Business Review*. https://hbr.org/2025/01/6-ways-ai-changed-business-in-2024-according-to-executives

Behrend, T. S., Selenko, E., & Donald, W. E. (2024). AI skills and employability: Evidence from a qualitative analysis. *Frontiers in Artificial Intelligence*, *7*, 1629320. DOI: 10.3389/frai.2025.1629320

Benabou, A., & Touhami, F. (2025). Artificial intelligence in human resource management: A PRISMA-based systematic review. *Acta Informatica Pragensia*, *14*(3), 489–505. DOI: 10.18267/j.aip.264

Benjamin, R. (2019). Race after technology: Abolitionist tools for the new Jim code. *Polity*. https://www.politybooks.com/bookdetail?book_id=1634

Brynjolfsson, E., & McAfee, A. (2014). The second machine age: Work, progress, and prosperity in a time of brilliant technologies. *W. W. Norton*. https://mindfultechnics.com/the-second-machine-age/

Budhwar, P., Malik, A., De Silva, M. T. T., & Thevisuthan, P. (2022). Artificial intelligence – challenges and opportunities for international HRM: A review and research agenda. *International Journal of Human Resource Management*, *33*(6), 1065–1097. DOI: 10.1080/09585192.2022.2035161

Bughin, J., Seong, J., Manyika, J., Chui, M., & Joshi, R. (2023). The future of work in the age of AI: Scenarios, trends, and policy responses. *McKinsey Global Institute*. https://www.mckinsey.com/featured-insights/future-of-work/jobs-lost-jobs-gained-what-the-future-of-work-will-mean-for-jobs-skills-and-wages

Burton, S. L. (2019). Grasping the cyber-world: Artificial intelligence and human capital meet to inform leadership. *International Journal of Economics, Commerce and Management, 7*(12), 707–729. https://www.researchgate.net/publication/338249804

Caldarini, G., Jaf, S., & McGarry, K. (2022). A literature survey of recent advances in chatbots. *Information (Basel)*, *13*(1), 41. DOI: 10.3390/info13010041

Cave, S., Dihal, K., & Dillon, S. (2019). *AI narratives: A history of imaginative thinking about intelligent machines*. Oxford University Press., https://global.oup.com/academic/product/ai-narratives-9780198846666

Chalmers, D., MacKenzie, N. G., & Carter, S. (2021). Artificial intelligence and entrepreneurship: Implications for venture creation in the fourth industrial revolution. *Entrepreneurship Theory and Practice*, *45*(5), 1028–1053. DOI: 10.1177/1042258720934581

Chen, E. (2024). Empowering artificial intelligence for knowledge management augmentation. *Issues in Information Systems*, *25*(1), 409–416. DOI: 10.48009/1_iis_2024_132

Corrêa, D., Moraes, T., & Teixeira, J. (2023). AI governance and regulation: Closing the gap between declarative ethics and pragmatic implementation. *Journal of Information. Communication and Ethics in Society*, *21*(5), 704–721. DOI: 10.1108/JICES-08-2022-0120

Criado, J. I., Sandoval-Almazán, R., & Gil-Garcia, J. R. (2025). Artificial intelligence and public administration: Understanding actors, governance, and policy from micro, meso, and macro perspectives. *Public Policy and Administration, 40*(2), 173–184. DOI: 10.1177/09520767241272921

Cunningham, N., & Carmichael, T. (2017). Sampling, interviewing and coding: Lessons from a constructivist grounded study. In *ECRM 2017: Proceedings of the 16th European Conference on Research Methods in Business and Management* (pp. 1–10). ACPI., https://research.manchester.ac.uk/en/publications/sampling-interviewing-and-coding-lessons-from-a-constructivist-gr/?utm_source=copilot.com

Dasgupta, S., Roy, S., & Saha, S. (2021). AI and human capital in developing economies: Barriers and opportunities. *Development Policy Review, 39*(6), 900–915. DOI: 10.1111/dpr.12567

Deming, D., & Summers, L. H. (2025). Is AI already shaking up the labor market? *Harvard Gazette.* https://news.harvard.edu/gazette/story/2025/02/is-ai-already-shaking-up-labor-market-a-i-artificial-intelligence/

Demir, K. A., Döven, G., & Sezen, B. (2023). Industry 5.0 and human-centric digital transformation. *Journal of Manufacturing Systems, 68*, 51–63. DOI: 10.1016/j.jmsy.2023.03.007

Donald, S., Selenko, E., & Baruch, Y. (2024). Artificial intelligence skills and their impact on employability and organizational success. *Frontiers in Artificial Intelligence, 7*, 1629320. Advance online publication. DOI: 10.3389/frai.2025.1629320

Ersanlı, C. Y., Çelik, F., Barjesteh, H., Duran, V., & Manoochehrzadeh, M. (2025). A review of global reskilling and upskilling initiatives in the age of AI. *AI and Ethics, 5*(6), 5719–5728. DOI: 10.1007/s43681-025-00767-9

Fathi, E., & MacKinnon, P. (2024). Is society ready for the impact of AI on the workforce? *Centre for International Governance Innovation.* https://www.cigionline.org/articles/is-society-ready-for-the-impact-of-ai-on-the-workforce/

Floridi, L. (2022). Ethical aspects of AI: Between risk management and trustworthy design. *AI & Society, 37*, 1497–1508. DOI: 10.1007/s00146-021-01244-4

Fogaça, D. R., Grijalvo, M., & Sacomano Neto, M. (2024). What are Industry 4.0 and Industry 5.0 all about? An integrative institutional model for the new industrial paradigms. *Administrative Sciences, 15*(4), 118. https://www.mdpi.com/2076-3387/15/4/118. DOI: 10.3390/admsci15040118

Frenette, J. (2023). Ensuring human oversight in high-performance AI systems: A framework for control and accountability. *World Journal of Advanced Research and Reviews, 20*(2), 1507–1516. DOI: 10.30574/wjarr.2023.20.2.2194

Gadimah Consulting. (2023). The 5th Industrial Revolution (5IR): A Shift from 'Technology for the People' to 'Technology with the People.' *Gadimah Consulting.* https://gadimah.consulting/blog/the-5th-industrial-revolution-5ir

Glikson, E., & Woolley, A. W. (2023). Human trust in AI: A review of empirical research. *The Academy of Management Annals, 17*(1), 484–516. https://www.researchgate.net/publication/340605601_Human_trust_in_artificial_intelligence_Review_of_empirical_research_Academy_of_Management_Annals_in_press

Grasso, A. (2024, March 27). Industry 5.0 will bridge automation to human-machine collaboration. *DeltalogiX.* https://deltalogix.blog/en/2024/03/27/industry-5-0-will-bridge-automation-to-human-machine-collaboration

Gupta, R., & Kim, S. (2022). Strategic deployment of artificial intelligence in enterprise operations: Evidence from global industries. *Journal of Business Research, 144*, 198–210. DOI: 10.1016/j.jbusres.2022.01.030

Holley, P. (2018, May 17). The Boston restaurant where robots have replaced the chefs. The Washington Post. https://www.washingtonpost.com/news/innovations/wp/2018/05/17/will-robots-replace-chefs-at-this-new-boston-restaurant-they-already-have/

Holley, P. (2019, July 2). This seafood restaurant's latest catch: Chinese robots that greet customers and deliver food. The Washington, Post. https://www.washingtonpost.com/technology/2019/07/02/this-seafood-restaurants-latest-catch-chinese-robots-that-greet-customers-deliver-food/

Hong, R.-Y., Shneiderman, B., & Sowa, S. (2023). Synergy between human and artificial intelligence: The future of collaborative work. *Computers in Human Behavior, 142*, 107677. DOI: 10.1016/j.chb.2022.107677

Hui, X., & Reshef, O. (2025). Is generative AI a job killer? Evidence from the freelance market. *The Brookings Institure.* https://www.brookings.edu/articles/is-generative-ai-a-job-killer-evidence-from-the-freelance-market/

Irmatova, G., Lysova, E., & Richardson, J. (2024). Digital readiness and AI adoption in HR: A comparative study. *Personnel Review, 54*(2), 285–305. DOI: 10.1108/PR-02-2022-0074

Jia, X., Ye, Y., & Chen, Z. (2024). Human–AI collaboration and work disengagement. *Journal of Organizational Behavior, 45*(4), 503–520. DOI: 10.1002/job.2725

Kenytinc. (2024, June 19). Major challenges of Natural Language Processing (NLP). *Author* https://www.kenyt.ai/blog/conversational-ai/major-challenges-of-natural-language-processing-nlp/

Kraus, S., Jones, P., Kailer, N., Weinmann, A., Chaparro-Banegas, N., & Roig-Tierno, N. (2021). Digital transformation: An overview of the current state of the art of research. *SAGE Open*, *11*(3), 1–15. DOI: 10.1177/21582440211047576

Kujala, J., Leinonen, H., Sachs, S., Heikkinen, A., & Laude, D. (2022). Stakeholder engagement: Past, present, and future. *Business & Society*, *61*(5), 1136–1196. DOI: 10.1177/00076503211066595

Lane, J. N., Leonardi, P. M., Contractor, N. S., & DeChurch, L. A. (2024). Teams in the digital workplace: Technology's role for communication, collaboration, and performance. *Small Group Research*, *55*(1), 139–183. DOI: 10.1177/10464964231200015

Levy, K., & Barocas, S. (2018). Refractive surveillance: Monitoring customers to manage workers. *International Journal of Communication*, *12*, 1166–1188. https://docslib.org/doc/2009570/refractive-surveillance-monitoring-customers-to-manage-workers

Luperti, G. (2025, October 3). The truth of AI in HR: A wake-up call for the people function. Forbes. https://www.forbes.com/councils/forbeshumanresourcescouncil/2025/10/03/the-truth-of-ai-in-hr-a-wake-up-call-for-the-people-function/

Madanchian, M., & Taherdoost, H. (2025). Barriers and Enablers of AI Adoption in Human Resource Management: A Critical Analysis of Organizational and Technological Factors. *Information (Basel)*, *16*(51), 51. Advance online publication. DOI: 10.3390/info16010051

Marr, B. (2025, June 30). How is AI really impacting jobs in 2025? *Forbes*. https://www.forbes.com/sites/bernardmarr/2025/06/30/how-is-ai-really-impacting-jobs-in-2025/

Merrill, K.Jr, Kim, J., & Collins, C. (2022). AI companions for lonely individuals and the role of social presence. *Communication Research Reports*, *39*(2), 93–103. DOI: 10.1080/08824096.2022.2045929

Nahavandi, S. (2019). Industry 5.0—A Human-Centric Solution. *Sustainability (Basel)*, *11*(16), 4371. DOI: 10.3390/su11164371

Noble, S. M., Mende, M., Grewal, D., & Parasuraman, A. (2022). The fifth industrial revolution: How harmonious human–machine collaboration is triggering a retail and service revolution. *Journal of Retailing*, *98*(2), 199–216. DOI: 10.1016/j.jretai.2022.04.003

Ochis, K. (2024, January, 23). AI organizational revolutions to watch in 2024: Navigating the transformative winds of organizational change. *Forbes*. https://www.forbes.com/councils/forbescoachescouncil/2024/01/23/ai-organizational-revolutions-to-watch-in-2024-navigating-the-transformative-winds-of-organizational-change/

OECD. (2023). Artificial intelligence and the labor market: Policy considerations for inclusive development. *OECD Publishing*. https://www.oecd-ilibrary.org/employment/oecd-employment-outlook-2023_9c86de40-en

Pegalajar-Palomino, M. C. (2022). Implications of mobile learning for sustainable inclusive education: A systematic review. *Journal of Educational Technology & Society*, *20*(5), 538–553. https://files.eric.ed.gov/fulltext/EJ1373433.pdf

Przegalińska, A., Triantoro, T., Kovbasiuk, A., Ciechanowski, L., Freeman, R. B., & Sowa, K. (2025). Collaborative AI in the workplace: Enhancing organizational performance through resource-based and task-technology fit perspectives. *International Journal of Information Management*, *81*, 102853. DOI: 10.1016/j.ijinfomgt.2024.102853

Purohit, A. (2025). Breaking down barriers to AI accessibility. *InformationWeek*. https://www.informationweek.com/machine-learning-ai/breaking-down-barriers-to-ai-accessibility

Raisch, S., & Krakowski, S. (2021). Artificial intelligence and management: The automation–augmentation paradox. *Academy of Management Review*, *46*(1), 192–210. DOI: 10.5465/amr.2018.0072

Saldaña, J. (2025). *The coding manual for qualitative researchers* (5th ed.). SAGE Publications Ltd. DOI: 10.4135/9781036235611

Salifu, A., Mensah, H. N., Tchao, E. T., Acheampong, F. A., Agbemenu, A. S., & Kponyo, J. J. (2025). Enhancing speech recognition through diverse shared features accent classification. *International Journal of Speech Technology*, *28*(2), 461–481. Advance online publication. DOI: 10.1007/s10772-025-10198-w

Seeber, I., Bittner, E., Briggs, R. O., de Vreede, T., de Vreede, G. J., Elkins, A., Maier, R., Merz, A. B., Oeste-Reiß, S., Randrup, N., Schwabe, G., & Söllner, M. (2020). Machines as teammates: A research agenda on AI in team collaboration. *Information & Management*, *57*(2), 103174. DOI: 10.1016/j.im.2019.103174

Shergill, P. S. (2025, April 18). AI can reshape enterprises—but the need for human involvement remains. *Forbes Human Resources Council*. https://www.forbes.com/councils/forbeshumanresourcescouncil/2025/04/18/ai-can-reshape-enterprises-but-the-need-for-human-involvement-remains/

Skelton-Wilson, S., Sandoval-Lunn, M., Zhang, X., Stern, F., & Kendall, J. (2021). Methods and emerging strategies to engage people with lived experience: Improving federal research, policy, and practice. *Office of the Assistant Secretary for Planning and Evaluation, U.S. Department of Health and Human Services*. https://aspe.hhs.gov/sites/default/files/documents/62e7a64c60e10c47484b763aa9868f99/lived-experience-brief.pdf

Smith, S. M., Tate, M., Freeman, K., Walsh, A., Ballsun-Stanton, B., & Lane, M. (2025). A university framework for the responsible use of generative AI in research. *Journal of Higher Education Policy and Management*, *47*(5), 623–639. DOI: 10.1080/1360080X.2025.2509187

Society for Human Resource Management [SHRM]. (2025). From adoption to empowerment: Shaping the AI-driven workforce of tomorrow. *Society for Human Resource Management [SHRM]*. https://www.shrm.org/content/dam/en/shrm/topics-tools/research/from-adoption-to-empowerment-shaping-the-ai-driven-workforce-of-tomorrow.pdf

Stanford Institute for Human-Centered Artificial Intelligence. (2025). AI index report 2025. *Stanford University*. https://aiindex.stanford.edu

Tarafdar, R. (2025). Human-AI collaboration in workflow optimization: A framework for hybrid decision systems in automation-heavy industries. *International Journal of Scientific Research in Computer Science. Engineering and Information Technology*, *11*(1), 3594–3613. DOI: 10.32628/CSEIT251112384

UNESCO. (2024). Recommendation on the ethics of artificial intelligence. *UNESCO*. https://www.unesco.org/en/artificial-intelligence/recommendation-ethics

United Nations. [UN]. (2023). Global digital compact: Open, free and secure digital future for all. *Author*. https://www.un.org/techenvoy/global-digital-compact

United Nations Conference on Trade and Development [UNCTAD]. (2025). Technology and innovation report 2023: Opening green windows. *Author*. https://unctad.org/publication/technology-and-innovation-report-2023

U.S. Department of War. (2025, April 24). Defense officials outline AI's strategic role in national security. *Author*. https://www.defense.gov/News/News-Stories/Article/Article/4165279/defense-officials-outline-ais-strategic-role-in-national-security/

Valenzuela, A., Puntoni, S., Hoffman, D., Castelo, N., De Freitas, J., Dietvorst, B., Hildebrand, C., Huh, Y. E., Meyer, R., Sweeney, M. E., Talaifar, S., Tomaino, G., & Wertenbroch, K. (2024). How Artificial Intelligence Constrains the Human Experience. *Journal of the Association for Consumer Research.* https://www.journals.uchicago.edu/doi/full/10.1086/730709

Wachter, S., Mittelstadt, B. D., & Russell, C. (2021). Why fairness cannot be automated: Bridging the gap between EU non-discrimination law and AI. *Computer Law & Security Review*, *37*, 105567. 2005.05906. DOI: 10.1016/j.clsr.2021.105567

Workday. (2025). Elevating human potential: The AI skills revolution. *Workday.* https://forms.workday.com/en-us/reports/elevating-human-potential/form.html?_gl=1*kmr1eq*_up*MQ.*_gs*MQ.&gclid=Cj0KCQjw7IjOBhDyARIsAFzrWQwqvwHl_05zgUozuVr00I0354lMfkNKcOEDP0GSIJSOwk5rwUJYtc0aArPeEALw_wcB&gclsrc=aw.ds&gbraid=0AAAAADgCFKdiii6KzcTgvB6NEeSFnh--k&step=step1_default

World Bank. (2021). World development report 2021: Data for better lives. *Author.* https://www.worldbank.org/en/publication/digital-progress-and-trends-report?utm_source=chatgpt.com

World Economic Forum. (2023, May). The future of jobs report 2023. *Author.* https://www.weforum.org/publications/the-future-of-jobs-report-2023/

World Economic Forum. (2025, January 21). Advancing AI transformation: A roadmap for businesses and governments. *Author.* https://www.weforum.org/press/2025/01/advancing-ai-transformation-a-roadmap-for-businesses-and-governments/

Xu, Z., Zhou, Z.-H., & Zhu, W. (2024). Machine learning automation. *National Science Review*, *11*(8), nwae288. Advance online publication. DOI: 10.1093/nsr/nwae288 PMID: 39262924

Youssef, F. E. A. (2022). Industry 4.0 and its implications: Concept, opportunities, and future directions. In Bányai, T., Bányai, Á., & Kaczmar, I. (Eds.), *Supply Chain – Recent Advances and New Perspectives in the Industry 4.0 Era* (pp. 1–22). IntechOpen., DOI: 10.5772/intechopen.102520

Zhou, E., & Lee, D. (2024). Generative artificial intelligence, human creativity, and art. *PNAS Nexus*, *3*(3), 52. DOI: 10.1093/pnasnexus/pgae052 PMID: 38444602

Zysman, J., & Nitzberg, M. (2020). Governing AI: Understanding the limits, possibility, and risks of AI in an era of intelligent tools and systems. *Berkeley Roundtable on the International Economy*. https://www.wilsoncenter.org/publication/governing-ai-understanding-limits-possibilities-and-risks-ai-era-intelligent-tools-and

KEY TERMS AND DEFINITIONS

Artificial intelligence: Artificial intelligence (AI) refers to the field of computer science and engineering dedicated to creating systems and algorithms capable of performing tasks that typically require human cognitive abilities, such as reasoning, learning, perception, and decision-making.

Digital transformation: Digital transformation is the ongoing, strategic process by which organizations and societies leverage digital technologies—including data analytics, cloud computing, and AI—to fundamentally change business models, operational processes, and stakeholder experiences.

Ethics: Ethics encompasses the principles, norms, and frameworks that guide the responsible design, deployment, and governance of technology, ensuring that human values, fairness, accountability, and societal well-being are prioritized in organizational and technological decision-making.

Human capital: Human capital represents the collective value derived from the skills, knowledge, competencies, creativity, and experience possessed by individuals within an organization, considered essential to fostering innovation, productivity, and competitive advantage.

Leadership: Leadership signifies the process by which individuals or groups influence, guide, and support others toward achieving shared objectives, often emphasizing vision, adaptability, ethical responsibility, and the ability to navigate organizational change in dynamic technological contexts.

Organizational change: Organizational change describes the planned or emergent transformation in an organization's structures, cultures, technologies, or processes, often undertaken to enhance effectiveness, respond to external pressures, or capitalize on new technological opportunities.

Qualitative research: Qualitative research is an interpretive approach to inquiry focused on comprehending the meaning, context, and complexity of phenomena, typically through methods such as interviews, case studies, and thematic analysis, with an emphasis on depth over breadth.

Workforce development: Workforce development refers to the comprehensive strategies, policies, and practices enacted by organizations, governments, or communities to equip people with the evolving skills, knowledge, and support needed to succeed in current and future labor markets shaped by digital and technological change.

Chapter 8
Rethinking Governance in the Digital Age: A Public Policy Perspective

Dana-Marie Ramjit
http://orcid.org/0000-0003-1369-8121
St. Mary's Univeristy, Canada

ABSTRACT

The governance landscape of the 21st century is increasingly shaped by the pressures of digitalization, civic innovation, and emergent forms of participatory democracy. Traditional administrative paradigms, grounded in top-down bureaucratic authority and legitimacy, are being challenged by a digital public sphere characterized by horizontal information flows, decentralized civic action, and algorithmic decision-making. This chapter argues that these changes represent a historically contingent shift in the foundations of governance, and a reconceptualization of public authority in a digitally networked era. These processes have initiated a structural transformation in which governance is increasingly disaggregated, responsive, and contested, demanding a new framework that moves beyond traditional models of legitimacy. This chapter situates these developments within the broader context of public policy and administrative theory, arguing for a rethinking of governance that centers on responsiveness, transparency, and equity in a complex, multi-nodal policy environment.

DOI: 10.4018/979-8-2600-1016-7.ch008

INTRODUCTION: GOVERNANCE IN AN ERA OF DIGITAL TRANSFORMATION

The digital age has precipitated a fundamental transformation in the architecture of governance, unsettling long-standing models of public administration grounded in centralized, hierarchical authority. For much of the twentieth century, governance was conceived through a state-centric lens, wherein legitimacy, control, and administrative capacity emanated from top-down bureaucratic structures. However, this paradigm is increasingly being destabilized by the intersecting forces of digitalization, civic innovation, and participatory democracy, all of which are recalibrating the citizen–state relationship in profound ways (Gardenier et al., 2024; Zuboff, 2022). What was once regarded as a dominant and durable model of governance is now revealed to be historically contingent, conceptually limited, and increasingly misaligned with the decentralized, networked, and contested nature of governance in the twenty-first century.

Since the early 2000s, a convergence of three interrelated developments, the empowerment of digitally engaged citizens, the fragmentation of governance across hybrid public–private domains, and the rise of platform-mediated modes of coordination, has fundamentally restructured the contours of public administration. These forces have unveiled a process of digital disaggregation, wherein authority and accountability are no longer monopolized by hierarchical state institutions but are instead dispersed across a complex and fluid network of actors. Central to this transformation is the figure of the digital citizen, whose participatory agency disrupts conventional notions of the passive, state-defined subject (Griffiths, 2015). As citizens assume more active roles in deliberative and co-productive processes, public services are increasingly reimagined through frameworks of transparency, responsiveness, and collective stewardship (Pūraitė et al., 2020; Moskatova et al., 2021).

At the core of this digital revolution is the increasing involvement of private digital actors in spaces traditionally governed by the state, complicating the boundaries of accountability and democratic oversight. As these private entities assume a larger role in governance, concerns arise about the erosion of public authority and potential for undue influence in policy decisions (Nair, 2024; Thi Duyen, 2021). Collectively, these dynamics produce a spectrum of participatory processes that are multi-nodal and transboundary, reshaping conventional understandings of authority and accountability. In this emergent landscape, public institutions are increasingly compelled to navigate volatile technological terrains and recalibrated civic expectations. What emerges is a call for a governance paradigm that abandons the static hierarchies of traditional bureaucracy in favour of fluid, ethically anchored frameworks capable of sustaining inclusive and adaptive policymaking (Fu & Barbour, 2023).

The reconfiguration of power through digital platforms introduces a duality, one of opportunity and another of risk. On the one hand, digital technologies have empowered citizens in unprecedented ways, enabling new forms of engagement, oversight, and collective action. On the other, they have generated complex ethical and institutional challenges that strain the foundations of traditional governance. Algorithmic bias, pervasive surveillance, data commodification, and emerging asymmetries of power between public institutions and private platforms exemplify the risks embedded in this transformation (Maksimenko et al., 2021). These developments underscore the need for a new governance paradigm, one that is not only adaptive to technological change but also anchored in transparency, equity, and democratic accountability.

In an era marked by rapid digital transformation, traditional governance models are increasingly inadequate to address the complexities of modern public administration. The proliferation of digital technologies, platforms, and private actors has decentralized authority, diluting hierarchical control, and reshaping the relationships between the state, citizens, and private entities. This shift raises critical challenges related to transparency, accountability, inclusivity, and ethical governance.

Despite these developments, there exists a critical demand for a holistic framework capable of adapting to the evolving dynamics while simultaneously upholding the fundamental principles of democracy. This conceptual analysis aims to critically examine how digital transformation is reshaping governance structures, practices, and legitimacy in contemporary public administration, while also addressing the pressing need for a holistic framework that adapts to these changes while upholding democratic principles. The analysis will advance specific recommendations for developing more resilient and inclusive digital governance frameworks capable of navigating these challenges while enhancing ethical integrity and legitimacy in public administration.

THEORETICAL FOUNDATIONS OF DIGITAL GOVERNANCE

In rethinking public administration for a digital era marked by global interdependence, it becomes imperative to depart from the traditional state-centric paradigms that have long dominated the field. Emerging scholarship calls for a theoretical reconfiguration grounded in the intersecting logics of postinternationalism, multicentric governance and digital transformation. Together, these concepts converge to shape a networked, adaptive, and ethically attuned framework of governance that acknowledges the erosion of rigid territorial boundaries and the rise of polycentric authority (Roe, 2020).

At the conceptual core of this redirection is the notion of *postinternationalism*, as articulated by Rosenau (2003), which captures the growing impact of communication technologies on political agency and identity. In contrast to the static image of the citizen as a subject of the nation-state, the postinternational citizen is fluid, mobile, and connected to multiple communities across digital, local, and transnational spaces (Ichijo, 2023). This citizen's engagement is not bound by national allegiances but is driven by issue-based affiliations and technologically mediated solidarity. The public sphere, once confined within the borders of the state, is now diffuse and expansive, challenging the state's monopoly over political discourse and policy formation (Emden, 2022; Antonakis, 2019). In this evolving landscape, citizenship is pluralized, redefined through acts of digital engagement, and anchored in the capacity for collective action beyond traditional state structures.

Multicentric governance offers a theoretical lens through which to understand the fragmentation and redistribution of authority in a hyperconnected world. Governance today is less about command and control, and more about coordination, negotiation, and reciprocity among an array of actors, state agencies, private corporations, NGOs, civic tech initiatives, and transnational advocacy networks (du Plessis et. al., 2024). As Cerny (2022) and Ramjit (2022) argue, power now circulates through webs of relationships that transcend traditional vertical hierarchies, giving rise to a model of public administration that is dialogical, relational, and situational. Legitimacy in such a system no longer emanates solely from institutional mandate but is increasingly derived from an actor's capacity to mediate between competing interests, facilitate co-production, and respond to emergent societal needs with agility and transparency (Harfst & Wiesner, 2024; Peter, 2023; 2020).

Digital transformation, the third axis of this framework, operates as both a catalyst and a disruptor of governance. The proliferation of AI, data analytics, blockchain, and cloud-based platforms has reshaped not only the mechanics of service delivery but also the epistemologies underpinning administrative decision-making (Badiger et. al., 2024). On the one hand, these innovations enhance transparency, streamline operations, and enable participatory mechanisms that amplify citizen voices (Ruthvika, 2025). On the other, they usher in complex ethical dilemmas surrounding algorithmic governance, digital equity, data sovereignty, and environmental sustainability (Avancha et. al., 2023). As such, digital transformation must be approached not as a technocratic fix, but as a domain requiring guidance and reflexive governance, where justice, and accountability remain at the forefront.

These theoretical currents gain salience considering global challenges, such as climate change, pandemics, migration, and economic volatility, that defy territorial solutions and demand integrative governance frameworks. In response, public administration must evolve into a hybrid system capable of global-local alignment. The figure of the global digital citizen is a critical agent in this process, mobilizing across borders, organizing through digital frames, and co-creating solutions to shared global concerns (Katapally, 2020; Fitzwater, 2022). This paradigm not only decentralizes authority but also reimagines governance as a dynamic relationship between local and global communities, mediated by digital tools and transnational solidarities.

Ultimately, this reconfigured framework calls for a public administration that is porous, participatory, and principled, capable of navigating the fluid and disputed terrain of global governance while remaining anchored in democratic accountability and ethical responsibility. By embedding the principles of postinternationalism, multicentricity, and digital transformation into public administration perspectives, scholars and practitioners are better positioned to confront the complexities and contradictions of governance in the twenty-first century.

TECHNOLOGICAL INNOVATIONS RESHAPING PUBLIC ADMINISTRATION

The digital revolution has redefined the rules of public administration, not merely by streamlining bureaucratic operations but by recalibrating the relationship between state institutions and the citizenry. At the forefront of this transformation are data analytics and artificial intelligence (AI), whose integration into administrative systems signals a paradigmatic shift from hierarchical control to algorithmic governance (Radha et. al., 2024; Kosuru et. al., 2023). For example, the city of Boston has deployed AI-enhanced traffic systems that adaptively manage congestion and reduce emissions, exemplifying how data-driven governance can yield tangible improvements in service delivery and environmental quality (Kumara et. al., 2023).

Digital platforms now operate as intermediaries of transparency and empowerment, offering citizens immediate access to state processes and enabling new forms of deliberative participation (Mirghaderi, et. al., 2023). As Ramezani et al. (2023) observe, these technological innovations signal the emergence of a participatory ethos, wherein governance is not merely enacted upon populations but increasingly co-produced with them. Yet such advancements, while promising, unveil a series of tensions that complicate the narrative of digital triumphalism (College & Bajpai, 2021).

Foremost among these are the distributive dilemmas accompanying with digital adoption. The proliferation of smart technologies presupposes a baseline of digital literacy, equitable access, and infrastructural readiness, conditions that remain unevenly distributed across socio-economic and geographic lines (Shabbir & Porwal,

2025; Eden et. al., 2024) Without targeted interventions, digital innovation risks exacerbating the very inequalities it seeks to ameliorate. Further compounding these concerns are the environmental costs of AI, particularly the carbon-intensive demands of training large-scale machine learning models. As Halsband (2022) cautions, the pursuit of administrative efficiency must be tempered by an awareness of its ecological footprint.

In this context, the challenge for public administrators is twofold: to harness the value of digital technologies while implementing frameworks of ethical governance and ecological stewardship (Alakitan & Makinde, 2024). This requires more than technical adaptation; it calls for a conceptual realignment in which innovation is not measured solely by speed or efficiency, but by its capacity to promote inclusion, accountability, and sustainability (Sibuea, 2025; Alim, 2024).

Such a recalibration calls for the application of digital ethics as a foundational pillar of public administration. Practices must be developed that prioritize privacy by design, implement transparent algorithmic accountability, and highlight environmental sustainability in technological procurement and deployment (Gao et. al., 2024; Mensah & Lbg, 2024). Moreover, inclusivity must become a guiding principle, ensuring that digital participation is not confined to the privileged, but extended to marginalized communities historically excluded from governance processes (Maheshwari et al., 2024).

In reimagining public administration through the lens of digital innovation, it becomes clear that technology is not a neutral tool but a force that reshapes institutional values, redistributes power, and redefines what it means to govern in the twenty-first century. A digitally empowered public administration, therefore, must be as much about justice as it is about performance and efficiency.

SOCIAL MOVEMENTS AND THE RECONFIGURATION OF PUBLIC AUTHORITY

The explosion of social movements in the digital age marks a critical inflection point in the evolution of governance. Increasingly, citizens are mobilizing to contest the authority of conventional top-down state structures, ushering in a heterarchical configuration of power, characterized by distributed and interdependent forms of authority (Gray & Warren, 2024; Thiel, 2023). This transformation is fuelled by digital platforms, which have become vital instruments for organizing dissent, amplifying marginalized voices, and constructing alternative political imaginaries (Cutolo & Vang, 2021; Fadlallah & Phillips, 2020). These platforms dissolve the spatial and temporal constraints that once limited collective action, thereby extending the arena of political engagement beyond borders (Hondros at. al., 2023).

The Arab Spring and the Black Lives Matter movements are representative of this new politics of visibility and participation (Saaida, 2024; Brown et. al., 2025). Both exploited the connective capacity of social media to galvanize widespread protest, disrupt entrenched power structures, and insert grassroots narratives into global policy discourse (Intentilia, 2023). Such mobilizations not only reveal the diminishing monopoly of the state over political voice but also point to the emergence of digitally-mediated civic agency, fluid, adaptive, and transnational in scope (Meikle, 2023). As Oghogho and Osazuwa (2024) argue in their analysis of the #EndSARS movement in Nigeria, digital activism operates across spatial scales, transforming national grievances into global imperatives and reinforcing a sense of shared political identity among dispersed actors. Estonia's e-Residency initiative (2014) exemplifies how a digital public space can expand access to governance and services globally. Launched in 2014, it allows entrepreneurs worldwide to access Estonian e-governance services, fostering international digital citizenship and transparent administration. This approach not only enhances citizen engagement but also demonstrates the potential of digital platforms to create a more inclusive and borderless model of governance.

This emergent paradigm of global citizenship, defined not by territorial allegiance but by solidarity, challenges the bounded rationality of state-centric governance (Saleem et. al., 2022; Biccum, 2020; Attfield, 2018). It calls forth a model of engagement through which individuals align around thematic affinities, rather than geopolitical boundaries, stressing the collective responsibility to confront issues of systemic injustice, environmental degradation, and democratic backsliding (Özen, H., & Konucuk, 2024).

However, the shift from hierarchical to heterarchical governance, while generative, is not without complications. Movements such as Occupy Wall Street, which powerfully refocused the discourse on economic inequality, simultaneously revealed the structural limitations of decentralized mobilization: fragmentation, coordination discrepancies, and strategic incoherence (Miller, 2019). The openness and fluidity that define heterarchical networks can also hinder the formation of sustained agendas and coherent institutional alternatives.

In navigating these complexities, public administrators are confronted with a dilemma. On one hand, they must acknowledge and accommodate the pluralistic nature of contemporary civic engagement. On the other, they must develop adaptive governance strategies capable of channeling diverse inputs into cohesive, actionable frameworks. This imposes a move toward bottom-up, governance models that prioritize continuous feedback, open-source decision-making, and flexible resource allocation.

Gardenier et al. (2024) offer a compelling approach to public administration empowerment and resilience. This framework suggests that a dynamically engaged citizenry, equipped with digital tools, and rooted in trans-local networks, can act as stewards of the public good, safeguarding democratic values in an era defined by uncertainty and flux. The rise of networked social movements compels a rethinking of governance as an iterative and collaborative process. Far from being a passive recipient of policy, the citizen becomes a co-architect of public life, redefining the contours of authority in ways that reflect the lived complexities of the digital, globalized age.

GLOBAL INTERDEPENDENCE AND THE SHIFTING TERRAIN OF PUBLIC ADMINISTRATION

The concept of global citizenship presents a vision of political and ethical belonging that transcends territorial boundaries, grounded in interconnectedness, shared values, and collective responsibility for addressing transnational challenges. Departing from the conventional mechanism of the nation-state, this perspective champions a multicentric model of governance wherein authority is distributed across an array of state and non-state actors. The diffusion of political power across these interlocking networks reflects the complexity of an emerging global order (Radovanović, 2024), as influence is no longer anchored solely in national institutions but extends through transnational circuits of activism, policy, and communication (Wuthnow, 2023).

Within this postinternational landscape, the meaning of citizenship is profoundly reconfigured. No longer synonymous with allegiance to a singular polity, citizenship becomes a pluralistic construct, embedded in global governance mechanisms, and enacted through participation in cross-border networks (Ferguson & Mansbach, 2010; 2004; Parker, 2009). These developments signify an exemplary shift from bounded sovereignty toward relational and networked modalities of political agency.

Social movements are at the vanguard of this transformation, serving as critical agents in shaping and disseminating new forms of global civic identity. By mobilizing across spatial divides and forging solidarities that cut across linguistic, cultural, and geopolitical lines, these movements contest dominant narratives, articulate alternative political visions, and champion shared power on a global scale (Lynn, 2025; Giugni, 2023; Rucht, 2023). In doing so, they promote a shared ethical orientation toward global justice, environmental sustainability, and human rights. As individuals engage in these movements, traditional notions of loyalty and identity are reshaped, compelling both citizens and institutions to navigate an increasingly interdependent political terrain (Fontana, 2023; Orr et. al., 2023).

This reconceptualization of citizenship exerts a profound influence on public administration. Contemporary citizens expect not only competent responses to local needs but also a moral and operational alignment with global priorities (Boels et. al., 2025; Chow & Ren, 2023). In this context, legitimacy is no longer derived solely from compliance or service delivery, but from an institution's ability to orchestrate inclusive dialogues, mediate across transnational interests, and respond adaptively to global crises (Brinkmann, 2024; Ferret Mas, 2023).

Shultz and Karsgaard (2023) clarify this dynamic by examining the rise of the attention economy, fueled by social media platforms that mediate public discourse and control the flow of information and influence. These technologies amplify voices across borders and reconstitute the public sphere as a digitally mediated, global network. Consequently, governance is increasingly performed not just through bureaucratic channels but through the curation of narratives that circulate within these hyperconnected arenas (Joinau, 2023).

Forging a balance between global and local obligations thus emerges as a central challenge for public administration in the digital age. Responsive governance demands the integration of diverse epistemologies and the cultivation of institutional capacities capable of operating simultaneously at multiple scales. In this reimagined paradigm, the global citizen is not a peripheral figure but a pivotal actor, one whose agency, affiliations, and expectations are reshaping the contours of democratic governance.

CONCLUSION AND RECOMMENDATIONS

The rise of an engaged, digitally-empowered public, shaped by the convergence of technology, transnational activism, and an emergent ethos of global citizenship, requires a reconsideration of the foundational principles of public administration. This evolving landscape presents a constitutive tension: while digital platforms and networks have radically expanded the horizons of citizen participation, collaborative governance, and democracy, they have simultaneously ushered in new vectors of complexity, such as algorithmic bias, information overload, data sovereignty dilemmas, and socio-digital stratification (Congge at. al., 2023; Amicelle, 2022; Machen & Nost, 2021; Hogan et. al., 2017).

In this context, governance legitimacy is no longer grounded solely in formal authority, but increasingly depends on the ethical awareness, flexibility, and forward-looking capacity of administrative systems. The rational-legal authority typical of bureaucracy is steadily giving way to more decentralized and adaptive forms of governance that reflect the complex, overlapping structures of today's socio-political landscape.

At the core of this shift is the digital public space, a dynamic arena in which participatory technologies and algorithmically mediated conversations play a fundamental role in shaping both policy agendas and institutional accountability. Social media platforms, open-source civic technologies, and interactive digital tools are not peripheral to governance, they are integral to a reconfigured state-citizen interface, where citizens emerge not merely as passive recipients of services, but as active co-producers of knowledge, oversight, and democratic legitimacy.

The digital transformation of governance is driving new forms of transparency, inclusion, and responsiveness in policymaking. As Araby (2024) explains, the move from traditional bureaucratic models to digital governance systems is reshaping the very nature of the state, embedding continuous feedback and citizen participation into how decisions are made. Similarly, Mkrtchyan and Melkumyan (2023) show that digital tools have significantly improved how public services are delivered and how quickly institutions can respond to citizens, while also creating more opportunities for public dialogue and debate in the policy process.

To respond effectively to the demands of a digitally mediated public sphere and the heterarchical dynamics of modern governance, public administration must undergo a strategic re-design. At the core of this move is the need to institutionalize decentralized decision-making processes and participatory platforms that embed deliberative democracy into the heart of policy processes (Mendonça & Asenbaum, 2025; Dryzek, 2020). These systems must move beyond tokenistic consultation, advancing genuine co-creation grounded in the diversity and lived realities of affected communities. In doing so, they not only enhance democratic legitimacy but also cultivate deeper collective ownership of policy in a time of institutional complexity and flux.

Equally essential is the development of permanent citizen advisory networks, composed of representatives from varied socio-economic, cultural, and regional constituencies (Reitstatter & Galter, 2025; Podder et. al., 2025). These bodies must function not as symbolic gestures but as integral nodes in the policymaking apparatus, sources of normative critique, anticipatory insight, and community-grounded intelligence. Their integration into institutional workflows would serve to enhance the state's cognitive agility and adaptive capacity amidst a rapidly shifting social contract.

Moreover, transparency must be radically expanded. Open data ecosystems, algorithmic accountability frameworks, and real-time information-sharing platforms constitute essential mechanisms for renewing trust (Samarawickrama, 2022). These tools help reduce the information gaps that once shaped public administration, empowering citizens to participate, monitor, and challenge decisions in the digital public space.

The growing digital divide demands immediate attention and investment in digital equity programs. These efforts should go beyond just providing access to technology and focus on improving digital literacy, participation skills, and creating the necessary support systems to ensure marginalized communities are not excluded from digital governance (Bhimavarapu, 2025; Wilson et al., 2024). Tackling these inequalities is not just about inclusion; it is a key part of maintaining the legitimacy of the governance system.

Finally, agile policy innovation labs should be integrated into administrative systems as active spaces for experimental governance. These labs, operating within a responsive policy framework, should collaborate with affected communities to co-design, test, and refine policy solutions (Bogdanova et al., 2025; Kocot & Kłak, 2024). Their core values must include humility, adaptability, and democratic responsiveness, with public institutions seen not as rigid, technocratic entities, but as learning organizations capable of addressing the complexities of social life.

Combined, these interventions do not merely modernize administrative practice, they reimagine governance as a co-evolutionary process, where the state functions not as the apex of authority, but as a nodal actor within a wider ecosystem of democratic innovation. Such a reorientation affirms that the future of public administration lies not in retreat, but in building resilient, inclusive, and ethically grounded governance systems capable of navigating uncertainty while remaining radically attuned to the diverse and evolving realities of contemporary society.

This discussion contributes to the evolving discourse on digital governance by highlighting the opportunities and risks associated with digital transformation in public administration. Its significance lies in providing a nuanced understanding of how digital technologies, citizen participation, and private actors influence governance processes, accountability, and legitimacy. Recognizing the importance of ethical considerations, inclusivity, and ecological sustainability is crucial for designing governance frameworks that are resilient and equitable in the digital age. Policymakers, scholars, and practitioners can leverage these insights to foster innovative, transparent, and participatory governance systems capable of effectively responding to the demands of our increasingly interconnected and complex world.

REFERENCES

Alakitan, M., & Makinde, E. (2024). *Where are the ethical guidelines? Examining the governance of digital technologies and AI in Nigeria. Policy &amp.* Internet., DOI: 10.1002/poi3.416

Alim, M. (2024). Examining the Interplay Between Innovation Index, Innovation Efficiency and Sustainability Index: A Cross-Group Analysis of G7 and E7 Countries. Verimlilik Dergisi, 77–88. https://doi.org/DOI: 10.51551/verimlilik.1344038

Amicelle, A. (2022). Big data surveillance across fields: Algorithmic governance for policing & regulation. *Big Data & Society*, *9*(2), 20539517221112431. Advance online publication. DOI: 10.1177/20539517221112431

Antonakis, A. (2019). The Structural Dimension of the Public Sphere (pp. 115–150). Springer fachmedien wiesbaden. https://doi.org/DOI: 10.1007/978-3-658-25639-5_8

Araby, M. A. A. A. (2024). Transforming citizen engagement in e- governance framework: a conceptual analysis. *JAKPP* (Jurnal Analisis Kebijakan &Amp; Pelayanan Publik), 213 235. https://doi.org/DOI: 10.31947/jakpp.v10i2.35497

Attfield, R. (2018). Global Citizenship. 1–10. https://doi.org/DOI: 10.1002/9781444367072.wbiee842

Avancha, S., Pandian, P., & Jain, S. (2023). Risk Management in IT Service Delivery Using Big Data Analytics. *Universal Research Reports*, *10*(2), 272–285. DOI: 10.36676/urr.v10.i2.1330

Badiger, M., Naik, A., Singh, C., Mehnaz, F. C., Smitha, A. B., Adiga, S., & Shetty, S. (2024). *AI in Healthcare Data Analytics Trends and Transformative Innovations*. IGI Global., DOI: 10.4018/979-8-3693-7277-7.ch001

Bhimavarapu, U. (2025). Artificial Intelligence and Digital Health Equity (pp. 319–336). Igi global. https://doi.org/DOI: 10.4018/979-8-3373-3384-7.ch013

Biccum, A. R. (2020). Global Citizenship. https://doi.org/DOI: 10.1093/acrefore/9780190846626.013.556

Boels, L., Boels, A., Alberto, R., & Hoogland, K. (2025). Citizens' data-ing with contemporary data in their daily life. *ZDM Mathematics Education*, *57*(1), 87–101. Advance online publication. DOI: 10.1007/s11858-025-01665-4

Bogdanova, M., Parashkevova, E., Smokova, M., & Stoyanova, M. (2025). Agile management of innovation networks—A theoretical approach. *Journal of Infrastructure. Policy and Development*, *9*(1), 10517. DOI: 10.24294/jipd10517

Brinkmann, M. (2024). *An Instrumentalist Theory of Political Legitimacy.* Oxford University Press Oxford., DOI: 10.1093/9780198901174.001.0001

Brown, B., Davila, M. A., & Hartley, D. J. (2025). What happened to Black Lives Matter? Public support for Black Lives Matter and the politics of police reform. *Contemporary Justice Review, 28*(1), 44–68. Advance online publication. DOI: 10.1080/10282580.2025.2484710

Cerny, P. (2022). *Heterarchy in world politics.* Routledge & CRC Press. https://www.routledge.com/Heterarchy-inWorldPolitics/Cerny/p/book/9781032403410

Chow, C., & Ren, L. (2023). Negotiating civic identity across different political contexts: Immigrant participation in social movements and political incorporation. *Sociology Compass, 17*(12), e13140. Advance online publication. DOI: 10.1111/soc4.13140

College, A., & Bajpai, A. (2021). Digital Tension: A Comparison Between Democracies and Authoritarian Regimes. *Political Expertise: POLITEX, 17*(4), 330–340. DOI: 10.21638/spbu23.2021.401

Congge, U., Guillamón, M., Nurmandi, A., Salahudin, N., & Sihidi, I. T. (2023). Digital democracy: A Systematic Literature Review. *Frontiers in Political Science, 5*, 972802. Advance online publication. DOI: 10.3389/fpos.2023.972802

Cutolo, D., & Vang, J. (2021). *Digital platforms.* Edward Elgar., DOI: 10.4337/9781839104145.00017

Dryzek, J. (2020). *Global deliberative democracy.* Routledge., DOI: 10.4324/9780367816681-42

Eden, C., Adeniyi, I., & Chisom, O.Chima Abimbola EdenOnyebuchi Nneamaka ChisomIdowu Sulaimon Adeniyi. (2024). Promoting Digital Literacy And Social Equity In Education: Lessons From Successful Initiatives. *International Journal of Management &amp. Entrepreneurship Research, 6*(3), 687–696. DOI: 10.51594/ijmer.v6i3.880

Emden, C. J. (2022). Changing Perceptions of the Public Sphere. berghahn books. https://doi.org/DOI: 10.1515/9780857455017

Estonia's e-Residency initiative. (2014). *Estonia's e-Residency: Digital nation.* https://eresident.gov.ee/

Fadlallah, H., & Phillips, R. A. (2020). Governance of Voice in Digital Platforms. *Proceedings of the International Association for Business and Society, 31*, 24–36. DOI: 10.5840/iabsproc2020314

Ferguson, Y., & Mansbach, R. (2004). *Postinternational politics*. Cambridge University., DOI: 10.1017/CBO9780511491344.002

Ferguson, Y. H., & Mansbach, R. W. (2010). Postinternational Theory. https://doi.org/DOI: 10.1093/acrefore/9780190846626.013.467

Ferret Mas, J. (2023). Distributive Justice, Political Legitimacy, and Independent Central Banks. *Res Publica (Liverpool, England)*, *30*(2), 249–266. DOI: 10.1007/s11158-023-09619-x

Fitzwater, L. (2022). *The Global Citizen, Globalized Lifestyles and Pedagogy*. Springer., DOI: 10.1007/978-3-031-10928-7_4

Fontana, L. B. (2023). *Identity in Latin American Social Movements*. Oxford University., DOI: 10.1093/oxfordhb/9780190870362.013.30

Fu, J. S., & Barbour, J. B. (2023). Contextualizing communication for digital innovation and the future of work. *Journal of Communication*, *74*(1), 36–47. DOI: 10.1093/joc/jqad031

Gao, D. K., Mittal, S., Haverly, A., Chen, J., & Wu, J. (2024). AI Ethics. *International Journal of Business Analytics*, *11*(1), 1–19. DOI: 10.4018/IJBAN.338367

Gardenier, A. M., Est, R., & Royakkers, L. (2024). Technological citizenship in times of digitization: An integrative framework. *Digital Society : Ethics, Socio-Legal and Governance of Digital Technology*, *3*(2), 21. Advance online publication. DOI: 10.1007/s44206-024-00106-1

Giugni, M. (2023). *Social Movements*. Oxford University., DOI: 10.1093/oxfordhb/9780192871787.013.18

Gray, S. W. D., & Warren, M. E. (2024). What kind of power can citizens exercise beyond the state? Globalizing democracy through representative claim-making. *International Theory*, *16*(3), 1–28. DOI: 10.1017/S175297192400006X

Griffiths, M. (2015). Empowering citizens. In Editor(s) (Eds.), Title of the work (pp. xx–xx). Publisher. https://doi.org/DOI: 10.4018/978-1-4666-8358-7.ch071

Halsband, A. (2022). Sustainable AI and intergenerational justice. *Sustainability (Basel)*, *14*(7), 3922. Advance online publication. DOI: 10.3390/su14073922

Harfst, P., & Wiesner, C. (2024). Measuring political legitimacy in two dimensions: Internal and external measures. *Frontiers in Political Science*, *6*, 999743. Advance online publication. DOI: 10.3389/fpos.2024.999743

Hogan, M.. (2017). Governance, Transparency and the Collaborative Design of Open Data Collaboration Platforms: Understanding Barriers, Options, and Needs. In Ojo, A., & Millard, J. (Eds.), *Government 3.0 – Next Generation Government Technology Infrastructure and Services. Public Administration and Information Technology* (Vol. 32). Springer., DOI: 10.1007/978-3-319-63743-3_12

Hondros, K., Schiemer, B., & Vogelgsang, L. (2023). Beyond personal safe spaces: Creating and maintaining collective environments for meaning and identity on digital platforms. *Organization, 30*(5), 809–829. DOI: 10.1177/13505084231168094

Ichijo, A. (2023). *The Nation State and Multicultural Citizenship*. Oxford University., DOI: 10.1093/hepl/9780192846051.003.0004

Intentilia, A. A. M. (2023). Foreign Policy, Public Diplomacy, and Social Media. Nation State. *Journal of International Students, 6*(1), 1–17. DOI: 10.24076/nsjis.v6i1.1062

Joinau, B. (2023). Cultural Governance and New Forms of Governmentality Focus on the South Korean Case. *The Journal of Arts Management, Law, and Society, 53*(6), 358–374. DOI: 10.1080/10632921.2023.2280646

Katapally, T. R. (2020). A Global Digital Citizen Science Policy to Tackle Pandemics Like COVID-19. *Journal of Medical Internet Research, 22*(5), e19357. DOI: 10.2196/19357 PMID: 32408267

Kocot, M., & Kłak, D. (2024). Employee Engagement In Innovation Processes In An Agile Organization. *Zeszyty Naukowe Wyższej Szkoły Humanitas Zarządzanie, 25*(4), 119–134. DOI: 10.5604/01.3001.0054.9665

Kosuru, S. K., Tadi, S., G, J., K, S., D, G., & K, S. S. S. (2023). Data Analytics and Artificial Intelligence. *Journal of Clinical and Pharmaceutical Research, 15–17*, 15–17. Advance online publication. DOI: 10.61427/jcpr.v3.i3.2023.112

Kumara, I., Mundt, P., Kayes, A. S. M., & Schneider, R. (2023). *Data Governance*. Springer., DOI: 10.1007/978-3-031-19554-9_3

Lynn, T. J. (2025). Social Movements. 1–11. https://doi.org/DOI: 10.1002/9781405165518.wbeoss159.pub3

Machen, R., & Nost, E. (2021). Thinking algorithmically: The making of hegemonic knowledge in climate governance. *Transactions of the Institute of British Geographers, 46*(3), 555 569. https://doi.org/DOI: 10.1111/tran.12441

Maheshwari, K., Jedan, C., Christiaans, I., Van Gijn, M., Maeckelberghe, E., & Plantinga, M. (2024). AI-Inclusivity in Healthcare: Motivating an Institutional Epistemic Trust Perspective. *Cambridge Quarterly of Healthcare Ethics*, •••, 1–15. DOI: 10.1017/S0963180124000215 PMID: 38682483

Maksimenko, I., Vashko, T., Zdrestova-Zakharenkova, S., & Nazarov, A. D. (2021). Digital transformation and its challenges to the strategic management system. *SHS Web of Conferences,* 106, 01035. https://doi.org/DOI: 10.1051/shsconf/202110601035

Meikle, G. (2023). Social Media. https://doi.org/DOI: 10.1093/obo/9780199791286-0369

Mendonça, R. F., & Asenbaum, H. (2025). Decolonizing deliberative democracy. *European Journal of Social Theory*. Advance online publication. DOI: 10.1177/13684310241297906

Mensah, G. B., & Lbg, A. (2024). AI Ethics. *Africa Journal For Regulatory Affairs*. https://doi.org/DOI: 10.62839/AJFRA/2024.v1.I1.32-45

Miller, J. E. (2019). *Occupy Wall Street*. Springer., DOI: 10.1007/978-3-030-17391-3_6

Mirghaderi, L., Hildt, E., & Sziron, M. (2023). Ethics and Transparency Issues in Digital Platforms: An Overview. *AI*, *4*(4), 831–844. DOI: 10.3390/ai4040042

Mkrtchyan, T., & Melkumyan, N. (2023). The foundations of digital transformation of the public administration system. *Alternative*, •••, 118–127. DOI: 10.55528/18292828-2023.2-118

Moskatova, I., Polze, A., & Reichert, R. (2021). Introduction. Digital Culture & Society., DOI: 10.14361/dcs-2021-070202

Nair, S. K. (2024). *Digital Transformation and Its Challenges in the Hospitality Industry in Malaysia*. IGI Global., DOI: 10.4018/979-8-3693-7683-6.ch017

Oghogho, E., & Osazuwa, S. (2024). The #EndSARS movement and the reshaping of political discourse in a digital age: A Nigerian case study. *International Journal of Research and Innovation in Applied Science*. Advance online publication. DOI: 10.51584/IJRIAS.2024.906017

Orr, L. V., Fowler, A., & Huber, G. A. (2023). Is Affective Polarization Driven by Identity, Loyalty, or Substance? *American Journal of Political Science*, *67*(4), 948–962. DOI: 10.1111/ajps.12796

Özen, H., & Konucuk, E. (2024). *Global Citizenship Identity*. IGI Global., DOI: 10.4018/979-8-3373-0402-1.ch012

Parker, N. (2009). From Borders to Margins: A Deleuzian Ontology for Identities in the Postinternational Environment. *Alternatives*, *34*(1), 17–39. DOI: 10.1177/030437540903400102

Peter, F. (2020). The Grounds of Political Legitimacy. *Journal of the American Philosophical Association*, *6*(3), 372–390. DOI: 10.1017/apa.2020.6

Peter, F. (2023). Political Legitimacy (pp. 3-C1P65). oxford university pressoxford. https://doi.org/DOI: 10.1093/oso/9780198872382.003.0001

Podder, A., Roy, P., Ghosh, S., Sarkar, S. K., & Choudhury, R. R. (2025). *Citizen Engagement and Smart Governance*. IGI Global., DOI: 10.4018/979-8-3693-9030-6.ch002

Pūraitė, A., Zuzevičiūtė, V., Bereikienė, D., Skrypko, T., & Shmorgun, L. (2020). Algorithmic governance in public sector: is digitization a key to effective management. Retrieved from http://www.ijmp.jor.br/index.php/ijmp/article/view/1400

Radha, C., Midunkumar, R., Muralibabu, S., Partheeban, V., & Praveenkumar, T. (2024). Role of artificial intelligence in big data analytics. *Int J Adv Res Sci Commu Technol*, *4*, 586–591.

Radovanović, M. (2024). Political Power and Its Representation. *AM Journal of Art and Media Studies*, *35*(35), 37–48. DOI: 10.25038/am.v0i28.603

Ramezani, M., Takian, A., Bakhtiari, A., Rabiee, H. R., Ghazanfari, S., & Mostafavi, H. (2023). The application of artificial intelligence in health policy: A scoping review. *BMC Health Services Research*, *23*(1), 1416. DOI: 10.1186/s12913-023-10462-2 PMID: 38102620

Ramjit, D. (2022). *From Postinternationalism to Heterarchy: Turbulence and Distance Proximities in a World of Globalization and Fragmentation* (P. G. Cerny, Ed.). Heterarchy in World Politics. Routledge.

Reitstatter, L., & Galter, K. (2025). Learning From Listening To A Citizen Board. *Museological Review*, *27*(27), 174–191. DOI: 10.29311/mr.vi27.4894

Roe, M. (2020). Polycentrism. In *Governance, Policy and Juxtaposition*. Springer., DOI: 10.1007/978-3-030-31848-2_5

Rosenau, J. N. (2003). Distant proximities. In *Princeton University Press eBooks*. https://doi.org/DOI: 10.1515/9780691231112

Roy, J. (2008). Beyond Westminster Governance: Bringing Politics And Public Service Into The Networked Era. *Canadian Public Administration*, *51*(4), 541–568. DOI: 10.1111/j.1754-7121.2008.00041.x

Rucht, D. (2023). *Social Movements*. Oxford University Press Oxford., DOI: 10.1093/oso/9780198877400.001.0001

Ruthvika, M. (2025). AI-Powered Data Analytics: A Game Changer. *International Journal of Advanced Research in Science. Tongxin Jishu*, •••, 97–102. DOI: 10.48175/IJARSCT-24409

Saaida, M. (2024). *The Role of External Actors in the Arab Spring*. Qeios., DOI: 10.32388/PPNEK0

Saleem, A., Raza, M., & Deeba, F. (2022). Global Citizenship Education: A New Approach to Global Citizenship Development. *Perennial Journal of History*, 3(2), 392 409. https://doi.org/DOI: 10.52700/pjh.v3i2.131

Samarawickrama, M. (2022). AI Governance and Ethics Framework for Sustainable AI and Sustainability. Cornell University. https://doi.org//arxiv.2210.08984DOI: 10.48550

Shabbir, N., & Porwal, S. (2025). Digital Literacy: A Necessity In The 21st Century For India. *Information Technologies and Learning Tools*, *105*(1), 222–231. DOI: 10.33407/itlt.v105i1.5883

Shultz, L., & Karsgaard, C. (2023). Taming global citizenship education within twitter's attention economy. *Journal of Creative Communications*, *19*(1), 13–31. DOI: 10.1177/09732586231198960

Sibuea, N. (2025). Digital Innovation as the Key to Efficiency and Accountability of Public Administration in Medan City, Indonesia. *Golden Ratio of Data in Summary*, *5*(1), 24–31. DOI: 10.52970/grdis.v5i1.821

Thi Duyen, H. (2021). Digital transformation in higher education in Vietnam and its challenges nowadays. *Vinh University Journal of Science*, *50*(4B). Advance online publication. DOI: 10.56824/vujs.2021ed19

Thiel, A. (2023). *Polycentric Governing and Polycentric Governance*. Oxford University Press Oxford., DOI: 10.1093/oso/9780192866837.003.0005

Wilson, S., Mc Ardle, R., Slight, R., Slight, S., Hassan, N., & Tolley, C. (2024). Strategies To Advancing Digital Health Equity: Perspectives From Underserved Groups. *European Journal of Public Health*, *34*(Suppl 3), ckae144.1123. Advance online publication. DOI: 10.1093/eurpub/ckae144.1123

Wuthnow, R. (2023). *Religion and Political Power*. Oxford University Press New York., DOI: 10.1093/oso/9780197652534.001.0001

Zuboff, S. (2022). Surveillance Capitalism or Democracy? The Death Match of Institutional Orders and the Politics of Knowledge in Our Information Civilization. *Organization Theory, 3*(3). Advance online publication. DOI: 10.1177/26317877221129290

Chapter 9
AI Governance Failures in Health Payers

Roderick Head
http://orcid.org/0009-0006-4344-3217
Marymount University, USA

ABSTRACT

EthosCare Systems, a mid-sized healthcare payer, faced severe reputational and regulatory fallout after deploying an AI-based claims review system that disproportionately denied claims for Black and Hispanic policyholders. This case study analyzes the root causes of that failure through a multi-framework lens, integrating Lean Six Sigma, ADKAR, Kotter's Change Model, COSO ERM, COBIT, the NIST AI Risk Management Framework, and Technology Business Management. The analysis shows how technical blind spots, absent governance structures, and weak cross-functional accountability allowed ethical risk to scale across the enterprise. The proposed solution includes a comprehensive governance redesign, creation of an AI Governance Council, and integration of fairness metrics into operational KPIs and leadership incentives. By combining organizational, technical, and financial perspectives, the case offers a practical roadmap for embedding ethical AI into enterprise strategy and aligning innovation with equity, transparency, and regulatory compliance.

INTRODUCTION

Healthcare payers increasingly use artificial intelligence (AI) systems to streamline operations and reduce administrative costs. However, when deployed without robust governance and ethical oversight, these technologies can cause significant harm to vulnerable populations and expose organizations to reputational, opera-

DOI: 10.4018/979-8-2600-1016-7.ch009

tional, and legal risks (NIST, 2023; Burt et al., 2022). This chapter explores such a scenario through the lens of EthosCare Systems, a mid-sized healthcare payer that implemented an AI-powered claims review system, resulting in disproportionately high denial rates for Black and Hispanic policyholders (Raji et al., 2020). The case serves as a powerful illustration of how well-intentioned digital innovation, when not grounded in risk-aware design, can produce outcomes that contradict ethical, legal, and organizational standards.

Internal audits later confirmed that the AI model had been trained on non-representative datasets and lacked sufficient bias testing and governance oversight during development and deployment (ISO, 2023). These weaknesses were not addressed during the system's integration, in part due to siloed implementation processes and the absence of cross-functional risk review. Each functional area prioritized short-term efficiency over ethical foresight. Data science teams focused on speed, compliance teams remained uninformed, and leadership lacked visibility into emerging bias risks.

The absence of integrated governance created blind spots that allowed the system's flaws to remain invisible until damage was done. As a result, the tool functioned as designed. It was technically efficient but ethically blind, triggering widespread operational and reputational fallout. More importantly, the failure illustrates how AI performance metrics can overshadow deeper concerns around fairness, accountability, and social impact. When oversight mechanisms are fragmented or absent, efficiency becomes a dangerous substitute for equity, especially in sectors with high human stakes.

EthosCare's failure reveals more than a biased algorithm. It exposes a fragmented organizational structure that could not manage innovation responsibly. Governance, ethics, and operations functioned in silos, each unaware of the risks brewing in the gaps between them. This lack of integration turned a technical oversight into a systemic failure. In highly regulated sectors like healthcare, where decisions carry both financial and human consequences, innovation without coordination becomes a liability rather than a competitive advantage.

Rebuilding trust after an AI failure demands more than a technical patch or a checklist approach to compliance. It calls for a coordinated strategy that embeds ethical foresight into operational processes and aligns risk management with enterprise goals. Without these structural changes, organizations risk repeating the same mistakes under different technologies. At EthosCare, the solution requires more than isolated improvements. It involves integrating change leadership, enterprise risk models, and AI-specific governance tools into a unified response framework. These elements form the foundation for meaningful transformation that restores stakeholder trust and prevents future harm.

The failures at EthosCare require more than isolated corrections or surface-level compliance. They demand a systemic response that integrates ethical foresight, operational discipline, and enterprise-level risk governance. This analysis applies three complementary frameworks: the NIST AI Risk Management Framework, COSO's Enterprise Risk Management model, and Kotter's 8-Step Change Model, to reengineer how AI oversight is structured and executed in healthcare environments (Harvard Business Publishing, 2020; TBM Council, 2023). Each framework addresses a distinct layer of failure, including technical bias, organizational silos, and leadership inertia. Together, they provide a strategic blueprint for restoring trust, embedding accountability, and building institutional resilience around AI adoption.

BACKGROUND OF THE STUDY

EthosCare Systems, a mid-sized U.S. healthcare payer, launched an artificial intelligence (AI) powered claims review system to improve processing efficiency and reduce administrative workload. The technology was designed to automate approvals and shorten turnaround times. However, within months of deployment, internal audits and external complaints revealed a critical failure: the system disproportionately denied claims submitted by Black and Hispanic policyholders (Raji et al., 2020). What began as a digital transformation quickly escalated into a public controversy, raising serious concerns about the organization's ethical and operational readiness.

The model had been trained on incomplete and demographically skewed data, with no meaningful bias testing or governance controls in place during development (NIST, 2023). As a result, the system met its technical objectives but failed on ethical grounds. The issue extended beyond flawed code or biased inputs. It reflected deeper structural problems, including the lack of cross-functional oversight, isolated decision-making, and inadequate mechanisms for post-deployment monitoring. By prioritizing operational speed over responsible implementation, EthosCare inadvertently created a system that magnified inequity while delivering efficiency.

Public fallout came swiftly. Affected policyholders filed complaints with civil rights organizations and government regulators, leading to multiple investigations into possible violations of anti-discrimination laws. Advocacy groups raised national concerns about the legality and transparency of AI use in healthcare. Social media amplified the backlash, dragging the organization into a reputational crisis it was unprepared to manage. Internally, employee morale plummeted as staff expressed frustration over the lack of transparency and the disjointed communication from leadership. The absence of a defined escalation path or unified command structure allowed a technical error to spiral into a full-blown organizational breakdown.

This failure is not unique to EthosCare. It reflects a broader pattern in the healthcare industry, where AI tools are often implemented with limited governance outside of technical performance benchmarks. While the system increased processing speed, it did so at the expense of fairness, explainability, and accountability. The lack of ethical oversight and stakeholder engagement created fertile ground for unintended harm. EthosCare's experience demonstrates the risks of uncoordinated digital transformation, particularly in regulated environments. What was framed as innovation revealed brittle governance structures, narrow risk foresight, and an inability to navigate complex change.

The consequences of this failure were not confined to operational disruption. They extended into potential legal liabilities, reputational damage, and eroded public trust in both the organization and the technology it deployed. Without adaptive governance structures, EthosCare lacked the resilience to detect early warning signs, contain damage, or recover credibility. This case serves as a cautionary tale about the organizational costs of ignoring ethical AI governance and underscores the urgent need for integrated frameworks that prioritize transparency, inclusion, and accountability from the outset.

PROBLEM STATEMENT

Artificial intelligence (AI) is reshaping healthcare operations by automating workflows, enabling predictive analytics, and enhancing patient engagement. However, when these systems are implemented without strong ethical safeguards and formal governance, they can generate outcomes that reinforce structural inequities and erode public trust. In a high-stakes industry like healthcare, algorithmic bias is not simply a technical flaw. It presents serious risks to patient safety, civil rights, and organizational credibility (Raji et al., 2020). Despite increased regulatory scrutiny and academic concern, many healthcare organizations continue to lack operationalized governance practices that can prevent such harm (Burt et al., 2022).

Many payers adopt AI tools focused on efficiency, but often neglect to embed risk mitigation throughout the model lifecycle. As a result, gaps emerge around explainability, data integrity, and monitoring of downstream impacts. Metrics such as throughput or automation rate often take precedence over fairness, equity, and legal compliance (Mehrabi et al., 2021). Organizational silos further exacerbate these issues, separating compliance functions from technical teams and executive leadership. This fragmentation leads to delays in identifying problems, ambiguity around accountability, and inconsistent responses when harm occurs (Obermeyer et al., 2019).

EthosCare Systems experienced this failure firsthand. The organization deployed an AI claims review tool that disproportionately denied claims submitted by Black and Hispanic policyholders. It lacked a formal enterprise risk management strategy, had no AI governance policy, and failed to establish internal escalation pathways. The underlying issues were not malicious but stemmed from skewed training data, limited validation procedures, and an absence of oversight across functional boundaries (Wilson et al., 2023). By the time external stakeholders raised concerns and regulatory scrutiny intensified, the organization had already lost credibility, alienated employees, and exposed itself to legal and financial risk.

This case demonstrates that AI-related failures are rarely technical in isolation. They are more often symptoms of fragmented governance, poor risk foresight, and a resistance to culture change. Addressing these challenges requires an integrated, multidisciplinary strategy. This study applies Lean Six Sigma's DMAIC framework to diagnose root causes and drive measurable improvements (Antony et al., 2019). Kotter's 8-Step Change Model and the ADKAR framework support organizational alignment and behavioral transformation (Hiatt, 2020; Kotter, 2012). COSO's ERM model provides risk structure, while COBIT 2019 and NIST's AI Risk Management Framework enhance technical accountability and ethical foresight (COSO, 2017; ISACA, 2019; NIST, 2023). Together, these tools offer a blueprint for responsible AI deployment grounded in transparency, resilience, and cross-functional accountability.

FOCUS OF THE CHAPTER

This chapter examines the organizational failures, ethical oversights, and governance breakdowns that enabled EthosCare Systems' AI-powered claims review system to harm historically marginalized populations at a disproportionately high rate. The analysis takes a systems-thinking approach, emphasizing that the algorithm's biased outcomes were not isolated technical glitches. Instead, they were symptoms of deeper issues such as fragmented leadership, siloed implementation processes, and a lack of cross-functional accountability. In heavily regulated sectors like healthcare, innovation without ethical foresight or integrated risk governance can escalate into enterprise-wide crises with legal, reputational, and operational consequences (Raji et al., 2020; Burt et al., 2022).

Rather than framing the issue as a coding error that can be resolved through technical fixes, this chapter positions AI bias as a multidimensional governance failure. It argues that an effective response requires an integrated, cross-disciplinary approach. A curated set of frameworks is used to examine organizational dysfunction across strategic, operational, and behavioral dimensions. The NIST AI Risk Management Framework and COSO's Enterprise Risk Management (ERM) model provide the foundation for ethical oversight, enterprise alignment, and risk awareness (NIST, 2023; COSO, 2017). To drive cultural and behavioral change, Kotter's 8-Step Change Model and the ADKAR framework offer practical methods to shift leadership mindset, increase organizational readiness, and reinforce ethical accountability at scale (Kotter, 2012; Hiatt, 2020). Operational and technical gaps are further addressed through Lean Six Sigma's DMAIC method and the IDEAL model, which support fairness auditing, structured improvement, and root cause diagnosis (Antony et al., 2019; Nickols, 2020).

Together, these frameworks form a comprehensive strategy that goes beyond compliance checklists or one-time remediation. They are not presented as isolated solutions but as interdependent elements within a unified governance architecture. The chapter underscores that ethical risk must be prioritized alongside financial and clinical risk if healthcare organizations want to adopt AI responsibly. By integrating these frameworks, institutions can shift from reactive crisis response to proactive prevention and long-term resilience. Through the EthosCare case, this chapter contributes to broader conversations about responsible AI by offering a practical and actionable governance model. The upcoming sections demonstrate how this integrated approach can restore trust, prevent future harm, and support the sustainable deployment of AI in high-risk healthcare environments (Jobin, Ienca, & Vayena, 2019; Floridi et al., 2018).

ORGANIZATIONAL TRAUMA & INTERNAL IMPACT

The algorithmic failure at EthosCare Systems triggered more than external scrutiny. It catalyzed deep internal dysfunction, revealing unresolved organizational trauma driven by ethical misalignment and breakdowns in communication. When institutions experience public ethical failures, employee trust often unravels quickly. This deterioration leads to disengagement, internal reputational harm, and a collapse of collective purpose and confidence in leadership (Edmondson, 2019).

At EthosCare, employees reported widespread confusion about oversight responsibilities and uncertainty about when or how to escalate concerns. Risk indicators that emerged during both the development and deployment phases were routinely ignored due to the absence of formal escalation protocols and psychologically safe feedback mechanisms. Psychological safety is a prerequisite for ethical accountability in complex systems, yet it was markedly absent at EthosCare. Staff feared retaliation, dismissal, or reputational damage if they raised concerns, which led to silence in the face of clear ethical red flags.

The internal climate worsened as public messaging on fairness and equity diverged sharply from the organization's actions. EthosCare had positioned itself as a champion of patient equity, yet its AI system produced discriminatory outcomes that leadership failed to acknowledge. When institutional behavior betrays declared values, morale declines, and cynicism spreads across teams (Gino & Pierce, 2021). In the context of AI, this misalignment is especially corrosive because it diminishes internal awareness, silences ethical dissent, and obstructs organizational learning.

Repairing this internal damage requires more than issuing apologies or updating policy documents. EthosCare must lead a structured recovery process that restores ethical culture, rebuilds trust, and addresses the root causes of trauma. Research underscores that successful ethical recovery depends on leadership visibility, transparent communication, and employee participation in decision-making (Edmondson, 2019). If these elements are absent, reforms risk being perceived as superficial, leading to further disengagement and distrust.

Long-term institutional resilience depends on restoring psychological safety, reestablishing open communication, and cultivating ethical leadership that models accountability. Employees must be empowered to challenge decisions, question assumptions, and participate in shaping oversight mechanisms. Governance frameworks alone are insufficient if the organizational culture does not support ethical vigilance. Without cultural repair, the structural integrity of AI oversight will remain fragile, and the organization will be prone to repeating the same failures under new technologies.

CRISIS MANAGEMENT & LEADERSHIP GAPS

The AI failure at EthosCare Systems did not escalate into a full-blown reputational and legal crisis solely because of a flawed algorithm. The deeper issue was the organization's inability to detect, escalate, and respond to early warning signals. This leadership vacuum created a delay in acknowledging harm, a lack of coordinated response, and ultimately, an erosion of both internal and external trust. Organizational resilience requires more than anticipating risk; it also demands predefined response structures that activate when those risks manifest.

One of the most critical breakdowns at EthosCare was the absence of an integrated crisis governance plan. There were no clear escalation protocols for surfacing ethical concerns, no designated crisis response team, and no established communication pathways between technical teams, compliance officers, and executive leadership. As a result, individual departments operated in silos, each uncertain of who was responsible for addressing the issue or how to coordinate a response. Kotter's 8-Step Change Model emphasizes the need for a guiding coalition to lead transformational efforts. At EthosCare, that coalition did not exist until reputational damage had already taken hold (Kotter, 2012).

COSO's Enterprise Risk Management (ERM) framework identifies the control environment as a foundational component of governance. It sets the tone at the top, establishes integrity and ethical values, and defines authority structures (COSO, 2017). EthosCare's control environment was fragmented and reactive. No individual or team had the authority or visibility to act decisively when bias concerns emerged. The absence of centralized risk ownership prevented early intervention and magnified the damage.

Equally concerning was the lack of scenario planning and simulated response exercises. In AI-integrated environments, ethical failures are not hypothetical; they are foreseeable events. Nevertheless, EthosCare had not invested in proactive crisis simulations or ethical readiness drills to prepare teams for bias-related incidents. This reactive posture left the organization flat-footed, scrambling to respond under public scrutiny without a coherent message or coordinated plan.

Moving forward, crisis governance cannot be treated as an afterthought. Organizations must implement structured escalation procedures, designate cross-functional response teams, and regularly test their readiness through ethical scenario planning. Leadership accountability should be tied to preparedness and ethical foresight, not just profitability. Only by anticipating failure and rehearsing response mechanisms can healthcare organizations maintain trust in the face of rapid technological change.

SOLUTIONS AND RECOMMENDATIONS

EthosCare Systems must evolve from reactive crisis containment to a proactive, integrated governance approach that embeds fairness, transparency, and risk awareness at every layer of its operations. The AI-driven claims denial issue revealed more than technical deficiencies. It exposed cultural complacency, fractured communication between departments, and a lack of ethical foresight. Addressing these failures requires more than surface-level changes. EthosCare must invest in enterprise-wide transformation that touches leadership behavior, organizational structure, and technical development practices.

A critical first step is establishing an Ethical AI Governance Council with cross-functional authority. This body should include representatives from legal, compliance, data science, patient advocacy, and executive leadership. Its role would extend beyond procedural audits and include oversight of AI model development, enforcement of fairness metrics, and monitoring of demographic impacts across algorithms. The council should be empowered to pause deployments, redirect resources, and enforce organizational standards for fairness and explainability, and to explain them. It must operate with transparency and accountability, publishing internal and external fairness reports that reflect both technical outcomes and stakeholder impacts (Floridi & Cowls, 2019; Jobin, Ienca, & Vayena, 2019).

In parallel, EthosCare should embed structured risk governance using frameworks such as COSO ERM, COBIT 2019, and the NIST AI Risk Management Framework. These models provide mechanisms to identify, assess, and respond to algorithmic risks before they affect vulnerable populations. Specific measures include conducting bias audits before model deployment, implementing fairness checkpoints throughout the development lifecycle, and creating escalation protocols for flagged issues. Governance must also be codified through documented standards and shared responsibility between business units, with oversight integrated into board-level reporting (COSO, 2017; ISACA, 2019; NIST, 2023).

Organizational culture also requires urgent repair. EthosCare must foster an internal climate where responsible AI use is treated as a shared value, not a compliance burden. Applying models like Kotter's 8-Step Change Model and the ADKAR framework enables targeted change at both leadership and employee levels. Training, storytelling, and two-way communication channels should be used to raise awareness, shift mindsets, and equip staff with tools to detect bias in their everyday work. Leaders must visibly commit to change by linking promotions, performance reviews, and departmental goals to outcomes of fairness and transparency (Kotter, 2012; Hiatt, 2020).

To ensure continuous improvement, EthosCare should adopt the DMAIC cycle from Lean Six Sigma. This approach supports rigorous process definition, measurement, root cause analysis, solution testing, and control. The organization must treat bias detection and mitigation as ongoing quality improvement efforts rather than one-time interventions. Data collection efforts should focus on tracking outcomes by race, gender, and geography, while improvement strategies should include retraining algorithms, adjusting business rules, and adding human oversight at decision points. These changes must be maintained through clearly assigned roles, regular audit schedules, and updated policies (Antony et al., 2019; Fraser & Simkins, 2016).

External engagement also plays a pivotal role in restoring trust and credibility. EthosCare should build formal partnerships with civil rights organizations, academic institutions, and regulatory bodies to co-develop solutions and benchmark performance. External audits and third-party reviews should be performed routinely, and findings should be published in formats accessible to both technical and non-technical stakeholders. Transparency is not only a reputational safeguard but also a mechanism for public accountability and ethical learning.

Implementing these recommendations will require not only strategic alignment but sustained accountability across all functions. EthosCare must transition from episodic risk response to a disciplined culture of ethical vigilance. That means building mechanisms to detect, prevent, and remediate harm across the AI lifecycle, not just during public crises. If executed correctly, this transformation positions EthosCare as a model for responsible innovation, capable of balancing operational efficiency with equity, transparency, and regulatory trustworthiness.

FRAMEWORK JUSTIFICATION

The systemic failures at EthosCare did not stem from a single decision or department. They emerged from a series of organizational breakdowns involving leadership alignment, technical oversight, cultural readiness, and operational execution. No single framework could adequately address this range of dysfunction. A coordinated blend of risk, governance, change, and quality improvement frameworks was required to deliver meaningful, sustained reform across the enterprise.

The COSO Enterprise Risk Management (ERM) framework was selected for its capacity to align ethical oversight with performance management. COSO emphasizes internal controls, tone at the top, and enterprise-wide accountability for risk. At EthosCare, these elements were either fragmented or absent, which allowed bias risks to escalate without early detection or intervention. COSO provides the structural foundation for formalizing authority lines, integrating ethical considerations into business decisions, and normalizing risk awareness across all levels of the organization. Its focus on culture, control activities, and information flow is essential for rebuilding trust and operational integrity (COSO, 2017).

The NIST AI Risk Management Framework complements COSO by addressing the specific risks introduced by artificial intelligence systems. It is organized around four core functions: Map, Measure, Manage, and Govern. These guide organizations through the lifecycle of AI development and deployment. This model helps identify where harms can emerge, implement technical and procedural controls, and monitor real-world outcomes. EthosCare's failure to engage in post-deployment monitoring or to provide stakeholder transparency could have been mitigated by this framework. NIST also emphasizes documentation, participatory engagement, and iterative learning, which are essential for institutions seeking to future-proof their AI systems (NIST, 2023).

The DMAIC model, drawn from Lean Six Sigma, introduces process discipline and continuous improvement into algorithmic governance. It follows a structured cycle that includes Define, Measure, Analyze, Improve, and Control. This approach is beneficial for diagnosing sources of bias and performance breakdowns in automated systems. At EthosCare, where bias signals were missed and remediation efforts were not systematically tracked, DMAIC offers a corrective process grounded in data. It transforms abstract fairness goals into measurable, repeatable interventions and supports cross-functional collaboration through its evidence-based structure (Antony et al., 2019).

To address leadership inertia and organizational resistance, Kotter's 8-Step Change Model provides a blueprint for guiding transformation. The model emphasizes creating urgency, forming a guiding coalition, and strategic communication to overcome inertia. EthosCare lacked an empowered leadership team to drive ethical reform, which prolonged reputational damage and internal confusion. Applying Kotter's model enables organizations to build momentum, mobilize cross-functional champions, and embed ethical priorities into institutional culture. The model helps move change from vision to practice by fostering alignment at every level of leadership (Kotter, 2012).

The ADKAR model brings change management to the individual level by focusing on Awareness, Desire, Knowledge, Ability, and Reinforcement. At EthosCare, employees were uncertain about their role in risk detection or ethical reporting. ADKAR supports workforce transformation by offering a roadmap for training, behavior change, and performance reinforcement. It ensures that staff not only understand new expectations but are also equipped and motivated to act on them. This model is particularly important for sustaining change over time because it addresses the human factors often overlooked in governance reform (Hiatt, 2020).

Together, these frameworks offer more than a patchwork solution. They form a comprehensive governance infrastructure that links strategic priorities, technical safeguards, cultural change, and operational discipline. Each framework addresses a critical failure point exposed by the EthosCare case. Their integration creates a resilient system capable of preventing, detecting, and responding to future risks. By institutionalizing these practices, EthosCare can shift from reactive crisis response to proactive ethical leadership, positioning itself as a model for responsible AI governance in healthcare.

APPLICATION OF INTEGRATED GOVERNANCE AND CHANGE FRAMEWORKS

EthosCare Systems cannot resolve its AI-related crisis with superficial fixes or isolated technical corrections. The failure was not purely algorithmic. It was systemic, driven by fragmented oversight, siloed decision-making, and the absence of ethical foresight. To rebuild trust and prevent recurrence, the organization requires an integrated governance and change management strategy that addresses root causes and embeds responsible AI principles across operations, culture, and leadership.

The COSO Enterprise Risk Management (ERM) framework provides a foundational structure for aligning AI risk with organizational performance objectives.

COSO outlines a holistic approach through components such as risk identification, assessment, control activities, information and communication, and monitoring (COSO, 2017). For EthosCare, this means defining algorithmic bias as a strategic risk category, mapping control points across departments, and embedding risk ownership at multiple levels. The framework supports consistent oversight of fairness and transparency, enabling the organization to shift from reactive responses to proactive risk anticipation. COSO also positions ethical AI governance as a core business function that requires sustained leadership attention and cross-functional coordination.

To strengthen technical integrity, EthosCare must implement the DMAIC methodology from Lean Six Sigma. This framework promotes disciplined process improvement through five steps: Define, Measure, Analyze, Improve, and Control (Antony et al., 2019). Applying DMAIC allows the organization to isolate bias in training data, quantify performance gaps, and implement validated corrective actions. For instance, the "Define" phase would focus on identifying demographic disparities in claim approvals, while the "Analyze" phase would pinpoint specific model inputs contributing to biased outcomes. In the "Control" phase, monitoring dashboards and human-in-the-loop oversight ensure sustained improvements. DMAIC enables data-driven remediation while reinforcing fairness audits and quality control.

Behavioral change at both leadership and employee levels is equally essential. Kotter's 8-Step Change Model provides a top-down roadmap for organizational transformation, beginning with establishing urgency and culminating in embedding new norms into company culture (Kotter, 2012). EthosCare must use this model to position ethical reform as a strategic imperative. It can build guiding coalitions, communicate a clear vision for responsible AI, and pursue short-term wins that build momentum. Kotter's model supports aligning leadership behavior with stated ethical commitments, thereby increasing visibility, credibility, and internal cohesion during the recovery process.

To support behavioral shifts at the individual level, the ADKAR framework targets the human side of change management. ADKAR stands for Awareness, Desire, Knowledge, Ability, and Reinforcement (Hiatt, 2020). During the AI crisis, many staff members lacked the clarity and confidence to report issues or question algorithmic outcomes. ADKAR provides a blueprint for guiding individuals through personal change. Awareness-building initiatives can highlight the ethical stakes of AI use. Desire can be nurtured through storytelling and executive transparency. Training boosts knowledge and skill development, while reinforcement comes through performance evaluations, incentives, and formal accountability structures. When paired with Kotter's model, ADKAR ensures change takes root from the ground up.

Technical governance must also be reinforced through the NIST AI Risk Management Framework (AI RMF), which offers structured guidance for identifying, assessing, managing, and monitoring AI-specific risks (NIST, 2023). The framework's four core functions, Map, Measure, Manage, and Govern, outline a process for clarifying system objectives, evaluating potential impacts, and applying continuous oversight. For EthosCare, NIST's model can be used to document the intended use of algorithms, assess impact across demographic groups, and define clear escalation paths when anomalies or bias signals appear. It also requires lifecycle-based monitoring to ensure governance is maintained long after deployment. This approach elevates explainability, accountability, and user trust throughout the AI pipeline.

The IDEAL model further enhances these frameworks by providing structure for reflective problem-solving. IDEAL stands for Identify, Define, Explore, Act, and Look back (Nickols, 2020). While not traditionally used for AI governance, it is especially valuable in situations where technical, cultural, and ethical issues intersect. EthosCare can apply IDEAL during root-cause retrospectives and cross-functional debriefs, helping teams dissect past governance breakdowns and co-design preventive strategies. The model also supports adaptive learning, making it well-suited for addressing novel and ambiguous challenges in AI ethics.

These frameworks are not meant to function in isolation. Their effectiveness lies in deliberate integration and coordinated deployment. COSO addresses enterprise risk at the strategic level. DMAIC and NIST reinforce technical accuracy and iterative oversight. Kotter and ADKAR enable leadership alignment and individual behavior change. IDEAL facilitates reflective learning and long-term improvement. Together, they create a unified architecture that transforms AI governance from fragmented compliance to institutional resilience.

This integrated approach is not simply about preventing another crisis. It is about positioning EthosCare as a leader in responsible digital transformation. By embedding these frameworks across systems, people, and strategy, the organization can restore credibility, improve fairness, and ensure regulatory preparedness. As AI becomes more entrenched in healthcare decision-making, this level of governance maturity will distinguish ethical innovators from those who fail to learn from their mistakes.

CONTINUOUS LEARNING AND IMPROVEMENT

Continuous learning is essential for building adaptive resilience in AI-governed systems, especially in high-stakes environments such as healthcare. EthosCare's failure to institutionalize structured learning processes allowed algorithmic bias to go undetected and uncorrected over time. This case underscores that a one-time technical fix is insufficient when the underlying problems are sociotechnical. The complexity and evolving dynamics of AI systems demand learning models that go beyond compliance checklists. Frameworks such as the IDEAL model and the

DMAIC methodology offer structured mechanisms for reflection, iterative process improvement, and error correction, ensuring that governance remains dynamic and forward-looking rather than reactive and static (Antony et al., 2019; Nickols, 2020).

To foster a culture of responsible innovation, healthcare organizations must operationalize continuous learning loops that span the entire AI lifecycle. These loops should enable the detection of model drift, the auditing of long-term performance trends, and the integration of lessons learned from real-world failures into enterprise policy. Importantly, learning must encompass both quantitative performance metrics and qualitative ethical insights. Organizations need systems that track demographic disparities in outcomes, identify latent patterns of inequity, and connect this intelligence to accountability structures. Governance decisions must also be informed by input from stakeholders beyond data and compliance teams. Impacted communities, bioethicists, and civil society representatives can provide critical context and foresight that internal teams may lack.

Interdisciplinary retrospectives are a particularly valuable mechanism for advancing institutional learning. When conducted regularly and with intention, these reviews bring together data scientists, clinicians, compliance professionals, and patient advocates to deconstruct adverse events and near-misses. These sessions promote shared ownership of ethical outcomes, facilitate cross-functional knowledge transfer, and expose operational blind spots that might otherwise go unrecognized. Moreover, retrospectives provide a psychologically safe space to challenge assumptions, explore value tensions, and refine decision-making norms across technical and non-technical domains. Over time, this practice builds a muscle of ethical vigilance and strengthens institutional memory, both of which are critical for managing AI systems at scale.

A growing body of literature supports integrating ethical reflection into agile learning systems. Effective AI governance demands an ongoing recalibration of risk models to reflect shifts in technology, regulation, and societal expectations. Institutions that embed learning mechanisms across development, deployment, and monitoring phases are more likely to catch anomalies early, adapt swiftly to external changes, and avoid reputational harm. These organizations treat governance not as a static function but as a living system that evolves in sync with external complexity. For EthosCare, the absence of such adaptive infrastructure transformed a preventable bias issue into a systemic failure. Without mechanisms for continuous improvement, ethical breaches are likely to recur, often with amplified consequences and reduced opportunity for recovery.

In the context of responsible AI, continuous learning is not a discretionary best practice. It is a strategic imperative. Organizations must commit to learning cultures that are data-informed, ethically grounded, and structurally embedded. This includes codifying lessons learned into policy, incorporating them into onboarding and professional development programs, and aligning incentives with improvement goals. For EthosCare to rebuild trust and avoid future harm, it must invest not only in technical upgrades but in a sustained learning infrastructure that integrates insights from every corner of the organization. Only then can the institution evolve from crisis management toward ethical maturity and innovation resilience.

LESSONS LEARNED

The case of EthosCare Systems demonstrates that AI implementation failures are not primarily rooted in technical shortcomings but in systemic leadership and governance breakdowns. The organization's effort to improve claims processing through automation exposed structural weaknesses, including siloed operations, fragmented oversight, and a lack of ethical foresight. These gaps allowed algorithmic bias to scale unchecked, damaging public trust and internal cohesion. One of the most important takeaways is that operational efficiency cannot be pursued in isolation from equity, transparency, and accountability. When left ungoverned, technology can magnify institutional blind spots and historical inequities (Raji et al., 2020; NIST, 2023).

A central failure was the absence of cross-functional governance capable of identifying early risk signals across the AI lifecycle. Concerns raised during development and deployment were not ignored maliciously; instead, they fell through the cracks of siloed teams that lacked shared accountability. COSO's Enterprise Risk Management framework emphasizes the need for risk ownership across the organization, particularly in high-impact sectors such as healthcare, where operational and ethical risks intersect (COSO, 2017). The EthosCare case illustrates why governance must be embedded proactively to anticipate harm, not just retroactively document it.

Leadership inertia further compounded the crisis. Executives failed to establish urgency, articulate ethical priorities, or mobilize a coherent institutional response. This vacuum undermined employee morale, delayed corrective action, and exposed the organization to reputational and regulatory risk. Kotter's 8-Step Model and the ADKAR framework emphasize the necessity of leadership-driven transformation, where ethical accountability is modeled visibly and reinforced structurally (Kotter, 2012; Hiatt, 2020). Without that leadership alignment, even the most advanced technical interventions will falter.

Another enduring lesson is that fairness cannot be bolted onto AI systems after deployment. Ethical design must begin at the data selection stage and continue through development, validation, and post-launch monitoring. This requires not only technical bias mitigation but also inclusive stakeholder engagement and transparency tools such as fairness dashboards, model cards, and public impact disclosures. These mechanisms are not optional features; they are essential infrastructure for ensuring that innovation aligns with public interest and legal standards.

Ultimately, the EthosCare crisis reinforces that AI governance is not a checklist or a compliance hurdle. It is an organizational imperative that demands cultural, operational, and strategic alignment. Long-term resilience depends on whether institutions treat ethical oversight as an afterthought or as a central pillar of innovation. Only those organizations that embed fairness, accountability, and transparency into their leadership practices, technical protocols, and governance architecture will be equipped to navigate the evolving demands of AI in healthcare.

IMPLICATIONS FOR PRACTICE AND FUTURE READINESS

The case of EthosCare Systems demonstrates that AI-related failures reveal not only technical deficiencies but also deeper ethical, cultural, and structural vulnerabilities. In healthcare, where algorithmic systems shape decisions with life-altering consequences, such failures escalate into institutional crises. The organization's inability to anticipate and mitigate algorithmic bias underscores the critical need to integrate governance, ethics, and cross-functional leadership into every layer of innovation. Surface-level fixes cannot correct systemic failures. What is needed is a reconfiguration of institutional behavior, accountability mechanisms, and workforce capabilities.

Healthcare organizations must begin by embedding ethical foresight into each phase of AI deployment. This involves implementing continuous risk identification processes, interdisciplinary collaboration, and pre-deployment fairness assessments. Governance frameworks such as the NIST AI Risk Management Framework and COSO's Enterprise Risk Management model must be operationalized across policies, procedures, and product development cycles (NIST, 2023; COSO, 2017). Ethical oversight should be linked directly to organizational performance metrics. When fairness and transparency are embedded into evaluation criteria, they move from abstract ideals to measurable priorities.

Early and sustained stakeholder engagement is another essential practice. Technical teams should not operate in isolation from compliance professionals, patient advocates, or impacted communities. EthosCare's inability to anticipate demographic bias stemmed in part from the absence of inclusive input during model development. Future-ready institutions must formalize stakeholder involvement through structures like advisory councils, co-design sessions, and participatory risk reviews. These mechanisms introduce alternative perspectives and help identify hidden assumptions and ethical blind spots that internal teams may overlook.

Workforce readiness must also evolve. Employees across all functions need more than technical proficiency. They require the capacity to identify algorithmic harm, navigate escalation pathways, and make informed judgments about trade-offs between automation and equity. Middle managers play a particularly critical role in bridging strategic intent and day-to-day implementation. Organizations should invest in AI governance literacy through structured training, scenario-based learning, and values-based leadership development. Staff must be empowered to challenge assumptions, raise concerns, and participate in shaping responsible innovation (van de Poel & Kukla, 2021; Mitchell et al., 2023).

Transparency must evolve into a proactive governance mechanism, not just a reactive public relations strategy. This includes real-time audit logs, fairness reporting, and plain-language documentation of AI system capabilities and limitations. Internally, a culture of transparency enhances psychological safety, making it more likely that employees will report issues without fear of retaliation. At EthosCare, the breakdown in internal communication and the absence of safe reporting channels contributed to the crisis. Ethical integrity must be reinforced through open dialogue, clear escalation procedures, and accountability at all levels (Edmondson, 2019).

Finally, responsible AI should be treated as an enterprise-wide competency. Governance structures must extend into procurement, vendor management, and executive oversight. Boards should receive regular briefings on AI risks and hold leadership accountable for ethical outcomes. Organizations that develop maturity models for AI governance will be better equipped to adapt to evolving regulatory landscapes. As international bodies expand legal mandates around fairness, explainability, and algorithmic transparency, institutions with embedded best practices will be more resilient and less susceptible to disruption (European Commission, 2024; Deloitte, 2023).

EthosCare's failure serves as both a cautionary tale and a call to action. Institutions that continue to approach governance reactively will remain vulnerable to similar crises. Those who invest in strategic foresight, inclusive governance, and cultural transformation will be positioned to lead. Fairness, accountability, and operational excellence are not mutually exclusive. When properly aligned, they define the future of responsible AI in healthcare.

STAKEHOLDER ENGAGEMENT AND EXTERNAL COLLABORATION

Building effective AI governance in healthcare cannot occur in isolation. Healthcare payers operate within complex ecosystems that include regulators, advocacy groups, academic researchers, legal experts, and affected communities. To ensure ethical alignment and long-term social legitimacy, organizations like EthosCare must engage stakeholders early, frequently, and meaningfully. This engagement is not merely a reputational safeguard. It is a strategic asset that enhances system design, strengthens transparency, and reduces the risk of unintended harm.

Stakeholder engagement should begin during the model design and development phase. Technical teams, legal advisors, civil rights organizations, and domain experts can co-develop evaluation criteria and risk matrices to identify harm vectors that internal teams may overlook. These collaborative processes introduce diverse perspectives and help mitigate tunnel vision that can arise from institutional blind spots. For example, EthosCare could establish a multidisciplinary external advisory board composed of bioethicists, health equity scholars, patient advocates, and data governance specialists. This type of collaboration fosters inclusive innovation and ensures that ethical foresight is embedded from the outset rather than retrofitted after deployment.

Transparent communication is essential throughout the AI system lifecycle. Organizations must publish accessible documentation such as model cards, fairness audits, and risk summaries tailored for both technical and non-technical audiences. These documents should clearly disclose the system's purpose, logic, limitations, intended users, known risks, and any applied mitigation strategies. By making this information public, EthosCare would not only align with emerging regulatory expectations from the European Union AI Act and the U.S. Office of Science and Technology Policy (OSTP), but also enhance its legitimacy with patients, watchdog groups, and oversight bodies. Transparency signals institutional maturity and reflects a willingness to be scrutinized, challenged, and continuously improved (NIST, 2023; OSTP, 2022).

Substantive collaboration must also extend beyond episodic consultation or symbolic compliance exercises. EthosCare should form formal partnerships with civil society organizations, academic institutions, and community health networks through standing memoranda of understanding, ethics co-labs, or participatory governance councils. These collaborations should be continuous and iterative, enabling external stakeholders to contribute to periodic audits, fairness reviews, and system recalibrations. This approach reinforces a culture of accountability and prevents governance from becoming static or performative. Effective collaboration builds shared ownership of outcomes and supports adaptive oversight systems that evolve alongside changing legal frameworks and public expectations (Jobin, Ienca, & Vayena, 2019).

Public engagement must also reach beyond institutional or technical elites. Patients and community members who are directly affected by automated decision-making systems deserve structured, accessible pathways to participate in governance. Mechanisms such as grievance portals, public comment periods, feedback hotlines, and regional listening forums allow impacted populations to raise concerns, share lived experiences, and inform AI policy and practice. EthosCare can use these inputs to surface unanticipated harms, validate system impact, and strengthen procedural fairness. When historically marginalized communities are empowered to shape algorithmic decisions, the result is not only a stronger ethical foundation but also a tangible increase in public trust and organizational credibility (Morley et al., 2020).

FUTURE OUTLOOK AND ETHICAL FORESIGHT

The lessons from EthosCare's failure must shape not only how organizations respond to AI crises but also how they design their future governance and innovation strategies. As artificial intelligence becomes more deeply embedded in healthcare operations, ethical foresight must evolve from a theoretical principle into a daily operational standard. This requires institutionalizing mechanisms that anticipate harm, detect risk early, and adapt systems before damage occurs. AI governance cannot be reactive. It must be predictive, iterative, and closely aligned with the organization's ethical commitments.

One emerging imperative is integrating ethical foresight into strategic planning cycles. This includes scenario-based forecasting, stakeholder-inclusive risk modeling, and proactive evaluations of how AI systems may affect vulnerable populations over time. Simulation-based audits and fairness stress tests should become part of standard pre-deployment protocols rather than post-crisis diagnostics. By embedding ethical considerations into planning, organizations can identify misalignments between innovation and equity goals before systems are deployed. This approach reflects recent guidance from the World Health Organization and the U.S. National Institute of Standards and Technology, both of which emphasize ongoing risk monitoring as a cornerstone of AI system stewardship (NIST, 2023; WHO, 2021).

Another forward-looking priority is treating ethical governance as a critical capability that must develop alongside technical sophistication. Many organizations invest heavily in machine learning infrastructure while neglecting the leadership development, cultural alignment, and process maturity required to manage the ethical dimensions of these systems. Ethical AI competency should be built into executive onboarding, leadership development curricula, and board governance training. Oversight cannot remain the domain of legal or compliance units alone. Leaders across all departments must understand the societal trade-offs and risks embedded in AI tools and be held accountable for ethical outcomes, not just operational or financial performance (Burt et al., 2022).

The regulatory environment will also demand greater ethical foresight. Policies emerging across the European Union, the United States, and global health coalitions are tightening expectations around transparency, explainability, and bias mitigation in algorithmic systems (European Parliament, 2023; HHS, 2024). Institutions that postpone ethical reform risk being unprepared for these mandates, exposing themselves to legal penalties and reputational harm. EthosCare's collapse serves as a case study in what happens when governance is treated as an afterthought. Organizations that act now to institutionalize ethical foresight will be positioned to lead responsibly in the next wave of healthcare transformation.

Lastly, the future of AI governance depends on moving from isolated compliance to collective responsibility. Ethical foresight requires cross-sector collaboration and sustained input from patients, regulators, community leaders, and civil society. Healthcare payers must participate in shared learning networks, contribute to open standards, and co-design safeguards with those most affected by automated decisions. These partnerships will improve oversight, strengthen system resilience, and build public trust. In doing so, organizations can transition from defending their reputations to defining what responsible innovation looks like.

LIMITATIONS AND FUTURE RESEARCH

While this chapter provides a comprehensive analysis of AI governance failures and recovery strategies at EthosCare Systems, several limitations restrict the broader applicability of its findings. First, the study centers on a single case from a U.S.-based healthcare payer organization. Although the case offers rich contextual insights, the lessons may not generalize to healthcare providers, international systems, or non-healthcare sectors. Comparative research across industries and jurisdictions is needed to test whether the frameworks presented here perform consistently under different regulatory, cultural, and operational conditions.

Second, the retrospective nature of the case presents challenges around data completeness and perspective bias. Much of the analysis draws from internal reports, leadership retrospectives, and after-action reviews. While these sources provide important details, they may reflect hindsight rationalization or exclude dissenting voices. Future research should incorporate prospective, longitudinal, or ethnographic methods to capture a broader range of experiences and insights before, during, and after algorithmic failures.

Third, the frameworks applied throughout this chapter, including COSO ERM, NIST AI RMF, DMAIC, Kotter's 8-Step Model, and the ADKAR framework, were initially developed outside the context of AI governance. Their adaptation to this case is both innovative and experimental. While these models bring structure and clarity, their combined use in managing ethical AI risk has not yet been validated through large-scale empirical studies. Future inquiry should evaluate the effectiveness, scalability, and interoperability of these frameworks across different organizational sizes, AI maturity levels, and risk profiles.

In addition, this chapter focused primarily on algorithmic bias in claims review processes. It did not address other classes of AI risk, such as data drift, adversarial manipulation, or emergent behaviors in generative models. As healthcare increasingly adopts AI for diagnostics, clinical decision support, and personalized medicine, new risk categories will demand equally robust governance responses. Research must explore how governance structures adapt when the stakes and complexity of AI use escalate.

Finally, this chapter does not offer a formal maturity model or benchmarking instrument to help organizations evaluate their AI governance readiness. While the frameworks presented serve as a guide, they do not provide a diagnostic structure for measuring baseline performance, tracking progress, or comparing across peers. Future scholarship should develop practical assessment tools, implementation roadmaps, and metrics that support organizations in operationalizing AI governance principles.

Further research should also examine the long-term impact of governance reforms on cultural recovery, ethical leadership, and AI system performance. Understanding whether governance interventions improve organizational trust, reduce the recurrence of harm, and promote continuous learning is critical to advancing the field. This will require interdisciplinary collaboration across regulatory science, behavioral psychology, data ethics, and organizational theory. Only by examining these intersections can we build a robust and evidence-based foundation for responsible AI in healthcare.

CONCLUSION

The EthosCare case exposes a growing fault line in the digital transformation of healthcare: the unchecked adoption of algorithmic tools without sufficient governance, ethical safeguards, or cultural readiness. The fallout from biased claim denials was not simply a technical error. It reflected leadership inertia, fragmented accountability, and a misplaced belief that innovation can thrive without equity as a guiding principle. This case serves as a wake-up call for any organization that treats AI oversight as a compliance checkbox rather than a strategic imperative.

Fixing these failures demanded more than algorithm retraining or reputational damage control. It required a deliberate, multidimensional response that rebuilt governance infrastructure, recalibrated risk management priorities, and redefined how ethical readiness is integrated into operations. The frameworks explored throughout this chapter, including COSO ERM, NIST AI RMF, Kotter's 8-Step Model, ADKAR, and DMAIC, offered more than procedural remedies. They provided a blueprint for institutional transformation, guiding EthosCare from reactive damage control to proactive ethical leadership.

At a broader level, this case illustrates a critical leadership mandate for the AI era: algorithmic systems must be governed with the same seriousness as financial, operational, and clinical risks. That includes embedding cross-functional oversight, prioritizing transparency, and holding senior leadership accountable for fairness, explainability, and social impact. These are not optional enhancements. They are core requirements in a sector where public trust, legal scrutiny, and reputational capital are tightly linked. Organizations that fail to meet this threshold risk becoming cautionary tales in an increasingly regulated and transparent digital health landscape.

The implications extend well beyond health insurers. Providers, vendors, and policymakers must recognize that AI deployment is not solely a technical task. It is a cultural, strategic, and ethical undertaking that demands participation from diverse stakeholders. Those who institutionalize inclusive governance and ethical foresight will be better equipped to meet the demands of emerging regulatory frameworks, including the European Union's AI Act and related global standards. Those who do not may face costly corrections, reputational erosion, or exclusion from innovation ecosystems where responsible AI is the price of entry.

In the end, AI governance cannot be reduced to a static policy or a one-time initiative. It must operate as a living system of controls, values, and interdisciplinary collaboration that evolves alongside technological advancement. For organizations like EthosCare, success will depend on whether they treat ethical risk as a constraint to manage or a catalyst for growth. Those that embrace governance maturity as a strategic asset will not only avoid future crises but will also define what trustworthy innovation looks like in healthcare. This demands ongoing leadership commitment, cultural investment, and system-level accountability that extends from daily operations to boardroom decisions. Ethical governance is no longer a regulatory formality. It is the foundation for sustainable value creation and long-term resilience in digital health.

REFERENCES

Antony, J., Snee, R. D., & Hoerl, R. (2019). Lean Six Sigma: Yesterday, today and tomorrow. *International Journal of Quality & Reliability Management*, *36*(8), 1536–1554. DOI: 10.1108/IJQRM-03-2018-0065

Burt, A., Knight, M., & Sandler, J. (2022). Beyond bias: Re-imagining the governance of artificial intelligence. *Harvard Kennedy School* Working Paper. https://carrcenter.hks.harvard.edu

COSO. (2017). Enterprise risk management: Integrating with strategy and performance. https://www.coso.org/enterprise-risk-management

Council, T. B. M. (2023). *Technology business management: Taxonomy and best practices*. TBM Council.

Deloitte. (2023). *2023 global human capital trends*. https://www2.deloitte.com

Edmondson, A. (2019). *The fearless organization: Creating psychological safety in the workplace for learning, innovation, and growth*. Wiley.

European Parliament. (2023). EU AI Act: First regulation on artificial intelligence. https://www.europarl.europa.eu/topics/en/article/20230601STO93804/eu-ai-act-first-regulation-on-artificial-intelligence

Floridi, L., & Cowls, J. (2019). A unified framework of five principles for AI in society. *Harvard Data Science Review*, *1*(1). Advance online publication. DOI: 10.1162/99608f92.8cd550d1

Floridi, L., Cowls, J., Beltrametti, M., Chatila, R., Chazerand, P., Dignum, V., Luetge, C., Madelin, R., Pagallo, U., Rossi, F., Shafer, B., & Vayena, E. (2018). AI4People—An ethical framework for a good AI society: Opportunities, risks, principles, and recommendations. *Minds and Machines*, *28*(4), 689–707. DOI: 10.1007/s11023-018-9482-5 PMID: 30930541

Fraser, J., & Simkins, B. (2016). *Enterprise risk management: Today's leading research and best practices for tomorrow's executives*. Wiley.

Harvard Business Publishing. (2020). *Leading change: A simulation by Kotter* [Simulation]. Harvard Business School Publishing.

HHS. (2024). Artificial intelligence strategy. U.S. Department of Health and Human Services. https://www.hhs.gov/sites/default/files/hhs-artificial-intelligence-strategy.pdf

Hiatt, J. (2020). *ADKAR: A model for change in business, government and our community* (2nd ed.). Prosci.

ISACA. (2019). *COBIT 2019 framework: Governance and management objectives*. ISACA.

ISO. (2023). ISO/IEC 42001:2023 Artificial intelligence management systems. International Organization for Standardization. https://www.iso.org/standard/42001

Jobin, A., Ienca, M., & Vayena, E. (2019). The global landscape of AI ethics guidelines. *Nature Machine Intelligence*, *1*(9), 389–399. DOI: 10.1038/s42256-019-0088-2

Kotter, J. P. (2012). *Leading change*. Harvard Business Review Press.

Mehrabi, N., Morstatter, F., Saxena, N., Lerman, K., & Galstyan, A. (2021). A survey on bias and fairness in machine learning. *ACM Computing Surveys*, *54*(6), 115. Advance online publication. DOI: 10.1145/3457607

Morley, J., Floridi, L., Kinsey, L., & Elhalal, A. (2020). From what to how: An initial review of publicly available AI ethics tools, methods and research to translate principles into practice. *AI and Ethics*, *1*(1), 1–20. DOI: 10.1007/s43681-020-00005-3

Nickols, F. (2020). The IDEAL problem-solving model. In *The knowledge in knowing* (pp. 125–134). Distance Consulting.

NIST. (2023). Artificial intelligence risk management framework (AI RMF 1.0) (NIST AI 100-1). U.S. Department of Commerce. https://nvlpubs.nist.gov/nistpubs/ai/nist.ai.100-1.pdf

Obermeyer, Z., Powers, B., Vogeli, C., & Mullainathan, S. (2019). Dissecting racial bias in an algorithm used to manage the health of populations. *Science*, *366*(6464), 447–453. DOI: 10.1126/science.aax2342 PMID: 31649194

OSTP. (2022). Blueprint for an AI Bill of Rights: Making automated systems work for the American people. The White House. https://bidenwhitehouse.archives.gov/ostp/ai-bill-of-rights/

Raji, I. D., Scheuerman, M. K., & Amironesei, R. (2020). The fallacy of AI functionality. *Proceedings of the Conference on Fairness, Accountability, and Transparency* (FAT*20), 272–281.

Topol, E. J. (2019). High-performance medicine: The convergence of human and artificial intelligence. *Nature Medicine*, *25*(1), 44–56. DOI: 10.1038/s41591-018-0300-7 PMID: 30617339

WHO. (2021). Ethics and governance of artificial intelligence for health. World Health Organization. https://iris.who.int/server/api/core/bitstreams/f780d926-4ae3-42ce-a6d6-e898a5562621/content

Wilson, T., Smith, A., & Jones, L. (2023). Algorithmic bias in health insurance claims: Legal exposure and governance strategies. *Journal of Health Law & Policy, 18*(2), 45–72.

KEY TERMS AND DEFINITIONS

Algorithmic Bias: Systematic and repeatable errors in a computer system that create unfair outcomes, particularly for marginalized groups. These biases often stem from flawed training data, unrepresentative sampling, or embedded societal assumptions (Mehrabi et al., 2021).

Artificial Intelligence (AI): A field of computer science focused on developing systems capable of performing tasks that typically require human intelligence. In healthcare, AI can automate decisions such as claims processing, diagnostics, and patient engagement (Topol, 2019; NIST, 2023).

Bias Auditing: The systematic evaluation of algorithms to detect and mitigate unfair treatment across demographic groups. These audits assess model inputs, decision thresholds, and outcomes to identify whether protected classes are disproportionately impacted. In healthcare, bias audits are crucial for preventing discriminatory outcomes in claims processing or clinical decision-making systems (Raji et al., 2020).

Change Management: A structured process for transitioning individuals, teams, and organizations from a current state to a desired future state. Frameworks like Kotter's 8-Step Model and ADKAR support both leadership-driven and employee-centered transformation (Hiatt, 2020; Kotter, 2012).

Continuous Improvement: An ongoing effort to enhance products, services, or processes through incremental and data-informed change. Models like DMAIC and IDEAL help structure these efforts to promote sustainability and resilience (Antony et al., 2019; Nickols, 2020).

Cross-Functional Escalation Pathways: Structured communication channels that enable staff across different departments to report, assess, and escalate emerging risks, particularly ethical or algorithmic risks, in real time. In AI governance, cross-functional escalation is critical to ensure that legal, compliance, technical, and operational teams respond to failures or red flags before they cause systemic harm (ISO, 2023; Fraser & Simkins, 2016).

Enterprise Risk Management (ERM): A structured approach used by organizations to identify, assess, manage, and monitor risks. The COSO ERM framework integrates risk awareness with strategic objectives across the enterprise (COSO, 2017).

Ethical AI: The practice of designing, developing, and deploying AI systems in ways that align with human values, fairness, transparency, and accountability. Ethical AI ensures that innovation does not compromise equity or stakeholder trust (Floridi & Cowls, 2019).

Ethical Foresight: The proactive identification and mitigation of moral risks during technology design and deployment. It requires organizations to anticipate unintended consequences, engage diverse stakeholders, and embed ethical values into system development lifecycles. Ethical foresight transforms governance from reactive compliance to a strategic imperative (Jobin, Ienca, & Vayena, 2019).

Fairness Metrics: Quantitative indicators used to measure the equity of algorithmic outcomes. Common examples include demographic parity, equal opportunity, and disparate impact ratios. These metrics help data scientists and compliance teams evaluate whether AI systems treat individuals equitably across race, gender, and socioeconomic lines (Mehrabi et al., 2021).

Governance: The system of rules, practices, and processes by which an organization directs and controls technology use, including AI. Strong governance ensures accountability, transparency, and alignment between innovation and ethical standards (ISACA, 2019).

NIST AI Risk Management Framework (AI RMF): A set of guidelines developed by the U.S. National Institute of Standards and Technology to help organizations manage risks associated with AI systems. It includes four key functions: Map, Measure, Manage, and Govern (NIST, 2023).

Psychological Safety: A shared belief that individuals can speak up about ideas, concerns, or mistakes without fear of retribution. It is essential for ethical accountability, especially in high-risk or highly regulated environments such as healthcare (Edmondson, 2019).

Chapter 10
Bridging the Digital Divide: Enhancing Organizational Agility for Equitable Access in Urban and Rural Post-Secondary Education

Jagneet Kour
http://orcid.org/0009-0003-0341-3636
Akal University, Talwandi Sabo, India

Raino Bhatia
http://orcid.org/0000-0002-5379-3003
Eternal University, India

ABSTRACT

The transition towards digitally enhanced education in post-secondary institutions has intensified the need for organizational agility, especially in addressing digital equity between urban and rural learners. This chapter examines how educational institutions can leverage technology adoption and agile strategies to bridge the urban-rural digital divide in post-secondary education. Focusing on a comparative case study approach, the research investigates disparities in infrastructure, digital literacy, device accessibility, and internet connectivity across urban and rural settings. Drawing on interviews with administrators, faculty, and students, the study highlights organizational responses such as mobile learning solutions, low-bandwidth content delivery, community-based digital hubs, and policy reforms aimed at promoting inclusivity. The chapter further explores how leadership agility, adaptive decision-making, and stakeholder collaboration contribute to institutional resilience and responsiveness in the face of digital inequities.

DOI: 10.4018/979-8-2600-1016-7.ch010

INTRODUCTION

Background and Rationale

The global shift towards digitalization has transformed virtually every aspect of human activity, with education standing out as one of the most meaningfully pretentious realms. Post-secondary foundations such as universities, colleges, and vocational training centers have embraced technological innovations to reimagine teaching and learning processes. These changes include the rise of online education, blended learning models, digital assessment systems, and the integration of artificial intelligence and data analytics into academic operations (OECD, 2021; Zawacki-Richter et al., 2019). Yet, while technology has opened new opportunities for accessibility and innovation, it has simultaneously highlighted and exacerbated pre-existing inequalities. A central challenge within this transformation is the digital divide, a term that refers to disparities in access to digital technologies, internet connectivity, and the skills required to effectively utilize these resources (Warschauer, 2003). This chapter explores the complexities of the digital divide in the context of post-secondary education, with a specific focus on India and a comparative lens on global disparities. It begins by examining the conceptual foundations of the digital divide, followed by an analysis of its dimensions: physical access, digital literacy, and institutional readiness. The chapter then discusses how these inequalities manifest between urban and rural learners, between socio-economic groups, and across global regions, including their profound psychosocial impacts. Subsequently, the discussion evaluates the academic, social, and psychological consequences of the divide, with special attention to equity in higher education. The final sections consider policy initiatives, institutional responses grounded in organizational agility, and future directions for bridging the divide, ensuring that digitalization becomes a tool for inclusion rather than exclusion.

In the Indian context, the disparities between urban and rural educational institutions are particularly stark. While urban universities such as the University of Delhi have rapidly embraced digital transformation, rural institutions like Himachal Pradesh University and Eternal University in Himachal Pradesh face multiple infrastructural and socio-economic challenges that hinder technology adoption. According to the Digital India Progress Report (Government of India, 2022), only 30% of rural households in India have access to internet facilities, compared to over 70% in urban areas. Such discrepancies directly impact student learning experiences, retention rates, and overall academic performance. The COVID-19 pandemic further exposed these gaps, forcing institutions to adopt emergency remote teaching practices without adequate preparation. The crisis highlighted the need for educational institutions to become more agile in their organizational structures and decision-making processes to effectively manage unforeseen challenges and promote digital equity (Hodges et al., 2020; Tadesse & Muluye, 2020).

Conceptual Foundations of the Digital Divide

The term digital divide emerged in the 1990s as scholars, policymakers, and technologists recognized that technological advancements were not evenly distributed across populations. Warschauer (2003) described the divide as not merely a binary condition of having or not having technology, but rather as a complex interplay of access, skills, and social context. Later frameworks expanded the concept to include three levels:

- First-level digital divide states the differences in physical access to devices and internet connectivity.
- Second-level digital divide states the disparities in digital skills, literacy, and the ability to use technologies effectively.
- Third-level digital divide – inequalities in the outcomes and benefits derived from using technology, such as academic success or employability (van Dijk, 2006; Scheerder et al., 2017).

In higher education, these dimensions intersect with issues of socio-economic status, geographic location, institutional capacity, and cultural factors, shaping how students engage with digital learning. For instance, a rural student with limited broadband access not only faces difficulties attending synchronous online classes but may also lack the digital fluency to maximize learning platforms, leading to reduced academic outcomes and significant stress.

The Digital Transformation of Post-Secondary Education

Online Education and Blended Learning

The advent of Massive Open Online Courses (MOOCs) in the early 2010s signaled a new era in higher education, democratizing access to high-quality content from prestigious universities. This innovation was later expanded through institution-led online programs and blended learning models that combined face-to-face and virtual instruction. These pedagogies allowed flexibility in pacing, location, and delivery, aligning with the demands of a globalized knowledge economy (Garrison & Vaughan, 2008; Cai, Y., 2020).During the COVID-19 pandemic, online education shifted from being an alternative mode to becoming the primary modality of instruction. While this accelerated digital transformation, it also exposed glaring inequities: students without devices or internet access were effectively excluded from the learning process. A UNESCO (2020) report estimated that 40% of learners worldwide were unable to participate in remote education due to lack of digital resources, a figure that rose dramatically in regions like Sub-Saharan Africa and South Asia.

Digital Assessment Systems

Beyond teaching, assessment has also been digitalized. Tools such as learning management systems (LMS), online proctoring, and AI-enabled grading systems are now common in universities. While these tools enable scalability and efficiency, they presuppose stable connectivity and access to functioning hardware. Students from disadvantaged groups often report challenges in adapting to such systems, contributing to stress, anxiety, and reduced academic performance (Jisc, 2021; Williamson et al., 2020).

Dimensions of the Digital Divide in Higher Education

1. Access to Devices and Connectivity

At the most basic level, students require functional devices (laptops, tablets, or smartphones) and reliable internet connections. In many rural or underdeveloped regions, internet penetration remains inadequate. For instance, in India, urban areas report a 70% internet penetration rate, while rural areas lag at 37% (IAMAI, 2022). Even within developed countries, rural broadband infrastructure often trails behind urban areas (Pew Research Center, 2021). This fundamental gap is the first barrier to digital equity.

2. Digital Literacy

Possessing a device and internet access does not automatically translate to meaningful participation in digital education. Digital literacy, the ability to navigate software, manage online communication, critically evaluate information, and practice cyber safety is crucial. Frameworks such as Eshet-Alkalai's (2004) and more recent models by UNESCO (2018) emphasize that literacy involves cognitive and technical skills. Studies show that first-generation college students often exhibit lower digital literacy compared to peers from higher socio-economic backgrounds (Gorski, 2009). This skill gap limits their ability to maximize online learning tools, reducing engagement and performance and fostering feelings of inadequacy.

3. Institutional Readiness

Institutions themselves play a role in the divide. Well-resourced universities in urban centers often provide campus-wide high-speed Wi-Fi, digital libraries, and IT support services. In contrast, smaller or rural colleges may lack robust infrastructure, leaving students with fewer opportunities for digitally enriched learning. Institutional readiness also encompasses the digital competency of faculty and the availability of professional development to foster effective digital pedagogy (Selwyn, 2021).

Urban-Rural Disparities in Post-Secondary Education

The urban-rural digital divide is one of the most pressing challenges in higher education. Rural students often face multiple barriers simultaneously as inadequate connectivity, fewer institutional resources, and limited exposure to digital environments during earlier schooling. While this is stark in India, it is a global phenomenon. In Brazil, rural universities struggle with similar connectivity issues (OECD, 2021), while in parts of the United States, the rural broadband gap remains a significant policy challenge (FCC, 2021). This comparative perspective underscores that the challenges faced by Indian institutions are part of a larger, global inequity in digital infrastructure.

Socio-Economic Inequalities and the Digital Divide

Socio-economic status (SES) plays a critical role in digital access. Students from wealthier households can afford multiple devices, private internet connections, and supplementary digital tools such as software licenses or online tutoring. In contrast, low-income students may share a single device among multiple family members or rely on mobile data plans with limited bandwidth. During the pandemic, surveys from the Pew Research Center (2020) revealed that 59% of low-income students in the U.S. struggled with homework due to lack of devices or internet, compared to only 13% of students from high-income households. This gap reinforces existing inequalities in academic performance and persistence rates and is mirrored in the Indian context, where low-SES students in both urban and rural settings face compounded disadvantages.

Academic, Social, and Psychological Consequences

Academic Outcomes

The digital divide directly affects academic outcomes through reduced access to resources, difficulties in attending virtual lectures, and challenges in submitting assessments. Students on the disadvantaged side of the divide often exhibit lower grades, higher dropout rates, and reduced participation in advanced digital learning opportunities such as virtual labs or online internships (OECD, 2021; UNESCO, 2021).

Social Inclusion

Digital education also facilitates social networks, collaboration, and professional networking. Students excluded from these digital spaces risk missing out on building academic and professional communities, which are vital for employability (Rajendra et al., 2022).

Psychological Impacts

The psychological toll of the digital divide is considerable and warrants deeper exploration. Students struggling with connectivity or device issues often report stress, anxiety, and feelings of inadequacy compared to peers. The constant struggle to stay connected can lead to digital fatigue and burnout (Sahu, 2020; Wiederhold, 2021). Moreover, the stigma of technological disadvantage can further isolate marginalized students, exacerbating mental health concerns and hindering their adjustment to the learning environment, which is a known factor in academic performance (Kaur & Bhatia, 2024; Sahu, 2020).

Significance of the Study

Addressing digital inequity is crucial for achieving the United Nations Sustainable Development Goal 4 (Quality Education for All) and for promoting inclusive higher education systems (UNESCO, 2021). By focusing on organizational agility as a key mechanism for change, this chapter offers a unique contribution to existing literature on digital equity and educational leadership. It provides a framework for understanding how institutions can proactively respond to digital challenges, making it relevant for policymakers, administrators, and educators globally.

The Digital Divide as a Global Equity Issue

The divide is not confined within nations but manifests globally. Students in developed countries generally enjoy stronger infrastructure and institutional support, while learners in developing nations often face systemic barriers. The World Bank (2020) notes that in Sub-Saharan Africa, fewer than 25% of higher education students have reliable internet access, compared to over 90% in Europe and North America. Such disparities undermine global initiatives for inclusive and equitable education, as envisioned in the UN Sustainable Development Goal 4. The recent pandemic has made it clear that digital equity is not a national but a global imperative, requiring international collaboration and knowledge sharing.

Organizational Agility in Education

Organizational agility refers to an institution's ability to quickly sense environmental changes and respond effectively through adaptive strategies (Overby et al., 2006). In the context of post-secondary education, agility means the capacity to adjust teaching methods, technological infrastructure, and support services to meet students' evolving needs. Agile institutions demonstrate characteristics such as flexible decision-making, rapid deployment of technology solutions, stakeholder collaboration, and continuous feedback integration (Denning, 2018; Holbeche, 2018). Organizational agility, initially conceptualized in the business and management domains, has been critically adapted to education to reflect how institutions respond to rapid changes in technology, learner needs, and socio-economic challenges.

Organizational Agility and Digital Equity in Post-Secondary Education

The transition to digitalized education requires institutions to demonstrate not only technological readiness but also organizational agility, which encompasses the capacity to rapidly respond, adapt, and innovate in times of change. Denning (2018) outlines three dimensions of organizational agility that are strategic, operational, and leadership agility, all of which are crucial in bridging the digital divide in education. These dimensions provide a framework for analyzing how post-secondary institutions can ensure equitable access to digital learning opportunities.

1. Strategic Agility: Anticipating and Addressing Environmental Changes

Strategic agility refers to the institution's ability to anticipate shifts in the external environment such as pandemics, technological disruptions, or socio-economic inequalities and proactively address them (Denning, 2018). In the context of digital equity, this involves:

- **Forecasting digital needs**: Institutions that engage in long-term planning are more likely to recognize potential disparities in student access to devices, internet connectivity, and digital literacy. For example, universities that had already invested in digital infrastructure before COVID-19 (such as digital libraries and online course platforms) were better prepared to transition to fully remote learning.

- **Developing inclusive policies**: Strategic agility requires policies that prioritize inclusion, such as providing subsidized laptops or ensuring rural students can access offline learning resources. This is evident in Scandinavia's national frameworks for equal access (OECD, 2021) and India's NEP 2020.
- **Adapting curricula**: Anticipating that the future of education will increasingly blend physical and digital learning, agile institutions redesign curricula to be flexible and equally effective in in-person, online, or hybrid delivery.

A clear example of strategic agility can be seen in initiatives like the Commonwealth of Learning's digital resource-sharing programs, which allowed developing nations to quickly access educational materials when traditional instruction was disrupted. Institutions that lacked such foresight often found themselves scrambling to address inequities only after disparities had widened.

2. Operational Agility: Adapting Internal Processes and Infrastructure

Operational agility emphasizes efficiency in internal processes, systems, and technological infrastructure to support rapid adaptation (Denning, 2018). For post-secondary institutions, this plays a direct role in narrowing the digital divide:

- **Digital Infrastructure**: Agile institutions prioritize investments in reliable learning management systems (LMS), cloud-based platforms, and secure networks that can handle large-scale online instruction. For example, the University of Cape Town shifted to mobile-compatible LMS tools to reach students in low-bandwidth regions.
- **Support Systems**: Operational agility involves creating robust student support mechanisms, such as digital help desks, peer-support networks, and IT troubleshooting services, ensuring students can effectively engage with digital platforms regardless of their prior experience.
- **Flexible Assessment Models**: Institutions demonstrated operational agility during the pandemic by adopting open-book online exams, project-based assessments, and continuous evaluation methods, which reduced reliance on high-stakes in-person testing that disadvantaged rural or low-income learners.
- **Partnerships**: Operational agility often requires collaborating with governments and private partners to expand access. For example, some universities partnered with telecom companies to provide free or discounted internet data packages to students. Such multi-stakeholder partnerships are crucial

for scaling innovative solutions and bridging resource gaps (Bhatia & Kaur, 2024).

Without operational agility, even the most inclusive policies can fail. For instance, distributing laptops without creating technical support structures leaves students unequipped to resolve basic problems, furthering inequity.

3. Leadership Agility: Fostering a Culture of Adaptability and Resilience

Leadership agility refers to the ability of institutional leaders to inspire, mobilize, and cultivate resilience among stakeholders (Denning, 2018). This dimension is critical because technology-driven transformation requires not just new tools but also profound cultural change and emotional intelligence to guide communities through periods of stress and uncertainty (Kour & Bhatia, 2025).

- **Visionary Leadership**: Leaders who recognize digital equity as a fundamental right frame it not as a temporary challenge but as part of the institution's mission. This helps ensure sustained efforts, such as long-term investment in digital access, rather than short-term crisis management.
- **Inclusive Decision-Making**: Agile leaders engage diverse stakeholders as students, faculty, administrators, and policymakers in designing digital solutions. For instance, participatory approaches to course redesign ensure that both technologically advanced and disadvantaged students' needs are considered.
- **Professional Development**: Leadership agility fosters adaptability by investing in continuous faculty training in digital pedagogy. Equipping educators with the skills to teach online or in hybrid modes reduces disparities in learning outcomes.
- **Crisis Management and Resilience**: During COVID-19, leaders who quickly communicated clear strategies, offered mental health resources, and mobilized financial aid for students exemplified leadership agility. Their actions reassured students and minimized the sense of exclusion experienced by those struggling with digital access.

An example comes from **India's National Education Policy (NEP 2020)**, where leaders emphasized digital inclusion as part of the policy vision, encouraging innovation while stressing affordability and accessibility.

Theoretical Framework: Organizational Agility Theory in Higher Education

Organizational agility has emerged as a crucial framework for understanding how institutions adapt in rapidly changing environments. Overby et al. (2006) define organizational agility as the capacity of an institution to sense environmental changes, seize emerging opportunities, and transform operations accordingly. Within the context of higher education, agility refers to the institution's ability to modify academic programs, pedagogical strategies, and administrative processes in response to external disruptions such as technological innovations, policy reforms, or global crises like the COVID-19 pandemic. Holbeche (2018) emphasizes that organizational agility extends beyond operational flexibility; it involves strategic foresight and the ability to embed adaptability into the institutional culture. In universities and colleges, this often manifests in the redesign of curricula to include digital competencies, the adoption of hybrid learning models, and the restructuring of administrative systems to support flexible delivery. Post-secondary institutions, traditionally criticized for bureaucratic rigidity, are increasingly realizing the importance of agility in sustaining their relevance in a competitive and digitally driven landscape (Cai, 2020).

Denning's (2018) three dimensions collectively demonstrate how agility is not merely about technological readiness but about an institution's capacity to align vision, operations, and culture. Cai (2020) highlights that agile post-secondary institutions were able to:

- Rapidly distribute devices and internet solutions to disadvantaged students.
- Redesign programs for blended and asynchronous delivery.
- Scale up student support services, including digital literacy training.
- Foster resilience in academic communities by encouraging collaboration and inclusivity.

Thus, organizational agility offers a lens through which institutions can proactively reduce digital inequities rather than reactively responding after disparities have taken root.

Linking Organizational Agility and Digital Equity

The rapid digitalization of education has amplified both opportunities and challenges for post-secondary institutions. While digital technologies have created avenues for innovation in teaching, assessment, and student support, the uneven distribution of access and skills has widened disparities between socio-economic, rural–urban, and institutional contexts. In this scenario, organizational agility becomes a critical enabler of digital equity, allowing institutions to adapt, innovate, and ensure inclusive participation in the digital learning ecosystem.

Conceptualizing the Nexus between Agility and Equity

Organizational agility, as Denning (2018) outlines, consists of three interrelated dimensions strategic agility, operational agility, and leadership agility. These capacities enable organizations to anticipate changes, modify internal structures efficiently, and foster adaptability in human capital. When applied to post-secondary education, agility becomes the foundation through which institutions can respond to digital inequities. For instance, strategic agility allows universities to anticipate inequities such as rural learners' limited internet connectivity or students' inability to afford expensive devices. By proactively investing in hybrid or offline-compatible learning platforms, institutions preempt exclusion. Operational agility ensures the rapid development and deployment of cost-effective solutions such as mobile-first applications, downloadable e-learning modules, or device-lending schemes. Meanwhile, leadership agility cultivates a climate of collaboration among faculty, administrators, and policymakers to co-create solutions that address systemic disparities. Alavi et al. (2014) argue that agility in education is inherently tied to organizational learning, where continuous adaptation based on stakeholder feedback fuels institutional resilience. Applied to digital equity, this means that institutions that learn from students' lived experiences of technological marginalization are better positioned to bridge the digital divide.

Strategic Agility and Long-term Policy Shifts

Strategic agility requires foresight in aligning institutional policies with broader goals of inclusion and accessibility. Institutions that demonstrate this capability often move beyond temporary fixes and create systemic frameworks to promote digital equity.

For example:

- Universities in Scandinavia have adopted national frameworks mandating equal access to digital learning resources, regardless of students' socio-economic status (OECD, 2021).
- Strategic agility here is reflected in long-term investments such as partnerships with telecommunication providers to subsidize internet access for students in remote regions.

- Policy innovations, such as mandating universal design principles in courseware development, ensure that digital learning resources are accessible to students with disabilities.

In essence, strategic agility institutionalizes equity into the DNA of educational systems, transforming it from an optional initiative into a structural imperative.

Operational Agility: Scaling Rapid Responses

Operational agility translates strategic intent into tangible, scalable practices. During the COVID-19 pandemic, many institutions exemplified this dimension by deploying emergency remote teaching (ERT) within weeks. However, operational agility is not just about speed, it is also about efficiency and inclusivity.

- Some Indian universities rapidly developed low-bandwidth platforms to deliver lectures to students in rural areas, where internet speeds are inconsistent.
- African post-secondary institutions have leveraged mobile phone–based learning systems, given that mobile penetration far exceeds laptop ownership (Cai, 2020).
- Operational agility also manifests in student support systems such as digital helpdesks, peer tutoring, and digital literacy bootcamps, which help students adapt to new technologies.

Thus, operational agility ensures that technological adoption is not merely reactive but sensitive to diverse student contexts, preventing the exclusion of marginalized groups.

Leadership Agility: Driving a Culture of Inclusivity

Leadership agility is arguably the linchpin of organizational responsiveness. Leaders who embrace agility foster cultures where experimentation, collaboration, and adaptability are valued.

- Faculty members encouraged by agile leadership often co-design learning innovations with students, ensuring that solutions are grounded in lived realities rather than abstract policy goals.
- Leaders who prioritize inclusivity may direct resources toward device-lending programs, mental health support for digital stress, or staff training in inclusive pedagogy.

- By promoting open channels of communication, agile leaders ensure that feedback loops from marginalized students shape institutional decision-making.

Denning (2018) emphasizes that leadership agility is about resilience and adaptability, qualities that are indispensable in ensuring that digital transformation does not deepen inequalities but rather becomes a tool for empowerment.

Organizational Learning as a Mediator

Alavi et al. (2014) underscore that agility in education is inherently tied to the organization's ability to learn and adapt continuously. This idea is particularly relevant to digital equity, where inequities are dynamic and context-specific.

- For instance, feedback from students during the pandemic revealed not only issues of internet access but also psychological barriers to online learning, such as digital fatigue and social isolation. Institutions that engaged in iterative learning cycles were able to redesign courses to include asynchronous participation options and integrate well-being check-ins (Wiederhold, 2021).
- Continuous monitoring of data on student engagement, dropout rates, and performance further informs agile decision-making, allowing institutions to refine equity strategies.

Thus, organizational learning functions as a bridge between agility and equity, ensuring that solutions evolve alongside challenges.

Practical Implications for Post-secondary Institutions

Linking organizational agility with digital equity has several implications:

1. Technology Adoption Strategies: Agile institutions do not adopt technologies uniformly; instead, they tailor adoption strategies to ensure maximum accessibility, such as offering both high- and low-tech options.
2. Collaborative Innovation: Leadership agility fosters interdisciplinary collaborations, where IT specialists, faculty, and students co-create inclusive digital platforms.
3. Scalability and Cost-efficiency: Operational agility ensures that solutions are scalable across departments and sustainable for institutions with limited resources.
4. Policy Advocacy: Strategic agility positions institutions as advocates for national-level reforms, such as universal broadband access or subsidized digital tools for students.

The intersection of organizational agility and digital equity represents both a challenge and an opportunity for post-secondary institutions. Agility equips institutions with the capacity to sense inequities early, respond through innovative practices, and institutionalize long-term equity frameworks. By leveraging strategic, operational, and leadership agility, educational organizations can ensure that digital transformation does not exacerbate existing divides but rather becomes a pathway toward inclusivity and resilience. Ultimately, in an era where education is increasingly mediated by technology, organizational agility is not merely a managerial advantage but a moral imperative one that enables the creation of equitable and sustainable digital learning ecosystems. This chapter explores the intersection between organizational agility and digital equity in post-secondary education. By examining the case of two contrasting Indian institutions, one urban (Delhi University) and one rural (Himachal Pradesh University/Eternal University). This study aims to identify how organizational agility has enabled or hindered efforts to bridge the digital divide.

METHODOLOGY

Research Design

This chapter employs a comparative qualitative case study design to investigate how organizational agility supports digital equity initiatives in urban and rural post-secondary education institutions in India. The case study method allows for an in-depth exploration of institutional contexts, leadership responses, technology adoption strategies, and stakeholder experiences (Yin, 2018). This design is particularly suited to capturing the nuanced, context-dependent nature of organizational agility.

Case Selection

Two post-secondary institutions were purposefully selected to represent urban and rural educational contexts, providing a stark contrast in resources and challenges:

1. **Urban Case: University of Delhi (DU), New Delhi**

As a leading urban institution with a wide range of digital infrastructure, DU offers insights into technology adoption strategies in resource-rich environments and how agility is operationalized with relative advantage.

2. **Rural Case: Eternal University (EU), Baru Sahib, Himachal Pradesh**

A private rural university serving first-generation learners from remote villages in North India. EU faces typical rural challenges such as low bandwidth, limited device access, and students from low socio-economic backgrounds, offering a critical view of agility under significant constraints.

This urban-rural comparison provides a meaningful contrast to analyze how organizational agility affects digital equity initiatives under differing resource constraints.

Participants

A total of 70 participants were involved across both institutions, ensuring a diversity of perspectives from key stakeholder groups:

Table 1.

Participant Group	University of Delhi (Urban)	Eternal University (Rural)
Administrators	5	5
Faculty Members	10	10
Students	20	20
Total	35	35

Participants were selected using purposive sampling, ensuring a diversity of academic departments and socio-economic backgrounds among students.

Data Collection Methods

Three primary data sources were used:

1. Semi-structured Interviews: Conducted with administrators, faculty, and students to gather firsthand narratives on digital access challenges and institutional responses, and the psychosocial impact of these challenges. Interview guides were tailored to each stakeholder group.
2. Document Analysis: Institutional reports, technology policy documents, Digital India-related communications, and internal memoranda on COVID-19 response were reviewed to understand the formal strategic posture of each institution.
3. Secondary Data: Statistical reports from the Ministry of Education, Digital India dashboard, and internal surveys from both universities were analyzed to contextualize the qualitative findings.

Interviews were conducted via Zoom and phone calls due to COVID-19 restrictions, and were recorded and transcribed verbatim for analysis.

Data Analysis

Data were analyzed using **thematic analysis** following Braun and Clarke's (2006) six-phase model:

1. Familiarization with data
2. Coding
3. Identifying initial themes
4. Reviewing themes
5. Defining and naming themes
6. Writing up the report

NVivo software was used to facilitate the coding process and visualize relationships between themes, ensuring a systematic and rigorous approach.

Ethical Considerations

The study adhered to strict ethical standards. Participants were assured of confidentiality and anonymity. Institutional permission and informed consent were obtained before data collection. Ethical approval was secured from both institutions' Research Ethics Committees.

FINDINGS

Thematic analysis revealed four major themes across the two case studies, highlighting how organizational agility manifested in different ways to address digital equity challenges.

Theme 1: Disparities in Digital Infrastructure

Urban Institution (Delhi University):

- High-speed internet across campus.
- Well-equipped smart classrooms.
- Students mostly owned smartphones, laptops, or tablets.
- Use of platforms like Google Classroom, Moodle, and Zoom.

Rural Institution (Eternal University):

- Frequent power cuts and internet outages.
- Limited smart classrooms.
- Many students owned only basic smartphones.
- Low bandwidth often limited video-based learning.

Student Quote (EU):
"I had to seek higher ground to catch internet signals during online classes."
Discussion:
The infrastructure gap significantly shaped students' learning experiences. For many in remote areas or restricted spaces like hostels, internet connectivity was nonexistent or highly unstable, resulting in lost signals and cracked audio during crucial lessons. Organizational agility at DU allowed rapid scaling up of online services. In direct response to these challenges, EU adopted low-data tools like WhatsApp-based teaching and Google meet which eliminated the need for students to search for elevated spots just to find a connection.

Theme 2: Agile Leadership and Decision-Making Processes

Delhi University:

- Rapid adoption and scaling of Learning Management Systems (LMS) across colleges.
- Formation of an Emergency Digital Learning Committee within two weeks of lockdown to coordinate response.
- Quick policy shifts allowing flexibility in assessment submissions and alternative assignment formats.

Eternal University:

- Leadership created micro-learning modules in PDF format, downloadable for offline study.
- Faculty were encouraged to develop audio lectures distributed via mobile applications like Telegram and WhatsApp.
- Proactive partnerships with local telecom providers to enhance campus bandwidth and provide discounted data packs for students.

Administrator Quote (EU):
"We realized that sticking to conventional online platforms wasn't feasible, so we adopted whatever low-cost tools worked for our students. Our strategy was flexibility, not perfection."

Discussion:

Both institutions demonstrated leadership agility, but contextual limitations profoundly shaped their strategies. DU's agility was characterized by rapid deployment of existing robust systems. EU's solutions were more grassroots-driven, adaptive, and innovative, born directly from technological constraints.

Theme 3: Faculty Adaptation and Capacity Building

Delhi University:

- University-organized faculty development programs (FDPs) and webinars on digital pedagogy and tools.
- Faculty quickly transitioned to flipped classrooms and interactive online assessments leveraging the stable infrastructure.

Eternal University:

- Peer-to-peer faculty training emerged due to limited access to external FDPs. Tech-savvy faculty mentored colleagues.
- Focus on asynchronous teaching methods (recorded lectures, reading materials) to accommodate connectivity issues.
- Faculty innovation in content compression (e.g., creating 2MB PDFs) to reduce data consumption for students.

Faculty Quote (EU):

"We used to share lecture summaries in 2 MB PDFs because many students couldn't download large files. We had to be creative with every byte of data."

Discussion:

Faculty agility became a critical frontline response in both settings. While urban faculty leveraged institutional support to enhance teaching, rural faculty agility was a necessity, leading to context-specific, low-tech innovations that were crucial for maintaining educational continuity.

Theme 4: Student Support Systems and Digital Literacy Initiatives

Delhi University:

- Established online student helplines and chat support for technical issues.

- Conducted digital orientation programs for new students on using the LMS and e-library resources.
- Provided access to institutional Wi-Fi and extensive digital libraries.

Eternal University:

- Conducted basic digital literacy workshops on how to use learning apps, submit assignments online, and participate in video calls.
- Created a Student Peer Mentor Program where digitally skilled students supported others, fostering a community-based approach.
- Set up an "Offline Resource Corner" where students could collect printed study material, USB drives with lectures, and submit assignments physically.

Student Quote (DU):
"We had online tutorials on how to use LMS and access e-library resources. It was very systematic."
Student Quote (EU):
"Our seniors helped us learn how to attend Google Meet classes and submit assignments by email."
Discussion:

Both institutions recognized that access alone was insufficient without support. DU's approach was formalized and centralized, while EU's was informal, community-driven, and often hybrid (mixing digital and physical), directly addressing the lack of reliable digital access. The peer-mentoring model at EU was particularly effective in building confidence and reducing the anxiety associated with digital learning, thereby facilitating student adjustment and creating conditions more conducive to academic success (Kaur & Bhatia, 2024).

Table 2. **Summary of Comparative Findings**

Aspect	Delhi University (Urban)	Eternal University (Rural)
Infrastructure	High bandwidth, advanced tools	Limited, low-cost, offline-focused tools
Leadership Response	Rapid digital transition	Contextual, low-tech innovations
Faculty Adaptation	Structured online pedagogy training	Informal, peer-driven digital teaching skills
Student Support	Centralized digital helpdesks	Peer mentors, offline resource distribution

Integrative Reflection

The case studies demonstrate that organizational agility is not a monolithic concept but manifests differently depending on context. Urban institutions like DU focus on leveraging and scaling existing technological infrastructure. Rural institutions like EU prioritize creative, low-resource, and often hybrid solutions to maximize access and inclusion. In both contexts, leadership flexibility, stakeholder engagement, and a willingness to innovate were central to overcoming digital equity barriers. These findings align with Denning's (2018) assertion that agile organizations adapt their strategies based on environmental constraints while keeping learner needs at the center. Furthermore, the findings highlight that agility in resource-constrained environments often requires a more profound level of creativity and community mobilization, turning constraints into catalysts for contextually relevant innovation.

DISCUSSION

The findings from this comparative case study of Delhi University (urban) and Eternal University (rural) reveal significant insights into how organizational agility can help post-secondary institutions address digital equity challenges across diverse contexts. The discussion situates these findings within the broader theoretical framework and existing literature.

Organizational Agility as a Catalyst for Change

Organizational agility emerged as a critical enabler in responding to digital disparities. In line with Overby et al. (2006), both institutions demonstrated varying degrees of sensing, decision-making, and adaptive response. At Delhi University, agility manifested through rapid deployment of LMS tools, digital faculty training, and online student support systems. Eternal University, despite infrastructural constraints, exhibited agility through grassroots innovations, flexible teaching approaches, and community-driven solutions. These examples affirm Denning's (2018) perspective that agility is not limited to resource-rich settings but can be operationalized in resource-constrained environments through creativity and stakeholder engagement.

Contextual Differences and Similarities

A notable finding is the stark divergence in digital infrastructure readiness, which shaped the expression of agility. The urban-rural divide reflected substantial differences in bandwidth availability, device ownership, and institutional technological capabilities. However, both universities shared a common commitment to minimizing student learning disruptions, demonstrating that the imperative for agility is universal, even if its execution is not. Whereas Delhi University leveraged its advanced infrastructure for efficiency and scale, Eternal University compensated through frugal innovation and offline resource distribution. This aligns perfectly with Holbeche's (2018) argument that agility is context-dependent and may take different operational forms in different institutional settings. The EU case proves that a lack of resources does not preclude agility; it redefines it.

Faculty and Leadership Agility

Faculty members in both settings demonstrated remarkable adaptability, which was a cornerstone of the institutional response. This reflects Cai's (2020) model of organizational learning agility. At DU, faculty embraced and were trained in flipped classroom models and interactive online assessments. At EU, faculty agency was even more critical, as they developed compressed learning materials and audio-based lessons suitable for low-bandwidth environments, often with peer-supported rather than institutional training. Leadership agility was evident in the creation of rapid-response committees, pragmatic policy revisions for digital learning, and resource reallocation to support students facing digital access issues. These adaptive governance structures support the proposition that leadership flexibility is a core pillar of organizational agility (Overby et al., 2006). The EU leadership's willingness to embrace "low-tech" solutions was a key factor in maintaining inclusivity.

Digital Literacy as an Equity Factor

Digital literacy gaps were more pronounced among rural students, corroborating findings from Gorski (2009) and Warschauer (2003). Both institutions initiated digital literacy programs, but the methods differed significantly: DU offered structured workshops, while EU relied on informal peer support models, which proved highly effective in building trust and reducing anxiety. The study also confirmed the severe psychosocial impacts of the digital divide, particularly in the rural context, where students reported significant stress, isolation, and feelings of inadequacy (Sahu, 2020). This demonstrates that institutional agility must not only address infrastructural and skill gaps but also actively integrate psychological and peer support mechanisms to address the holistic wellbeing of students.

Implications for Higher Education Policy

This study underscores the need for policy frameworks that support contextually nuanced agility and digital equity simultaneously. The Government of India's Digital India initiative (Government of India, 2022) provides macro-level support, but institutional-level agility is essential for contextual implementation. Policies must be flexible enough to empower rural institutions to adopt innovative models suited to their unique challenges, rather than imposing one-size-fits-all technological mandates. Funding schemes should support sustainable agility projects in rural institutions, such as partnerships for affordable connectivity and grants for developing offline-digital hybrid learning resources. Without supporting this localized agility, top-down policy initiatives may fail to translate into ground-level impact (Selwyn, 2021).

STRATEGIES AND RECOMMENDATIONS

Based on the findings and discussion, the following actionable recommendations are proposed for policymakers, institutional leaders, and educators:

Infrastructure Development for Rural Institutions

- Government and private sector partnerships (PPP models) should prioritize improving internet connectivity and power stability in rural campuses through dedicated initiatives.
- Low-cost hardware programs (e.g., subsidized tablets, laptops, or smartphone financing schemes) should be initiated specifically for economically disadvantaged students in both rural and urban areas.

Contextualized Digital Pedagogy

- Institutions, especially in rural areas, should prioritize the design of teaching resources that are compatible with low-bandwidth environments (e.g., text-based modules, compressed audio lessons).
- Asynchronous and offline learning modes should be strengthened and formally integrated into curriculum planning to support students with intermittent internet access.

Comprehensive Faculty Capacity Building

- Nationwide digital pedagogy training programs (e.g., by the UGC) must include special modules focused on teaching in low-resource settings, digital inclusivity, and mental health awareness.
- Formalized peer-mentoring and twinning networks between urban and rural institutions can facilitate continuous knowledge-sharing and support.

Integrated Digital Literacy and Wellbeing Programs

- Institutions should conduct regular, mandatory digital literacy workshops for both students and faculty, moving beyond tool use to critical digital citizenship.
- Student support systems must integrate psychosocial support, such as counseling services that address digital stress and anxiety, and peer mentor programs to foster belonging.

Leadership Training for Organizational Agility

- Higher education leadership development programs should incorporate principles of agile leadership, such as rapid decision-making, iterative planning, and stakeholder engagement.
- Establishing internal "Digital Equity Task Forces" with representatives from all stakeholders can help continuously monitor challenges, gather feedback, and implement solutions.

Policy Support for Institutional Agility

- Regulatory bodies like the University Grants Commission (UGC) should introduce flexible policy guidelines that encourage innovative academic practices (e.g., blended learning, alternative assessments) during digital disruptions.
- Government funding schemes should specifically support agile technology adoption projects in rural institutions, with a focus on sustainability and local capacity building.

FUTURE DIRECTIONS

The journey towards digital equity is ongoing and must evolve with new technologies and challenges. Future directions include:

Artificial Intelligence and Adaptive Learning

As AI becomes integrated into education (e.g., through adaptive learning platforms and automated feedback), ensuring equitable access is critical. Research and policy must focus on developing low-cost, offline-capable AI tools and preventing the emergence of a new "AI divide." Ethical frameworks for AI in education are needed to ensure fairness and transparency.

Digital Wellbeing and Inclusivity

Future digital initiatives must incorporate a focus on digital wellbeing, combating issues like screen fatigue and promoting healthy digital habits. Technologies and pedagogies must be designed to be inclusive of learners with disabilities from the outset, adhering to universal design for learning (UDL) principles.

Global Collaboration

International organizations (e.g., UNESCO, World Bank) should foster global collaborations to share best practices, innovative low-cost solutions, and policy frameworks. South-South collaboration can be particularly valuable in sharing contextually relevant strategies for digital equity.

Longitudinal Impact Research

Future research should employ longitudinal designs to track the long-term impact of agile strategies on student academic outcomes, retention, and employability. Further comparative studies across different national contexts will deepen our understanding of how agility functions in varied cultural and economic landscapes.

CONCLUSION

This chapter has explored how organizational agility enables post-secondary institutions to address digital equity challenges across urban and rural contexts in India. Through comparative case studies of Delhi University and Eternal University, the research highlights that while resource availability shapes technology adoption strategies, agility in leadership, faculty adaptation, and stakeholder collaboration play equally critical roles. The study contributes to both theoretical and practical discourses by integrating organizational agility and digital equity frameworks. The findings emphasize that agility is not a one-size-fits-all solution; instead, it requires contextual adaptation grounded in institutional realities and a deep understanding of student needs. By integrating organizational agility and digital equity, the theoretical framework underscores that agility is not only about survival in a volatile environment but also about justice and inclusion. Post-secondary institutions must view agility not as an isolated administrative skill but as a moral and strategic commitment to reducing inequities in digital learning. The lessons from India, with its stark contrasts, offer insights for global audiences facing similar, if less pronounced, disparities. The imperative is clear: building agile, equitable, and resilient educational systems is fundamental to ensuring that the future of digital learning is inclusive for all. Future research could expand on this work by exploring the longitudinal impacts of agile strategies, by conducting cross-national comparisons, and by delving deeper into the role of emerging technologies like AI. The findings hold significant value for policymakers, institutional leaders, and educators worldwide who are seeking to create inclusive, technology-enabled learning environments that serve every learner equitably.

REFERENCES

Alavi, S., Amini, A., Jandaghi, G., & Hoseini, S. M. (2014). The effect of organizational agility on performance with a case study in hospitals. *International Journal of Academic Research in Business & Social Sciences*, *4*(4), 171–180.

Bhatia, R., & Kaur, J. (2024). Collaborating Academia, Industry, and Government: Enhancing Business Practices Through Innovative Pedagogies. In Fostering Industry-Academia Partnerships for Innovation-Driven Trade (pp. 40-53). IGI Global.

Braun, V., & Clarke, V. (2006). Using thematic analysis in psychology. *Qualitative Research in Psychology*, *3*(2), 77–101. DOI: 10.1191/1478088706qp063oa

Cai, L. (2020). Agile transformation in higher education: Organizational agility in universities. *Journal of Organizational Change Management*, *33*(6), 1132–1144.

Cai, W. (2020). Building agility into higher education: Theory and practice. *International Journal of Educational Management*, *34*(4), 755–769.

Cai, Y. (2020). The impact of COVID-19 on higher education: A review of emerging evidence. *International Higher Education*, (102), 6–8.

Denning, S. (2018). *The age of agile: How smart companies are transforming the way work gets done*. AMACOM.

Eshet-Alkalai, Y. (2004). Digital literacy: A conceptual framework for survival skills in the digital era. *Journal of Educational Multimedia and Hypermedia*, *13*(1), 93–106.

FCC. (2021). 2021 Broadband Deployment Report. Federal Communications Commission. https://www.fcc.gov/reports-research/reports/broadband-progress-reports/2021-broadband-deployment-report

Garrison, D. R., & Vaughan, N. D. (2008). *Blended learning in higher education: Framework, principles, and guidelines*. Jossey-Bass.

Gorski, P. C. (2009). Insisting on digital equity: Reframing the dominant discourse on multicultural education and technology. *Urban Education*, *44*(3), 348–364. DOI: 10.1177/0042085908318712

Government of India. (2022). *Digital India Progress Report*. Ministry of Electronics and Information Technology.

Hodges, C., Moore, S., Lockee, B., Trust, T., & Bond, A. (2020). The difference between emergency remote teaching and online learning. *EDUCAUSE Review*, •••, 27.

Holbeche, L. (2018). *The agile organization: How to build an innovative, sustainable and resilient business*. Kogan Page Publishers.

IAMAI. (2022). *Internet in India Report*. Internet and Mobile Association of India.

Jisc. (2021). Digital experience insights survey. Jisc.

Kaur, J., & Bhatia, R. (2024). Synchrony in Learning: Investigating the Connection between Student Adjustment and Academic Performance. *Journal of Research in Education and Pedagogy*, *1*(2), 132–139. DOI: 10.70232/jrep.v1i2.16

Kour, J., & Bhatia, R. (2025). From self-awareness to social skills: The journey of emotionally intelligent leadership. In *Emotionally intelligent methods for meaningful leadership* (pp. 173–196). IGI Global Scientific Publishing.

OECD. (2021). *Education in the Digital Age: Healthy and Happy Children*. OECD Publishing.

OECD. (2021). *The state of higher education: One year into the COVID-19 pandemic*. OECD Publishing.

Overby, E., Bharadwaj, A., & Sambamurthy, V. (2006). Enterprise agility and the enabling role of information technology. *European Journal of Information Systems*, *15*(2), 120–131. DOI: 10.1057/palgrave.ejis.3000600

Pew Research Center. (2020). Digital divide persists even as lower-income Americans make gains in tech adoption. Pew.

Pew Research Center. (2021). Mobile Technology and Home Broadband 2021. Pew.

Rajendra, R., Mishra, S., & Tripathi, S. (2022). Social isolation and digital connectedness: A study of Indian students during the COVID-19 pandemic. *Journal of Educational Technology Systems*, *50*(4), 495–514.

Sahu, P. (2020). Closure of universities due to COVID-19: Impact on education and mental health. *Cureus*, *12*(4). PMID: 32377489

Scheerder, A., van Deursen, A., & van Dijk, J. (2017). Determinants of Internet skills, uses and outcomes. A systematic review of the second- and third-level digital divide. *Telematics and Informatics*, *34*(8), 1607–1624. DOI: 10.1016/j.tele.2017.07.007

Selwyn, N. (2004). Reconsidering political and popular understandings of the digital divide. *New Media & Society*, *6*(3), 341–362. DOI: 10.1177/1461444804042519

Selwyn, N. (2021). *Education and Technology: Key Issues and Debates* (3rd ed.). Bloomsbury Academic.

Tadesse, S., & Muluye, W. (2020). The impact of COVID-19 pandemic on education system in developing countries: A review. *Open Journal of Social Sciences*, *8*(10), 159–170. DOI: 10.4236/jss.2020.810011

UNESCO. (2018). *A global framework of reference on digital literacy skills for indicator 4.4.2*. UNESCO Institute for Statistics.

UNESCO. (2020). *Education in a post-COVID world: Nine ideas for public action*. UNESCO.

UNESCO. (2021). *Education and Digital Transformation Report*. United Nations Educational, Scientific and Cultural Organization.

Van Dijk, J. (2006). Digital divide research, achievements and shortcomings. *Poetics*, *34*(4–5), 221–235. DOI: 10.1016/j.poetic.2006.05.004

Warschauer, M. (2003). *Technology and social inclusion: Rethinking the digital divide*. MIT Press. DOI: 10.7551/mitpress/6699.001.0001

Wiederhold, B. K. (2021). The Role of Psychology in Enhancing Cybersecurity. *Cyberpsychology, Behavior, and Social Networking*, *24*(5), 291–292. PMID: 34003012

Williamson, B., Eynon, R., & Potter, J. (2020). Pandemic politics, pedagogies and practices: Digital technologies and distance education during the coronavirus emergency. *Learning, Media and Technology*, *45*(2), 107–114. DOI: 10.1080/17439884.2020.1761641

World Bank. (2020). The COVID-19 pandemic: Shocks to education and policy responses. World Bank.

Yin, R. K. (2018). *Case study research and applications: Design and methods* (6th ed.). SAGE Publications.

Zawacki-Richter, O., Marin, V. I., Bond, M., & Gouverneur, F. (2019). Systematic review of research on artificial intelligence applications in higher education – where are the educators? *International Journal of Educational Technology in Higher Education*, *16*(1), 39. DOI: 10.1186/s41239-019-0171-0

Chapter 11
Studying and Researching the Psychology Dynamics of Organizational Cybercrime and Cybersecurity

Sharon L. Burton
http://orcid.org/0000-0003-1653-9783
Embry-Riddle Aeronautical University, USA

Darrell Norman Burrell
http://orcid.org/0000-0002-4675-9544
Marymount University, USA

Adina Lundy
http://orcid.org/0000-0001-7564-2110
University of Rhode Island, USA

Calvin Nobles
http://orcid.org/0000-0003-4002-1108
University of Maryland Global Campus, USA

Maurice Dawson
http://orcid.org/0000-0003-4609-3444
Illinois Institute of Technology, USA

Laura A. Jones
http://orcid.org/0000-0002-0299-370X
Capitol Technology University, USA

Samantha Thibodeau
http://orcid.org/0009-0000-4639-9166
Marymount University, USA

Chitra N. Perera
http://orcid.org/0009-0005-3431-4969
Marymount University, USA

Philip Reed
http://orcid.org/0009-0000-1266-0151
Marymount University, USA

Gregory Karl Smith
http://orcid.org/0009-0000-5122-2250
Marymount University, USA

Kylei L. Conti
http://orcid.org/0009-0009-0495-6601
Marymount University, USA

DOI: 10.4018/979-8-2600-1016-7.ch011

Julia DeFrance
http://orcid.org/0009-0005-8105-2594
Marymount University, USA

ABSTRACT

This qualitative study examines healthcare cybercrime through the lens of criminal psychology and cybersecurity risk management, emphasizing the behavioral dynamics that enable repeated system compromise. Using semi-structured Zoom interviews with ten professionals holding graduate education in cyberpsychology, criminal psychology, criminal justice, cybersecurity, and human factors, the study explored offender strategies, organizational decision-making, and guardianship effectiveness. Findings indicate that cybercriminals systematically exploit cognitive overload, authority bias, and normalized risk behaviors within healthcare environments, while organizational fragmentation and short-term risk perceptions weaken defensive capacity. Participants emphasized that cybersecurity failures are rarely technical in isolation but emerge from predictable human and cultural vulnerabilities.

INTRODUCTION

The accelerated digitization of healthcare has produced a profound and increasingly dangerous paradox in which technologies designed to enhance patient care simultaneously amplify exposure to cybercrime (Burrell, 2024; Burton, 2024; Burrell, 2023; Burrell et al., 2023). Electronic health records, interoperable clinical platforms, cloud-based infrastructures, and network-connected medical devices have reshaped healthcare delivery into a data-intensive enterprise, yet this transformation has also expanded the cognitive and technical terrain available to motivated offenders (Burrell, 2024). From a criminal psychology perspective, healthcare systems represent ideal targets because they combine high-value, immutable data with environments characterized by urgency, trust, and uneven cybersecurity literacy. Cybercriminals do not merely exploit software vulnerabilities; they deliberately study organizational behavior, staff routines, and institutional stress points to identify moments when human judgment is most likely to fail. In this sense, modern healthcare cybercrime is best understood not as a purely technical phenomenon, but as a behavioral one in which adversaries weaponize psychology as effectively as malware threats.

Healthcare cybercrime increasingly reflects sophisticated patterns of psychological manipulation rooted in principles of persuasion, coercion, and risk calculus (Burrell, 2024). Attackers routinely leverage authority bias by impersonating executives, vendors, or regulatory bodies, knowing that hierarchical cultures discourage challenge and delay. Urgency is deliberately manufactured through ransomware countdowns, spoofed emergency requests, or fabricated system alerts that compel rapid action without verification. Workflow fatigue, an endemic condition in clinical environments, further degrades attentional capacity, increasing susceptibility to phishing emails and credential harvesting schemes. These tactics are not incidental; they reflect a rational, adaptive threat model in which cybercriminals assess human behavior as a predictable system vulnerability (Burrell, 2024). Real-world incidents in which ransomware attacks forced hospital diversions, delayed surgeries, or disrupted emergency care demonstrate that these psychologically engineered intrusions now pose direct threats to patient safety, blurring the boundary between cyber risk and clinical risk (Burrell, 2024; Burton, 2024; Burrell, 2023; Burrell et al., 2023).

Equally consequential, yet often underexamined, is the psychology of cybersecurity risk management within healthcare organizations. Risk mitigation strategies are shaped by cognitive biases, organizational culture, and leadership perception as much as by formal policy or technical capability. Normalization of deviance, where repeated exposure to minor security incidents diminishes perceived severity, can lead institutions to tolerate unsafe practices until catastrophic failure occurs. Optimism bias may cause decision-makers to underestimate the likelihood or impact of a breach, particularly when competing priorities such as patient throughput, regulatory compliance, and cost containment dominate strategic planning. Furthermore, cybersecurity investments are frequently evaluated through short-term financial lenses rather than long-term risk exposure, creating structural incentives to defer critical controls. These psychological dynamics can produce a false sense of security that cybercriminals readily exploit, reinforcing a cycle in which defenses remain static while adversarial strategies evolve.

As cybercriminals adopt increasingly adaptive, behavior-driven methods that outpace institutional defenses, healthcare organizations face an urgent imperative to reconceptualize cybersecurity risk management through a psychological and behavioral lens. Effective risk mitigation must extend beyond compliance-based checklists or reactive incident response to encompass an understanding of adversarial intent, human-system interaction, and decision-making under pressure. Without explicitly integrating criminal psychological risk into cybersecurity governance, digital transformation initiatives may unintentionally magnify systemic fragility rather than resilience (Burrell, 2024; Burton, 2024; Burrell, 2023; Burrell et al., 2023). In this context, cybersecurity emerges not merely as a technical safeguard but as a socio-technical discipline that demands insight into how humans perceive risk, respond to threat, and adapt, or fail to adapt, under conditions of uncertainty. Addressing this challenge is essential to protecting not only sensitive data, but the integrity, continuity, and ethical foundations of modern healthcare delivery.

PROBLEM STATEMENT

Healthcare organizations continue to face an intensifying cyber threat environment in which criminal actors deliberately exploit both system weaknesses and human cognitive vulnerabilities to access sensitive patient data. Protected health information commands high value on illicit markets, not only for financial fraud but also for identity reconstruction, blackmail, and long-term exploitation, making healthcare systems particularly attractive targets (Gordon et al., 2022). Attackers frequently employ social engineering techniques that mimic trusted internal communications or medical vendors, knowing that clinical personnel operate under constant time pressure and may lack specialized cybersecurity training. HYG Health Services, a fictional name used to protect the privacy of the actual organization central to this intervention, has experienced three cybersecurity breaches within a five-year period, signaling persistent failures in risk governance and threat mitigation. The most recent incident resulted in the unauthorized access and theft of personal data belonging to two thousand patients, compounding reputational harm and eroding public trust. The organization's repeated exposure demonstrates how insufficiently adaptive cybersecurity risk management can undermine operational credibility, regulatory compliance, and long-term organizational viability.

SIGNIFICANCE OF THE INQUIRY

The scale and trajectory of healthcare cybercrime underscore the critical need for cybersecurity risk management strategies that explicitly incorporate criminal psychology, threat behavior, and human-system interaction. Since the beginning of 2023, nearly 250 healthcare data breaches affecting more than 24 million individuals have been reported to the U.S. Department of Health and Human Services, representing a 56% increase over the same period in 2022 (Fortified Health Security, 2023). Healthcare organizations experience approximately twice the number of cyberattacks observed in other industry sectors, a disparity driven by both intensified criminal targeting and the continued reliance on legacy security controls that fail to address behavioral exploitation (CSO, 2018). Concurrently, the expanding electronic collection, storage, and exchange of health data through analytics, interoperability initiatives, and regulatory mandates further amplifies systemic exposure (Blanke & McGrady, 2016). Real-world incidents in which ransomware attacks have halted clinical operations or compromised patient care reveal that cybersecurity failures now produce tangible harm with ethical, legal, and public health implications. This inquiry is significant because it positions cybersecurity not solely as a technical function but as a risk management discipline that must account for adversarial intent, psychological manipulation, and organizational behavior. Without the immediate adoption of evidence-based, behaviorally informed cybersecurity measures, healthcare organizations such as HYG Health Services face escalating financial losses, regulatory sanctions, and irreversible damage to patient trust.

RATIONAL CHOICE THEORY

Rational Choice Theory posits that offenders engage in criminal behavior after evaluating perceived risks, rewards, and effort (Cornish et al., 1989; Hechter & Kanazawa, 1997; Hayward, 2007). Crime occurs when the anticipated benefits outweigh the anticipated costs, given the offender's available information and constraints (Cornish et al., 1989; Hechter & Kanazawa, 1997; Hayward, 2007). Cybercriminals targeting healthcare organizations engage in deliberate cost–benefit analyses (Cornish et al., 1989; Hechter & Kanazawa, 1997; Hayward, 2007). Protected health information offers high, enduring value because it cannot be invalidated like financial credentials, while healthcare environments often exhibit inconsistent defenses and slow response cycles. Repeated breaches signal low deterrence, reinforcing offender perceptions that the probability of success outweighs the risk of punishment (Cornish et al., 1989; Hechter & Kanazawa, 1997; Hayward, 2007). From a risk management standpoint, inadequate controls unintentionally function as criminogenic signals, encouraging repeated victimization (Cornish et al., 1989; Hechter & Kanazawa, 1997; Hayward, 2007). Effective mitigation therefore alters offender calculations by increasing perceived effort, reducing reward, and elevating detection certainty (Cornish et al., 1989; Hechter & Kanazawa, 1997; Hayward, 2007).

Healthcare cybercrime exemplifies rational choice dynamics. Cybercriminals target healthcare organizations because protected health information is highly valuable, difficult to invalidate, and often poorly defended relative to its worth. From a psychological perspective, attackers assess not only technical defenses but also organizational behaviors, such as delayed patching, fragmented governance, and overworked staff, that lower perceived detection risk. Repeated breaches at organizations like HYG signal to adversaries that defensive controls are insufficient or inconsistently enforced, reinforcing the rational calculation that further attacks are likely to succeed. Risk management failures therefore function as psychological cues to offenders, inadvertently signaling permissiveness rather than deterrence.

ROUTINE ACTIVITY THEORY

Routine Activity Theory conceptualizes crime as the predictable outcome of environmental conditions rather than solely the product of deviant motivation, emphasizing the convergence of a motivated offender, an attractive target, and insufficient guardianship as the catalyst for criminal action (Yar, 2005; Reyns, 2017; Leukfeldt & Yar, 2016). When applied to healthcare cybercrime, this framework reveals how digital transformation has unintentionally engineered criminogenic conditions by normalizing routines that cyber adversaries systematically observe, model, and exploit. Modern healthcare environments generate continuous streams of high-value data, operate under intense temporal pressure, and rely on complex socio-technical systems that frequently outpace their own security governance. These conditions do not merely invite cybercrime; they structure opportunity in ways that align precisely with offender rationality and behavioral adaptation.

From the offender's psychological perspective, healthcare institutions represent ideal targets because routine organizational behaviors reduce uncertainty and effort. Cybercriminals monitor predictable activity patterns such as shift changes, billing cycles, software updates, and vendor communications, timing attacks to coincide with periods of maximal cognitive load and minimal scrutiny. Phishing campaigns disguised as electronic health record alerts or supplier invoices exploit habitual email triage behaviors, while ransomware attacks are often launched during weekends or holidays when security staffing is reduced. These tactics illustrate how offenders leverage routine activity not randomly, but strategically, transforming normal operations into attack vectors. High-profile incidents in which ransomware has forced hospitals to divert emergency patients or revert to paper records demonstrate that offenders understand not only system architecture but institutional rhythms, exploiting moments when guardianship is weakest.

The suitability of healthcare data as a criminal target further amplifies risk within this theoretical framework. Unlike financial information, which can be canceled or reissued, protected health information is immutable, comprehensive, and enduring, making it exceptionally valuable for identity reconstruction, insurance fraud, and long-term exploitation. This permanence alters offender motivation by increasing the perceived reward of successful intrusion while simultaneously lowering moral inhibition, as harm is temporally and spatially distant from the offender. For organizations such as HYG, repeated exposure of patient data signals to offenders that the target remains viable, reinforcing attack persistence and escalation. In this way, routine activity dynamics become self-reinforcing where each breach strengthens offender confidence while eroding institutional credibility.

Risk mitigation strategies grounded in this theory prioritize strengthening guardianship by reducing predictability, increasing surveillance visibility, and embedding cybersecurity awareness into everyday practice. Rather than relying on post-incident punishment or compliance-driven controls, this approach reframes cybersecurity as continuous crime prevention; one that disrupts offender opportunity by reshaping the routine conditions under which crime emerges. When guardianship becomes active, adaptive, and culturally reinforced, the convergence necessary for cybercrime is no longer assured, fundamentally altering the psychological calculus of would-be offenders.

CRIME PATTERN THEORY

Crime Pattern Theory explains criminal behavior as an adaptive process shaped by familiarity, repetition, and environmental cues, arguing that offenders do not act randomly but instead exploit predictable spatial and temporal patterns where opportunity routinely emerges (Brantingham & Brantingham, 2013). When translated into the cyber domain, this theory provides a powerful lens for understanding how cybercriminals cognitively map healthcare organizations as navigable environments rather than abstract technical systems. Through reconnaissance, prior intrusions, and shared criminal intelligence, offenders develop mental representations of digital terrain that include common access points, response delays, and behavioral blind spots. Healthcare institutions that rely on standardized workflows and interconnected systems inadvertently provide the structural consistency necessary for these criminal maps to stabilize and evolve.

From a criminal psychological perspective, cyber offenders derive efficiency and confidence from familiarity. Entry mechanisms such as third-party vendor portals, remote access interfaces, and email gateways function as recurring 'nodes' that attackers probe and revisit across campaigns. Temporal regularities, including shift transitions, billing deadlines, software patch windows, and emergency surges, form predictable 'paths' of vulnerability that inform attack timing. Ransomware incidents that occur during weekends or overnight hours, when technical staff availability is limited, illustrate how offenders exploit these temporal edges to maximize disruption while minimizing resistance. Well-documented attacks on hospital networks during pandemic surges further demonstrate that cybercriminals intentionally synchronize intrusions with periods of institutional strain, leveraging operational chaos as a strategic advantage.

Repeated victimization significantly accelerates the refinement of offender crime patterns. When organizations such as HYG experience multiple breaches, attackers interpret these events as confirmation of persistent structural weaknesses rather than isolated failures. Each successful intrusion enhances offender spatial knowledge, enabling the identification of stable attack routes and secondary targets within the network. This iterative learning process mirrors physical-world crime patterns, where offenders return to locations that previously yielded reward with minimal risk. In cybersecurity contexts, unresolved vulnerabilities and inconsistent remediation practices transform digital infrastructure into a criminogenic environment that invites repeated exploitation. Over time, this familiarity reduces offender uncertainty and lowers the psychological threshold for escalation, including broader data exfiltration or ransomware deployment.

Risk mitigation strategies informed by Crime Pattern Theory seek to disrupt offender cognition by destabilizing environmental predictability. Effective cybersecurity governance introduces friction into offender mapping through network segmentation, randomized access controls, rotating credentials, and adaptive monitoring protocols (Brantingham & Brantingham, 2016). Just as urban crime prevention reduces offending by altering lighting, access routes, and visibility, cyber risk management reduces intrusion by eliminating habitual access paths and obscuring system regularities. Embedding this approach within organizational culture further strengthens guardianship by ensuring that security practices evolve in tandem with threat behavior. By continually reshaping the digital landscape, healthcare organizations can prevent offenders from forming stable crime patterns, thereby transforming cybersecurity from reactive defense into proactive crime prevention.

SITUATIONAL CRIME PREVENTION THEORY

Situational Crime Prevention Theory frames criminal behavior as a function of opportunity shaped by environmental conditions, emphasizing that crime is most effectively reduced when the situational contexts that facilitate offending are systematically altered (Akinbowale et al., 2024; Beebe & Rao, 2005; Eck & Clarke, 2019; Ho, 2024). Within the realm of healthcare cybercrime, this perspective shifts analytical focus away from abstract offender motivation and toward the concrete conditions that make cyber intrusions cognitively efficient and operationally attractive. Cybercriminals operate as adaptive problem solvers who seek environments characterized by low resistance, predictable defenses, and high payoff. Healthcare organizations that rely on legacy systems, inconsistent access controls, or compliance-only security measures inadvertently construct digital environments in which criminal opportunity flourishes."

From a criminal psychological standpoint, situational manipulation is central to cyber offending. Attackers are acutely sensitive to effort thresholds, detection likelihood, and reward magnitude, continuously recalibrating tactics in response to environmental cues. For example, the absence of multi-factor authentication dramatically lowers the cognitive and technical effort required to compromise user accounts, while limited real-time monitoring reduces perceived risk of detection. Conversely, robust logging, behavioral analytics, and rapid incident response increase offender uncertainty and anxiety, often deterring further engagement. Real-world ransomware campaigns targeting hospitals have demonstrated that attackers routinely abandon attempts when encryption, network segmentation, or endpoint detection complicate lateral movement, redirecting their efforts toward less fortified organizations. These behavioral responses underscore that cybercriminals respond predictably to situational barriers, validating the preventive logic of the theory.

Reducing criminal reward is equally central to effective cybersecurity risk management. Healthcare data hold exceptional value because of their permanence and richness, enabling long-term identity exploitation and insurance fraud. Encryption at rest and in transit, strict data minimization practices, and segmented storage architectures directly undermine the payoff of successful breaches by rendering stolen data unusable or incomplete. From the offender's perspective, diminished reward alters the risk–reward calculus, weakening motivation even when access is technically achievable. Publicized enforcement actions and regulatory penalties further amplify this effect by signaling that healthcare data theft carries escalating consequences. These measures collectively erode the perceived profitability of healthcare cybercrime, reinforcing the deterrent value of situational controls.

Situational Crime Prevention Theory also addresses the psychological rationalizations that offenders and insiders use to justify misconduct. Clear, enforced cybersecurity policies remove ambiguity that might otherwise be exploited to neutralize responsibility, particularly in cases of insider threat or negligent behavior. When organizations such as HYG establish unambiguous standards for access, authentication, and data handling, and visibly enforce them, offenders encounter fewer cognitive pathways for excuse-making or moral disengagement. Risk mitigation strategies grounded in this theory therefore function not merely as technical safeguards but as behavioral constraints that reshape decision-making environments. In this way, cybersecurity emerges as a form of institutional crime prevention infrastructure, designed to disrupt opportunity structures before criminal intent can translate into harm. By systematically increasing effort, elevating risk, reducing reward, and eliminating excuses, healthcare organizations can transform their digital ecosystems from permissive targets into resilient environments that actively repel cybercrime.

Guardianship Theory situates crime prevention within the presence, visibility, and effectiveness of actors capable of observing, intervening, and responding to deviant behavior, emphasizing that crime is less likely to occur when oversight is active and credible rather than symbolic (Kikerpill, 2021; Leukfeldt & Yar, 2016; Reynald et al., 2018). Within the context of cybercrime, guardianship is not confined to physical presence but extends to socio-technical systems and human decision-makers who collectively shape an offender's perception of risk. Cybercriminals are acutely sensitive to signals of supervision, assessing whether an organization demonstrates awareness, responsiveness, and coordinated control. Where guardianship appears fragmented or dormant, offenders interpret this absence as an invitation rather than a barrier, adjusting their tactics to exploit perceived blind spots.

From a criminal psychological perspective, the absence of effective guardianship lowers cognitive inhibition by reducing the perceived likelihood of interruption or consequence. In healthcare environments, where operational urgency and complex workflows dominate daily activity, cybercriminals exploit moments when oversight is diffused across departments or relegated to understaffed security teams. Real-world ransomware attacks on hospitals frequently occur during nights, weekends, or holiday period; temporal windows in which security operations are scaled back and decision-making authority is unclear. These attacks reveal that offenders not only monitor technical defenses but also evaluate organizational vigilance, deliberately timing intrusions to coincide with diminished supervisory presence. Such behavior underscores that cybercrime is shaped as much by perceived organizational attentiveness as by technological capability.

In healthcare cybersecurity, guardianship manifests through layered oversight mechanisms that include security operations centers, SIEM platforms, trained personnel, and executive-level engagement. Each of these components contributes to a shared perception of watchfulness that directly influences offender decision-making. When employees are educated to recognize and report anomalies, when alerts are actively monitored rather than passively logged, and when leadership visibly prioritizes cybersecurity governance, offenders encounter uncertainty that disrupts attack planning. Conversely, under-resourced security teams, inconsistent enforcement of access controls, and ambiguous reporting structures fragment guardianship and create exploitable gaps. For organizations such as HYG, repeated security incidents signal to offenders that guardianship remains insufficiently coordinated, reinforcing perceptions of low resistance and encouraging reoffending.

Effective cybersecurity risk management therefore requires the deliberate strengthening of guardianship as a continuous, organization-wide function rather than a reactive technical role. Centralized monitoring, routine training, and clearly assigned accountability increase the probability of early detection and rapid intervention, compressing the temporal window in which offenders can operate. From a psychological standpoint, this heightened guardianship elevates offender anxiety and forces recalibration of risk, often diverting attacks toward less vigilant targets. By embedding guardianship into daily operations and institutional culture, healthcare organizations transform cybersecurity into an active form of crime prevention—one that reduces opportunity not through fear alone, but through the sustained presence of capable, engaged, and adaptive oversight.

COMPLEXITIES AND CONTEXTS OF HEALTHCARE CYBERCRIME

Healthcare cybercrime produces cascading consequences that extend well beyond compromised data systems, exerting psychological, professional, and organizational pressure on the human actors embedded within those systems. Employees often occupy the most psychologically vulnerable position in the cyber risk ecosystem, functioning simultaneously as targets, vectors, and casualties of cyberattacks. From a criminal psychology standpoint, cyber adversaries deliberately exploit cognitive overload, role ambiguity, and fear of authority to induce security lapses, while institutions frequently respond by assigning blame to individual employees rather than addressing systemic risk conditions. In healthcare environments such as HYG, employee errors associated with phishing or improper data handling may result in reprimands, retraining mandates, or termination depending on the perceived severity of the incident (Yeo & Banfield, 2022). However, punitive responses alone fail to account for the reality that cybercriminals engineer conditions under which error becomes statistically probable. As repeated breaches occur, employees experience heightened anxiety, job insecurity, and moral distress, particularly when their professional futures become intertwined with the organization's ability to maintain operational credibility. This dynamic not only undermines morale but also paradoxically increases risk, as fear-based cultures discourage incident reporting and proactive engagement with cybersecurity protocols.

At the organizational level, cybercrime operates as a reputational weapon, intentionally designed to erode trust rather than merely extract data. Healthcare organizations rely on public confidence in their ability to safeguard deeply personal information, and repeated breaches signal institutional vulnerability that adversaries are quick to exploit. For HYG, multiple security incidents within a relatively short time horizon reflect not only technical deficiencies but also failures in risk perception and governance. Research demonstrates that reputational damage following data breaches drives patient attrition and long-term revenue loss as consumers seek alternatives perceived as safer (Decker & Galer, 2013). Real-world enforcement actions illustrate the material consequences of such failures. In 2021, Excellus Health Plan paid $5.1 million following a breach affecting over nine million individuals (U.S. Department of Health and Human Services, 2021), while Oklahoma State University incurred an $875,000 penalty in 2022 after malware exposure compromised sensitive health data (U.S. Department of Health and Human Services, 2022). These cases underscore that cybercrime imposes enduring financial and legal liabilities that threaten organizational sustainability when risk mitigation strategies remain reactive rather than anticipatory.

Effective cybersecurity risk management therefore requires methodologies that align technical controls with behavioral insight. Continuous improvement frameworks such as Lean Six Sigma offer value when applied not merely to process efficiency but to the systematic identification of human-system vulnerabilities. Within healthcare contexts like HYG, structured assessment of confidentiality, integrity, and availability controls, as required under HIPAA, must be coupled with analysis of how training gaps, leadership priorities, and cultural norms create exploitable weaknesses (Antony et al., 2017; Momani et al., 2017). Cybercriminals routinely exploit inconsistent enforcement, outdated controls, and fragmented accountability structures, making organizational commitment a decisive factor in mitigation success. Improvements grounded in expert consultation, targeted training, and formalized response mechanisms represent not isolated interventions but iterative defenses that evolve alongside threat behavior.

Change management models further reinforce the necessity of embedding cybersecurity into organizational culture. Incremental improvement philosophies emphasize workforce participation, leadership accountability, and standardization as mechanisms for reducing error and waste (Singh & Singh, 2009). In cybersecurity contexts, this translates into disciplined hygiene practices, elimination of redundant or insecure workflows, and shared ownership of data protection responsibilities. Criminal actors rely on organizational inertia and fragmented communication; continuous improvement disrupts these patterns by reducing ambiguity and reinforcing collective vigilance. When leadership visibly prioritizes cybersecurity, employees internalize risk awareness as part of professional identity rather than external compliance.

Enterprise-level risk frameworks provide the structural backbone necessary to sustain these efforts. Comprehensive risk management approaches emphasize governance, strategy alignment, performance monitoring, and transparent communication as interdependent components of resilience (COSO, 2017a; COSO, 2017b). For HYG, integrating cybersecurity into enterprise risk governance reframes breaches not as isolated IT failures but as predictable outcomes of unmanaged risk exposure. This perspective aligns resource allocation with threat severity and shifts decision-making away from short-term cost avoidance toward long-term risk reduction. As COSO notes, the cost of proactive risk management is consistently outweighed by the financial and reputational damage incurred in its absence.

Organizational culture ultimately determines whether technical safeguards succeed or fail. Models linking cultural traits to performance demonstrate that adaptability, involvement, consistency, and mission clarity directly influence employee behavior and risk awareness (Denison et al., 2014). A risk-averse cybersecurity culture at HYG would require visible leadership engagement, predictable enforcement of security standards, continuous learning, and a shared mission centered on patient privacy.

Without such alignment, even advanced security technologies remain underutilized or circumvented.

Technological controls nonetheless remain critical, particularly when informed by behavioral threat intelligence. Security Information and Event Management systems enhance situational awareness by correlating events across systems and identifying patterns consistent with adversarial behavior (Bhatt et al., 2014; González-Granadillo et al., 2021). When integrated into a centralized Security Operations Center, these systems enable rapid detection and response while supporting strategic analysis of evolving threats (Vielberth & Pernul, 2018). Investment decisions surrounding such technologies must reflect an organization's defined risk tolerance, acknowledging that underinvestment effectively transfers power to adversaries who face minimal marginal costs to attack.

Sustainable cybersecurity resilience further depends on policies, information sharing, and workforce education. Clear standards governing access control, authentication, data classification, and incident response establish baseline expectations that reduce ambiguity exploited by cybercriminals (Liveri et al., 2015). Collaborative intelligence sharing among healthcare organizations enhances collective defense by distributing lessons learned from breach events (Hautamaki & Kokkonen, 2020). Finally, continuous training transforms employees from passive liabilities into active defenders. Given that many healthcare professionals enter practice with limited cybersecurity education (Swede et al., 2019), structured awareness programs incorporating simulations, reporting protocols, and regular reinforcement are essential to mitigating psychologically engineered attacks (Kim, 2017).

Taken together, these elements illustrate that healthcare cybersecurity is fundamentally a contest of human behavior. Criminal actors succeed not because organizations lack technology, but because they exploit misaligned incentives, cognitive bias, and cultural weakness. Addressing cybercrime therefore requires risk management strategies that integrate psychological insight, organizational discipline, and adaptive learning. For HYG, as for the healthcare sector broadly, resilience will depend on recognizing cybersecurity not as a technical problem to be solved, but as a human system to be understood, governed, and continually reinforced.

METHODS AND STUDY DESIGN

This qualitative study employed an interpretive research design to examine how criminal psychological risk manifests in healthcare cybercrime and how risk management and mitigation are understood across related professional disciplines. Individual, semi-structured interviews were selected to capture nuanced experiential knowledge, subjective interpretation, and cross-disciplinary insight into cybercriminal behavior and defensive decision-making. This approach was appropriate given the study's focus on cognition, perception of risk, and adaptive behavior rather than quantifiable outcomes.

PARTICIPANTS AND SAMPLING

The study consisted of ten participants recruited through purposive sampling to ensure disciplinary diversity and professional expertise relevant to cybercrime and cybersecurity risk management. Participants met two inclusion criteria: (a) possession of graduate-level education in a relevant field and (b) a minimum of three years of professional experience within that field. The final sample included:

- Two participants with graduate education in **cyberpsychology**
- Two participants with graduate education in **criminal psychology**
- Two participants with graduate education in **criminal justice**
- Two participants with graduate education in **cybersecurity**
- Two participants with graduate education in **human factors**

This interdisciplinary composition was intentional, allowing the study to triangulate perspectives on offender behavior, system vulnerability, human decision-making, and institutional risk.

Data Collection Procedures

Data were collected through individual interviews conducted via Zoom to accommodate geographic dispersion and professional schedules. Each interview lasted between 45 and 70 minutes and was audio-recorded with participant consent. The virtual format was selected not only for logistical efficiency but also because it reflects the same mediated environments in which cybercrime and cybersecurity operations frequently occur.

A semi-structured interview protocol was used to balance consistency across interviews with flexibility to probe emergent insights. Participants were informed that the study focused on psychological and behavioral dimensions of cybercrime and cybersecurity risk management in healthcare contexts, including experiences related to organizational response, offender behavior, and mitigation practices.

Data Collection Questions

Only three core questions guided all interviews:

1. How do you perceive the psychological strategies cybercriminals use when targeting healthcare organizations?
2. How do human decision-making and organizational culture influence cybersecurity risk management and mitigation?
3. What factors most significantly weaken or strengthen cybersecurity guardianship in healthcare environments?

Data Analysis

Interviews were transcribed verbatim and analyzed using thematic analysis. Coding was iterative and inductive, allowing themes to emerge directly from participant narratives while remaining informed by criminological and psychological theory. Patterns were examined both within and across disciplines to identify converging and diverging interpretations of cyber risk. Credibility was enhanced through analyst reflexivity and comparison of themes across professional backgrounds.

FINDINGS

Question 1: Psychological Strategies Used by Cybercriminals

Theme 1: Exploitation of Cognitive Overload

Definition: Cybercriminals intentionally target moments of fatigue, urgency, and divided attention to increase the likelihood of human error.

Participant Quote:

"Honestly, they're not hacking people at their best, they're hacking people when they're tired, stressed, and juggling ten things at once. In healthcare, that's basically all the time. The emails don't have to be perfect; they just have to land when someone's brain is fried and they're trying to move fast. That's when people click without thinking."

Recommendations:

1. Design workflows that reduce unnecessary cognitive burden during high-risk tasks.
2. Implement just-in-time security prompts during peak workload periods.
3. Align staffing models to ensure security oversight during high-stress operational windows.

Theme 2: Psychological Manipulation Through Authority and Urgency

Definition: Offenders leverage authority bias and artificial urgency to suppress critical thinking.

Participant Quote:

"They're really good at pretending to be someone you don't want to question. A supervisor, IT, a vendor. Add a deadline or a threat and suddenly logic shuts off. It's not stupidity, it's pressure. People are trying to do the 'right thing' fast."

Recommendations:

1. Train staff to pause and verify authority-based requests regardless of urgency.
2. Normalize challenge and verification within organizational culture.
3. Use simulations that replicate high-pressure manipulation tactics.

Question 2: Human Decision-Making and Organizational Risk Management

Theme 1: Normalization of Risky Behavior

Definition: Repeated exposure to minor security lapses reduces perceived severity and urgency.

Participant Quote:

"When nothing bad happens the first few times, people stop seeing it as risky. It becomes normal. That's when the real danger starts, because by the time something serious happens, the habits are already baked in."

Recommendations:

1. Track and report near-miss security events as learning opportunities.
2. Incorporate behavioral metrics into risk assessments.
3. Reinforce consequences without defaulting to blame.

Theme 2: Short-Term Thinking in Risk Decisions

Definition: Immediate operational pressures outweigh long-term security considerations.

Participant Quote:

"Cybersecurity always loses to whatever fire is burning today. Budgets, patient flow, compliance audits. The breach feels abstract until it's not, and by then it's too late."

Recommendations:

1. Frame cybersecurity investments as loss prevention rather than optional costs.
2. Integrate cyber risk into enterprise-level decision-making.
3. Use scenario-based planning to personalize future risk.

Question 3: Factors Influencing Cybersecurity Guardianship

Theme 1: Fragmented Ownership of Security

Definition: Lack of clear accountability weakens collective vigilance.
Participant Quote:
"Everyone thinks security is someone else's job. IT thinks it's leadership, leadership thinks it's IT, and staff just try not to mess up. That gap is exactly where attackers operate."
Recommendations:

1. Clearly define cybersecurity roles across organizational levels.
2. Embed security responsibilities into job descriptions.
3. Promote shared accountability rather than siloed control.

Theme 2: Visibility of Oversight as Deterrence

Definition: Active, visible guardianship alters offender behavior and internal compliance.
Participant Quote:
"When people know someone is actually watching and responding, behavior changes. And attackers notice that too. Silence looks like weakness."
Recommendations:

1. Increase transparency around monitoring and response efforts.
2. Publicize internal security improvements to reinforce deterrence.
3. Maintain consistent leadership engagement with cybersecurity initiatives.

CONCLUSION

This study demonstrates that healthcare cybercrime is fundamentally a human-centered phenomenon driven by offender psychology, environmental opportunity, and organizational decision-making rather than by technical failure alone. Findings from interdisciplinary participant interviews reveal that cybercriminals deliberately exploit predictable cognitive vulnerabilities such as fatigue, authority bias, and urgency, while healthcare organizations often reinforce these vulnerabilities through fragmented accountability, normalized risk behavior, and short-term decision-making. Cybersecurity failures within healthcare settings therefore emerge not as isolated incidents, but as predictable outcomes of misaligned incentives, insufficient guardianship, and underdeveloped risk cultures. The convergence of criminal psychological strategy and organizational vulnerability creates an ecosystem in which cybercrime thrives unless actively disrupted. By integrating criminological theory with practitioner insight, this study reinforces the necessity of reframing cybersecurity as a continuous behavioral risk management challenge rather than a static technical function. Sustainable resilience will depend on organizations' willingness to address how humans perceive, prioritize, and respond to risk under pressure.

Organizational Implications

At the organizational level, the findings suggest that cybersecurity resilience is inseparable from institutional culture, workflow design, and governance structures. Organizations that treat cybersecurity as a specialized technical responsibility rather than a shared operational function inadvertently create gaps that cybercriminals exploit. Normalization of risky behaviors, inconsistent enforcement of security protocols, and unclear ownership of cyber risk weaken collective vigilance and lower the perceived cost of offending. Healthcare organizations must therefore adopt a systems-oriented approach that aligns technology, policy, training, and culture around a unified risk management strategy. Embedding cybersecurity into everyday operations, through routine communication, behavioral metrics, and cross-functional collaboration, reduces reliance on individual vigilance and strengthens organizational guardianship. Without this integration, even advanced technical controls remain vulnerable to predictable human failure.

Leadership Implications

Leadership plays a decisive role in shaping how cybersecurity risk is perceived, prioritized, and acted upon within healthcare organizations. The findings indicate that when leaders frame cybersecurity as an abstract or secondary concern, employees internalize this hierarchy of risk, often prioritizing speed and productivity over security. Conversely, visible leadership engagement, consistent messaging, and active participation in cybersecurity governance signal institutional commitment and elevate perceived importance. Leaders must recognize that their decisions influence not only resource allocation but also risk normalization and ethical accountability.

Effective leadership in cybersecurity requires moving beyond compliance-driven oversight toward behavioral stewardship, where leaders model secure practices, support reporting without fear of reprisal, and align cybersecurity objectives with patient safety and organizational mission. Failure to do so risks perpetuating a culture in which cyber threats are underestimated until damage becomes unavoidable.

Policy Implications

The findings also carry significant implications for cybersecurity policy at organizational and regulatory levels. Policies that focus exclusively on compliance checklists or post-incident penalties fail to address the behavioral dynamics that enable cybercrime. Effective policy must incorporate principles from situational crime prevention, guardianship, and human factors psychology to reduce opportunity, clarify responsibility, and eliminate ambiguity. This includes policies that mandate continuous training, define clear reporting pathways, and require visible monitoring and response capabilities. At a broader level, regulatory frameworks should incentivize proactive risk management and information sharing rather than reactive punishment alone. Policies that support transparency, cross-organizational collaboration, and adaptive learning strengthen collective defense and reduce systemic vulnerability across the healthcare sector. Ultimately, cybersecurity policy must evolve from a static regulatory obligation into a dynamic instrument of crime prevention grounded in an understanding of human behavior.

Recommendations for Future Research

Future research on healthcare cybersecurity would benefit substantially from the application of organizational ethnography as a primary methodological approach. Organizational ethnography is a qualitative research method grounded in prolonged, immersive observation of organizational settings, practices, interactions, and meaning-making processes. Rather than relying solely on interviews or retrospective self-report, organizational ethnography involves the systematic study of how people actually behave within institutional environments over time, including how norms, routines, power relations, and informal practices shape decision-making. In the context of healthcare cybersecurity, this method is particularly well suited to examining how security risks emerge through everyday work practices, cultural expectations, and structural constraints that are often invisible in policy documents or formal risk assessments.

The value of organizational ethnography for advancing cybersecurity research lies in its capacity to capture the lived realities of healthcare work as it unfolds in real time. The findings of this study demonstrate that cybercriminals exploit cognitive overload, authority structures, urgency, and normalized risk behaviors, all of which are embedded in routine organizational life. Ethnography allows researchers to observe these dynamics directly rather than inferring them after the fact. For example, it can reveal how clinical time pressure competes with security verification, how informal workarounds become normalized in response to workflow inefficiencies, and how leadership messaging about productivity or patient throughput implicitly shapes security behavior. This depth of contextual insight is difficult to achieve through interviews alone, as participants may be unaware of how habitual practices contribute to vulnerability or may rationalize behaviors that feel unavoidable within their professional roles.

Organizational ethnography also offers distinct advantages over more traditional qualitative approaches by situating cybersecurity risk within its broader socio-technical ecosystem. Healthcare cybercrime, as demonstrated throughout this study, is not merely the result of individual error or technical failure but is produced through the interaction of human cognition, organizational culture, institutional priorities, and adaptive threat behavior. Ethnographic research enables scholars to examine how these layers intersect, including how security policies are interpreted at different organizational levels, how responsibility for cyber risk is informally distributed, and how employees negotiate competing demands between care delivery and compliance. By foregrounding context, ethnography helps avoid the tendency to individualize blame and instead illuminates how systemic conditions make error predictable.

As applied to the topic of healthcare cybersecurity risk management, an organizational ethnographic research process would unfold in several interrelated stages. The first stage would involve gaining sustained access to a healthcare organization, such as a hospital or integrated health system, and establishing trust with leadership and staff across clinical, administrative, and technical roles. This access is essential to observe cybersecurity practices not only during formal training or incident response exercises, but during routine operations where vulnerabilities most often emerge. The researcher would then engage in prolonged participant observation, spending time in clinical units, administrative offices, and IT or security operations environments to document how cybersecurity considerations are incorporated, deprioritized, or bypassed in daily work.

The next stage would focus on tracing how cybersecurity-related decisions are made under conditions of pressure, uncertainty, and competing organizational goals. This would include observing moments of heightened risk, such as shift changes, system outages, vendor communications, or emergency surges, which this study identified as prime windows for cyber exploitation. Fieldnotes would capture not only observable actions, but also language, emotional tone, and informal reasoning, providing insight into how staff interpret risk, authority, and accountability in practice. Interviews would be integrated as a complementary method, allowing participants to reflect on observed behaviors and articulate the rationales behind them, thereby deepening analytic interpretation.

The final stage of the ethnographic process would involve iterative analysis linking observed organizational behavior to criminological and psychological theory. Patterns identified through observation could be mapped onto frameworks such as routine activity theory, situational crime prevention, and guardianship, all of which underpin the theoretical foundations of this study. This approach would enable future research to move beyond identifying that human factors matter, toward explaining precisely how organizational structures and cultures create criminogenic conditions that cybercriminals rationally exploit. Importantly, ethnographic findings could directly inform the design of interventions by revealing which practices are realistically modifiable and which constraints require structural change rather than individual retraining.

In sum, organizational ethnography represents a powerful and underutilized methodological pathway for advancing healthcare cybersecurity research. By capturing the complex, embedded, and often contradictory realities of healthcare work, this approach aligns closely with the study's conclusion that cybersecurity is fundamentally a human and organizational problem rather than a purely technical one. Future research employing organizational ethnography would deepen theoretical understanding, improve the ecological validity of cybersecurity interventions, and support the development of risk management strategies that are responsive to how healthcare organizations actually function in practice rather than how they are assumed to operate.

REFERENCES

Akinbowale, O. E., Zerihun, M. F., & Mashigo, P. (2024). Application of situational crime prevention framework for cybercrime mitigation. [IJCBPL]. *International Journal of Cyber Behavior, Psychology and Learning*, *14*(1), 1–23. https://www.igi-global.com/article/application-of-situational-crime-prevention-framework-for-cybercrime-mitigation/353436. DOI: 10.4018/IJCBPL.353436

Antony, J., Snee, R., & Hoerl, R. (2017). Lean Six Sigma: Yesterday, today and tomorrow. *International Journal of Quality & Reliability Management*, *34*(7), 1073–1093. DOI: 10.1108/IJQRM-03-2016-0035

Beebe, N. L., & Rao, V. S. (2005, December). Using situational crime prevention theory to explain the effectiveness of information systems security. In *Proceedings of the 2005 SoftWars Conference, Las Vegas, NV* (pp. 1-18). https://www.researchgate.net/profile/Nicole-Beebe/publication/237264626_Using_Situational_Crime_Prevention_Theory_to_Explain_the_Effectiveness_of_Information_Systems_Security/links/570e47a508aee76b9dade7a1/Using-Situational-Crime-Prevention-Theory-to-Explain-the-Effectiveness-of-Information-Systems-Security.pdf

Bhatt, S., Manadhata, P. K., & Zomlot, L. (2014). The operational role of Security Information and Event Management systems. *IEEE Security and Privacy*, *12*(5), 35–41. DOI: 10.1109/MSP.2014.103

Blanke, S. J., & McGrady, E. (2016). When it comes to securing patient health information from breaches, your best medicine is a dose of prevention: A cybersecurity risk assessment checklist. *Journal of Healthcare Risk Management*, *36*(1), 14–24. DOI: 10.1002/jhrm.21230 PMID: 27400172

Brantingham, P., & Brantingham, P. (2013). Crime pattern theory. In *Environmental criminology and crime analysis* (pp. 100–116). Willan., https://www.taylorfrancis.com/chapters/edit/10.4324/9780203118214-13/crime-pattern-theory-paul-brantingham-patricia-brantingham

Brantingham, P. J., & Brantingham, P. L. (2016). The geometry of crime and crime pattern theory. In *Environmental criminology and crime analysis* (pp. 117–135). Routledge., https://www.taylorfrancis.com/chapters/edit/10.4324/9781315709826-12/geometry-crime-crime-pattern-theory-paul-brantingham-patricia-brantingham

Burrell, D. N. (2023). Cybersecurity in healthcare through the 7-S model strategy. *Scientific Bulletin-Nicolae Balcescu Land Forces Academy, 28*(1), 26-35. https://reference-global.com/download/article/10.2478/bsaft-2023-0003.pdf

Burrell, D. N. (2024). Understanding Cognitive and Behavioral Psychological Factors that Lead to Cybersecurity Breaches in Healthcare. *RAIS Journal for Social Sciences, 8*(2), 43-53. https://ideas.repec.org/a/smo/jornl1/v8y2024i2p43-53.html

Burrell, D. N., Burton, S. L., Nobles, C., Springs, D., Huff, A. J., Brown-Jackson, K. L., Richardson, K., Wright, J. B., Muller, S. R., & Jones, A. J. (2023). The Managerial Ethical and Operational Challenges of Hospital Cybersecurity. In Burrell, D. (Ed.), *Transformational Interventions for Business, Technology, and Healthcare* (pp. 444–458). IGI Global Scientific Publishing., DOI: 10.4018/979-8-3693-1634-4.ch026

Burton, S. L. (2024). Securing tomorrow: Synergizing change management and cybersecurity in the digital era. *Holistica, 15*(1), 1. https://reference-global.com/download/article/10.2478/hjbpa-2024-0001.pdf

Cornish, D. B., & Clarke, R. V. (1989). Crime specialisation, crime displacement and rational choice theory. In *Criminal behavior and the justice system: Psychological perspectives* (pp. 103–117). Springer Berlin Heidelberg., https://link.springer.com/chapter/10.1007/978-3-642-86017-1_7 DOI: 10.1007/978-3-642-86017-1_7

COSO. (2017a, June). *Enterprise Risk Management – integrated framework.* Retrieved from https://www.coso.org/_files/ugd/3059fc_61ea5985b03c4293960642fdce408eaa.pdf

COSO. (2017b, June). *Enterprise Risk Management – integrating with strategy and performance.* Retrieved from https://www.coso.org/_files/ugd/3059fc_61ea5985b03c4293960642fdce408eaa.pdf

CSO. (2018, March 06). *Healthcare experiences twice the number of cyber attacks as other industries.* https://www.csoonline.com/article/564763/healthcare-experiences-twice-the-number-of-cyber-attacks-as-other-industries.html

Decker, A., & Galer, D. (2013). *Enterprises and business risks control techniques (risk control & risk management techniques*. ERMSTTP.

Denison, D., Nieminen, L., & Kotrba, L. (2014). Diagnosing organizational cultures: A conceptual and empirical review of culture effectiveness surveys. *European Journal of Work and Organizational Psychology, 23*(1), 145–161. DOI: 10.1080/1359432X.2012.713173

Denison. *Introduction to the Denison model* (2019). https://denisonconsulting.com/wp-content/uploads/2019/08/introduction-to-the-denison-model.pdf

Eck, J. E., & Clarke, R. V. (2019). Situational crime prevention: Theory, practice and evidence. In *Handbook on crime and deviance* (pp. 355–376). Springer International Publishing., https://link.springer.com/chapter/10.1007/978-3-030-20779-3_18 DOI: 10.1007/978-3-030-20779-3_18

Fortified Health Security. (2023, July 18). *Fortified Health Security releases 2023 mid-year horizon report* https://fortifiedhealthsecurity.com/horizon-report/2023-mid-year-horizon-report/

González-Granadillo, G., González-Zarzosa, S., & Diaz, R. (2021). Security Information and Event Management (SIEM): Analysis, trends, and usage in critical infrastructures. *Sensors (Basel), 21*(14), 4759. DOI: 10.3390/s21144759 PMID: 34300500

Gordon, W. J., Ikoma, N., Lyu, H., Jackson, G. P., & Landman, A. B. (2022). Protecting procedural care—Cybersecurity considerations for robotic surgery. *NPJ Digital Medicine*, *5*(1), 148. DOI: 10.1038/s41746-022-00693-8 PMID: 36127420

Hautamaki, J., & Kokkonen, T. (2020). Model for cyber security information sharing in healthcare sector. *2020 International Conference on Electrical, Communication, and Computer Engineering (ICECCE)*, 1–5. https://doi.org/DOI: 10.1109/ICECCE49384.2020.9179175

Hayward, K. (2007). Situational crime prevention and its discontents: Rational choice theory versus the 'culture of now'. *Social Policy and Administration*, *41*(3), 232–250. https://onlinelibrary.wiley.com/doi/abs/10.1111/j.1467-9515.2007.00550.x?casa_token=Afo7niSFlw8AAAAA%3AIn0vcW4nNsNjCqF3BEwDQI_hSq7ytkRzDhriVbZvrbth-R3bLm9ewu7G_MMzMhP16hYfV3cxM0XGgxYI. DOI: 10.1111/j.1467-9515.2007.00550.x

Hechter, M., & Kanazawa, S. (1997). Sociological rational choice theory. *Annual Review of Sociology*, *23*(1), 191–214. https://www.annualreviews.org/content/journals/10.1146/annurev.soc.23.1.191. DOI: 10.1146/annurev.soc.23.1.191

Ho, H. (2024). *Using Situational Crime Prevention (SCP) to prevent cybercrimes* (Doctoral dissertation, Singapore Institute of Technology). https://espace.library.uq.edu.au/view/UQ:c6c6fc3

Kikerpill, K. (2021). The individual's role in cybercrime prevention: Internal spheres of protection and our ability to safeguard them. *Kybernetes*, *50*(4), 1015–1026. https://www.emerald.com/k/article-abstract/50/4/1015/263657/The-individual-s-role-in-cybercrime-prevention?redirectedFrom=fulltext. DOI: 10.1108/K-06-2020-0335

Kim, L. (2017). Cybersecurity awareness: Protecting data and patients. *Nursing, 47*(6), 65–67. DOI: 10.1097/01.NURSE.0000516242.05454.b4 PMID: 28538357

Leukfeldt, E. R., & Yar, M. (2016). Applying routine activity theory to cybercrime: A theoretical and empirical analysis. *Deviant Behavior, 37*(3), 263–280. https://www.tandfonline.com/doi/full/10.1080/01639625.2015.1012409. DOI: 10.1080/01639625.2015.1012409

Liveri, D., Sarri, A., & Skouloudi, C. (2015). Security and resilience in eHealth: Security challenges and risks. *European Union Agency For Network and Information Security*. https://data.europa.eu/doi/10.2824/217830

Momani, A., Hirzallah, M., & Mumani, A. (2017). Improving employees' safety awareness in healthcare organizations using the DMAIC quality improvement approach. *Journal for Healthcare Quality, 39*(1), 54–63. DOI: 10.1097/JHQ.0000000000000049 PMID: 27579603

Reynald, D. M., Moir, E., Cook, A., & Vakhitova, Z. (2018). Changing perspectives on guardianship against crime: An examination of the importance of micro-level factors. *Crime Prevention and Community Safety, 20*(4), 268–283. https://link.springer.com/article/10.1057/s41300-018-0049-4. DOI: 10.1057/s41300-018-0049-4

Security Standards. General Rules, 45 C.F.R. § 164.306 (2011). https://www.govinfo.gov/content/pkg/CFR-2011-title45-vol1/pdf/CFR-2011-title45-vol1-sec164-306.pdf

Singh, J., & Singh, H. (2009). Kaizen philosophy: A review of literature. *The Icfai University Journal of Operations Management, 3*(2), 51–72. https://cdn.chools.in/LEAN_PDF/Kaizen%20Toolkit/Kaizen_Philosophy_A_Review_of_Literature.pdf

Swede, M. J., Scovetta, V., & Eugene-Colin, M. (2019). Protecting patient data is the new scope of practice: A recommended cybersecurity curricula for healthcare students to prepare for this challenge. *Journal of Allied Health, 48*(2), 148–156. https://www.ingentaconnect.com/content/asahp/jah/2019/00000048/00000002/art00013 PMID: 31167018

Tin, D., Hata, R., Granholm, F., Ciottone, R. G., Staynings, R., & Ciottone, G. R. (2023). Cyberthreats: A primer for healthcare professionals. *The American Journal of Emergency Medicine, 68*, 179–185. DOI: 10.1016/j.ajem.2023.04.001 PMID: 37061434

Tripwire. (2020, October 25). *HIPAA breach notification – what you need to know*. https://www.tripwire.com/state-of-security/hipaa-breach-notification-what-need-know

U.S. Department of Health and Human Services. (2021, January 14). *Insurer pays $5.1 million to settle data breach affecting over 9.3 million people.* U.S. Department of Health and Human Services. https://www.hhs.gov/hipaa/for-professionals/compliance-enforcement/agreements/excellus/index.html

U.S. Department of Health and Human Services. 2022, July 14). *Oklahoma State University – Center for Health Services pays $875,000 to settle hacking breach.* U.S. Department of Health and Human Services. https://www.hhs.gov/about/news/2022/07/14/oklahoma-state-university-center-health-services-pays-875000-settle-hacking-breach.html

Vielberth, M., & Pernul, G. (2018). A Security Information and Event Management pattern. *12th Latin American Conference on Pattern Languages of Programs.* HILLSIDE 978-1-941652-11-4. https://epub.uni-regensburg.de/41139/1/A%20Security%20Information%20and%20Event%20Management%20Pattern.pdf

Yeo, L. H., & Banfield, J. (2022). Human factors in electronic health records cybersecurity breach: An exploratory analysis. *Perspectives in Health Information Management, 19,* •••. https://pubmed.ncbi.nlm.nih.gov/35692854/PMID: 35692854

Chapter 12
Evaluating the Effectiveness of AI and Machine Learning Models in Preventing Financial Fraud in E-Commerce

Lawrence E. Iweriebor
http://orcid.org/0009-0004-4812-3787
Capitol Technology University, USA

Eugene Lewis
http://orcid.org/0000-0002-2956-0760
Capitol Technology University, USA

ABSTRACT

The rapid expansion of e-commerce has introduced significant challenges in the detection and prevention of financial fraud. As fraudulent techniques evolve in complexity and coordination, traditional rule-based systems have proven increasingly inadequate. This study examines the effectiveness of machine learning models, specifically Random Forest and XGBoost, in detecting fraudulent transactions within highly imbalanced credit card data representative of online commerce environments. The analysis focuses on the impact of resampling methods, including Synthetic Minority Oversampling Technique (SMOTE) and random undersampling, in addressing class imbalance. Results indicate that both techniques improved model performance, with SMOTE yielding higher F1-scores and recall. Among the models evaluated, XGBoost

DOI: 10.4018/979-8-2600-1016-7.ch012

trained on SMOTE-balanced data demonstrated the most effective performance. The study also incorporated interpretability analysis through SHAP values to identify key contributing features, thereby enhancing model transparency.

INTRODUCTION

Payment-card fraud losses worldwide reached $33.83 billion in 2023 (The Nilson Report, 2025). In 2024, U.S. consumers reported more than $12.5 billion in fraud losses, a 25% year-over-year increase (Federal Trade Commission, 2025). In 2022, the Canadian Anti-Fraud Centre recorded 91,190 fraud reports and 57,055 victims, with losses surpassing $531 million. Such figures illustrate how financial fraud inflicts substantial economic harm while undermining confidence in financial systems (Motie & Raahemi, 2024).

The widespread adoption of e-commerce has significantly changed how consumers and businesses interact. Platforms such as Amazon, eBay, and numerous mobile-based marketplaces have transformed global retail by offering speed, convenience, and accessibility. However, this evolution has also brought about new and sophisticated forms of digital fraud. As online platforms grow in complexity, so do the methods used by fraudsters to exploit them, ranging from account takeovers and fake listings to phishing schemes and coordinated scam networks (Mutemi & Bacao, 2024). Every day, people make millions of purchases and payments online, and each one can be a target for fraud. These transactions cover the full range of digital finance, and the risks come in many forms: credit-card misuse, doctored bank statements, insurance scams, and even automated attacks on banking systems (Reddy, 2022).

The increasing volume of digital transactions, especially since the COVID-19 pandemic, has led to a sharp rise in cybercrime and financial fraud within the e-commerce landscape. As Mutemi and Bacao (2024) explain, this trend places not only businesses but also consumers at heightened risk, impacting trust, financial security, and mental well-being. Traditional fraud detection strategies, largely rule-based systems, often fall short in addressing today's dynamic and highly adaptable fraud tactics. These rule-based systems rely on predefined thresholds, such as transaction limits or geolocation mismatches, which are easily bypassed by sophisticated fraud actors. Furthermore, static models do not evolve with emerging fraud patterns, making them less effective in real-world environments (Verma & Gupta, 2025). As a result, e-commerce platforms must look beyond conventional tools and embrace more adaptive technologies that can analyze behaviors, patterns, and connections in real time.

Machine learning-based fraud detection systems offer a promising alternative. Unlike fixed-rule systems, they can identify complex patterns within transactional data and adjust to new threats without manual intervention. Recent studies have emphasized the increasing role of intelligent detection mechanisms in identifying fraudulent activities across digital ecosystems (Baisholan et al., 2025; Li & Yang, 2023). These approaches also show potential for reducing false positives, improving decision-making, and offering better fraud insights through behavior-based analytics (Ahmed et al., 2025).

The scope of fraud is not limited to high-profile platforms alone; smaller online retailers, payment processors, and digital service providers are equally vulnerable. As fraud continues to evolve in both form and frequency, the need for more responsive, transparent, and scalable fraud detection solutions becomes critical.

This study explores how fraud detection frameworks, particularly those grounded in machine learning, can help address the growing threat of financial fraud in e-commerce. It also highlights the importance of explainability, scalability, and practical deployment in ensuring that these systems are not only accurate but also usable and trustworthy.

PROBLEM STATEMENT

The rise of digital commerce has amplified both the scale and complexity of financial fraud. Payment-card fraud losses worldwide reached $33.83 billion in 2023 (The Nilson Report, 2025). While many businesses have implemented fraud detection systems, these systems are frequently reactive and static, unable to keep pace with the evolving tactics of modern cybercriminals. This disconnect is particularly evident in e-commerce platforms, where fraudsters exploit vulnerabilities, behavioral patterns, and system gaps (Mutemi & Bacao, 2024). Also, cashless payments are higher today than at any point since the start of the digital age. This is great for convenience, but it also opens more doors for fraud.

In 2024, U.S. consumers reported more than $12.5 billion in fraud losses, a 25% year-over-year increase (Federal Trade Commission, 2025). One of the core challenges is the heavy reliance on rule-based or traditional fraud detection systems. These systems are limited in their ability to adapt to new fraud techniques. As a result, many fraudulent transactions go undetected, while legitimate users are sometimes wrongly flagged, creating customer friction and operational inefficiencies (Verma & Gupta, 2025). This limitation is reinforced by findings in Becker (2025), who noted that rule-based systems fall short in detecting adaptive fraud schemes such as fake reviews and account takeovers, especially when fraud evolves over time.

Another significant issue lies in the scarcity of real-world data available for building robust detection models. According to Mutemi and Bacao (2024), many fraud detection strategies are constrained by the lack of accessible, labeled datasets, which is due to the proprietary nature of fraud-related data. This shortage limits both research and practical model development, making it difficult to design systems that reflect the true behavior of fraud in dynamic e-commerce environments. As Vasant et al. (2025) point out, dataset imbalance continues to affect performance, with fraudulent activities making up a small fraction of total transactions, resulting in biased learning unless properly addressed.

Furthermore, existing fraud models often lack interpretability (Zhou et al., 2023). As Baisholan et al. (2025) point out, businesses and regulators are increasingly concerned about the "black box" nature of many detection algorithms, which offer little insight into how fraud decisions are made. This lack of transparency can erode trust in the system, impede regulatory compliance, and complicate analysts' efforts to justify or investigate suspicious transactions. The same issue is echoed in Mendonça et al. (2025), who highlight that graph-based models, though effective, often face scrutiny due to limited model explainability unless paired with reinforcement learning or attention mechanisms. Collectively, these problems underscore the need for fraud detection systems that are adaptive, explainable, and capable of operating effectively even in data-constrained environments.

SIGNIFICANCE OF THE PROJECT

Fraud in the e-commerce ecosystem is not just a technical problem; it is a financial, reputational, and societal issue. Its impact is felt by a wide range of stakeholders, including consumers, merchants, financial institutions, and regulatory bodies. With the growing use of mobile payments, digital wallets, and cross-platform shopping, the number of potential fraud vectors continues to expand (Li & Yang, 2023).

This study is significant because it explores how advanced, data-driven techniques, particularly machine learning, can improve the detection and prevention of fraud in e-commerce systems. Unlike static, rule-based models, machine learning algorithms can process large volumes of real-time data, recognize patterns, and flag anomalies that would otherwise go unnoticed (Baisholan et al., 2025). This aligns with findings from Byrapu Reddy et al. (2024), who argue that big data analytics and machine learning are essential in uncovering hidden fraud patterns and enabling timely interventions in digital marketplaces.

Moreover, this study emphasizes the importance of system interpretability. As Verma and Gupta (2025) argue, the ethical and regulatory implications of fraud detection technologies demand that such systems offer transparency in their decision-making. When customers are denied transactions or subjected to reviews, both businesses and users benefit from having clear explanations for those decisions. Becker (2025) strengthens this point, noting that using graph attention mechanisms can help flag transactions while maintaining traceable decision paths, especially when combined with GRU for temporal modeling.

Importantly, this study also considers scalability. While large e-commerce platforms may have the resources to deploy complex fraud systems, small and medium-sized businesses face cost and implementation barriers. By highlighting adaptable and transparent frameworks, the study seeks to provide practical guidance for a broader range of organizations operating in digital marketplaces. Mendonça et al. (2025) support this perspective, demonstrating that graph-based architectures can scale across various platform sizes without sacrificing detection accuracy.

Ultimately, this research contributes to the ongoing conversation about financial cybersecurity in the digital age by presenting solutions that are accurate, scalable, and explainable—thereby fostering greater trust and resilience across the e-commerce sector.

Research Gaps

While machine learning and data-driven methods have gained popularity in financial fraud detection, significant gaps persist in their application to e-commerce and financial cybersecurity. A major concern is the limited use of real-world, imbalanced datasets. Many existing studies rely on synthetic or publicly available datasets that do not reflect the complexity, noise, and fraud sparsity found in actual transaction environments. This practice restricts the generalizability and effectiveness of fraud models in live e-commerce platforms (Mutemi & Bacao, 2024).

In their evaluation of hybrid machine learning models, Vasant et al. (2025) emphasize that dataset imbalance remains a critical limitation. They highlight how oversampling techniques such as SMOTE, when not paired with effective feature extraction methods like LDA, can result in biased classifiers. This highlights the ongoing difficulty of building detection models that perform well across both rare and common transaction types.

Another gap lies in the underrepresentation of emerging fraud types, such as triangulation fraud, reseller abuse, and bot-based attacks. These fraud forms are increasingly prevalent in decentralized and mobile-first marketplaces, yet receive little scholarly attention. As a result, fraud detection models often fail to cover these high-impact risks, leaving significant vulnerabilities unaddressed (Mutemi & Bacao, 2024). Zeng et al. (2025) further reinforce this, stating that buyer-seller collusion and behavioral manipulation are not adequately addressed by conventional fraud detection systems, which tend to focus narrowly on transaction-level anomalies.

Equally concerning is the lack of interpretability in many high-performing fraud detection models. While ensemble and deep learning models offer high accuracy, they often operate as opaque systems that cannot explain how a transaction was classified. This creates barriers to regulatory compliance and limits their usability in high-stakes financial environments (Baisholan et al., 2025). Mendonça et al. (2025) echo these concerns, noting that while graph neural networks are highly effective, they often suffer from limited transparency unless attention weights or reinforcement strategies are incorporated.

Moreover, most studies treat fraud detection as a one-time task, ignoring the need for continuous model updates and adaptation to evolving threats. The dynamic nature of fraud necessitates systems that can learn and evolve over time (Hu et al., 2025; Agrahari et al., 2022). Yet, this requirement remains largely absent in existing research (Mutemi & Bacao, 2024). Becker (2025) adds that scalable and adaptive graph learning strategies are still in early stages of development, making this an area ripe for further exploration.

These research gaps directly affect the integrity of financial cybersecurity in e-commerce. Models that cannot adapt, explain decisions, or detect real-world fraud patterns leave digital platforms exposed to systemic risk. Addressing these issues is essential to building resilient, trustworthy fraud detection systems for the e-commerce industry.

This study examines how machine learning can be applied to improve financial fraud detection in e-commerce. It focuses on addressing common issues such as imbalanced data, the use of raw transaction details, and the need for models that are not only accurate but also understandable.

METHODOLOGY

This study analyzes a publicly available dataset comprising credit card transactions made by European cardholders over a two-day period in September 2013. The dataset includes 284,807 transactions, among which 492 are labeled as fraudulent. This translates to a fraud rate of approximately 0.17%, illustrating a substantial class imbalance, an important consideration in the development and evaluation of fraud detection models.

The study aims to compare Random Forest and XGBoost under SMOTE and random undersampling, evaluate performance with F1 and recall on an imbalanced dataset, and use SHAP to identify influential variables for interpretability.

The dataset consists of 31 numerical features. Features V1 through V28 are anonymized variables derived from a Principal Component Analysis (PCA) applied to the original data. The remaining features, Time and Amount, were retained in their raw form. Time measures the number of seconds elapsed since the first transaction, and Amount represents the monetary value of the transaction. The target variable, Class, is binary, where a value of 1 indicates a fraudulent transaction and 0 indicates a legitimate one.

A preliminary review of the dataset shows no missing values. All variables are numeric, which simplifies preprocessing and allows for straightforward integration with a range of machine learning models.

Scope and Feature Representation: This study focuses on transaction-level features to establish baseline ensemble performance on highly imbalanced fraud data. The dataset comprises individual credit card transactions, each represented by 31 numerical features. Features V1 through V28 are anonymized variables derived from Principal Component Analysis (PCA) applied to the original data by the dataset authors for privacy protection (Dal Pozzolo et al., 2015). While this anonymization is essential for ethical data sharing, it precludes reconstruction of entity-relationship graphs that would be necessary for relational modeling approaches. Specifically, the PCA transformation removes direct identifiers such as cardholder IDs, merchant IDs, device fingerprints, and IP addresses—the very entities that would form nodes in a fraud network graph.

Our analysis further applied PCA transformation (retaining 95% of variance) to compare model performance on raw versus dimensionally-reduced feature spaces. This additional PCA step, while useful for assessing feature representation robustness, reinforces the transaction-level scope of the study. As noted in the Literature Review, fraud often exhibits relational patterns such as device sharing across multiple accounts, coordinated attacks from bot networks, or collusion between buyers and sellers (Mendonça et al., 2025; Becker, 2025; Zeng et al., 2025). Graph-based approaches, including Graph Neural Networks and community detection algorithms, represent a promising extension for datasets where entity relationships are preserved.

However, for this foundational comparison of ensemble methods under resampling strategies, the transaction-level feature representation is appropriate and aligns with the majority of published fraud detection research on public datasets. Future research with access to proprietary data containing relational metadata should prioritize graph-based architectures to capture network effects and coordinated fraud schemes.

Data Preparation and Leakage Prevention: The dataset was split into training (80%) and testing (20%) sets using stratified random sampling with a fixed random seed (random_state=42) to ensure reproducibility. Stratification preserved the 0.17% fraud rate in both partitions. Importantly, the train-test split maintained the temporal ordering inherent in the dataset, as the Time feature measures seconds elapsed since the first transaction. This chronological structure ensures that the test set comprises transactions occurring after those in the training set, preventing the model from learning from future information—a critical consideration given that fraud patterns evolve over time (Hu et al., 2025).

To prevent data leakage, all preprocessing operations strictly followed the principle of fitting on training data and transforming test data. Specifically, StandardScaler normalization of Amount and Time features was fitted exclusively on training data, with the learned parameters (mean and standard deviation) then applied to scale the test set. This ensures that no information from the test set influenced the training process.

Similarly, resampling techniques—both SMOTE (Synthetic Minority Oversampling Technique) and Random Undersampling (RUS)—were applied exclusively to the training set after the train-test split. SMOTE generated synthetic minority-class samples by interpolating between existing fraud cases, while RUS reduced the majority class by random selection. In both cases, the test set remained completely unmodified, maintaining its original class distribution and ensuring unbiased performance evaluation. All sampling operations used fixed random seeds (random_state=42) for reproducibility.

Additionally, when PCA transformation was employed, the PCA model was fitted on the scaled training data (retaining 95% of variance) and then applied to transform the test data. This procedure, applied consistently across all experimental conditions, eliminates the risk of information leakage that could artificially inflate performance metrics.

Model Training and Configuration: Two ensemble classifiers were trained and evaluated: Random Forest (RF) and XGBoost. Random Forest serves as a baseline ensemble classifier against which XGBoost performance is benchmarked.

Random Forest models were configured with 300 trees (n_estimators=300), unrestricted maximum depth (max_depth=None), and parallel processing enabled (n_jobs=-1). All models used fixed random seeds (random_state=42) for reproducibility. Class weights were not manually adjusted, as class balance was instead addressed through the resampling strategies (SMOTE and RUS) applied to the training data.

XGBoost models were configured with 400 estimators (n_estimators=400), maximum tree depth of 6 (max_depth=6), a conservative learning rate of 0.05 (learning_rate=0.05), and regularization via L2 penalty (reg_lambda=1.0). Stochastic gradient boosting was employed with subsample=0.9 and colsample_bytree=0.9 to reduce overfitting. These hyperparameters were selected through preliminary cross-validation experiments on the training set to balance model complexity with generalization performance.

Each model was trained under four experimental conditions:

1. Random Forest + SMOTE (training on raw scaled features)
2. Random Forest + SMOTE (training on PCA-transformed features)
3. XGBoost + SMOTE (training on raw scaled features)

4. XGBoost + SMOTE (training on PCA-transformed features)

Additional experiments with Random Undersampling (RUS) were conducted to compare oversampling versus undersampling strategies. All training procedures maintained the strict separation between training and test data, with model fitting performed exclusively on the resampled training sets.

Evaluation Protocol: Model performance was evaluated on the held-out test set using precision, recall, and F1-score for the fraud class (positive class), along with the Area Under the ROC Curve (AUC). A fixed classification threshold of 0.5 was applied to predicted probabilities to generate binary predictions. Precision measures the proportion of flagged transactions that are truly fraudulent, recall measures the proportion of actual fraud cases successfully detected, and F1-score provides a harmonic balance between the two.

Given the extreme class imbalance (0.17% fraud rate), AUC was used as a threshold-independent metric to assess the model's ability to rank fraudulent transactions higher than legitimate ones across all possible decision thresholds. ROC curves were plotted for visual comparison of model discrimination performance.

The evaluation was conducted on the unmodified test set, which retained the original 99.83% / 0.17% class distribution. This approach ensures that performance metrics reflect real-world conditions where fraud is rare, providing a realistic assessment of operational effectiveness. All evaluation metrics were computed using scikit-learn's precision_recall_fscore_support and roc_auc_score functions with consistent parameter settings (average='binary', zero_division=0).

Interpretability Analysis with SHAP: To address the interpretability gap identified in the literature, SHAP (SHapley Additive exPlanations) analysis was employed to decompose model predictions into feature-level contributions (Lundberg & Lee, 2017). SHAP values provide a unified measure of feature importance grounded in cooperative game theory, quantifying each feature's marginal contribution to the model's output for individual predictions.

For computational efficiency while maintaining representativeness, a stratified sample was constructed from the test set comprising all fraud cases (n=98) plus up to 500 randomly selected legitimate transactions. This balanced evaluation set ensures that SHAP analysis captures the decision-making patterns for both classes without computational burden from the full 56,962-transaction test set. The sample was shuffled with a fixed random seed (random_state=42) to prevent ordering effects.

SHAP TreeExplainer was applied to all trained models (Random Forest and XGBoost on both raw and PCA-transformed features). TreeExplainer leverages the tree structure of ensemble models to efficiently compute exact SHAP values without approximation. For models trained on raw features, SHAP values were computed for all 31 original features (28 PCA-anonymized features V1-V28 plus Time and

Amount). For models trained on PCA components, SHAP values were computed for the principal components (retaining 95% of variance).

SHAP summary plots (bar plots showing mean absolute SHAP values) were generated to visualize global feature importance, highlighting which features most strongly influence fraud predictions across the dataset. Additionally, the raw SHAP values for each transaction in the evaluation sample were exported to CSV files, enabling further analysis of instance-level explanations and supporting regulatory compliance requirements for auditable decision-making.

This comprehensive SHAP implementation provides both global interpretability (which features matter most overall) and local interpretability (why individual transactions were flagged), directly addressing the "black box" concerns raised in recent literature (Baisholan et al., 2025; Zhou et al., 2023).

Reproducibility and Transparency: To facilitate independent replication and verification, all computational experiments followed strict reproducibility protocols:

1. **Dataset**: The publicly available Kaggle Credit Card Fraud Detection dataset (Dal Pozzolo et al., 2015) was used without modification. The dataset file creditcard.csv was read directly using pandas, ensuring exact replication of input data.
2. **Random Seed Control**: All stochastic operations used a fixed random seed (random_state=42), including:
   - o Train-test splitting (train_test_split)
   - o SMOTE oversampling
   - o Random undersampling
   - o Random Forest initialization
   - o XGBoost initialization
   - o PCA fitting
   - o SHAP sample selection
3. **Preprocessing Pipeline**: The exact sequence of operations was: a. Load dataset and separate features (X) from target (y) b. Split into training (80%) and test (20%) with stratification c. Fit StandardScaler on training data for Amount and Time features d. Transform both training and test data using fitted scaler e. Fit PCA (95% variance retention) on scaled training data f. Transform both training and test data using fitted PCA g. Apply SMOTE or RUS to training data only h. Train models on resampled training data i. Evaluate on unmodified test data
4. **Software Environment**: All experiments were conducted in Python 3.x with the following libraries:
   - o pandas (data manipulation)
   - o numpy (numerical operations)
   - o scikit-learn (train-test split, StandardScaler, PCA, RandomForestClassifier, metrics)

- imbalanced-learn (SMOTE, RandomUnderSampler)
    - xgboost (XGBClassifier)
    - shap (TreeExplainer, summary plots)
    - matplotlib and seaborn (visualization)
5. **Artifacts and Outputs**: The analysis generated the following reproducible artifacts:
    - res_summary.csv: Performance metrics for all model configurations
    - roc_top_models.png: ROC curves comparing top-performing models
    - shap_bar_*.png: SHAP feature importance plots (4 files, one per model)
    - shap_sample_*.csv: Raw SHAP values for all transactions in evaluation sample (4 files)
    - interpretability_summary.csv: Index mapping models to their SHAP artifacts
6. **Code Availability and Data Access:** The complete analysis is documented in a Jupyter notebook containing all preprocessing, training, evaluation, and interpretation code. The dataset is publicly available on Kaggle (creditcard.csv from the "Credit Card Fraud Detection" dataset by the Machine Learning Group at ULB). All experiments can be fully reproduced using the documented methodology, hyperparameters, and random seed values provided in this manuscript. The computational pipeline uses only open-source Python libraries (scikit-learn, imbalanced-learn, xgboost, shap, pandas, numpy, matplotlib, seaborn), ensuring accessibility for independent verification. Code and supplementary materials are available from the corresponding author upon request.

This level of documentation aligns with emerging standards for reproducible machine learning research and ensures that all findings can be independently verified or extended.

PROJECT THEORY

This study draws on Routine Activity Theory (RAT) to align model design with how fraud occurs in practice. RAT holds that crime happens when a motivated offender meets a suitable target in the absence of a capable guardian (Cohen & Felson, 1979). In e-commerce, this maps directly onto system design: the fraud model functions as a guardian on the hot path (pre-authorization) so risky transactions can be stopped before settlement (Williams, Levi, & Brookman, 2016). RAT further supports risk-based controls, such as step-up authentication, temporary holds, or manual review, when scores exceed thresholds set to reflect asymmetric business costs (Williams, 2015).

Feature engineering follows the same logic by capturing target suitability (e.g., new accounts, unusually large baskets, rapid purchase bursts, device/location mismatches) and guardianship strength (e.g., verified identity, stable device binding, reliable history) (Pratt, Holtfreter, & Reisig, 2010; Leukfeldt & Yar, 2016; Parti, 2023). Evaluation then emphasizes recall on the fraud class, PR-AUC, cost-aware threshold analysis, and latency checks to confirm the guardian can act in real-time. Together with anomaly detection, ensembles, graph methods, and interpretability, RAT provides the behavioral rationale for where to place the model, which signals to prioritize, and how to operationalize actions once risk is detected.

LITERATURE REVIEW

The increasing volume of digital transactions, especially since the COVID-19 pandemic, has led to a sharp rise in cybercrime and financial fraud within the e-commerce landscape. As Mutemi and Bacao (2024) explain, this trend places not only businesses but also consumers at heightened risk, impacting trust, financial security, and mental well-being.

Machine learning-based fraud detection systems offer a promising alternative (Baisholan et al., 2025). Unlike fixed-rule systems, they can identify complex patterns within transactional data and adjust to new threats without manual intervention. Recent studies have emphasized the increasing role of intelligent detection mechanisms in identifying fraudulent activities across digital ecosystems (Baisholan et al., 2025; Li & Yang, 2023).

One of the core challenges is the heavy reliance on rule-based or traditional fraud detection systems. As a result, many fraudulent transactions go undetected, while legitimate users are sometimes wrongly flagged, creating customer friction and operational inefficiencies (Verma & Gupta, 2025). This limitation is reinforced by findings in Becker (2025), who noted that rule-based systems fall short in detecting adaptive fraud schemes such as fake reviews and account takeovers, especially when fraud evolves over time.

Another significant issue lies in the scarcity of real-world data available for building robust detection models. According to Mutemi and Bacao (2024), many fraud detection strategies are constrained by the lack of accessible, labeled datasets, which is due to the proprietary nature of fraud-related data. As Vasant et al. (2025) point out, dataset imbalance continues to affect performance, with fraudulent activities making up a small fraction of total transactions, resulting in biased learning unless properly addressed.

Furthermore, existing fraud models often lack interpretability. This lack of transparency can erode trust in the system, impede regulatory compliance, and complicate analysts' efforts to justify or investigate suspicious transactions. The same issue is echoed in Mendonça et al. (2025), who highlight that graph-based models, though effective, often face scrutiny due to limited model explainability unless paired with reinforcement learning or attention mechanisms.

Another gap lies in the underrepresentation of emerging fraud types, such as triangulation fraud, reseller abuse, and bot-based attacks (Mutemi & Bacao, 2024). Zeng et al. (2025) further reinforce this, stating that buyer-seller collusion and behavioral manipulation are not adequately addressed by conventional fraud detection systems, which tend to focus narrowly on transaction-level anomalies. Moreover, most studies treat fraud detection as a one-time task, ignoring the need for continuous model updates and adaptation to evolving threats (Mutemi & Bacao, 2024).

The literature consistently notes that fraud datasets are severely imbalanced, that many systems remain opaque to investigators and regulators, and that findings on ensemble performance vary across settings. These issues create uncertainty about which algorithm–resampling combinations reliably improve recall without inflating false positives. To address this uncertainty, the study compares Random Forest and XGBoost trained with SMOTE and random undersampling and evaluates performance using F1 and recall. SHAP-based interpretability is then used to expose the drivers of model decisions, aligning the results with operational and compliance needs.

RESULTS

Each classifier was trained and tested under consistent preprocessing conditions, with resampling applied only to the training data. The evaluation metrics used were Precision, Recall, and F1-score, with a focus on the fraud class. These metrics help assess the model's ability to correctly identify fraudulent transactions without excessively misclassifying legitimate ones.

Table 1. Performance of Random Forest and XGBoost on Resampled Datasets Using SMOTE and Random Undersampling.

Model	Sampling Strategy	Precision	Recall	F1-Score
Random Forest	Random Undersampling	0.83	0.76	0.79
XGBoost	Random Undersampling	0.81	0.78	0.79
Random Forest	SMOTE	0.87	0.83	0.85
XGBoost	SMOTE	0.90	0.82	0.86

Uncertainty Quantification

The performance metrics reported in Table 1 represent mean values obtained through stratified k-fold cross-validation, ensuring that the class distribution was preserved across training and validation folds. Model selection involved systematic hyperparameter tuning conducted within cross-validation loops to prevent overfitting, with the final hyperparameters selected based on validation performance. While point estimates are reported here for clarity and interpretability, readers should note that confidence intervals for these metrics would provide additional insight into model stability and variance. Bootstrapping approaches, where the test set is resampled with replacement and metrics are recalculated across iterations, represent best practice for quantifying uncertainty in imbalanced classification tasks (Dal Pozzolo et al., 2015).

The absence of reported confidence intervals is acknowledged as a limitation; however, the consistent performance patterns observed across both resampling strategies (SMOTE and random undersampling) and both classifiers (Random Forest and XGBoost) suggest that the relative rankings are robust. Future validation protocols should incorporate nested cross-validation, where an outer loop evaluates model performance and an inner loop conducts hyperparameter optimization, thereby providing unbiased estimates of generalization performance along with variance measures.

Both SMOTE and random undersampling improved the recall scores of the models compared to training on imbalanced data (baseline not shown here), which is particularly important in fraud detection, where missing a fraud case is costly. SMOTE generally resulted in better F1-scores and precision, likely due to its ability to retain more information by synthetically generating minority class samples rather than discarding majority samples.

The XGBoost model combined with SMOTE achieved the highest F1-score (0.86), indicating it was the most balanced in detecting fraud while minimizing false positives. In contrast, models using random undersampling performed comparably in recall but slightly lower in precision, due to reduced training data size.

Table 2. Performance on SMOTE Data: Comparison of F1-scores for Random Forest and XGBoost under different resampling strategies.

Sampling Strategy	Random Forest F1	XGBoost F1
Random Undersampling	0.79	0.79
SMOTE	0.85	0.86

DISCUSSION

The results indicate that XGBoost slightly outperformed Random Forest in both resampling strategies. With SMOTE, the performance gap widened, with XGBoost achieving the highest F1-score. This suggests that XGBoost's gradient boosting mechanism may be more effective at leveraging the additional synthetic data created by SMOTE, improving generalization on the minority class. Although both models are viable options, XGBoost demonstrated more consistent and slightly superior performance across the board, especially when trained on SMOTE-balanced data.

INTERPRETABILITY AND ANALYST SUPPORT

SHAP (SHapley Additive exPlanations) analysis was employed to decompose model predictions into feature-level contributions, directly addressing the interpretability gap identified in the literature (Baisholan et al., 2025; Zhou et al., 2023). This approach enables fraud analysts to understand which transaction characteristics—such as Amount, Time, or specific PCA components—drive individual risk scores. In operational settings, SHAP values serve multiple critical functions: they support regulatory compliance by providing auditable explanations for declined transactions; they facilitate analyst investigation by highlighting suspicious patterns (e.g., unusually high V4 or V14 values that correlate with known fraud schemes); and they enable continuous model refinement through analyst feedback on false positives.

This aligns with the theoretical framework's discussion of guardianship mechanisms, where transparency strengthens the "capable guardian" role by ensuring that both automated systems and human analysts work cohesively to prevent fraud (Cohen & Felson, 1979; Williams, Levi, & Brookman, 2016). When customers dispute flagged transactions, SHAP-based explanations provide customer service representatives with intelligible reasons rather than opaque algorithmic outputs, reducing friction and maintaining trust. Future deployments should integrate SHAP outputs directly into fraud review dashboards, potentially with visualizations showing feature contributions for flagged transactions ranked by uncertainty or borderline scores.

COST-AWARE THRESHOLD CALIBRATION

Consistent with Routine Activity Theory's emphasis on asymmetric costs of fraud prevention (Williams, 2015), these performance metrics should inform threshold calibration in production environments. While F1-score provides a balanced view of precision and recall, real-world deployment requires explicit consideration of the relative costs of false positives (customer friction, manual review workload, potential account abandonment) versus false negatives (fraud losses, chargeback fees, reputational damage). For instance, if the average fraud loss is $500 and the cost of manually reviewing a flagged transaction is $5, organizations can tolerate a 100:1 false-positive-to-true-positive ratio before review costs exceed fraud savings.

The models presented here achieved precision rates of 0.83–0.90, suggesting that for every genuine fraud case detected, fewer than two legitimate transactions are incorrectly flagged—a favorable ratio in most cost scenarios. Organizations should conduct threshold analysis by plotting expected financial loss across varying decision thresholds, selecting the operating point that minimizes total cost. While this study focuses on F1-score for model comparison, the Area Under the Precision-Recall Curve (AUPRC) provides a threshold-independent assessment particularly suited to imbalanced datasets and was monitored during model development to ensure robust performance across varying decision points. Future work should explicitly model cost functions and report threshold recommendations calibrated to specific business contexts, potentially using decision curve analysis or expected value frameworks.

RECOMMENDATIONS

Building on the empirical results and findings from this research, the ensemble classifiers, particularly Random Forest and XGBoost, are the strongest classifiers recommended for production pilots and deployment, given their observed performance, with decision-threshold calibration to manage precision–recall trade-offs in rare-event detection. Training with SMOTE and benchmarking against random undersampling will evaluate models using complementary performance metrics to confirm stability across various settings, thereby addressing the issue of class imbalance.

To close the gap between offline experiments and real use, roll out in stages (shadow or A/B evaluation) before a full release. Because interpretability is essential for stakeholder trust and compliance, pair accuracy checks with clear explanations and review procedures. Finally, build in routine monitoring for drift and schedule periodic retraining so models keep pace with changing fraud patterns.

CONCLUSIONS AND LIMITATIONS

This study evaluated the effectiveness of two popular machine learning classifiers, Random Forest and XGBoost, for credit card fraud detection, using different strategies to address class imbalance: SMOTE (Synthetic Minority Oversampling

Technique) and Random Undersampling. Fraudulent transactions constituted a very small fraction of the dataset, making effective handling of imbalance critical to model performance. Although the results confirm the potential of ensemble methods and resampling strategies in e-commerce fraud detection, the study also underscores several limitations.

The reliance on a static, publicly available dataset from 2013 limits generalizability to current fraud tactics. The 11-year gap between data collection and analysis means emerging fraud vectors (e.g., mobile-wallet exploitation, cryptocurrency-linked schemes) are not represented. Out-of-time validation on more recent data would be essential before production deployment. The absence of real-time adaptation and relational modeling constrains the models' effectiveness against emerging fraud tactics.

The findings of this study highlight the effectiveness of ensemble classifiers, specifically Random Forest and XGBoost, in detecting financial fraud within imbalanced datasets. The performance gains observed through resampling techniques underscore the importance of addressing class imbalance in financial fraud detection. Nonetheless, several avenues for further investigation remain. First, while SMOTE significantly improved classification metrics, it introduces synthetic data that may not fully reflect the complexity of actual fraudulent behavior. Future research should explore hybrid approaches that combine SMOTE with techniques such as Tomek Links or Edited Nearest Neighbors to reduce overlap between classes and enhance data quality. Second, this study utilized a publicly available dataset, which, although valuable for benchmarking, does not replicate the full range of variables and conditions present in real-world e-commerce systems. Subsequent research should evaluate models using proprietary or live transactional data that reflect current fraud tactics, seasonal behaviors, and platform-specific vulnerabilities.

Third, the interpretability of machine learning models remains a significant concern, particularly in regulated sectors such as finance. While SHAP values were used to explain XGBoost predictions, a comparative analysis of different interpretability methods across multiple models was not conducted. Future studies should investigate the utility and consistency of interpretability frameworks, such as LIME, counterfactual explanations, and rule extraction, in the context of fraud detection. Fourth, the current research treated each transaction as an independent observation. However, many fraudulent schemes involve coordination across multiple accounts, devices, or entities. Graph-based modeling techniques, including Graph Neural Networks, should be considered to capture relationships and detect patterns indicative of organized or networked fraud. Fifth, the models applied in this study followed a static learning approach. Given the dynamic nature of e-commerce fraud, there is a need for adaptive systems that can update their parameters as new data becomes available. Online learning and incremental model updating should be explored to maintain detection accuracy over time.

Finally, the integration of expert knowledge into the model evaluation and refinement process should be prioritized. Human-in-the-loop frameworks, where analysts provide feedback on model outputs or assist in label verification, may improve both the precision of detection and the practical trustworthiness of deployed systems. Addressing these areas in future research will contribute to the development of more robust, scalable, and context-aware fraud detection systems for the e-commerce sector.

ACKNOWLEDGMENTS

This research utilized the publicly available Credit Card Fraud Detection dataset compiled by the Machine Learning Group at Université Libre de Bruxelles (ULB) and made available through Kaggle. We acknowledge the original data collectors (Dal Pozzolo et al., 2015) for making this resource available to the research community.

REFERENCES

Agrahari, S., & Singh, A. K. (2022). Concept drift detection in data stream mining: A literature review. *Journal of King Saud University. Computer and Information Sciences, 34*(10), 9523–9540. DOI: 10.1016/j.jksuci.2021.11.006

Ahmed, K. H., Axelsson, S., Li, Y., & Sagheer, A. M. (2025). A credit card fraud detection approach based on ensemble machine learning classifier with hybrid data sampling. *Machine Learning with Applications, 20*, 100675. DOI: 10.1016/j.mlwa.2025.100675

Baisholan, N., Dietz, J. E., Gnatyuk, S., Turdalyuly, M., Matson, E. T., & Baisholanova, K. (2025). FraudX AI: An interpretable machine learning framework for credit card fraud detection on imbalanced datasets. *Computers, 14*(120), 120. Advance online publication. DOI: 10.3390/computers14040120

Becker, L. (2025). Anomaly detection in e-commerce platforms via graph neural networks. *Asia Pacific Economic and Management Review, 15*(1), 44–61. DOI: 10.62177/apemr.v2i2.208

Byrapu Reddy, S. R., Sharma, R., & Patel, N. (2024). Effective fraud detection in e-commerce: Leveraging machine learning and big data analytics. *International Journal of Computer Applications, 182*(12), 1–8.

Cohen, L. E., & Felson, M. (1979). Social change and crime rate trends: A routine activity approach. *American Sociological Review, 44*(4), 588. DOI: 10.2307/2094589

Dal Pozzolo, A., Caelen, O., Johnson, R. A., & Bontempi, G. (2015). Calibrating probability with undersampling for unbalanced classification. In *2015 IEEE Symposium Series on Computational Intelligence* (pp. 159–166). https://doi.org/DOI: 10.1109/SSCI.2015.33

Federal Trade Commission. (2025, July 30). *New FTC data show a big Jump in reported losses to fraud to $12.5 billion in 2024*. https://www.ftc.gov/news-events/news/press-releases/2025/03/new-ftc-data-show-big-jump-reported-losses-fraud-125-billion-2024?utm_source=chatgpt.com

Hu, L., Lu, Y., & Feng, Y. (2025). Concept drift detection based on deep neural networks and Autoencoders. *Applied Sciences (Basel, Switzerland)*, *15*(6), 3056. DOI: 10.3390/app15063056

Leukfeldt, E. R., & Yar, M. (2016). Applying routine activity theory to cybercrime: A theoretical and empirical analysis. *Deviant Behavior*, *37*(3), 263–280. DOI: 10.1080/01639625.2015.1012409

Li, J., & Yang, D. (2023). Research on financial fraud detection models integrating multiple relational graphs. *Systems*, *11*(539), 539. Advance online publication. DOI: 10.3390/systems11110539

Mendonça, A. C. M., Silva, F. L., de Oliveira, L. E. C., Souza, J. A. C., & de Souza, J. T. (2025). Graph-based deep learning for e-commerce fraud detection. *Computers*, *14*(110). Advance online publication. DOI: 10.3390/computers14040110

Motie, S., & Raahemi, B. (2024). Financial fraud detection using graph neural networks: A systematic review. *Expert Systems with Applications*, *240*, 122156. DOI: 10.1016/j.eswa.2023.122156

Mutemi, A., & Bacao, F. (2024). E-commerce fraud detection based on machine learning techniques: Systematic literature review. *Big Data Mining and Analytics*, *7*(2), 419–444. DOI: 10.26599/BDMA.2023.9020023

Pratt, T. C., Holtfreter, K., & Reisig, M. D. (2010). Routine online activity and internet fraud targeting: Extending the generality of routine activity theory. *Journal of Research in Crime and Delinquency*, *47*(3), 267–296. DOI: 10.1177/0022427810365903

Reddy, D. H. (2022). An analysis of the supervised learning approach for online fraud detection. *Computational Intelligence and Machine Learning*, *3*(2), 47–56. DOI: 10.36647/CIML/03.02.A007

The Nilson Report. (2025, January 6). *Payment card fraud losses approach $34 billion*. GlobeNewswire News Room. https://www.globenewswire.com/news-release/2025/01/06/3004931/0/en/Payment-Card-Fraud-Losses-Approach-34-Billion.html?utm_source=chatgpt.com

Vasant, M., Rahim, N. A., & Rani, A. M. A. (2025). Enhancing e-commerce security: A hybrid machine learning approach to fraud detection. *Security and Privacy*, *8*(1), e194. DOI: 10.1002/spy2.194

Verma, A., & Gupta, M. (2025). Harnessing the use of artificial intelligence in financial fraud detection. *International Journal of Education & Management Studies*, *15*(1), 116–122.

Williams, M. L. (2015). Guardians upon high: An application of routine activities theory to online identity theft in Europe at the country and individual level. *British Journal of Criminology*, *56*(1), 21–48. DOI: 10.1093/bjc/azv011

Yazici, Y. (2020). Approaches to fraud detection on credit card transactions using artificial intelligence methods. *Computer Science and Information Technology*, •••, 235–244. DOI: 10.5121/csit.2020.101018

Zeng, Q., Jin, Y., Liu, Y., & Xu, X. (2025). NNEnsLeG: A novel approach for e-commerce payment fraud detection using ensemble learning and neural networks. *Information Sciences*, *646*, 17–32. DOI: 10.1016/j.ins.2023.119532

Zhou, Y., Li, H., Xiao, Z., & Qiu, J. (2023). A user-centered explainable artificial intelligence approach for financial fraud detection. *Finance Research Letters*, *58*, 104309. DOI: 10.1016/j.frl.2023.104309

APPENDIX A: MODEL DOCUMENTATION

Model Overview

Model Type: XGBoost Gradient Boosted Decision Trees with SMOTE resampling
Research Context: Academic study on fraud detection in imbalanced datasets
Dataset: Credit Card Fraud Detection Dataset (Dal Pozzolo et al., 2015)
Training Period: September 2013 (two-day transaction window)
Developed By: Lawrence Ejime Iweriebor & Eugene J. Lewis /Capitol Technology University
Date: 10/12/2025
Contact: leiweriebor@yahoo.com, eugenejmlewis@gmail.com

Research Purpose

Primary Objectives:

- Compare ensemble classifier performance (Random Forest vs. XGBoost) on highly imbalanced fraud data
- Evaluate resampling strategies (SMOTE vs. Random Undersampling) for class imbalance
- Demonstrate interpretable fraud detection using SHAP explanations
- Establish reproducible methodology for fraud detection research

Target Audience:

- Academic researchers in machine learning and fraud detection
- Graduate students studying imbalanced classification
- Scholars in financial cybersecurity
- Practitioners seeking evidence-based fraud detection approaches

Research Scope:

- Transaction-level fraud detection
- Comparative analysis of ensemble methods
- Interpretability via SHAP values
- Benchmarking on publicly available data

Dataset Characteristics

Source: Kaggle Credit Card Fraud Detection Dataset
Original Study: Dal Pozzolo et al. (2015)
Data Collection: European cardholders, September 2013
Size: 284,807 transactions
Class Distribution:

- Legitimate: 284,315 (99.83%)
- Fraudulent: 492 (0.17%)

Features:

- 28 PCA-transformed features (V1–V28) - anonymized by dataset authors
- Time: seconds elapsed since first transaction
- Amount: transaction monetary value
- Class: binary label (0=legitimate, 1=fraud)

Preprocessing Applied:

- StandardScaler normalization of Amount and Time (fitted on training data only)
- Additional PCA transformation (95% variance retention) for comparison experiments
- Stratified 80/20 train-test split (random_state=42)
- SMOTE and Random Undersampling applied to training set only

Known Data Limitations:

- The dataset is 11 years old (collected 2013, analyzed 2024-2025)
- PCA anonymization by original authors prevents entity-relationship analysis
- Geographic scope limited to European cardholders
- Temporal scope limited to two-day window
- No demographic, merchant category, or device information available

Model Configuration

Models Evaluated:

1. Random Forest (baseline ensemble)

- n_estimators=300
- max_depth=None (unrestricted)
- random_state=42
- n_jobs=-1 (parallel processing)

2. XGBoost (advanced ensemble)
   - n_estimators=400
   - max_depth=6
   - learning_rate=0.05
   - reg_lambda=1.0 (L2 regularization)
   - subsample=0.9
   - colsample_bytree=0.9
   - random_state=42

Experimental Conditions:

- Each classifier trained on: (a) raw scaled features, (b) PCA-transformed features
- Each trained with: (a) SMOTE resampling, (b) Random Undersampling
- Total configurations evaluated: 8 (2 classifiers × 2 feature types × 2 resampling strategies)

Performance Results

Evaluation Metrics: Precision, Recall, F1-Score (fraud class), Area Under ROC Curve (AUC)

Best Performing Configuration (XGBoost + SMOTE on raw features):

- Precision: 0.90
- Recall: 0.82
- F1-Score: 0.86

Table 3. Comparison Results

Model	Resampling	Features	F1-Score
XGBoost	SMOTE	Raw	0.86
Random Forest	SMOTE	Raw	0.85
XGBoost	Undersampling	Raw	0.79
Random Forest	Undersampling	Raw	0.79

Key Finding: SMOTE consistently outperformed Random Undersampling across both classifiers; XGBoost showed marginal advantage over Random Forest, especially with SMOTE.

Evaluation Context:

- Fixed threshold: 0.5
- Test set: Unmodified (99.83% / 0.17% distribution preserved)
- Cross-validation: Stratified k-fold on training set for hyperparameter selection
- Uncertainty: Point estimates reported; confidence intervals acknowledged as future work

Interpretability Analysis

Method: SHAP (SHapley Additive exPlanations) using TreeExplainer

Sample: All fraud cases (n=98) + 500 randomly selected legitimate transactions from test set

Artifacts Generated:

- SHAP bar plots showing global feature importance (4 plots: RF/XGB × Raw/PCA)
- CSV files with raw SHAP values for each transaction (4 files)
- Summary statistics mapping features to importance rankings

Key Insights:

- SHAP analysis reveals which PCA components and raw features (Time, Amount) most influence fraud predictions
- Enables both global interpretability (overall feature importance) and local interpretability (individual transaction explanations)
- Addresses "black box" concerns in machine learning literature

Research Limitations

Dataset Limitations:

1. Temporal Validity: 11-year gap between data collection (2013) and analysis (2024-2025); fraud patterns have evolved significantly
2. Feature Anonymization: PCA transformation by dataset authors prevents interpretation of business-meaningful features and graph-based analysis

3. Geographic Scope: European cardholders only; generalizability to other regions unknown
4. Narrow Time Window: Two days of transactions; seasonal and long-term patterns not captured
5. Class Imbalance: 0.17% fraud rate may not reflect all fraud contexts

Methodological Limitations:

1. Static Learning: Models do not adapt to concept drift over time
2. Transaction Independence: No modeling of relational patterns (e.g., coordinated fraud rings)
3. Synthetic Data: SMOTE generates artificial samples that may not reflect real fraud diversity
4. Fixed Threshold: 0.5 probability threshold used; threshold optimization not performed
5. Confidence Intervals: Point estimates reported; variance measures acknowledged as future work

Generalizability Concerns:

- Results specific to this dataset and fraud rate
- Performance on current fraud tactics unknown
- Applicability to non-credit-card fraud types (e.g., mobile wallets, cryptocurrency) not tested

Ethical and Scholarly Considerations

Data Privacy:

- Dataset already anonymized via PCA by original authors
- No re-identification possible from published results
- SHAP values reveal feature importance, not individual identities

Bias and Fairness:

- Cannot assess fairness across demographic groups due to anonymization
- Geographic bias: European cardholders only
- Temporal bias: 2013 fraud patterns may not reflect current demographics of fraud victims

Research Ethics:

- Public dataset used under open data license
- No human subjects involved beyond original data collection (governed by Dal Pozzolo et al., 2015)
- Results reported transparently including limitations

Scholarly Contribution:

- Advances understanding of ensemble methods for imbalanced classification
- Demonstrates value of SMOTE over Random Undersampling
- Provides reproducible methodology for fraud detection research
- Connects machine learning techniques to criminological theory (Routine Activity Theory)

Reproducibility
Complete reproducibility protocols documented in manuscript:

- Dataset: Publicly available on Kaggle
- Random seeds: random_state=42 for all stochastic operations
- Preprocessing: Step-by-step pipeline documented
- Software: Python 3.x with standard open-source libraries (scikit-learn, imbalanced-learn, xgboost, shap)
- Hyperparameters: All values explicitly specified
- Evaluation: Metrics computed with documented parameter settings

Artifacts Available:

- Performance summary (res_summary.csv)
- ROC curves (roc_top_models.png)
- SHAP importance plots (4 PNG files)
- SHAP values (4 CSV files)
- Model-artifact mapping (interpretability_summary.csv)

Code Availability: Computational notebooks documenting the complete pipeline are available from the corresponding author upon reasonable request.

Future Research Directions

Based on limitations identified in this study, future research should:

1. Temporal Validation: Evaluate models on recent fraud data (2023-2025) to assess concept drift
2. Graph-Based Modeling: Apply Graph Neural Networks to datasets with preserved entity relationships
3. Hybrid Resampling: Combine SMOTE with techniques like Tomek Links or Edited Nearest Neighbors
4. Threshold Optimization: Conduct cost-sensitive threshold calibration for different fraud contexts
5. Uncertainty Quantification: Report confidence intervals via bootstrapping or nested cross-validation
6. Comparative Interpretability: Evaluate LIME, counterfactual explanations alongside SHAP
7. Online Learning: Develop adaptive models that update parameters as new fraud patterns emerge
8. Real-World Validation: Partner with financial institutions to test on proprietary operational data

Contact and Correspondence

Principal Investigator: Lawrence Ejime Iweriebor & Eugene J. Lewis,
Institution: Capitol Technology University
Email: leiweriebor@yahoo.com, eugenejmlewis@gmail.com
ORCID: https://orcid.org/0009-0004-4812-3787, https://orcid.org/0000-0002-2956-0760

For questions about methodology, dataset access, or replication:

- Dataset: Available at https://www.kaggle.com/datasets/mlg-ulb/creditcardfraud
- Correspondence: leiweriebor@yahoo.com, eugenejmlewis@gmail.com
- Supplementary materials: Available upon reasonable request

Chapter 13
Healthcare Cybersecurity:
A Critical Analysis of the Prevalence of Ransomware and Phishing Attacks on Hospital Medical Records

Oladele Stephen Olawoye
http://orcid.org/0009-0003-1117-1374
Capitol Technology University, USA

Eugene J. Lewis
http://orcid.org/0000-0002-2956-0760
Capitol Technology University, USA

ABSTRACT

Hospitals face rising threats from ransomware and phishing attacks which reveal both system vulnerabilities and staff security weaknesses in their medical record systems. Healthcare sector has faced tremendous cyber-attacks since the inception of Electronic Health Records (EHRs) - digital versions of a patient's medical history, stored and accessed electronically. Healthcare environments face regular attacks from malware like ransomware, adware, spyware, trojan horses, worms, viruses, botnets, and rootkits, so organizations need to identify these threats. Attackers use system and network weaknesses to launch phishing email attacks and distribute harmful email attachments. Healthcare organizations need to establish both technical and non-technical security protocols which combine advanced threat detection with staff training and regulatory adherence and protected data backups. Digital healthcare requires advanced cybersecurity systems to achieve complete protection.

DOI: 10.4018/979-8-2600-1016-7.ch013

INTRODUCTION

EHRs, the Internet of Things (IoT) and Internet of Medical Things (IoMT) technologies have brought a healthcare revolution through their ability to track patient vital signs in real-time and improve data management and diagnostic accuracy for enhanced medical outcomes. The increasing number of IoT and IoMT systems has introduced new security risks which allow unauthorized access to medical records and critical healthcare systems for data theft. Healthcare organizations need to create complete security protocols because they experience sophisticated ransomware and phishing attacks that use generative and agentic AI. In addition, there is Ransomware-as-a-Service (RaaS) and Malware-as-a-Service, a criminal business model where cybercriminals operate which lets others use their ransomware tools to execute attacks (Kaspersky, n.d; KELA Cyber Threat Intelligence (2025).

Hospitals need to create multiple security protocols which unite sophisticated threat detection systems with employee training initiatives and strict regulatory compliance and reliable data protection solutions. Multiple security layers must be implemented to defend patient information and healthcare services from emerging cyber threats (Ponemon Institute, 2022).

Healthcare facilities that operate like hospitals and healthcare institutions maintain extensive collections of sensitive information which include both personally identifiable information (PII) and protected health information (PHI). The dark web values this information because cybercriminals use it to commit identity theft and insurance fraud against healthcare organizations (Ponemon Institute, 2022). The number of cyberattacks has grown significantly because attackers now use advanced methods which include ransomware and phishing schemes.

Healthcare facilities face major threats from ransomware attacks. The attackers gain access to hospital systems to encrypt essential patient information before asking for payment to restore access to the data. The disruption of these systems creates major issues for emergency responses because healthcare providers need immediate access to patient information to deliver proper medical treatment. Medical records that cannot be accessed lead to delayed treatment which poses serious health dangers to patients. Phishing attacks use deceptive methods to trick people into revealing their login credentials while also making them unknowingly download harmful software. The use of typical human actions by cybercriminals enables them to obtain unauthorized access to healthcare data which results in major privacy breaches for patients (CISA, 2019).

The number of cyberattacks grows because security breakdowns in cyberspace produce consequences which surpass monetary losses and regulatory fines. Medical deception in healthcare practice results in major issues that damage patient trust in medical providers which weakens the essential therapeutic bond needed for proper patient care. HIPAA (Health Insurance Portability and Accountability Act) non-compliance happens when data security breaches fail to meet the law's strict rules for protecting patient information and keeping it confidential (Ponemon Institute, 2022).

Healthcare organizations need to establish strong security systems because cybersecurity threats continue to grow in severity. Organizations must develop full cybersecurity plans which address both system vulnerabilities and human security weaknesses according to the plan. The protection of sensitive health information needs three fundamental components which include staff training programs and threat detection systems and data backup systems that provide resilience. Healthcare organizations need to take immediate action against digital transformation speed because they must defend both medical information and healthcare delivery systems.

To fully understand this concept, below are definitions of common terms used in the course of this write-up.

PROBLEM STATEMENT

The healthcare sector experiences increasing security threats because of ransomware and phishing attacks which lead to substantial medical record exposure and operational system failures. The Verizon (2020) report indicates that attackers exposed more than 29 million patient records through 655 data breaches which made up 27% of all malware incidents. DBIR (2020) reports that phishing attacks lead to 22% of all incidents which enables attackers to launch extensive cyberattacks. The disclosure of personal information during data breaches threatens patient privacy while causing operational disruptions that lead to financial losses and emotional suffering for affected patients (Verizon, 2020). The Privacy Act of 1974 and HIPAA offer protection, but numerous organizations lack proper cybersecurity systems according to NIST (2018). Organizations must identify various malware types and understand system weaknesses pathways of attacks, while considering technical and non-technical measures to harden attach surface. The significance of the study is important to know why this topic is relevant in today's world.

SIGNIFICANCE OF THE STUDY

The technical problems that ransomware and phishing attacks create produce additional impacts that extend past their direct effects. The healthcare system faces substantial financial and legal and clinical risks in this situation. The Ponemon Institute (2022) states that organizations need to spend $10.1 million on average to handle breach-related expenses which include legal fees and recovery costs and payment of fines. Noncompliance with HIPAA or GDPR regulations will lead to penalties and more regulatory oversight according (NIST, 2018.). The medical consequences of these events include postponed medical treatments and abandoned surgical procedures which happened during WannaCry and Scripps Health incidents that put patient safety at risk (Kwon et al. 2020; Health IT Security, 2021). The research demonstrates that healthcare facilities must establish robust security measures because it proves cyberattacks endanger patient welfare while damaging public confidence in medical services.

METHODOLOGY

The research design combines qualitative literature review with case study methods to study risk management systems. The research used non-human qualitative methods to combine results from previous studies. The research draws data from peer-reviewed journals and government reports and healthcare breach records which cover the period from 2018 to 2025. The research bases its analysis on the NIST Cybersecurity Framework together with recognized healthcare risk management concepts (NIST, 2018).

The WannaCry, Colonial Pipeline and Scripps Health cases show how ransomware and phishing attacks affect healthcare organizations. Healthcare organizations face rising numbers of cyberattacks which result in major medical record breaches and operational system interruptions. The Verizon (2020) report shows healthcare organizations experienced 655 data breaches which exposed 29 million patient records while ransomware attacks caused 27% of all malware-related incidents. The DBIR (2020) shows that phishing attacks represent 22% of all breaches because they enable attackers to launch more extensive cyberattacks. The two main security risks that emerge from these incidents involve patient privacy violations and permanent damage to operational business functions. Medical identity theft victims face multiple challenges which include severe mental distress and monetary losses and potential negative effects on their health (DBIR, 2020; Verizon, 2020).

Multiple healthcare organizations fail to establish strong cybersecurity frameworks despite having the Privacy Act of 1974 and HIPAA regulations in place (HHS, n.d.). The healthcare sector faces one main type of malware threat which includes ransomware. The identification of risk vectors enables organizations to understand how threats exploit system weaknesses through phishing emails and unsecured devices. Organizations need to combine technical security measures with non-technical approaches that include threat detection systems and secure data backups and staff training and regulatory compliance to achieve effective risk management. The combination of multiple security strategies enables organizations to identify cyber threats early and stop them from happening while protecting sensitive patient information (Ponemon Institute, 2022; Verizon, 2020).

THEORIES FROM THE LITERATURE

The Malware Threats section identifies various malware types which include ransomware and adware and spyware and trojan horses and worms and viruses and botnets and rootkits. Risk Vectors show the entry points through which threats access systems and networks to find weaknesses. Risk Management examines security protocols which unite technical solutions with non-technical measures to defend against advanced threats and train staff and follow regulations and protect backup data.

The WannaCry ransomware attack targeted Microsoft Windows systems during May 2017 marked the beginning of this specific ransomware variant. The EternalBlue exploit enabled WannaCry to spread between networks while it encrypted files and demanded Bitcoin payments from victims. The ransomware nature of this attack creates difficulties for healthcare organizations because it blocks their access to vital patient information (Gorman, 2023).

The DarkSide group conducted a ransomware attack against Colonial Pipeline during May 2021. The malware used encryption to lock down essential systems before demanding payment from the DarkSide group which resulted in major disruptions to US energy distribution. The Colonial Pipeline attack on critical infrastructure demonstrates how ransomware attacks can impact healthcare-connected systems which result in system-wide consequences (Gorman, 2023; Cohen, 2021).

Scripps Health became the target of a ransomware attack when it occurred in May 2021. The healthcare organization needed to disable multiple operational systems while redirecting patients to alternative medical facilities because of this security breach. The healthcare services experienced disruptions because of the malware attack which resulted in encrypted data and compromised patient care (Miller, 2021).

These three major cybersecurity incidents show how organizations across all sectors face widespread security threats with healthcare organizations being among the most vulnerable. Organizations need to understand malware types and adversary attack methods and implement strategic security measures to enhance their cybersecurity defenses. The next topic introduces Risk vendors that explain pathways of attacks.

Risk Vectors

Healthcare facilities experience rising cyber-attacks because of malware incidents which include ransomware and spyware threats. Healthcare organizations need to detect system vulnerabilities because attackers use phishing emails and malicious attachments to gain access to their systems. The three major cybersecurity incidents show how organizations across all industries face widespread security threats with healthcare organizations being among the most vulnerable. Organizations need to understand malware types and adversary attack methods and implement strategic countermeasures to enhance their cybersecurity defenses.

Healthcare organizations need to create detection methods for network pathways and system entry points which cyber threats use to attack patient data while maintaining healthcare regulatory compliance.

Phishing/ Social Engineering

Social engineering describes the methods cybercriminals use to extract confidential data from people through phishing attacks which represent their primary approach. The attackers in phishing attempts work to get sensitive information from victims by creating fake emergencies and using fear tactics to gain their trust. Healthcare networks face cyber-attacks through phishing attacks which result in unauthorized system access and data breaches according to research findings that show 22% of such incidents stem from these attacks. The combination of deceptive emails and malicious websites in phishing attacks leads to malware installation which reveals both PII and PHI data. Attackers create fake domains and basic email addresses to execute psychological manipulation which forces users to take actions without performing any verification checks (Ponemon Institute, 2022; Kaspersky, n.d.; Verizon, 2020).

Research evidence demonstrates that spear phishing targets specific individuals through customized messages, yet smishing attacks use deceptive text messages to steal confidential information. Attackers employ two primary methods to deceive users through fake security alerts about account threats which lead victims to dangerous links for protection (Ponemon Institute, 2022; Verizon, 2020).

Research indicates that healthcare cybersecurity has achieved some advancements yet continues to encounter persistent security problems. Organizations face difficulties in achieving information assurance because they do not have sufficient phishing attack awareness training programs. The healthcare industry requires enhanced training programs because current human vulnerability education fails to provide adequate protection. Healthcare organizations should develop targeted training programs for staff members to teach them phishing attack identification and response techniques which will reduce phishing attack incidents (Ponemon Institute, 2022; CISA, 2020; Verizon, 2020).

Malicious Insider

Research studies have identified malicious insiders as organization members who deliberately break security rules because they want financial benefits or seek revenge or follow ideological beliefs. The Ponemon Institute (2022) and Verizon (2020) report that insiders who harm security systems base their actions on financial rewards and organizational disputes and a need to reveal system weaknesses. The actions of these individuals result in major security incidents which harm organizational reputation while causing substantial financial damage and breaking customer trust.

Research findings demonstrate that accidental insiders include all personnel who work for the organization and its contractors who unintentionally reveal security weaknesses become visible. Security breaches occur because human errors combine with inadequate staff training and insufficient employee supervision. An employee faces risk from phishing attacks while simultaneously disclosing sensitive information because they do not recognize its importance (CISA, 2020). Organizations need to establish complete training programs and strong security awareness initiatives because accidental insiders do not have malicious intentions, yet they create major security threats (Verizon, 2020; Ponemon Institute, 2022).

Organizations experience their most severe security threats because malicious insiders represent their most dangerous security threat. The Verizon Protected Health Information Data Breach Report (PHIDBR, 2018) reveals healthcare organizations face the greatest risk of insider attacks because 58% of all insider incidents occur in this sector. The report defines insiders as all people who have permission to access or understand organizational resources which include staff members and facilities and information and equipment and networks and systems. Healthcare organizations face elevated security risks because their systems store vulnerable personally identifiable information (PII) and protected health information (PHI) which can be sold to black market operators (PHIDBR, 2018).

Research on cybersecurity shows that healthcare organizations do not have sufficient protection systems against malware attacks which include ransomware attacks. The healthcare sector needs to detect its current weaknesses before it can start fixing them. The healthcare industry faces increased cyberattack risks because it depends on outdated information technology systems. Healthcare organizations face two main challenges when they need to fix software vulnerabilities because they lack sufficient resources and specialized technical expertise. Healthcare facilities operate without proper cybersecurity protection because they cannot find enough IT staff to support their systems. Healthcare organizations choose to pay ransom demands because they want to prevent patient data exposure and maintain public trust (Craig & Corey, 2021).

Research findings show that insufficient employee training and lack of awareness about security protocols increase the risk of insider threats. The healthcare industry needs to solve its current information assurance and training deficits. Security breaches occur when staff members lack understanding of security protocols and procedures (CISA, 2020; NIST, 2018). The lack of proper training leads to errors which compromise the security of an organization (NIST, 2018).

Supply-Chain Attack

Cyber attackers exploit supply chain vulnerabilities to execute attacks which result in system breaches through indirect methods (Kaspersky, n.d.). Research findings demonstrate that hackers exploit third-party vendor vulnerabilities to gain access to target organizations through supply chain attacks. Security systems fail to detect these attacks because organizations trust their external vendors. The two main supply chain attack methods include software supply chain attacks which introduce malware during development or updates and hardware attacks which damage devices during manufacturing (Zhuoran, et al, 2025)

The healthcare sector experienced two major data breaches at CaptureRx and MedNetworx which exposed one million patient records and revealed weaknesses in risk evaluation and cybersecurity protection. Medical devices connected through networks create advanced security challenges because of their complex interdependent systems. Healthcare organizations need to perform complete vendor risk evaluations while implementing secure development practices for software and hardware and verifying component authenticity and delivering cybersecurity training to staff members (Basu et al., 2019; Kolbasuk, 2022).

The Target.com data breach demonstrates third-party vendor risks because it began with a vendor attack which resulted in $18.5 million settlement and exposed 70 million customer records; the incident proves healthcare organizations need to build robust vendor management systems and authentication protocols (StrongDM, 2025). Risk management concept explores ways to harden the security layer of healthcare IT infrastructure in the healthcare space.

RISK MANAGEMENT

Risk Management explores how organizations that harden their security layer with series of software, hardware, and organizational internal standards and policies that tend towards technical and non-technical approach. Risk Management investigates the following question: How can healthcare organizations create complete risk management systems which unite sophisticated technical security systems with non-technical protocols including staff education and regulatory adherence and protected data storage methods to identify and handle cyber threats and defend patient data?

Technical Measures

Patching and Updates

The process of updating software and systems through patching operations leads to improved functionality and security vulnerability fixes and system bug resolutions. System updates deliver new functionality and performance enhancements, but patches specifically address particular security vulnerabilities and system defects. Healthcare organizations must perform updates and patches as standard cybersecurity protocols because these practices defend systems from cyber threats while keeping them operational. Organizations in the healthcare sectors can reduce their security threat exposure through systematic patch implementation according to the incidents. The WannaCry attack showed that systems without proper patching become attack targets because organizations that follow proper patch management strategies can avoid such incidents (Kaspersky, n.d.; Roumani, 2021).

Network Segmentation

Network segmentation helps prevent WannaCry and Colonial Pipeline and Scripps Health ransomware attacks from spreading throughout networks. Healthcare organizations can protect their sensitive data better through the process of separating critical systems from each other. Network segmentation enables organizations to establish stronger access control systems. Organizations can apply security measures based on the level of sensitivity for each network segment they create. Organizations should establish separate segments for sensitive data which require advanced authentication systems and increased surveillance measures. The security system becomes more effective at stopping internal threats while simultaneously strengthening defenses against outside cyber threats (Cynet, 2022).

Endpoint detection and response (EDR)

EDR systems operate as fundamental cybersecurity solutions because they provide complete surveillance of all endpoint system activities. The tools help healthcare organizations detect threats immediately while enabling them to analyze and respond to incidents which healthcare organizations require for their sensitive information management (Klinghofer, 2022). The development of generative and agentic AI technology allows attackers to generate adaptive polymorphic malware and execute massive automated attacks. Extended Detection and Response (XDR) platforms detect and respond to complex threats through their ability to analyze data from multiple sources for fast threat identification. The XDR system fights against RaaS and MaaS cybercrime models which let threat actors launch AI-based attacks through simple deployment methods. XDR protects organizations from advanced AI threats and service-based attacks through its combination of behavioral analytics and threat intelligence capabilities (IBM, 2021).

Virtual Private Networks (VPNs)

Virtual Private Networks (VPNs) function as fundamental security measures which protect user privacy during online activities. The system encrypts internet data before it travels through protected servers which defend confidential information from potential interception. The healthcare sector can implement VPNs to defend protected health information (PHI) while following regulatory standards. (Cynet, 2022; Kaspersky, n.d).

Antivirus Software and Firewalls

All workstations used by employees need to receive antivirus software protection from their organizations. The software needs configuration to execute full host component scans which check files and boot records. The software system needs to run continuous file scans on all files users' access and download. The software system needs to monitor PDF downloads and macros because these files contain hidden malware according to Cynet (2022) and Kaspersky (n.d).

Research shows that next-generation antivirus (NGAV) represents an essential cybersecurity advancement which addresses the weaknesses of conventional antivirus software. The system receives security updates daily through publicly available vulnerability data which differentiates it from traditional antivirus software that relies on file signature detection and sporadic updates. The system enhances its ability to detect and block zero-day threats through its combination of threat intelligence and behavioral analytics. The new NGAV system detects and blocks newly emerging threats which include attacks that generative and agentic AI systems produce. The system achieves malware prevention through its use of real-time compromise indicator feeds and malware hash similarity analysis and machine learning-based file evaluation and behavior tracking. The sophisticated security capabilities of NGAV make it an optimal solution for protecting organizations against contemporary cyber threats (Cynet, 2022; Forrest et al., n.d.; Kaspersky, n.d).

Non-Technical Measures

Employee Training

Social engineering attacks through phishing emails and credential theft methods targeted Colonial Pipeline and Scripps Health. Healthcare organizations should reduce their social engineering attack exposure through continuous security awareness training for their employees. Healthcare healthcare organizations should perform complete risk assessments before implementing secure software development practices which include secure coding and testing according to NIST (2020). Healthcare organizations should perform complete verification of their hardware and software components to minimize their exposure to cyber threats (Basu et al., 2019).

Healthcare organizations need to train their staff members in advance about cybersecurity to minimize supply-chain attack vulnerabilities (Craig & Corey, 2021). Healthcare organizations need to train all their staff members because they serve as the primary non-technical defense against cyber threats. Security protocols become more effective when healthcare organizations use both positive and negative incentives for enforcement. Security systems depend on human behavior as their most vulnerable point even though security technology offers fundamental protection. The training program teaches staff members to recognize security threats and execute proper responses based on Verizon (2020) and Ponemon Institute (2019) research.

Incident Response Plans

A well-defined response plan serves as the essential element which solves all security incidents. Healthcare organizations that prepare themselves can achieve fast recovery while minimizing damage from attacks. 1.) Healthcare organizations should train their staff members to understand incident response protocols and basic cybersecurity principles. The combination of training programs with simulation-based exercises enables employees to understand their responsibilities better. 2.) Healthcare organizations that detect security incidents at their beginning stage achieve better threat identification capabilities. Healthcare organizations require monitoring systems which detect security threats and unusual system behavior. 3.) The first step of incident response requires immediate actions to stop threats while protecting system resources from further damage. 4.) Healthcare organizations must remove the incident source after containment by taking out malware and repairing system vulnerabilities and implementing security protocols to prevent future breaches. 5.) Healthcare organizations focus their resources on system recovery and operational restoration to build defenses for future threats. 6.) Healthcare organizations must perform a thorough assessment of their incident response plan following every security incident to identify areas for improvement (NIST Publication, 2025).

Two-factor authentication (2FA)

This is one of the defensive mechanism healthcare sectors can implement. Two-factor authentication (2FA) operates as an essential security mechanism which provides enhanced online protection through a two-step verification process before allowing system or user account access. Users must enter two separate verification elements to access systems or user accounts through their password or PIN and either a smartphone app-generated code or a hardware token (Wang et al., 2025; Johnson, 2020).

The security system of 2FA protects systems from unauthorized access because it functions optimally when protecting sensitive data including financial information and personal details and business secrets (Johnson, 2020). The security measure provides an effective defense system which protects users from cyber-attacks and data theft incidents. A user password theft by an attacker will not grant access to the account because they must provide both verification methods to succeed. The deployment of 2FA enhances individual account protection while healthcare organizations can use it to teach users about digital security best practices for their online activities (Verizon, 2020; Johnson, 2020).

RESEARCH DESIGN

Research design employed qualitative methods for data collection. The research design required qualitative methods because vendor vulnerabilities stem from social-technical elements which include regulatory systems and human conduct and organizational systems that quantitative methods fail to measure effectively (Yin, 2018). The research incorporated previous study findings through non-human qualitative methods. The research focused on U.S. hospitals that experienced ransomware or phishing attacks during the period from 2018 to 2025. The research base consisted of breach reports from the U.S. Department of Health and Human Services (HHS) and Verizon's Data Breach Investigations Report and forensic analysis of cyber incidents. The researchers applied thematic coding to their data analysis which produced three major cybersecurity incidents that show how healthcare organizations face widespread security threats particularly in healthcare settings. Healthcare organizations need to understand malware types and adversary attack methods and defensive strategies to enhance their cybersecurity resistance.

CASE SELECTION

The first case analyzed malware threats through identification of various malware types including ransomware and adware and spyware and trojan horses and worms and viruses and botnets and rootkits. Ransomware attacks appeared as a recurring pattern throughout all three reported incidents.

The WannaCry ransomware variant launched a Microsoft Windows system attack in May 2017 which spread through networks by using the EternalBlue exploit. The malware system encrypted all files while demanding Bitcoin payments which made it difficult for healthcare facilities to access their patient information (Gorman, 2023).

The DarkSide group conducted a ransomware attack against Colonial Pipeline during May 2021. The malware system used encryption to lock down vital systems while demanding payment from users which resulted in severe disruptions to the US energy network. The Colonial Pipeline attack on non-healthcare infrastructure demonstrated how ransomware attacks can create secondary impacts on healthcare operations (Gorman, 2023; Cohen, 2021).

Scripps Health experienced a ransomware attack in May 2021 which required them to disable operational systems and redirect patients to alternative facilities. The attack demonstrated healthcare organizations' susceptibility to malware-based disruptions which disabled essential services and compromised patient care quality (Miller, 2021).

The second case investigates risk vectors by showing how threats enter networks and use vulnerabilities to cause damage. The incidents involving WannaCry and Colonial Pipeline and Scripps Health demonstrated that phishing and social engineering attacks represent common attack methods.

The third case evaluates risk management approaches which implement both technological and non-technological solutions to enhance healthcare IT system security.

Scripps Health experienced a ransomware attack in May 2021 which required them to disable certain systems while patients needed to seek care at different facilities. The attack on Scripps Health demonstrates healthcare organizations' exposure to ransomware attacks which used malware encryption to disable essential services and compromise patient treatment (Miller, 2021).

RESULTS, RECOMMENDATIONS, CONCLUSIONS, AND SOLUTIONS

Results

Ransomware prevalence

The 2020 Verizon report showed that ransomware attacks caused 27% of all malware-related security breaches which demonstrated their increasing danger to healthcare organizations from different industries (Verizon, 2020). Ransomware attacks result in both data theft and operational breakdowns which lead to major financial damage. The security threat landscape shows phishing attacks will soon become the most prevalent threat. The WannaCry and Colonial Pipeline and Scripps health incidents all experienced ransomware attacks which appeared as a persistent threat throughout these events.

Phishing prevalence

Phishing attacks represented 22% of all security breaches which established them as a dominant technique for cybercriminals to breach system security. The first point of entry for ransomware attacks occurs when users fall victim to phishing scams which lead them to reveal sensitive information or download malware according to the DBIR (2020). Healthcare organizations must train their staff about cybersecurity threats because phishing attacks show the necessity of such training. Operational disruptions occur as a result of the direct impact (Alabdan, 2020).

Operational disruptions

The WannaCry ransomware attack from 2017 demonstrated how security breaches can result in major harm to critical infrastructure systems. It disabled over 80 hospitals in the National Health Service (NHS) in the UK, resulting in the cancellation of numerous surgeries and emergency services. The attack demonstrated how ransomware operations create instant operational breakdowns which result in extended damage to medical services and healthcare organization trust (Kwon et al.,2020). Healthcare costs continue to increase at a concerning pace (Gorman, 2023).

Healthcare costs

Healthcare organizations now face substantial financial damage because data breaches have become so expensive that they now cost $10.1 million annually according to 2022 statistics. The figure demonstrates various expense categories which include legal fees and regulatory fines and notification costs and remediation efforts to prove why healthcare organizations need robust cybersecurity protection for their patient data (Ponemon Institute, 2022). The organization needs to determine its future path by receiving recommendations for strategic development.

RECOMMENDATIONS

Technical Measures

Two Factor Authentical Implementation

The implementation of Multi-Factor Authentication (MFA) and Endpoint Detection/Response Tools requires healthcare organizations to use essential security protocols that verify user identity through multiple authentication methods which include password entry with text message verification codes and biometric authentication. The system implements a two-factor authentication process which minimizes unauthorized entry when login credentials become exposed. The implementation of endpoint detection and response tools will establish complete endpoint surveillance systems which detect abnormal system activities to enable fast threat response (Wang et al., 2025; Johnson, 2020).

Virtual Private Networks (VPNs)

Virtual Private Networks (VPNs) operate as essential security tools which protect user privacy throughout their online activities. The system protects internet data through encryption before it travels through protected servers which defend confidential information from potential interception (CISOMAG, 2020). Healthcare organizations use VPNs to protect protected health information (PHI) while meeting their mandatory regulatory requirements (Kaspersky, n.d). The encryption process of VPNs transforms data into encrypted content which protects it from interception and unauthorized access while creating a secure connection between devices and VPN servers. The encryption process transforms user IP addresses into untraceable addresses which protect their privacy and make it difficult for others to monitor their online activities. VPNs provide users with secure data transfer capabilities and geo-restriction bypassing and employee remote network access. The different VPN types include remote access VPNs for personal users and site-to-site VPNs for network connections and client-based VPNs that need software installation and browser-based VPNs that operate as web extensions. VPNs serve as fundamental security instruments which protect digital privacy by enabling users to send data safely (Kaur, 2022; Hossain, 2021).

Antivirus Software and Firewalls

Firewalls function as network traffic managers which monitor all incoming and outgoing network traffic. The system uses antivirus software to detect and remove harmful computer viruses. The protection of sensitive information depends on encryption while intrusion detection systems notify administrators about security threats. The implementation of technical security measures creates an efficient defense system which protects vital information systems (CISOMAG, 2020; Ponemon Institute, 2019; Verizon, 2020).

Next-generation antivirus (NGAV)

The system improves cybersecurity through advanced antivirus protection which fights Ransomware-as-a-Service (RaaS) and Malware-as-a-Service (MaaS) threats and maintains daily updates of public vulnerability data (Kaspersky, n.d). The system employs threat intelligence and behavior analysis and machine learning to identify zero-day threats while NGFWs provide deep packet inspection and intrusion detection and prevention and network segmentation and encrypted traffic inspection capabilities for enhanced security and response. Windows Defender Exploit Guard (WDEG) monitors network traffic while preventing unauthorized system changes and it now protects against sophisticated AI-based threats that use artificial intelligence to create RaaS and MaaS attacks which bypass traditional security measures (Cynet, 2022; Forrest et al., n.d.; Kaspersky, n.d.).

Data Encryption

Research evidence demonstrates that encryption technology prevents unauthorized users from accessing unprotected Protected Health Information (PHI) or Personally Identifiable Information (PII) (HHS, n.d.). The HIPAA security rules mandate that electronic PHI must receive encryption protection while encryption and decryption keys must be stored independently from the main data. The Department of Health and Human Services (HHS) implements National Institute of Standards and Technology (NIST) security standards which are detailed in NIST Special Publication 800-series (NIST, n.d.). Special Publication 800-53 from Hyperproof (2025) provides healthcare organizations with security and privacy controls for their information systems and operations.

Non-Technical Measures

Employee Training

Healthcare organizations need to maintain employee training and phishing simulation programs as their main cyber defense system through ongoing educational programs that teach staff about cyber threats and perform simulated phishing tests. The simulations present staff with suspicious emails and fraudulent links to teach them how to identify phishing tactics and demonstrate proper procedures for threat reporting and safe action avoidance. The training program needs periodic updates to stay effective against new cyber threats and security advancements. A cybersecurity culture requires leadership support through regular drills and performance evaluations which check employee compliance with security protocols including immediate software updates. A security-oriented organizational culture emerges when all personnel, including non-IT staff members grasp their responsibilities for protecting patient information while recognizing the necessity of strong authentication and encryption and regular software updates to fight external and internal security threats (Kamalanathan et al., 2025).

Implementing Zero-Trust Model

Healthcare organizations need to run their Zero-Trust Security Frameworks actively because this approach provides better cybersecurity protection. The zero-trust security model requires all users and devices to verify their access rights before they can connect to healthcare networks. The security approach demands healthcare organizations to view all users and systems as threats because threats can emerge from both inside and outside the network. Healthcare organizations can protect themselves from insider threats and unauthorized external attacks by performing regular audits and monitoring user activities and implementing strict access control systems (Alsuwaidi et al., 2024; Gupta et al. 2024).

Incident Response Playbook

Healthcare organizations should develop incident response playbooks which detail ransomware containment and data recovery procedures for various cyber incidents. The playbooks need to contain detailed instructions which help teams detect attacks immediately while performing threat blocking and starting data recovery and system functionality restoration procedures. Healthcare organizations can achieve fast recovery through established responses which provide all personnel with clear directions about their roles during security incidents thus enhancing operational efficiency and team coordination (Ponemon Institute, 2019; Verizon, 2020).

CONCLUSIONS

Medical records at hospitals remain under constant security threats because ransomware and phishing attacks continue to be the most common threats. The initial stage of these attacks involves using deceptive tactics including phishing and social engineering to take advantage of human mistakes which grants attackers entry to healthcare networks and systems. Ransomware attacks on healthcare systems result in medical data lockdowns which create operational problems and endanger patient safety while causing financial damage to facilities and eroding public confidence in healthcare institutions.

Healthcare organizations need to establish a defense system which consists of multiple security layers that follow a specific timeline to combat current and future threats. The initial defense measure requires healthcare organizations to establish technical security systems which combine strong authentication systems with continuous network monitoring to stop unauthorized access and detect potential security threats. Healthcare organizations need to follow regulatory requirements because these laws create a legal structure which protects patient information and maintains privacy standards.

Healthcare organizations need to establish extensive training programs which teach staff members to detect and handle cyber threats through phishing simulation exercises that enhance their awareness and readiness. Healthcare organizations need to develop effective emergency response plans with incident response playbooks to handle breaches and protect patient safety while restoring operational functions.

Analysis from incidents that ransomware malware threats along with other malware threats remain a major threat to healthcare facilities and essential infrastructure systems. Healthcare organizations can build digital security through risk vector identification and solutions that unite technical and organizational and regulatory aspects to protect patient data privacy and deliver high-quality healthcare services.

Solutions

Healthcare organizations must implement robust security measures to counter the growing threats of ransomware and phishing attacks.

IT Infrastructure Insurance

Healthcare organizations buy cybersecurity insurance to defend their financial stability against cyberattacks and data breaches because it pays for recovery expenses and legal fees and regulatory fines (Baharuddin et al., 2020). The insurance program helps healthcare organizations manage risks through fast recovery and business continuity services which include incident response and investigations and public relations and patient compensation. Healthcare organizations face difficulties when they try to evaluate new security threats and understand complicated insurance policies and fulfill necessary security standards. Healthcare providers need to implement strong cybersecurity measures alongside insurance coverage to protect their assets while preserving patient trust in digital healthcare (Baharuddin et al., 2020).

AI-Based Anomaly Detection

AI-based anomaly detection systems will strengthen cybersecurity protection because they can detect new threats that Generative and Agentic AI technologies create through their use of large language models (LLMs). The systems monitor user activities and network data streams to detect abnormal behavior which could signal phishing or ransomware attacks while fighting against Malware-as-a-Service (MaaS) and Ransomware-as-a-Service (RaaS) threats. The combination of predictive analytics with real-time monitoring enables healthcare organizations to detect and stop AI-based attacks before they reach sensitive data which reduces the damage from new cybercrime service models (Rippling, 2025; Parker, 2023).

Implement Block-Chain Technology

Blockchain technology enables medical record management to achieve better data protection and reliability through its implementation. The decentralized nature of blockchain systems enables secure patient data storage and sharing which protects data from unauthorized access while ensuring both accuracy and reliability. Zaabar et al. (2021) explained HealthBlock as a blockchain healthcare data management system which protects healthcare information including PHI and PII through improved privacy and security and data interoperability.

Intelligence Sharing

The Cybersecurity and Infrastructure Security Agency (CISA) work with other cybersecurity organizations to distribute threat intelligence through their established partnership programs. The cooperative initiatives between healthcare institutions provide them with essential resources and current threat information and security best practice recommendations (Radware, 2022).

RECOMMENDATIONS FOR FUTURE RESEARCH

AI and Machine Learning in Phishing and Ransomware Detection. The healthcare industry uses artificial intelligence (AI) and machine learning (ML) to combat phishing and ransomware cyber threats. The systems analyze large datasets to identify security threats by recognizing patterns and detecting unusual activity which enables threat detection before attacks occur. AI and ML systems track unusual email patterns and user actions to help healthcare organizations build instant monitoring systems which produce warning alerts. Healthcare organizations can minimize attack damage and accelerate their response through automated threat management which directly supports patient care delivery. The systems learn from new data to improve their accuracy and their capacity to handle evolving cyber threats. Healthcare organizations that implement AI and ML-based cybersecurity solutions will achieve better protection for patient data and improved resistance against cyber threats (AWS, 2025; Susnjara & Smalley, 2024).

The evaluation process between HIPAA and GDPR shows their different approaches to cybersecurity system protection. The two regulations protect different data types because GDPR provides extensive privacy protection that HIPAA lacks which demonstrates why the United States needs enhanced data protection standards (CISOMAG, 2020). The HIPAA system protects health information within U.S. healthcare operations, but GDPR protects all personal data across European Union sectors which enables users to control their information better. The HIPAA regulations fail to provide victims with all their rights to access and modify and remove their personal data. The current regulations expose significant weaknesses in U.S. data protection systems because they need to establish complete standards which fulfill international requirements for better patient information security. The rapid growth of healthcare cybersecurity threats demands stronger legal protections for sensitive digital healthcare information (CISOMAG, 2020).

Longitudinal Studies on Medical Identity Theft. Research needs to study medical identity theft in depth to understand its complete impact on victims throughout their entire experience with crime. Research shows that victims develop higher stress levels and anxiety which leads to long-term emotional consequences. The observation of these effects across time will reveal the full extent of victim consequences which will help develop enhanced healthcare support systems and preventive measures (Irvin-Erickson, 2024).

REFERENCES

Alabdan, R. (2020). Phishing Attacks Survey: Types, Vectors, and Technical Approaches. *Future Internet, 12*(10), 168. DOI: 10.3390/fi12100168

Alsuwaidi, N. Alharmoodi and H. A. Hamadi, (2024). "The Transformative Impact of Zero-Trust Architecture on Healthcare Security," *2024 2nd International Conference on Cyber Resilience (ICCR)*, Dubai, United Arab Emirates, pp. 1-8, DOI: 10.1109/ICCR61006.2024.10532794

Amazon Web Services. (2025). *Predictive Analytics and Machine Learning in Cybersecurity: Enhancing Reliability and Security.* AWS White Paper. https://aws.amazon.com/whitepapers

Basu, S., Liu, F., & Wang, C. (2019). Hardware supply chain security risks in healthcare systems. *Journal of Cybersecurity, 5*(3), 1–14. DOI: 10.1093/cybsec/tyz012

CISOMAG. (2020). *Healthcare data breaches and regulatory frameworks: A global perspective.* EC-Council.

Cohen, A. (2021). *Colonial Pipeline shuts down operations after ransomware attack.* The New York Times. Retrieved from https://www.nytimes.com/2021/05/08/us/colonial-pipeline-hack.html)

Corporation, I. B. M. (2021). *IBM launches QRadar XDR, a comprehensive open XDR solution.* IBM TechXchange Community. https://community.ibm.com/community/user/discussion/ibm-launches-qradar-xdr-a-comprehensive-open-xdr-solution?hlmlt=VT

Craig, R., & Corey, D. (2021). Cyber threats in healthcare: A comprehensive review. *Journal of Healthcare Information Management, 35*(2), 112–119.

Cyber Threat Intelligence, K. E. L. A. (2025*). Third-party risk in healthcare demands immediate attention.* https://www.kelacyber.com/blog/why-third-party-risk-in-healthcare-demands-immediate-attention/

Cybersecurity & Infrastructure Security Agency (CISA). (2019). *Phishing guidance for healthcare institutions.* U.S. Department of Homeland Security. https://www.cisa.gov

Cynet. (2022). *Cynet Next-Gen Antivirus (NGAV).* Retrieved from https://www.cynet.com/platform/next-gen-antivirus/

Federal Trade Commission. (n.d.). *Medical identity theft.* https://www.ftc.gov/identity-theft

Forrest, A., & Lindemulder, G. (n.d.). *What is a next-generation antivirus (NGAV)? IBM.* Retrieved from https://www.ibm.com/think/topics/next-generation-antivirus/#:~:text=Authors,IBM%20Think

Gorman, B. (2023). *EternalBlue: What is it and how does it work? AVG.* Retrieved from https://www.avg.com/en/signal/eternal-blue#:~:text=Exactly%20when%20the%20EternalBlue%20exploit,the%20hacker%20group%20Shadow%20Brokers

Gupta, D., Elluri, L., Jain, A., Moni, S. S., & Aslan, O. (2024). *Blockchain-enhanced framework for secure third-party vendor risk management and vigilant security controls.* arXiv preprint. https://arxiv.org/abs/2411.13447 DOI: 10.1109/BigData62323.2024.10825025

Health, I. T. Security. (2021). Scripps Health ransomware attack disrupts care. *HealthITSecurity.com.* https://healthitsecurity.com

Hossain, I. (2021). *Analysis the importance of VPN for Creating a Safe Connection Over the World of Internet.* IJARCCE., DOI: 10.17148/IJARCCE.2021.101017

Hyperproof. (2025). NIST 800-53: *Security and privacy controls for information systems and organizations.* https://hyperproof.io/nist-800-53/

Identity Theft Resource Center. (2016). *Medical identity theft: The impact on patients.* ITRC Report. https://www.idtheftcenter.org

Irvin-Erickson, Y. (2024). Consequences of Identity Theft Victimization: Disabilities and Mental Distress. *Crime and Delinquency*, *0*(0), 00111287241227926. Advance online publication. DOI: 10.1177/00111287241227926

Johnson, C., Kwon, J., & Liu, M. E. (2020). The impact of WannaCry ransomware attack on hospitals: Lessons learned. *Journal of Cybersecurity*, *6*(1). Advance online publication. DOI: 10.1093/cybsec/tyaa006

Kamalanathan, S., Rajan, S. M., & Schell, S. (2025). *Implementing zero trust in healthcare. Cognizant.* https://www.cognizant.com/en_us/industries/documents/cognizant-implementing-zero-trust-in-healthcare.pdf

Kaspersky. (n.d.). *Glossary.* Retrieved from https://encyclopedia.kaspersky.com/glossary/

Kaspersky. (n.d.). *Next Generation Firewall (NGAV).* Retrieved from https://encyclopedia.kaspersky.com/glossary/

Kaur, C. (2022). *The vital role of VPN in making secure connections over the Internet world. International Journal of Recent Technology and Engineering (IJRTE, 8(6).* DOI: 10.2139/ssrn.4032918

Klinghofer, B. (2022). *Introducing Microsoft Defender for Endpoint plan 1*. Retrieved from https://techcommunity.microsoft.com/t5/microsoft-defender-for-endpoint/introducing-microsoft-defender-for-endpoint-plan-1/ba-p/2636641

Marchal, S., Asokan, N., & Niemi, V. (2017). A survey of anti-phishing solutions. *ACM Computing Surveys*, *50*(6), 1–31. DOI: 10.1145/3131095

Miller, S. (2021). Scripps Health announces systems down after ransomware attack. San *Diego Union-Tribune*. Retrieved from https://www.sandiegouniontribune.com/news/story/2021-05-02/scripps-health-networks-hacked-in-ransomware-attack

National Institute of Standards and Technology. (2020). *Framework for improving critical infrastructure cybersecurity* (Version 1.1). U.S. Department of Commerce. DOI: 10.6028/NIST.CSWP.04162018

NIST. (2025). *Incident response recommendations and considerations for cybersecurity risk management: A CSF 2.0 community profile (NIST Special Publication 800-61r3)*. DOI: 10.6028/NIST.SP.800-61r3

Parker, J. (2023). *80% of ransomware attacks now use artificial intelligence. MIT Sloan School of Management*. https://mitsloan.mit.edu/ideas-made-to-matter/80-ransomware-attacks-now-use-artificial-intelligence

Ponemon Institute. (2022). *Cost of a data breach report*. IBM Security. https://www.ibm.com/reports/data-breach

Radware. (2022). *Supply chain attack trends and mitigation strategies in healthcare*. Radware Security Reports.

Rippling. (2025). Agentic AI security: *A guide to threats, risks & best practices*. Rippling Blog. https://www.rippling.com/blog/agentic-ai-security

Risk-Based Security. (2020). *Data breach quick view report*. Risk Based Security. https://www.riskbasedsecurity.com

Roumani, Y. (2021). Patching Zero-day vulnerabilities: An empirical analysis. *Journal of Cybersecurity*, *7*(1), tyab023. Advance online publication. DOI: 10.1093/cybsec/tyab023

Shacklett, M. (2021). The evolving cybersecurity threat landscape in healthcare. *Information Security Journal: A Global Perspective, 30*(4), 215–225. DOI: 10.1080/19393555.2021.1937999

Strong, D. M. (2025). *Target data breach: What happened and how to prevent it.* https://www.strongdm.com/what-is/target-data-breach

Susnjara, P., & Smalley, T. (2024). *Machine learning for healthcare security integration*. Springer.

Tan, Z., Parambath, S. P., Anagnostopoulos, C., Singer, J., & Marnerides, A. K. (2025). Advanced Persistent Threats Based on Supply Chain Vulnerabilities: Challenges, Solutions, and Future Directions. *IEEE Internet of Things Journal, 12*(6), 6371–6395. DOI: 10.1109/JIOT.2025.3528744

Verizon. (2020). *2020 Data breach investigations report (DBIR)*. Verizon Enterprise Solutions. https://www.verizon.com/business/resources/reports/dbir/

Wang P, Boodraj M, Baskerville R (2025;), "Beyond passwords: A review of the hidden risks in two-factor authentication". *Journal of Systems and Information Technology*, Vol. ahead-of-print No. ahead-of-print. DOI: 10.1108/JSIT-03-2025-0140

Yin, R. K. (2018). *Case study research and applications: Design and methods* (6th ed.). SAGE Publications.

KEY TERMS AND DEFINITIONS

Attack Vectors: Methods used by cybercriminals to gain unauthorized access, like phishing and medical device vulnerabilities (Kaspersky, n.d).

Cybersecurity Framework: Guidelines for managing cybersecurity risks, with the NIST framework commonly used in healthcare (Kaspersky, n.d).

Electronic health records (EHRs): They are digital versions of a patient's medical history, stored and accessed electronically

Healthcare IT Infrastructure: Hardware and software for managing digital information in healthcare, needing protection from cyber threats (Kaspersky, n.d).

Intrusion Detection Systems (IDS): A system that monitors malicious activities and alerts threats but does not take action (Kaspersky, n.d).

Intrusion Prevention Systems (IPS): A proactive system that blocks and prevents detected threats in real-time (Kaspersky, n.d).

Malware: Software intended to harm computers or networks, disrupting healthcare services and compromising patient data (Kaspersky, n.d).

Passkeys: The authentication system known as passkeys operates through cryptographic keys which function as a replacement for conventional password authentication (Kaspersky, n.d).

Patches: Patches are specific updates that fix known issues, vulnerabilities, or bugs in software. They address problems and often enhance security without major changes (Kaspersky, n.d.).

Personally Identifiable Information (PII): Data that can identify an individual, such as names and Social Security numbers, crucial for privacy in healthcare (Kaspersky, n.d).

Protected Health Information (PHI): Health data linked to individuals, protected under HIPAA, including medical records and personal identifiers (Kaspersky, n.d).

Ransomware: A type of malware that encrypts data and demands payment for decryption, critical in healthcare for maintaining access to patient information (Kaspersky, n.d).

Ransomware-as-a-Service (RaaS): Cybercriminals operate a business model which lets others use their ransomware tools to execute attacks (Kaspersky, n.d).

Social engineering: This is a tactic used by cybercriminals to manipulate individuals into revealing confidential information.

Updates: Updates are broader and may include new features, performance improvements, and multiple patches. They keep software current and enhance the overall user experience (Kaspersky, n.d.).

Zero-Day exploit: This term is used to describe exploit code that has been written to take advantage of a vulnerability before the software vendor knows about it and has had the chance to publish a patch for it (Kaspersky, n.d.).

Zero-trust Architectures: The security model demands authentication for all access requests because it treats all users and devices as potential security threats (Kaspersky, n.d).

Zero-trust Frameworks: The frameworks establish step-by-step guidelines to deploy zero-trust security through identity authentication and restricted access permissions (Kaspersky, n.d).

Personally Identifiable Information (PII): Data that can identify an individual, such as names and Social Security numbers, requiring privacy measures [illegible] (Kosinski, [illegible]).

Protected Health Information (PHI): Health data linked to individuals, protected under HIPAA, including medical records and personal identifiers [illegible].

[illegible]

Compilation of References

Abdavi, F., Fateh, H., & Pashaie, S. (2018). The Effects of Denison's Model of Organizational Culture on Customer Relationship Management (CRM): Case Study of Ministry of Sports and Youth in Iran. *International Journal of Management, Accounting & Economics, 5*(6), 461–472. https://www.researchgate.net/profile/Sajjad-Pashaie/publication/360791392_The_Effects_of_Denison's_Model_of_Organizational_Culture_on_Customer_Relationship_Management_CRM_Case_Study_of_Ministry_of_Sports_and_Youth_in_Iran/links/628ba1d739fa217031682af0/The-Effects-of-Denisons-Model-of-Organizational-Culture-on-Customer-Relationship-Management-CRM-Case-Study-of-Ministry-of-Sports-and-Youth-in-Iran.pdf

Agrahari, S., & Singh, A. K. (2022). Concept drift detection in data stream mining: A literature review. *Journal of King Saud University. Computer and Information Sciences, 34*(10), 9523–9540. DOI: 10.1016/j.jksuci.2021.11.006

Ahmady, G. A., Nikooravesh, A., & Mehrpour, M. (2016). Effect of organizational culture on knowledge management based on Denison Model. *Procedia: Social and Behavioral Sciences, 230*, 387–395. https://www.sciencedirect.com/science/article/pii/S1877042816311508. DOI: 10.1016/j.sbspro.2016.09.049

Ahmed, F. A., Gul, S., & Shahzad, S. (2025). Ensuring accountability and transparency in AI-driven corporate governance. *International Journal of Social Sciences Bulletin*. DOI: 10.5281/zenodo.15378921

Ahmed, K. H., Axelsson, S., Li, Y., & Sagheer, A. M. (2025). A credit card fraud detection approach based on ensemble machine learning classifier with hybrid data sampling. *Machine Learning with Applications, 20*, 100675. DOI: 10.1016/j.mlwa.2025.100675

AI Literacy Institute. (2024). Gender and age gaps in generative AI. https://ailiteracy.institute/gender-and-age-gaps-in-generative-ai

Ajunwa, I. (2020). The paradox of automation as anti-bias intervention. *Cardozo Law Review*, *41*(4), 1671–1742. https://cardozolawreview.com

Akinbowale, O. E., Zerihun, M. F., & Mashigo, P. (2024). Application of situational crime prevention framework for cybercrime mitigation. [IJCBPL]. *International Journal of Cyber Behavior, Psychology and Learning*, *14*(1), 1–23. https://www.igi-global.com/article/application-of-situational-crime-prevention-framework-for-cybercrime-mitigation/353436. DOI: 10.4018/IJCBPL.353436

Alabdan, R. (2020). Phishing Attacks Survey: Types, Vectors, and Technical Approaches. *Future Internet*, *12*(10), 168. DOI: 10.3390/fi12100168

Alakaş, E. Ö. (2024). Digital transformational leadership and organizational agility in digital transformation: Structural equation modelling of the moderating effects of digital culture and digital strategy. *The Journal of High Technology Management Research*, *35*(2), 100517. Advance online publication. DOI: 10.1016/j.hitech.2024.100517

Alakitan, M., & Makinde, E. (2024). *Where are the ethical guidelines? Examining the governance of digital technologies and AI in Nigeria. Policy &amp.* Internet., DOI: 10.1002/poi3.416

Alavi, S., Amini, A., Jandaghi, G., & Hoseini, S. M. (2014). The effect of organizational agility on performance with a case study in hospitals. *International Journal of Academic Research in Business & Social Sciences*, *4*(4), 171–180.

Alim, M. (2024). Examining the Interplay Between Innovation Index, Innovation Efficiency and Sustainability Index: A Cross-Group Analysis of G7 and E7 Countries. Verimlilik Dergisi, 77–88. https://doi.org/DOI: 10.51551/verimlilik.1344038

ALSaidi. K. S., AL'Abd AL-Busaidi, A., & Sundaravadivazhagan, B. (2024). Securing Embodied AI: Addressing Cybersecurity Challenges in Physical Systems. In: Raj, P., Rocha, A., Singh, S.P., Dutta, P.K., Sundaravadivazhagan, B. (eds) Building Embodied AI Systems: The Agents, the Architecture Principles, Challenges, and Application Domains. *Information Systems Engineering and Management, 14*. Springer, Cham. DOI: 10.1007/978-3-031-68256-8_21

Alsheibani, S., Cheung, Y., & Messom, C. (2018). Artificial Intelligence Adoption: AI-readiness at Firm-Level. *PACIS, 4*, 231-245. https://research.monash.edu/en/publications/artificial-intelligence-adoption-ai-readiness-at-firm-level/

Alsuwaidi, N. Alharmoodi and H. A. Hamadi, (2024). "The Transformative Impact of Zero-Trust Architecture on Healthcare Security," *2024 2nd International Conference on Cyber Resilience (ICCR)*, Dubai, United Arab Emirates, pp. 1-8, DOI: 10.1109/ICCR61006.2024.10532794

Amazon Web Services. (2025). *Predictive Analytics and Machine Learning in Cybersecurity: Enhancing Reliability and Security.* AWS White Paper. https://aws.amazon.com/whitepapers

Amicelle, A. (2022). Big data surveillance across fields: Algorithmic governance for policing & regulation. *Big Data & Society*, *9*(2), 20539517221112431. Advance online publication. DOI: 10.1177/20539517221112431

Antonakis, A. (2019). The Structural Dimension of the Public Sphere (pp. 115–150). Springer fachmedien wiesbaden. https://doi.org/DOI: 10.1007/978-3-658-25639-5_8

Antony, J., Snee, R. D., & Hoerl, R. (2019). Lean Six Sigma: Yesterday, today and tomorrow. *International Journal of Quality & Reliability Management*, *36*(8), 1536–1554. DOI: 10.1108/IJQRM-03-2018-0065

Araby, M. A. A. A. (2024). Transforming citizen engagement in e- governance framework: a conceptual analysis. *JAKPP* (Jurnal Analisis Kebijakan &Amp; Pelayanan Publik), 213 235. https://doi.org/DOI: 10.31947/jakpp.v10i2.35497

Ashrafian, H. (2023). Engineering a social contract: Rawlsian distributive justice through algorithmic game theory and artificial intelligence. *AI and Ethics*, *3*(4), 1447–1454. DOI: 10.1007/s43681-022-00253-6

Association of Certified Fraud Examiners. (2020). *Report to the nations: 2020 global study on occupational fraud and abuse.* https://acfepublic.s3-us-west-2.amazonaws.com/2020-Report-to-the-Nations.pdf

Attfield, R. (2018). Global Citizenship. 1–10. https://doi.org/DOI: 10.1002/9781444367072.wbiee842

Audretsch, D. B., Belitski, M., Caiazza, R., Drapeau, M. D., Menter, M., & Wales, W. J. (2023). Resilience and digitally-advanced entrepreneurship. *Entrepreneurship and Regional Development*, *36*(1–2), 1–9. DOI: 10.1080/08985626.2023.2275193

Avancha, S., Pandian, P., & Jain, S. (2023). Risk Management in IT Service Delivery Using Big Data Analytics. *Universal Research Reports*, *10*(2), 272–285. DOI: 10.36676/urr.v10.i2.1330

Babina, T., & Fedyk, A. (2025). The effects of AI on firms and workers. *Brookings Institution*. https://www.brookings.edu/articles/the-effects-of-ai-on-firms-and-workers/

Badiger, M., Naik, A., Singh, C., Mehnaz, F. C., Smitha, A. B., Adiga, S., & Shetty, S. (2024). *AI in Healthcare Data Analytics Trends and Transformative Innovations*. IGI Global., DOI: 10.4018/979-8-3693-7277-7.ch001

Baisholan, N., Dietz, J. E., Gnatyuk, S., Turdalyuly, M., Matson, E. T., & Baisholanova, K. (2025). FraudX AI: An interpretable machine learning framework for credit card fraud detection on imbalanced datasets. *Computers*, *14*(120), 120. Advance online publication. DOI: 10.3390/computers14040120

Bankins, S., Formosa, B., & Donald, W. E. (2024b). Human–machine collaboration in contemporary work. *Human Resource Management Review*, *34*(1), 100824. DOI: 10.1016/j.hrmr.2023.100824

Bankins, S., Ocampo, A. C. G., Marrone, J. A., Restubog, S. L. D., & Woo, S. E. (2024a). A multilevel review of artificial intelligence in organizations: Implications for organizational behavior research and practice. *Journal of Organizational Behavior*, *45*(2), 159–182. DOI: 10.1002/job.2735

Barkan, S. E. (2018). The Conflict Approach. *The Cambridge Handbook of Social Problems, 1*, 241. https://books.google.com/books?hl=en&lr=&id=g9tPDwAAQBAJ&oi=fnd&pg=PA241&dq=1.%09Barkan,+S.+E.+(2018).+The+Conflict+Approach.++The+Cambridge+Handbook+of+Social+Problems,+1,+241.&ots=Y3o2m68ZIU&sig=PGW9NqLpmOg7hTevn1Ynajy7Ag0#v=onepage&q&f=false

Barocas, S., Crawford, K., Shapiro, A., & Wallach, H. (2017). The problem with bias: Allocative versus representational harms in machine learning. In *Proceedings of the 9th Annual Conference of the Special Interest Group For Computing, Information And Society. [SIGCIS]*. Philadelphia, PA.

Barocas, S., Hardt, M., & Narayanan, A. (2023). *Fairness and machine learning: Limitations and opportunities*. MIT Press.

Barocas, S., & Selbst, A. D. (2016). Big data's disparate impact. *California Law Review*, *104*(3), 671–732. DOI: 10.15779/Z38BG31

Barocas, S., & Selbst, A. D. (2016). Big data's disparate impact. *SSRN*, *104*(3), 671–732. DOI: 10.2139/ssrn.2477899

Basson, M., & Botha, C. (2012). Towards meaning: Symbolic interactionism and workplace bullying. In *BULLYING: An assault on human dignity* (pp. 77–91). Brill., https://www.researchgate.net/publication/341240876_Towards_Meaning_Symbolic_Interactionism_and_Workplace_Bullying DOI: 10.1163/9781848881020_010

Basu, S., Liu, F., & Wang, C. (2019). Hardware supply chain security risks in healthcare systems. *Journal of Cybersecurity*, *5*(3), 1–14. DOI: 10.1093/cybsec/tyz012

Basu, S., Majumdar, B., Mukherjee, K., Munjal, S., & Palaksha, C. (2023). Artificial intelligence–HRM interactions and outcomes: A systematic review and causal configurational explanation. *Human Resource Management Review*, *33*(1), 100893. DOI: 10.1016/j.hrmr.2022.100893

Bean, R. (2025, January 2). 6 Ways AI changed business in 2024, According to executives. *Harvard Business Review*. https://hbr.org/2025/01/6-ways-ai-changed-business-in-2024-according-to-executives

Becker, L. (2025). Anomaly detection in e-commerce platforms via graph neural networks. *Asia Pacific Economic and Management Review*, *15*(1), 44–61. DOI: 10.62177/apemr.v2i2.208

Beebe, N. L., & Rao, V. S. (2005, December). Using situational crime prevention theory to explain the effectiveness of information systems security. In *Proceedings of the 2005 SoftWars Conference, Las Vegas, NV* (pp. 1-18). https://www.researchgate.net/profile/Nicole-Beebe/publication/237264626_Using_Situational_Crime_Prevention_Theory_to_Explain_the_Effectiveness_of_Information_Systems_Security/links/570e47a508aee76b9dade7a1/Using-Situational-Crime-Prevention-Theory-to-Explain-the-Effectiveness-of-Information-Systems-Security.pdf

Behrend, T. S., Selenko, E., & Donald, W. E. (2024). AI skills and employability: Evidence from a qualitative analysis. *Frontiers in Artificial Intelligence*, *7*, 1629320. DOI: 10.3389/frai.2025.1629320

Benabou, A., & Touhami, F. (2025). Artificial intelligence in human resource management: A PRISMA-based systematic review. *Acta Informatica Pragensia*, *14*(3), 489–505. DOI: 10.18267/j.aip.264

Benjamin, R. (2019). Race after technology: Abolitionist tools for the new Jim code. *Polity*. https://www.politybooks.com/bookdetail?book_id=1634

Bhatia, R., & Kaur, J. (2024). Collaborating Academia, Industry, and Government: Enhancing Business Practices Through Innovative Pedagogies. In Fostering Industry-Academia Partnerships for Innovation-Driven Trade (pp. 40-53). IGI Global.

Bhatt, S., Manadhata, P. K., & Zomlot, L. (2014). The operational role of Security Information and Event Management systems. *IEEE Security and Privacy*, *12*(5), 35–41. DOI: 10.1109/MSP.2014.103

Bhimavarapu, U. (2025). Artificial Intelligence and Digital Health Equity (pp. 319–336). Igi global. https://doi.org/DOI: 10.4018/979-8-3373-3384-7.ch013

Biccum, A. R. (2020). Global Citizenship. https://doi.org/DOI: 10.1093/acrefore/9780190846626.013.556

Binns, R., Veale, M., Van Kleek, M., Lyngs, U., Zhao, J., & Shadbolt, N. (2018). 'It's reducing a human being to a percentage': Perceptions of justice in algorithmic hiring. *Proceedings of the 2018 CHI Conference on Human Factors in Computing Systems*, 1–14. https://doi.org/DOI: 10.1145/3173574.3173951

Blanke, S. J., & McGrady, E. (2016). When it comes to securing patient health information from breaches, your best medicine is a dose of prevention: A cybersecurity risk assessment checklist. *Journal of Healthcare Risk Management*, *36*(1), 14–24. DOI: 10.1002/jhrm.21230 PMID: 27400172

Boels, L., Boels, A., Alberto, R., & Hoogland, K. (2025). Citizens' data-ing with contemporary data in their daily life. *ZDM Mathematics Education*, *57*(1), 87–101. Advance online publication. DOI: 10.1007/s11858-025-01665-4

Bogdanova, M., Parashkevova, E., Smokova, M., & Stoyanova, M. (2025). Agile management of innovation networks—A theoretical approach. *Journal of Infrastructure. Policy and Development*, *9*(1), 10517. DOI: 10.24294/jipd10517

Bolsin, S., Faunce, T., & Oakley, J. (2005). Practical virtue ethics: Healthcare whistleblowing and portable digital technology. *Journal of Medical Ethics*, *31*(10), 612–618. DOI: 10.1136/jme.2004.010603 PMID: 16199607

Bostrom, R. P., & Heinen, J. S. (1977). MIS problems and failures: A socio-technical perspective, Part I: The causes. *Management Information Systems Quarterly*, *1*(3), 17–32. DOI: 10.2307/248710

Boyd, D., & Crawford, K. (2012). Critical questions for Big Data: Provocations for a cultural, technological, and scholarly phenomenon. *Information Communication and Society*, *15*(5), 662–679. DOI: 10.1080/1369118X.2012.678878

Brantingham, P., & Brantingham, P. (2013). Crime pattern theory. In *Environmental criminology and crime analysis* (pp. 100–116). Willan., https://www.taylorfrancis.com/chapters/edit/10.4324/9780203118214-13/crime-pattern-theory-paul-brantingham-patricia-brantingham

Braun, V., & Clarke, V. (2006). Using thematic analysis in psychology. *Qualitative Research in Psychology, 3*(2), 77–101. DOI: 10.1191/1478088706qp063oa

Bridges, S. (2020, March 12). *Bridges transition model.* William Bridges Associates. Retrieved March 21, 2023, from https://wmbridges.com/about/what-is-transition/

Brinkmann, M. (2024). *An Instrumentalist Theory of Political Legitimacy.* Oxford University Press Oxford., DOI: 10.1093/9780198901174.001.0001

Brown, B., Davila, M. A., & Hartley, D. J. (2025). What happened to Black Lives Matter? Public support for Black Lives Matter and the politics of police reform. *Contemporary Justice Review, 28*(1), 44–68. Advance online publication. DOI: 10.1080/10282580.2025.2484710

Brynjolfsson, E., & McAfee, A. (2014). The second machine age: Work, progress, and prosperity in a time of brilliant technologies. *W. W. Norton.* https://mindfultechnics.com/the-second-machine-age/

Budhwar, P., Malik, A., De Silva, M. T. T., & Thevisuthan, P. (2022). Artificial intelligence – challenges and opportunities for international HRM: A review and research agenda. *International Journal of Human Resource Management, 33*(6), 1065–1097. DOI: 10.1080/09585192.2022.2035161

Bughin, J., Seong, J., Manyika, J., Chui, M., & Joshi, R. (2023). The future of work in the age of AI: Scenarios, trends, and policy responses. *McKinsey Global Institute.* https://www.mckinsey.com/featured-insights/future-of-work/jobs-lost-jobs-gained-what-the-future-of-work-will-mean-for-jobs-skills-and-wages

Buolamwini, J., & Gebru, T. (2018). Gender shades: Intersectional accuracy disparities in commercial gender classification. *Proceedings of the 1st Conference on Fairness, Accountability and Transparency, 81*, 77-91. https://proceedings.mlr.press/v81/buolamwini18a/buolamwini18a.pdf

Burrell, D. N. (2022). Creating inclusive, diverse, and psychologically safe workplaces for African-American women working in public health response supply chain and logistics. *Land Forces Academy Review, 27*(2), 134-140. https://www.armyacademy.ro/reviste/rev2_2022/Art_Burrell_Raft_2_2022.pdf

Burrell, D. N. (2023). Cybersecurity in healthcare through the 7-S model strategy. *Scientific Bulletin-Nicolae Balcescu Land Forces Academy, 28*(1), 26-35. https://reference-global.com/download/article/10.2478/bsaft-2023-0003.pdf

Burrell, D. N. (2024). Understanding Cognitive and Behavioral Psychological Factors that Lead to Cybersecurity Breaches in Healthcare. *RAIS Journal for Social Sciences, 8*(2), 43-53. https://ideas.repec.org/a/smo/jornl1/v8y2024i2p43-53.html

Burrell, D. N. (2023). Dynamic evaluation approaches to telehealth technologies and artificial intelligence (AI) telemedicine applications in healthcare and biotechnology organizations. *Merits*, *3*(4), 700–721. DOI: 10.3390/merits3040042

Burrell, D. N., Barrett, S. J., Lewis, E. J., Dawson, M., Bovell, K., & Crowe, M. (2021). Creating Inclusive Workplaces for Women in Health Organizations Engaging in Digital Economy-Driven Innovations. [IJIDE]. *International Journal of Innovation in the Digital Economy*, *12*(2), 18–31. https://www.igi-global.com/article/creating-inclusive-workplaces-for-women-in-health-organizations-engaging-in-digital-economy-driven-innovations/273608. DOI: 10.4018/IJIDE.2021040102

Burrell, D. N., Burton, S. L., Nobles, C., Springs, D., Huff, A. J., Brown-Jackson, K. L., Richardson, K., Wright, J. B., Muller, S. R., & Jones, A. J. (2023). The Managerial Ethical and Operational Challenges of Hospital Cybersecurity. In Burrell, D. (Ed.), *Transformational Interventions for Business, Technology, and Healthcare* (pp. 444–458). IGI Global Scientific Publishing., DOI: 10.4018/979-8-3693-1634-4.ch026

Burrell, D. N., Shufutinsky, A., Duncan, T. D., Springs, D., McLester, Q., & Mozes, R. (2021). Organizational Dynamics Around Sexual Harassment Interventions and Occurrences in Clinical Training Healthcare Environments. In Johnson, R. (Ed.), *Handbook of Research on Multidisciplinary Perspectives on Managerial and Leadership Psychology* (pp. 300–319). IGI Global., DOI: 10.4018/978-1-7998-3811-1.ch015

Burt, A., Knight, M., & Sandler, J. (2022). Beyond bias: Re-imagining the governance of artificial intelligence. *Harvard Kennedy School* Working Paper. https://carrcenter.hks.harvard.edu

Burton, S. L. (2019). Grasping the cyber-world: Artificial intelligence and human capital meet to inform leadership. *International Journal of Economics, Commerce and Management, 7*(12), 707–729. https://www.researchgate.net/publication/338249804

Burton, S. L. (2024). Securing tomorrow: Synergizing change management and cybersecurity in the digital era. *Holistica, 15*(1), 1. https://reference-global.com/download/article/10.2478/hjbpa-2024-0001.pdf

Burton, S. L. (2025). Integrating Cybersecurity and Artificial Intelligence: Adaptive Frameworks for Future-Ready Education. https://doi.org/10.5281/zenodo.16333218

Byrapu Reddy, S. R., Sharma, R., & Patel, N. (2024). Effective fraud detection in e-commerce: Leveraging machine learning and big data analytics. *International Journal of Computer Applications*, *182*(12), 1–8.

Cai, L. (2020). Agile transformation in higher education: Organizational agility in universities. *Journal of Organizational Change Management*, *33*(6), 1132–1144.

Cai, W. (2020). Building agility into higher education: Theory and practice. *International Journal of Educational Management, 34*(4), 755–769.

Cai, Y. (2020). The impact of COVID-19 on higher education: A review of emerging evidence. *International Higher Education*, (102), 6–8.

Caldarini, G., Jaf, S., & McGarry, K. (2022). A literature survey of recent advances in chatbots. *Information (Basel), 13*(1), 41. DOI: 10.3390/info13010041

Calderone, K. L. (1990). The influence of gender on the frequency of pain and sedative medication administered to postoperative patients. *Sex Roles, 23*(11-12), 713–725. DOI: 10.1007/BF00289259

Calo, Z. R. (2024). AI, medicine and Christian ethics. *Research Handbook on Health, AI and the Law*, 219-233.

Campbell, D. (2011). Diversity and job satisfaction: Reconciling conflicting theories and findings. *International Journal of Applied Management and Technology, 10*(1), 1. https://scholarworks.waldenu.edu/ijamt/vol10/iss1/1/

Caton, S., & Haas, C. (2020). Fairness in machine learning: A survey. https://arxiv.org/abs/2010.04053

Caulfield, J. L., & Brenner, E. F. (2020). Resolving complex community problems: Applying collective leadership and Kotter's change model to wicked problems within social system networks. *Nonprofit Management & Leadership, 30*(3), 509–524. https://onlinelibrary.wiley.com/doi/abs/10.1002/nml.21399?casa_token=SE49ZSKJpHUAAAAA%3AIx7MEpsN-No4ZQq24qjdlnajh3MB3vvPwz2Vqw8yPI7kfcEcRPvW1fi8kVByVvrP0OPsp7vVIFyRsva5. DOI: 10.1002/nml.21399

Cave, S., Dihal, K., & Dillon, S. (2019). *AI narratives: A history of imaginative thinking about intelligent machines*. Oxford University Press., https://global.oup.com/academic/product/ai-narratives-9780198846666

Cerny, P. (2022). *Heterarchy in world politics*. Routledge & CRC Press. https://www.routledge.com/Heterarchy-inWorldPolitics/Cerny/p/book/9781032403410

Chalmers, D., MacKenzie, N. G., & Carter, S. (2021). Artificial intelligence and entrepreneurship: Implications for venture creation in the fourth industrial revolution. *Entrepreneurship Theory and Practice, 45*(5), 1028–1053. DOI: 10.1177/1042258720934581

Chamorro-Premuzic, T., Polli, F., & Dattner, B. (2019). Building ethical AI for talent management. *Harvard Business Review*.

Chang, Y.-L., & Ke, J. (2023). Socially Responsible Artificial Intelligence Empowered People Analytics: A Novel Framework Towards Sustainability. *Human Resource Development Review*, *23*(1), 88–120. DOI: 10.1177/15344843231200930

Chen, E. (2024). Empowering artificial intelligence for knowledge management augmentation. *Issues in Information Systems*, *25*(1), 409–416. DOI: 10.48009/1_iis_2024_132

Cherns, A. (1976). The principles of sociotechnical design. *Human Relations*, *29*(8), 783–792. DOI: 10.1177/001872677602900806

Cherns, A. (1987). Principles of sociotechnical design revisited. *Human Relations*, *40*(3), 153–161. DOI: 10.1177/001872678704000303

Cheung, H. K., King, E., Lindsey, A., Membere, A., Markell, H. M., & Kilcullen, M. (2016). Understanding and reducing workplace discrimination. *Research in Personnel and Human Resources Management*, •••, 101–152. https://www.emerald.com/books/edited-volume/12777/chapter-abstract/83108905/Understanding-and-Reducing-Workplace?redirectedFrom=fulltext

Chomczyński, P. (2020). Mobbing from the standpoint of symbolic interactionism. *Qualitative Sociology Review, 16*(4), 52-62. https://www.ceeol.com/search/article-detail?id=909745

Chow, C., & Ren, L. (2023). Negotiating civic identity across different political contexts: Immigrant participation in social movements and political incorporation. *Sociology Compass*, *17*(12), e13140. Advance online publication. DOI: 10.1111/soc4.13140

CISOMAG. (2020). *Healthcare data breaches and regulatory frameworks: A global perspective*. EC-Council.

Cohen, A. (2021). *Colonial Pipeline shuts down operations after ransomware attack*. The New York Times. Retrieved from https://www.nytimes.com/2021/05/08/us/colonial-pipeline-hack.html)

Cohen, L. E., & Felson, M. (1979). Social change and crime rate trends: A routine activity approach. *American Sociological Review*, *44*(4), 588. DOI: 10.2307/2094589

College, A., & Bajpai, A. (2021). Digital Tension: A Comparison Between Democracies and Authoritarian Regimes. *Political Expertise: POLITEX*, *17*(4), 330–340. DOI: 10.21638/spbu23.2021.401

Collins, R. (2010). *A graphical method for exploring the business environment.* Henley Business School., http://dl1.icdst.org/pdfs/files/3debe72112ec5b1d1abd4f83ced389a8.pdf

Congge, U., Guillamón, M., Nurmandi, A., Salahudin, N., & Sihidi, I. T. (2023). Digital democracy: A Systematic Literature Review. *Frontiers in Political Science*, *5*, 972802. Advance online publication. DOI: 10.3389/fpos.2023.972802

Constantino, T. (2024, November 12) Women Make Up 29% Of The AI Workforce; Here's How To Fix It. Forbes. Retrieved from: https://www.forbes.com/sites/torconstantino/2024/11/12/women-make-up-29-of-the-ai-workforce---heres-how-to-fix-it/

Cornish, D. B., & Clarke, R. V. (1989). Crime specialisation, crime displacement and rational choice theory. In *Criminal behavior and the justice system: Psychological perspectives* (pp. 103–117). Springer Berlin Heidelberg., https://link.springer.com/chapter/10.1007/978-3-642-86017-1_7 DOI: 10.1007/978-3-642-86017-1_7

Corporation, I. B. M. (2021). *IBM launches QRadar XDR, a comprehensive open XDR solution.* IBM TechXchange Community. https://community.ibm.com/community/user/discussion/ibm-launches-qradar-xdr-a-comprehensive-open-xdr-solution?hlmlt=VT

Corrêa, D., Moraes, T., & Teixeira, J. (2023). AI governance and regulation: Closing the gap between declarative ethics and pragmatic implementation. *Journal of Information. Communication and Ethics in Society*, *21*(5), 704–721. DOI: 10.1108/JICES-08-2022-0120

COSO. (2017). Enterprise risk management: Integrating with strategy and performance. https://www.coso.org/enterprise-risk-management

COSO. (2017a, June). *Enterprise Risk Management – integrated framework.* Retrieved from https://www.coso.org/_files/ugd/3059fc_61ea5985b03c4293960642fdce408eaa.pdf

COSO. (2017b, June). *Enterprise Risk Management – integrating with strategy and performance.* Retrieved from https://www.coso.org/_files/ugd/3059fc_61ea5985b03c4293960642fdce408eaa.pdf

Council, T. B. M. (2023). *Technology business management: Taxonomy and best practices.* TBM Council.

Cowgill, B., Dell'Acqua, F., Deng, S., Hsu, D., Verma, N., & Chaintreau, A. (2020). *Biased programmers? Or biased data? A field experiment in operationalizing AI ethics.* DOI: /arXiv.2012.02394DOI: 10.1145/3391403.3399545

Craig, R., & Corey, D. (2021). Cyber threats in healthcare: A comprehensive review. *Journal of Healthcare Information Management, 35*(2), 112–119.

Crawford, K., Miltner, K., & Gray, M. L. (2014). Critiquing Big Data: Politics, ethics, epistemology. *International Journal of Communication, 8*, 1663–1672. https://ijoc.org/index.php/ijoc/article/view/2167/1164

Crenshaw, K. (1989). Demarginalizing the intersection of race and sex: A black feminist critique of antidiscrimination doctrine, feminist theory and antiracist politics. *University of Chicago Legal Forum, 1989*(1), 139–167. https://chicagounbound.uchicago.edu/uclf/vol1989/iss1/8

Criado, J. I., Sandoval-Almazán, R., & Gil-Garcia, J. R. (2025). Artificial intelligence and public administration: Understanding actors, governance, and policy from micro, meso, and macro perspectives. *Public Policy and Administration, 40*(2), 173–184. DOI: 10.1177/09520767241272921

CSO. (2018, March 06). *Healthcare experiences twice the number of cyber attacks as other industries*. https://www.csoonline.com/article/564763/healthcare-experiences-twice-the-number-of-cyber-attacks-as-other-industries.html

Cuevas, A. G., & Boen, C. (2021). Tip of the iceberg: Measuring racial discrimination in studies of health. *Stress and Health, 37*(5), 1043–1050. https://pmc.ncbi.nlm.nih.gov/articles/PMC8449795/. DOI: 10.1002/smi.3047 PMID: 33739613

Cunningham, N., & Carmichael, T. (2017). Sampling, interviewing and coding: Lessons from a constructivist grounded study. In *ECRM 2017: Proceedings of the 16th European Conference on Research Methods in Business and Management* (pp. 1–10). ACPI., https://research.manchester.ac.uk/en/publications/sampling-interviewing-and-coding-lessons-from-a-constructivist-gr/?utm_source=copilot.com

Cutolo, D., & Vang, J. (2021). *Digital platforms*. Edward Elgar., DOI: 10.4337/9781839104145.00017

Cyber Threat Intelligence, K. E. L. A. (2025). *Third-party risk in healthcare demands immediate attention*. https://www.kelacyber.com/blog/why-third-party-risk-in-healthcare-demands-immediate-attention/

Cybersecurity & Infrastructure Security Agency (CISA). (2019). *Phishing guidance for healthcare institutions*. U.S. Department of Homeland Security. https://www.cisa.gov

Cynet. (2022). *Cynet Next-Gen Antivirus (NGAV)*. Retrieved from https://www.cynet.com/platform/next-gen-antivirus/

Dal Pozzolo, A., Caelen, O., Johnson, R. A., & Bontempi, G. (2015). Calibrating probability with undersampling for unbalanced classification. In *2015 IEEE Symposium Series on Computational Intelligence* (pp. 159–166). https://doi.org/DOI: 10.1109/SSCI.2015.33

Dalton, C., & Thatcher, J. (2014). What does a Critical Data Studies look like, and why do we care? Seven points for a critical approach to 'big data.' *Environment and Planning D: Society and Space. Online journal companion.* https://societyandspace.com/material/commentaries/craig-dalton-and-jim-thatcher-what-does-a-critical-data-studies-look-like-and-why-do-we-care-seven-points-for-a-critical-approach-to-big-data/

Dasgupta, S., Roy, S., & Saha, S. (2021). AI and human capital in developing economies: Barriers and opportunities. *Development Policy Review, 39*(6), 900–915. DOI: 10.1111/dpr.12567

Dastin, J. (2018). *Amazon scrapped 'AI' recruiting tool that showed bias against women.* Reuters. https://www.reuters.com/article/us-amazon-com-jobs-automation-insight-idUSKCN1MK08G

Decker, A., & Galer, D. (2013). *Enterprises and business risks control techniques (risk control & risk management techniques.* ERMSTTP.

Deloitte, A. I. Institute. (2021). *Women in AI.* https://www2.deloitte.com/content/dam/Deloitte/us/Documents/deloitte-analytics/us-consulting-women-in-ai.pdf

Deloitte. (2023). *2023 global human capital trends.* https://www2.deloitte.com

Deming, D., & Summers, L. H. (2025). Is AI already shaking up the labor market? *Harvard Gazette.* https://news.harvard.edu/gazette/story/2025/02/is-ai-already-shaking-up-labor-market-a-i-artificial-intelligence/

Demir, K. A., Döven, G., & Sezen, B. (2023). Industry 5.0 and human-centric digital transformation. *Journal of Manufacturing Systems, 68*, 51–63. DOI: 10.1016/j.jmsy.2023.03.007

Denison. *Introduction to the Denison model* (2019). https://denisonconsulting.com/wp-content/uploads/2019/08/introduction-to-the-denison-model.pdf

Denison, D., Nieminen, L., & Kotrba, L. (2014). Diagnosing organizational cultures: A conceptual and empirical review of culture effectiveness surveys. *European Journal of Work and Organizational Psychology, 23*(1), 145–161. DOI: 10.1080/1359432X.2012.713173

Denning, S. (2018). *The age of agile: How smart companies are transforming the way work gets done*. AMACOM.

Dhatt, R., Theobald, S., Buzuzi, S., Ros, B., Vong, S., Muraya, K., Molyneux, S., Hawkins, K., González-Beiras, C., Ronsin, K., Lichtenstein, D., Wilkins, K., Thompson, K., Davis, K., & Jackson, C. (2017). The role of women's leadership and gender equity in leadership and health system strengthening. *Global Health, Epidemiology and Genomics, 2*, e8. https://www.cambridge.org/core/journals/global-health-epidemiology-and-genomics/article/role-ofwomens-leadership-and-gender-equity-in-leadership-and-health-systemstrengthening/A6AEB63AFE17295E0EF9E40741A2EC5B. DOI: 10.1017/gheg.2016.22 PMID: 29868219

Díaz-García, C., González-Moreno, A., & Sáez-Martínez, F. J. (2013). Gender diversity within R&D teams: Its impact on radicalness of innovation. *Innovation (North Sydney, N.S.W.), 15*(2), 149–160. DOI: 10.5172/impp.2013.15.2.149

Dill, J., & Duffy, M. (2022). Structural Racism And Black Women's Employment In The US Health Care Sector: Study examines structural racism and black women's employment in the US healthcare sector. *Health Affairs, 41*(2), 265–272. https://www.healthaffairs.org/doi/full/10.1377/hlthaff.2021.01400. DOI: 10.1377/hlthaff.2021.01400 PMID: 35130061

Dordunoo, L. (2025). Integrating organizational and social network theories to mitigate racial bias in facial recognition technology. In Burrell, D. (Ed.), *Organizational Readiness and Research: Security, Management, and Decision Making* (pp. 283–348). IGI Global Scientific Publishing., DOI: 10.4018/979-8-3693-8562-3.ch009

Doshi-Velez, F., & Kim, B. (2017). *Towards a rigorous science of interpretable machine learning. arXiv preprint*. https://arxiv.org/abs/1702.08608

Dryzek, J. (2020). *Global deliberative democracy*. Routledge., DOI: 10.4324/9780367816681-42

Dwork, C., Hardt, M., Pitassi, T., Reingold, O., & Zemel, R. (2011). *Fairness through awareness*. https://doi.org/DOI: 10.1145/2090236.2090255

Eck, J. E., & Clarke, R. V. (2019). Situational crime prevention: Theory, practice and evidence. In *Handbook on crime and deviance* (pp. 355–376). Springer International Publishing., https://link.springer.com/chapter/10.1007/978-3-030-20779-3_18 DOI: 10.1007/978-3-030-20779-3_18

Eden, C., Adeniyi, I., & Chisom, O.Chima Abimbola EdenOnyebuchi Nneamaka ChisomIdowu Sulaimon Adeniyi. (2024). Promoting Digital Literacy And Social Equity In Education: Lessons From Successful Initiatives. *International Journal of Management &amp. Entrepreneurship Research*, *6*(3), 687–696. DOI: 10.51594/ijmer.v6i3.880

Edmondson, A. (2019). *The fearless organization: Creating psychological safety in the workplace for learning, innovation, and growth.* Wiley.

Eisikovits, N., & Feldman, D. (2022). AI and phronesis. *Moral Philosophy and Politics*, *9*(2), 181–199. DOI: 10.1515/mopp-2021-0026

Ekbia, H., Mattioli, M., Kouper, I., Arave, G., Ghazinejad, A., Bowman, T., Suri, V.R., Tsou, A., Weingart, S. & Sugimoto, C.R. (2015), Big data, bigger dilemmas: A critical review. *Journal of The Association for Information Science & Technology, 66*(8), 1523-1545. (First published in 2014)DOI: 10.1002/asi.23294

El-Amin, A. (2022). Organizational climate change: diversity, equity, inclusion, and belonging. In *Implementing Diversity, Equity, Inclusion, and Belonging Management in Organizational Change Initiatives* (pp. 1–23). IGI Global. https://www.igi-global.com/chapter/organizational-climate-change/304638

Emdad, F. B., Ho, S. M., Ravuri, B., & Hussain, S. (2023). Towards a unified utilitarian ethics framework for healthcare artificial intelligence. *arXiv preprint arXiv:2309.14617.*

Emden, C. J. (2022). Changing Perceptions of the Public Sphere. berghahn books. https://doi.org/DOI: 10.1515/9780857455017

Epker, E. (2023, August 1). Artificial intelligence in women's health: The pros, the cons, and the guardrails needed to improve care. *Forbes*. https://www.forbes.com/sites/evaepker/2023/08/01/artificial-intelligence-in-womens-health-the-pros-the-cons-and-the-guardrails-needed-to-improve-care/?sh=3ecb29d34c87

Ersanlı, C. Y., Çelik, F., Barjesteh, H., Duran, V., & Manoochehrzadeh, M. (2025). A review of global reskilling and upskilling initiatives in the age of AI. *AI and Ethics*, *5*(6), 5719–5728. DOI: 10.1007/s43681-025-00767-9

Eshet-Alkalai, Y. (2004). Digital literacy: A conceptual framework for survival skills in the digital era. *Journal of Educational Multimedia and Hypermedia, 13*(1), 93–106.

Estonia's e-Residency initiative. (2014). *Estonia's e-Residency: Digital nation.* https://eresident.gov.ee/

European Parliament. (2023). EU AI Act: First regulation on artificial intelligence. https://www.europarl.europa.eu/topics/en/article/20230601STO93804/eu-ai-act-first-regulation-on-artificial-intelligence

Fadlallah, H., & Phillips, R. A. (2020). Governance of Voice in Digital Platforms. *Proceedings of the International Association for Business and Society*, *31*, 24–36. DOI: 10.5840/iabsproc2020314

Fathi, E., & MacKinnon, P. (2024). Is society ready for the impact of AI on the workforce? *Centre for International Governance Innovation*. https://www.cigionline.org/articles/is-society-ready-for-the-impact-of-ai-on-the-workforce/

FCC. (2021). 2021 Broadband Deployment Report. Federal Communications Commission. https://www.fcc.gov/reports-research/reports/broadband-progress-reports/2021-broadband-deployment-report

Federal Trade Commission. (2025, July 30). *New FTC data show a big Jump in reported losses to fraud to $12.5 billion in 2024*. https://www.ftc.gov/news-events/news/press-releases/2025/03/new-ftc-data-show-big-jump-reported-losses-fraud-125-billion-2024?utm_source=chatgpt.com

Federal Trade Commission. (n.d.). *Medical identity theft.* https://www.ftc.gov/identity-theft

Ferguson, Y. H., & Mansbach, R. W. (2010). Postinternational Theory. https://doi.org/DOI: 10.1093/acrefore/9780190846626.013.467

Ferguson, Y., & Mansbach, R. (2004). *Postinternational politics*. Cambridge University., DOI: 10.1017/CBO9780511491344.002

Ferret Mas, J. (2023). Distributive Justice, Political Legitimacy, and Independent Central Banks. *Res Publica (Liverpool, England)*, *30*(2), 249–266. DOI: 10.1007/s11158-023-09619-x

Figueiredo, J. M. P. C. (2024). *The Impact of Artificial Intelligence on the Stakeholder Theory: A Bibliometric Review Analysis*. PQDT-Global.

Fitzwater, L. (2022). *The Global Citizen, Globalized Lifestyles and Pedagogy*. Springer., DOI: 10.1007/978-3-031-10928-7_4

Floridi, L. (2022). Ethical aspects of AI: Between risk management and trustworthy design. *AI & Society*, *37*, 1497–1508. DOI: 10.1007/s00146-021-01244-4

Floridi, L., & Cowls, J. (2019). A unified framework of five principles for AI in society. *Harvard Data Science Review*, *1*(1). Advance online publication. DOI: 10.1162/99608f92.8cd550d1

Floridi, L., Cowls, J., Beltrametti, M., Chatila, R., Chazerand, P., Dignum, V., Luetge, C., Madelin, R., Pagallo, U., Rossi, F., Shafer, B., & Vayena, E. (2018). AI4People—An ethical framework for a good AI society: Opportunities, risks, principles, and recommendations. *Minds and Machines*, *28*(4), 689–707. DOI: 10.1007/s11023-018-9482-5 PMID: 30930541

Flynn, A., Powell, A., Scott, A. J., & Cama, E. (2022). Deepfakes and digitally altered imagery abuse: A cross-country exploration of an emerging form of image-based sexual abuse. *British Journal of Criminology*, *62*(6), 1341–1358. DOI: 10.1093/bjc/azab111

Fogaça, D. R., Grijalvo, M., & Sacomano Neto, M. (2024). What are Industry 4.0 and Industry 5.0 all about? An integrative institutional model for the new industrial paradigms. *Administrative Sciences*, *15*(4), 118. https://www.mdpi.com/2076-3387/15/4/118. DOI: 10.3390/admsci15040118

Fontana, L. B. (2023). *Identity in Latin American Social Movements*. Oxford University., DOI: 10.1093/oxfordhb/9780190870362.013.30

Forrest, A., & Lindemulder, G. (n.d.). *What is a next-generation antivirus (NGAV)? IBM.* Retrieved from https://www.ibm.com/think/topics/next-generation-antivirus/#:~:text=Authors,IBM%20Think

Fortified Health Security. (2023, July 18). *Fortified Health Security releases 2023 mid-year horizon report* https://fortifiedhealthsecurity.com/horizon-report/2023-mid-year-horizon-report/

Fraser, J., & Simkins, B. (2016). *Enterprise risk management: Today's leading research and best practices for tomorrow's executives.* Wiley.

Frenette, J. (2023). Ensuring human oversight in high-performance AI systems: A framework for control and accountability. *World Journal of Advanced Research and Reviews*, *20*(2), 1507–1516. DOI: 10.30574/wjarr.2023.20.2.2194

Fu, J. S., & Barbour, J. B. (2023). Contextualizing communication for digital innovation and the future of work. *Journal of Communication*, *74*(1), 36–47. DOI: 10.1093/joc/jqad031

Gadimah Consulting. (2023). The 5th Industrial Revolution (5IR): A Shift from 'Technology for the People' to 'Technology with the People.' *Gadimah Consulting*. https://gadimah.consulting/blog/the-5th-industrial-revolution-5ir

Gaebler, J. D., Goel, S., Huq, A., & Tambe, P. (2025). Auditing large language models for race & gender disparities: Implications for artificial intelligence-based hiring. *Behavioral Science & Policy*, *10*(2), 46–55. DOI: 10.1177/23794607251320229

Gagliardi, A. R., & Tomaselli, G. (2025). Aligning corporate social responsibility with artificial intelligence in healthcare in the context of the post-COVID-19 recovery: A viewpoint. *Journal of Health Organization and Management*. Advance online publication. DOI: 10.1108/JHOM-06-2024-0244 PMID: 39763013

Gao, D. K., Mittal, S., Haverly, A., Chen, J., & Wu, J. (2024). AI Ethics. *International Journal of Business Analytics*, *11*(1), 1–19. DOI: 10.4018/IJBAN.338367

Gardenier, A. M., Est, R., & Royakkers, L. (2024). Technological citizenship in times of digitization: An integrative framework. *Digital Society : Ethics, Socio-Legal and Governance of Digital Technology*, *3*(2), 21. Advance online publication. DOI: 10.1007/s44206-024-00106-1

Garrison, D. R., & Vaughan, N. D. (2008). *Blended learning in higher education: Framework, principles, and guidelines*. Jossey-Bass.

Geden, M., & Andrews, J. (2021). Fair and interpretable algorithmic hiring using evolutionary many-objective optimization. *The Thirty-Fifth AAAI Conference on Artificial Intelligence (AAAI-21)* 14795-14803. DOI: 10.1609/aaai.v35i17.17737

Gibelli, F., Maio, G., & Ricci, G. (2024). Healthcare in the age of sapient machines: Physician decision-making autonomy faced with artificial intelligence. Ethical, deontological and compensatory aspects. *Frontiers in Medicine*, *11*, 1477371. DOI: 10.3389/fmed.2024.1477371 PMID: 39267961

Giugni, M. (2023). *Social Movements*. Oxford University., DOI: 10.1093/oxfordhb/9780192871787.013.18

Glikson, E., & Woolley, A. W. (2020). Human trust in artificial intelligence: Review of empirical research. *The Academy of Management Annals*, *14*(2), 627–660. DOI: 10.5465/annals.2018.0057

Glikson, E., & Woolley, A. W. (2023). Human trust in AI: A review of empirical research. *The Academy of Management Annals*, *17*(1), 484–516. https://www.researchgate.net/publication/340605601_Human_trust_in_artificial_intelligence_Review_of_empirical_research_Academy_of_Management_Annals_in_press

González-Granadillo, G., González-Zarzosa, S., & Diaz, R. (2021). Security Information and Event Management (SIEM): Analysis, trends, and usage in critical infrastructures. *Sensors (Basel)*, *21*(14), 4759. DOI: 10.3390/s21144759 PMID: 34300500

Google, A. I. (n.d.). *Responsible AI practices*. https://ai.google/responsibility/responsible-ai-practices/

Gordon, W. J., Ikoma, N., Lyu, H., Jackson, G. P., & Landman, A. B. (2022). Protecting procedural care—Cybersecurity considerations for robotic surgery. *NPJ Digital Medicine*, *5*(1), 148. DOI: 10.1038/s41746-022-00693-8 PMID: 36127420

Gorman, B. (2023). *EternalBlue: What is it and how does it work? AVG.* Retrieved from https://www.avg.com/en/signal/eternal-blue#:~:text=Exactly%20when%20the%20EternalBlue%20exploit,the%20hacker%20group%20Shadow%20Brokers

Gorski, P. C. (2009). Insisting on digital equity: Reframing the dominant discourse on multicultural education and technology. *Urban Education*, *44*(3), 348–364. DOI: 10.1177/0042085908318712

Government of India. (2022). *Digital India Progress Report.* Ministry of Electronics and Information Technology.

Grasso, A. (2024, March 27). Industry 5.0 will bridge automation to human-machine collaboration. *DeltalogiX.* https://deltalogix.blog/en/2024/03/27/industry-5-0-will-bridge-automation-to-human-machine-collaboration

Grau, E., & Klien, K. (2025, January 29). Why We Need More Women In The AI Revolution. Time. Retrieved from: https://time.com/7210973/women-in-the-ai-revolution/

Graves, M. (2024). Apprehending AI moral purpose in practical wisdom. *AI & Society*, *39*(3), 1335–1348. DOI: 10.1007/s00146-022-01597-7

Gray, S. W. D., & Warren, M. E. (2024). What kind of power can citizens exercise beyond the state? Globalizing democracy through representative claim-making. *International Theory*, *16*(3), 1–28. DOI: 10.1017/S175297192400006X

Greenfield, B., & Jensen, G. M. (2010). Beyond a code of ethics: Phenomenological ethics for everyday practice. *Physiotherapy Research International*, *15*(2), 88–95. https://onlinelibrary.wiley.com/doi/abs/10.1002/pri.481?casa_token=1Q_foO-riuQAAAAA%3APHkMu5tnhGDQK03SiV9mlDFSlihwNac0UtYcxD8aGyKPwsK8AXU9vMLvs2Y2IX8nsh5PbQ-Vlm3Y4Kc2. DOI: 10.1002/pri.481 PMID: 20564757

Griffiths, M. (2015). Empowering citizens. In Editor(s) (Eds.), Title of the work (pp. xx–xx). Publisher. https://doi.org/DOI: 10.4018/978-1-4666-8358-7.ch071

GSMA. (2025). The mobile gender gap report 2025. https://www.gsma.com/r/gender-gap/

Gupta, D., Elluri, L., Jain, A., Moni, S. S., & Aslan, O. (2024). *Blockchain-enhanced framework for secure third-party vendor risk management and vigilant security controls*. arXiv preprint. https://arxiv.org/abs/2411.13447 DOI: 10.1109/BigData62323.2024.10825025

Gupta, R., & Kim, S. (2022). Strategic deployment of artificial intelligence in enterprise operations: Evidence from global industries. *Journal of Business Research, 144*, 198–210. DOI: 10.1016/j.jbusres.2022.01.030

Haley, P. (2025). Artificial intelligence and ethical dimensions of automated traffic enforcement: Implications for public health, healthcare equity, and social justice. *Health Economics and Management Review, 6*(2), 32-49. https://armgpublishing.com/wp-content/uploads/2025/07/HEM_2_2025_3.pdf

Haley, P., & Burrell, D. N. (2025). Integrating Artificial Intelligence into Law Enforcement: Socioeconomic and Ethical Challenges. *SocioEconomic Challenges, 9*(2), 60-77. https://armgpublishing.com/wp-content/uploads/2025/07/SEC_2_2025_4.pdf

Haley, P., & Burrell, D. N. (2025). Using Artificial Intelligence in Law Enforcement and Policing to Improve Public Health and Safety. *Law. Economics and Society, 1*(1), 46–p46. DOI: 10.30560/les.v1n1p46

Hall, P., & Ellis, D. (2023). A systematic review of socio-technical gender bias in AI algorithms. *Online Information Review*, *47*(7), 1264–1279. DOI: 10.1108/OIR-08-2021-0452

Halsband, A. (2022). Sustainable AI and intergenerational justice. *Sustainability (Basel), 14*(7), 3922. Advance online publication. DOI: 10.3390/su14073922

Harfst, P., & Wiesner, C. (2024). Measuring political legitimacy in two dimensions: Internal and external measures. *Frontiers in Political Science*, *6*, 999743. Advance online publication. DOI: 10.3389/fpos.2024.999743

Hartnett, K. (2022). Racially biased medical device results raise patient safety concerns. Modern Healthcare. Retrieved from: https://www.modernhealthcare.com/providers/bias-medical-device-results-raises-patient-safety-concerns

Harvard Business Publishing. (2020). *Leading change: A simulation by Kotter* [Simulation]. Harvard Business School Publishing.

Hautamaki, J., & Kokkonen, T. (2020). Model for cyber security information sharing in healthcare sector. *2020 International Conference on Electrical, Communication, and Computer Engineering (ICECCE)*, 1–5. https://doi.org/DOI: 10.1109/ICECCE49384.2020.9179175

Hayward, K. (2007). Situational crime prevention and its discontents: Rational choice theory versus the 'culture of now'. *Social Policy and Administration*, *41*(3), 232–250. https://onlinelibrary.wiley.com/doi/abs/10.1111/j.1467-9515.2007.00550.x?casa_token=Afo7niSFlw8AAAAA%3AIn0vcW4nNsNjCqF3BEwDQI_hSq7ytkRzDhriVbZvrbth-R3bLm9ewu7G_MMzMhP16hYfV3cxM0XGgxYI. DOI: 10.1111/j.1467-9515.2007.00550.x

Health, I. T. Security. (2021). Scripps Health ransomware attack disrupts care. *HealthITSecurity.com.* https://healthitsecurity.com

Hechter, M., & Kanazawa, S. (1997). Sociological rational choice theory. *Annual Review of Sociology*, *23*(1), 191–214. https://www.annualreviews.org/content/journals/10.1146/annurev.soc.23.1.191. DOI: 10.1146/annurev.soc.23.1.191

Hennein, R., Gorman, H., Chung, V., & Lowe, S. R. (2023). Gender discrimination among women healthcare workers during the COVID-19 pandemic: Findings from a mixed methods study. *PLoS One*, *18*(2), e0281367. https://journals.plos.org/plosone/article?id=10.1371/journal.pone.0281367. DOI: 10.1371/journal.pone.0281367 PMID: 36745623

Henry, N., Flynn, A., & Powell, A. (2020). Technology-facilitated sexual violence: A review of the literature. *Violence Against Women*, *26*(15–16), 1828–1854. DOI: 10.1177/1077801219875821

HHS. (2024). Artificial intelligence strategy. U.S. Department of Health and Human Services. https://www.hhs.gov/sites/default/files/hhs-artificial-intelligence-strategy.pdf

Hiatt, J. (2020). *ADKAR: A model for change in business, government and our community* (2nd ed.). Prosci.

Hillebrand, T. M. (2019). *The critical role of leadership in implementing the adequate change management model for effective organizational change* (Doctoral dissertation). https://opus.hs-furtwangen.de/frontdoor/index/index/docId/5958

Ho, H. (2024). *Using Situational Crime Prevention (SCP) to prevent cybercrimes* (Doctoral dissertation, Singapore Institute of Technology). https://espace.library.uq.edu.au/view/UQ:c6c6fc3

Hodges, C., Moore, S., Lockee, B., Trust, T., & Bond, A. (2020). The difference between emergency remote teaching and online learning. *EDUCAUSE Review*, •••, 27.

Hofmannn, B., Oortwijn, W., Lysdahl, K. B., Refolo, P., Sacchini, D., Van Der Wilt, G. J., & Gerhardus, A. (2015). Integrating ethics in health technology assessment: Many ways to Rome. *International Journal of Technology Assessment in Health Care, 31*(3), 131–137. DOI: 10.1017/S0266462315000276 PMID: 26063128

Hogan, M.. (2017). Governance, Transparency and the Collaborative Design of Open Data Collaboration Platforms: Understanding Barriers, Options, and Needs. In Ojo, A., & Millard, J. (Eds.), *Government 3.0 – Next Generation Government Technology Infrastructure and Services. Public Administration and Information Technology* (Vol. 32). Springer., DOI: 10.1007/978-3-319-63743-3_12

Holbeche, L. (2018). *The agile organization: How to build an innovative, sustainable and resilient business.* Kogan Page Publishers.

Holley, P. (2018, May 17). The Boston restaurant where robots have replaced the chefs. The Washington Post. https://www.washingtonpost.com/news/innovations/wp/2018/05/17/will-robots-replace-chefs-at-this-new-boston-restaurant-they-already-have/

Holley, P. (2019, July 2). This seafood restaurant's latest catch: Chinese robots that greet customers and deliver food. The Washington, Post. https://www.washingtonpost.com/technology/2019/07/02/this-seafood-restaurants-latest-catch-chinese-robots-that-greet-customers-deliver-food/

Hondros, K., Schiemer, B., & Vogelgsang, L. (2023). Beyond personal safe spaces: Creating and maintaining collective environments for meaning and identity on digital platforms. *Organization, 30*(5), 809–829. DOI: 10.1177/13505084231168094

Hong, R.-Y., Shneiderman, B., & Sowa, S. (2023). Synergy between human and artificial intelligence: The future of collaborative work. *Computers in Human Behavior, 142*, 107677. DOI: 10.1016/j.chb.2022.107677

Hossain, I. (2021). *Analysis the importance of VPN for Creating a Safe Connection Over the World of Internet.* IJARCCE., DOI: 10.17148/IJARCCE.2021.101017

Huff, A., Burrell, D. N., Richardson, K., Springs, D., Aridi, A. S., Crowe, M. M., & Lewis, E. (2023). Illegal Pregnancy Discrimination Is a Severe Business, Legal, and Public Health Issue. In Burrell, D. (Ed.), *Real-World Solutions for Diversity, Strategic Change, and Organizational Development: Perspectives in Healthcare, Education, Business, and Technology* (pp. 119–129). IGI Global., DOI: 10.4018/978-1-6684-8691-7.ch008

Hui, X., & Reshef, O. (2025). Is generative AI a job killer? Evidence from the freelance market. *The Brookings Institure.* https://www.brookings.edu/articles/is-generative-ai-a-job-killer-evidence-from-the-freelance-market/

Hu, L., Lu, Y., & Feng, Y. (2025). Concept drift detection based on deep neural networks and Autoencoders. *Applied Sciences (Basel, Switzerland), 15*(6), 3056. DOI: 10.3390/app15063056

Hyperproof. (2025). NIST 800-53: *Security and privacy controls for information systems and organizations*. https://hyperproof.io/nist-800-53/

IAMAI. (2022). *Internet in India Report*. Internet and Mobile Association of India.

Ichijo, A. (2023). *The Nation State and Multicultural Citizenship*. Oxford University., DOI: 10.1093/hepl/9780192846051.003.0004

Idemudia, I., & Onoshakpor, C. (2023). Gender, workforce and artificial intelligence. *2023 IEEE AFRICON*, 1-3. DOI: . https://ieeexplore.ieee.org/document/10293367DOI: 10.1109/AFRICON55910.2023.10293367

Identity Theft Resource Center. (2016). *Medical identity theft: The impact on patients*. ITRC Report. https://www.idtheftcenter.org

Iliadis, A., & Russo, F. (2016). Critical data studies: An introduction. *Big Data & Society, 3*(2). (Original work published 2016)DOI: 10.1177/2053951716674238

Innovations, G. Stanford University. (n.d.) *Facial recognition: Analyzing gender and intersectionality in machine learning*. https://genderedinnovations.stanford.edu/case-studies/facial.html#tabs-2

Intentilia, A. A. M. (2023). Foreign Policy, Public Diplomacy, and Social Media. Nation State. *Journal of International Students*, *6*(1), 1–17. DOI: 10.24076/nsjis.v6i1.1062

International Labour Organization (ILO). the World Health Organization (WHO). (2022, July 13). Women in the health and care sector earn 24 percent less than men. Retrieved from: https://www.who.int/news/item/13-07-2022-women-in-the-health-and-care-sector-earn-24-percent-less-than-men

Irmatova, G., Lysova, E., & Richardson, J. (2024). Digital readiness and AI adoption in HR: A comparative study. *Personnel Review*, *54*(2), 285–305. DOI: 10.1108/PR-02-2022-0074

Irvin-Erickson, Y. (2024). Consequences of Identity Theft Victimization: Disabilities and Mental Distress. *Crime and Delinquency*, *0*(0), 00111287241227926. Advance online publication. DOI: 10.1177/00111287241227926

ISACA. (2019). *COBIT 2019 framework: Governance and management objectives*. ISACA.

ISO. (2023). ISO/IEC 42001:2023 Artificial intelligence management systems. International Organization for Standardization. https://www.iso.org/standard/42001

Jaakkola, E. (2020). Designing conceptual articles: Four approaches. *AMS Review, 10*), 18–26. DOI: 10.1007/s13162-020-00161-0

Jia, X., Ye, Y., & Chen, Z. (2024). Human–AI collaboration and work disengagement. *Journal of Organizational Behavior*, *45*(4), 503–520. DOI: 10.1002/job.2725

Jisc. (2021). Digital experience insights survey. Jisc.

Jobin, A., Ienca, M., & Vayena, E. (2019). The global landscape of AI ethics guidelines. *Nature Machine Intelligence*, *1*(9), 389–399. DOI: 10.1038/s42256-019-0088-2

Johnson, C., Kwon, J., & Liu, M. E. (2020). The impact of WannaCry ransomware attack on hospitals: Lessons learned. *Journal of Cybersecurity*, *6*(1). Advance online publication. DOI: 10.1093/cybsec/tyaa006

Joinau, B. (2023). Cultural Governance and New Forms of Governmentality Focus on the South Korean Case. *The Journal of Arts Management, Law, and Society*, *53*(6), 358–374. DOI: 10.1080/10632921.2023.2280646

Kahsay, W. G., Negarandeh, R., Dehghan Nayeri, N., & Hasanpour, M. (2020). Sexual harassment against female nurses: A systematic review. *BMC Nursing*, *19*(1), 1–12. https://link.springer.com/article/10.1186/s12912-020-00450-w. DOI: 10.1186/s12912-020-00450-w

Kamalanathan, S., Rajan, S. M., & Schell, S. (2025). *Implementing zero trust in healthcare. Cognizant.* https://www.cognizant.com/en_us/industries/documents/cognizant-implementing-zero-trust-in-healthcare.pdf

Kaplan, R. S., & Norton, D. P. (1992). The balanced scorecard: Measures that drive performance. *Harvard Business Review*. PMID: 10119714

Kaplan, R. S., & Norton, D. P. (1996). *The balanced scorecard: Translating strategy into action*. Harvard Business School Press.

Kaspersky. (n.d.). *Glossary.* Retrieved from https://encyclopedia.kaspersky.com/glossary/

Kaspersky. (n.d.). *Next Generation Firewall (NGAV).* Retrieved from https://encyclopedia.kaspersky.com/glossary/

Katapally, T. R. (2020). A Global Digital Citizen Science Policy to Tackle Pandemics Like COVID-19. *Journal of Medical Internet Research*, *22*(5), e19357. DOI: 10.2196/19357 PMID: 32408267

Kaur, C. (2022). *The vital role of VPN in making secure connections over the Internet world. International Journal of Recent Technology and Engineering (IJRTE, 8(6).* DOI: 10.2139/ssrn.4032918

Kaur, J., & Bhatia, R. (2024). Synchrony in Learning: Investigating the Connection between Student Adjustment and Academic Performance. *Journal of Research in Education and Pedagogy, 1*(2), 132–139. DOI: 10.70232/jrep.v1i2.16

Kenytinc. (2024, June 19). Major challenges of Natural Language Processing (NLP). *Author* https://www.kenyt.ai/blog/conversational-ai/major-challenges-of-natural-language-processing-nlp/

Keyes, O. (2018). The misgendering machines: Trans/HCI implications of automatic gender recognition. *Proceedings of the ACM on Human-Computer Interaction, 2*(CSCW), 1–22. DOI: 10.1145/3274357

Khan, H., Pandey, S., Kumar, B. V., Akram, S. V., & Pal, P. (2024, March). Artificial Intelligence (AI) in the Field of Corporate Social Responsibility. In *2024 3rd International Conference on Sentiment Analysis and Deep Learning (ICSADL)* (pp. 164-168). IEEE.

Kikerpill, K. (2021). The individual's role in cybercrime prevention: Internal spheres of protection and our ability to safeguard them. *Kybernetes, 50*(4), 1015–1026. https://www.emerald.com/k/article-abstract/50/4/1015/263657/The-individual-s-role-in-cybercrime-prevention?redirectedFrom=fulltext. DOI: 10.1108/K-06-2020-0335

Kim, L. (2017). Cybersecurity awareness: Protecting data and patients. *Nursing, 47*(6), 65–67. DOI: 10.1097/01.NURSE.0000516242.05454.b4 PMID: 28538357

Kleiner, J. (2025). The social contract theory meets cybersecurity: Systematic literature review. *Digital Policy. Regulation & Governance, 27*(4), 446–465.

Klinghofer, B. (2022). *Introducing Microsoft Defender for Endpoint plan 1*. Retrieved from https://techcommunity.microsoft.com/t5/microsoft-defender-for-endpoint/introducing-microsoft-defender-for-endpoint-plan-1/ba-p/2636641

Kocot, M., & Kłak, D. (2024). Employee Engagement In Innovation Processes In An Agile Organization. *Zeszyty Naukowe Wyższej Szkoły Humanitas Zarządzanie, 25*(4), 119–134. DOI: 10.5604/01.3001.0054.9665

Kosuru, S. K., Tadi, S., G, J., K, S., D, G., & K, S. S. S. (2023). Data Analytics and Artificial Intelligence. *Journal of Clinical and Pharmaceutical Research, 15–17,* 15–17. Advance online publication. DOI: 10.61427/jcpr.v3.i3.2023.112

Kotter, J. P. (1996). *Leading change*. Harvard Business School Press.

Kotter, J. P. (2017). What leaders really do. In *Leadership perspectives* (pp. 7–15). Routledge. DOI: 10.4324/9781315250601-2

Kour, J., & Bhatia, R. (2025). From self-awareness to social skills: The journey of emotionally intelligent leadership. In *Emotionally intelligent methods for meaningful leadership* (pp. 173–196). IGI Global Scientific Publishing.

KPMG. (2022). *A triple threat across the Americas: 2022 KPMG fraud outlook.* https://assets.kpmg.com/content/dam/kpmg/xx/pdf/2022/01/fraud-survey.pdf

Krause, M. E. (2015). *The role of personal values in shaping leaders' experiences with employee engagement: A qualitative phenomenological study* (Doctoral dissertation, University of Phoenix). https://www.proquest.com/openview/18c17edefb1935f4a07a2ca309ce11f5/1?pq-origsite=gscholar&cbl=18750

Kraus, S., Jones, P., Kailer, N., Weinmann, A., Chaparro-Banegas, N., & Roig-Tierno, N. (2021). Digital transformation: An overview of the current state of the art of research. *SAGE Open, 11*(3), 1–15. DOI: 10.1177/21582440211047576

Kubiak, E., Efremova, M. I., Baron, S., & Frasca, K. J. (2023). Gender equity in hiring: Examining the effectiveness of a personality-based algorithm. *Frontiers in Psychology, 14*, 1219865. DOI: 10.3389/fpsyg.2023.1219865 PMID: 37655204

Kujala, J., Leinonen, H., Sachs, S., Heikkinen, A., & Laude, D. (2022). Stakeholder engagement: Past, present, and future. *Business & Society, 61*(5), 1136–1196. DOI: 10.1177/00076503211066595

Kumara, I., Mundt, P., Kayes, A. S. M., & Schneider, R. (2023). *Data Governance.* Springer., DOI: 10.1007/978-3-031-19554-9_3

Kusuma, P. G., & Madasu, S. (2015). 'A Great Place to Work': A comparison of Employee Engagement Practices of select companies with David Zinger Engagement Pyramid. *Aweshkar Research Journal, 19*(1). https://www.semanticscholar.org/paper/%27A-Great-Place-to-Work%27-%3A-A-comparison-of-Employee-Kusuma-Madasu/dca59a224130758224dc04e66711fc00ec0d3fad

Lane, J. N., Leonardi, P. M., Contractor, N. S., & DeChurch, L. A. (2024). Teams in the digital workplace: Technology's role for communication, collaboration, and performance. *Small Group Research, 55*(1), 139–183. DOI: 10.1177/10464964231200015

Lebcir, R., Hill, T., Atun, R., & Cubric, M. (2021). Stakeholders' views on the organisational factors affecting application of artificial intelligence in healthcare: A scoping review protocol. *BMJ Open, 11*(3), e044074. DOI: 10.1136/bmjopen-2020-044074 PMID: 33753441

Lee, N. T., Resnick, P., & Barton, G. (2019). Algorithmic bias detection and mitigation: Best practices and policies to reduce consumer harms. https://www.brookings.edu/articles/algorithmic-bias-detection-and-mitigation-best-practices-and-policies-to-reduce-consumer-harms/

Leukfeldt, E. R., & Yar, M. (2016). Applying routine activity theory to cybercrime: A theoretical and empirical analysis. *Deviant Behavior*, *37*(3), 263–280. https://www.tandfonline.com/doi/full/10.1080/01639625.2015.1012409. DOI: 10.1080/01639625.2015.1012409

Levy, K., & Barocas, S. (2018). Refractive surveillance: Monitoring customers to manage workers. *International Journal of Communication*, *12*, 1166–1188. https://docslib.org/doc/2009570/refractive-surveillance-monitoring-customers-to-manage-workers

Li, J., & Yang, D. (2023). Research on financial fraud detection models integrating multiple relational graphs. *Systems*, *11*(539), 539. Advance online publication. DOI: 10.3390/systems11110539

Liveri, D., Sarri, A., & Skouloudi, C. (2015). Security and resilience in eHealth: Security challenges and risks. *European Union Agency For Network and Information Security*. https://data.europa.eu/doi/10.2824/217830

Lloyd's Register Foundation & Gallup. (2022). *World risk poll 2021: A digital world perceptions of risk from AI and misuse of personal data.* https://wrp.lrfoundation.org.uk/LRF_2021_report_a-digtial-world-ai-and-personal-data_online_version.pdf

Lundy, D., Burrell, D. N., McCargo, T., Lima, F. M., Harris, N., Eke, H., & Prunella, K. 2025, November. Understanding the Psychology of Pregnancy Discrimination as a Challenging Womanâ€™ s Mental Health Workplace Dynamic. In *RAIS Conference Proceedings 2022-2025* (No. 0608). Research Association for Interdisciplinary Studies. https://ideas.repec.org/p/smo/raiswp/0608.html

Luperti, G. (2025, October 3). The truth of AI in HR: A wake-up call for the people function. Forbes. https://www.forbes.com/councils/forbeshumanresourcescouncil/2025/10/03/the-truth-of-ai-in-hr-a-wake-up-call-for-the-people-function/

Lussier, R. N., & Achua, C. F. (2012). *LEADERSHIP Theory, Application, & Skill Development.* Cengage Learning.

Lynn, T. J. (2025). Social Movements. 1–11. https://doi.org/DOI: 10.1002/9781405165518.wbeoss159.pub3

Machen, R., & Nost, E. (2021). Thinking algorithmically: The making of hegemonic knowledge in climate governance. *Transactions of the Institute of British Geographers, 46*(3), 555 569. https://doi.org/DOI: 10.1111/tran.12441

Mack, P. (2004). Utilitarian ethics in healthcare. *International journal of the computer, the internet and management, 12*(3), 63-72.

Madanchian, M., & Taherdoost, H. (2025). Barriers and Enablers of AI Adoption in Human Resource Management: A Critical Analysis of Organizational and Technological Factors. *Information (Basel), 16*(51), 51. Advance online publication. DOI: 10.3390/info16010051

Maheshwari, K., Jedan, C., Christiaans, I., Van Gijn, M., Maeckelberghe, E., & Plantinga, M. (2024). AI-Inclusivity in Healthcare: Motivating an Institutional Epistemic Trust Perspective. *Cambridge Quarterly of Healthcare Ethics*, •••, 1–15. DOI: 10.1017/S0963180124000215 PMID: 38682483

Maksimenko, I., Vashko, T., Zdrestova-Zakharenkova, S., & Nazarov, A. D. (2021). Digital transformation and its challenges to the strategic management system. *SHS Web of Conferences,* 106, 01035. https://doi.org/DOI: 10.1051/shsconf/202110601035

Manyika, J., Silberg, J., & Presten, B. (2019, October 25). What do we do about the biases in AI? *Harvard Business Review.* https://hbr.org/2019/10/what-do-we-do-about-the-biases-in-ai

Marchal, S., Asokan, N., & Niemi, V. (2017). A survey of anti-phishing solutions. *ACM Computing Surveys, 50*(6), 1–31. DOI: 10.1145/3131095

Marr, B. (2025, June 30). How is AI really impacting jobs in 2025? *Forbes.* https://www.forbes.com/sites/bernardmarr/2025/06/30/how-is-ai-really-impacting-jobs-in-2025/

Martin, N. (2022). Image-based sexual abuse and deepfakes: A survivor turned activist's perspective. In *The Palgrave handbook of gendered violence and technology* (pp. 55–72). Springer., DOI: 10.1007/978-3-030-83734-1_4

Maslej, N., Fattorini, L., Brynjolfsson, E., Etchemendy, J., Ligett, K., Lyons, T., Manyika, J., Ngo, H., Niebles, J. C., Parli, V., Shoham, Y., Wald, R., Clark, J., & Perrault, R. (2023). *Artificial Intelligence Index Report 2023.* Stanford University, Human-Centered Artificial Intelligence. https://aiindex.stanford.edu/wp-content/uploads/2023/04/HAI_AI-Index-Report_2023.pdf

McClain, T. S., Kammer-Kerwick, M., Wood, L., Temple, J. R., & Busch-Armendariz, N. (2021). Sexual harassment among medical students: Prevalence, prediction, and correlated outcomes. *Workplace Health & Safety*, *69*(6), 257–267. https://journals.sagepub.com/doi/full/10.1177/2165079920969402. DOI: 10.1177/2165079920969402 PMID: 33331247

McKinsey & Company. (2023). *The state of AI in 2023: Generative AI's breakout year.* https://www.mckinsey.com/capabilities/quantumblack/our-insights/the-state-of-ai-in-2023-generative-ais-breakout-year

McLester, Q., Burrell, D. N., Nobles, C., & Castillo, I. (2021). Advancing Knowledge About Sexual Harassment Is a Critical Aspect of Organizational Development for All Employees. [IJKBO]. *International Journal of Knowledge-Based Organizations*, *11*(4), 48–60. DOI: 10.4018/IJKBO.2021100104

McMahon, J. M., & Harvey, R. J. (2007). The effect of moral intensity on ethical judgment. *Journal of Business Ethics, 72*(4), 335-357. Retrieved from ABI/INFORM Global database. (Document ID: 1247251681). https://link.springer.com/article/10.1007/s10551-006-9174-6

Mehrabi, N., Morstatter, F., Saxena, N., Lerman, K., & Galstyan, A. (2021). A survey on bias and fairness in machine learning. *ACM Computing Surveys*, *54*(6), 1–35. DOI: 10.1145/3457607

Meikle, G. (2023). Social Media. https://doi.org/DOI: 10.1093/obo/9780199791286-0369

Mendonça, A. C. M., Silva, F. L., de Oliveira, L. E. C., Souza, J. A. C., & de Souza, J. T. (2025). Graph-based deep learning for e-commerce fraud detection. *Computers*, *14*(110). Advance online publication. DOI: 10.3390/computers14040110

Mendonça, R. F., & Asenbaum, H. (2025). Decolonizing deliberative democracy. *European Journal of Social Theory*. Advance online publication. DOI: 10.1177/13684310241297906

Mensah, G. B., & Lbg, A. (2024). AI Ethics. *Africa Journal For Regulatory Affairs*. https://doi.org/DOI: 10.62839/AJFRA/2024.v1.I1.32-45

Merrill, K.Jr, Kim, J., & Collins, C. (2022). AI companions for lonely individuals and the role of social presence. *Communication Research Reports*, *39*(2), 93–103. DOI: 10.1080/08824096.2022.2045929

Mik-Meyer, N., Mik-Meyer, N., & Järvinen, M. (2020). Symbolic interactionism, stigma, and othering. *Qualitative analysis: Eight approaches for the social sciences*, 51-72. https://www.researchgate.net/publication/348677705_Symbolic_interactionism_stigma_and_othering

Miller, J. L. (2017). Managing transitions: Using William Bridges' transition model and a change style assessment instrument to inform strategies and measure progress in organizational change management. In *The 12th International Conference on Performance Measurement in Libraries Proceedings* (p. 357). https://digitalcommons.butler.edu/librarian_papers/74/

Miller, S. (2021). Scripps Health announces systems down after ransomware attack. San *Diego Union-Tribune.* Retrieved from https://www.sandiegouniontribune.com/news/story/2021-05-02/scripps-health-networks-hacked-in-ransomware-attack

Miller, J. E. (2019). *Occupy Wall Street.* Springer., DOI: 10.1007/978-3-030-17391-3_6

Mirghaderi, L., Hildt, E., & Sziron, M. (2023). Ethics and Transparency Issues in Digital Platforms: An Overview. *AI*, *4*(4), 831–844. DOI: 10.3390/ai4040042

Mkrtchyan, T., & Melkumyan, N. (2023). The foundations of digital transformation of the public administration system. *Alternative*, •••, 118–127. DOI: 10.55528/18292828-2023.2-118

Momani, A., Hirzallah, M., & Mumani, A. (2017). Improving employees' safety awareness in healthcare organizations using the DMAIC quality improvement approach. *Journal for Healthcare Quality*, *39*(1), 54–63. DOI: 10.1097/JHQ.0000000000000049 PMID: 27579603

Monlezun, D. J., Sotomayor, C., Peters, N. J., Steigner, L., Gallagher, C. M., & García, A. (2022). The global AI ethics of COVID-19 recovery: Narrative review and Personalist Social Contract ethical analysis of AI-driven optimization of public health effectiveness and social equities. *Medicina y Etica : Revista Internacional de Bioetica, Deontologia y Etica Medica*, *33*(2), 357–394. DOI: 10.36105/mye.2022v33n2.02

Monroe, J. (2024). Corporate Social Responsibility in the MedTech Industry, the Emergence of Artificial Intelligence in the ERA of COVID-19. *American Journal of Artificial Intelligence*, *8*(1), 1–4. DOI: 10.11648/j.ajai.20240801.11

Morgenroth, T., & Ryan, M. K. (2018). Addressing gender inequality: Stumbling blocks and roads ahead. *Group Processes & Intergroup Relations*, *21*(5), 671–677. https://journals.sagepub.com/doi/full/10.1177/1368430218786079?casa_token=9ZRbr3InQZ4AAAAA%3Ahze0HaTkvuFWSh9R9MN1x0OiRDKnEHY3lirKO2A_zYJ2AN22jEPwCmKjlbDHR190n0i1mAFb_VF3mw. DOI: 10.1177/1368430218786079

Morley, J., Floridi, L., Kinsey, L., & Elhalal, A. (2020). From what to how: An initial review of publicly available AI ethics tools, methods and research to translate principles into practice. *AI and Ethics*, *1*(1), 1–20. DOI: 10.1007/s43681-020-00005-3

Moskatova, I., Polze, A., & Reichert, R. (2021). Introduction. Digital Culture & Society., DOI: 10.14361/dcs-2021-070202

Motie, S., & Raahemi, B. (2024). Financial fraud detection using graph neural networks: A systematic review. *Expert Systems with Applications*, *240*, 122156. DOI: 10.1016/j.eswa.2023.122156

Muduli, A., & Choudhury, A. (2025). Exploring the role of workforce agility on digital transformation: A systematic literature review. *Benchmarking*, *32*(2), 492–512. DOI: 10.1108/BIJ-02-2023-0108

Mullin, A. E., Coe, I. R., Gooden, E. A., Tunde-Byass, M., & Wiley, R. E. (2021). Inclusion, diversity, equity, and accessibility: From organizational responsibility to leadership competency. *Healthcare Management Forum*, *34*(6), 311–315. DOI: 10.1177/08404704211038232 PMID: 34535064

Mutemi, A., & Bacao, F. (2024). E-commerce fraud detection based on machine learning techniques: Systematic literature review. *Big Data Mining and Analytics*, *7*(2), 419–444. DOI: 10.26599/BDMA.2023.9020023

Nahavandi, S. (2019). Industry 5.0—A Human-Centric Solution. *Sustainability (Basel)*, *11*(16), 4371. DOI: 10.3390/su11164371

Nair, S. K. (2024). *Digital Transformation and Its Challenges in the Hospitality Industry in Malaysia*. IGI Global., DOI: 10.4018/979-8-3693-7683-6.ch017

National Institute of Standards and Technology. (2020). *Framework for improving critical infrastructure cybersecurity* (Version 1.1). U.S. Department of Commerce. DOI: 10.6028/NIST.CSWP.04162018

Nguyen, T. N., Le, C. V., Nguyen, M., Nguyen, G., Lien, T. T. H., & Nguyen, O. (2025). The organisational impact of agility: A systematic literature review. *Management Review Quarterly*, *75*(3), 2709–2757. DOI: 10.1007/s11301-024-00446-9

Nickols, F. (2020). The IDEAL problem-solving model. In *The knowledge in knowing* (pp. 125–134). Distance Consulting.

Nicotera, A. M. (2019). Human relations theory. In *Origins and Traditions of Organizational Communication* (pp. 106–127). Routledge. DOI: 10.4324/9780203703625-8

NIST. (2023). Artificial intelligence risk management framework (AI RMF 1.0) (NIST AI 100-1). U.S. Department of Commerce. https://nvlpubs.nist.gov/nistpubs/ai/nist.ai.100-1.pdf

NIST. (2025). *Incident response recommendations and considerations for cybersecurity risk management: A CSF 2.0 community profile (NIST Special Publication 800-61r3).* DOI: 10.6028/NIST.SP.800-61r3

Noble, S. M., Mende, M., Grewal, D., & Parasuraman, A. (2022). The fifth industrial revolution: How harmonious human–machine collaboration is triggering a retail and service revolution. *Journal of Retailing*, *98*(2), 199–216. DOI: 10.1016/j.jretai.2022.04.003

Noble, S. U. (2018). *Algorithms of oppression: How search engines reinforce racism.* NYU Press. DOI: 10.18574/nyu/9781479833641.001.0001

O'Connor, S., & Liu, H. (2023). Gender bias perpetuation and mitigation in AI technologies: Case studies and lessons learned. *AI & Society*, *29*, 2045–2057. DOI: 10.1007/s00146-023-01675-4

O'Neil, C. (2016). *Weapons of math destruction: How big data increases inequality and threatens democracy*. Crown Publishing Group.

Obermeyer, Z., Powers, B., Vogeli, C., & Mullainathan, S. (2019). Dissecting racial bias in an algorithm used to manage the health of populations. *Science*, *366*(6464), 447–453. DOI: 10.1126/science.aax2342 PMID: 31649194

Ochis, K. (2024, January, 23). AI organizational revolutions to watch in 2024: Navigating the transformative winds of organizational change. *Forbes.* https://www.forbes.com/councils/forbescoachescouncil/2024/01/23/ai-organizational-revolutions-to-watch-in-2024-navigating-the-transformative-winds-of-organizational-change/

OECD. (2021). *Education in the Digital Age: Healthy and Happy Children*. OECD Publishing.

OECD. (2021). *The state of higher education: One year into the COVID-19 pandemic*. OECD Publishing.

OECD. (2023). Artificial intelligence and the labor market: Policy considerations for inclusive development. *OECD Publishing*. https://www.oecd-ilibrary.org/employment/oecd-employment-outlook-2023_9c86de40-en

Oghogho, E., & Osazuwa, S. (2024). The #EndSARS movement and the reshaping of political discourse in a digital age: A Nigerian case study. *International Journal of Research and Innovation in Applied Science*. Advance online publication. DOI: 10.51584/IJRIAS.2024.906017

Okolie, C. (2023). Artificial intelligence-altered videos (deepfakes), image-based sexual abuse, and data privacy concerns. *Journal of International Women's Studies*, *25*(2), 11. https://vc.bridgew.edu/jiws/vol25/iss2/11

Omar, M., & Burrell, D. N. (2024). Organizational Dynamics and Bias in Artificial Intelligence (AI) Recruitment Algorithms. In E. Lewis (Ed.), Evolution of Cross-Sector Cyber Intelligent Markets (pp. 269-290). IGI Global Scientific Publishing. DOI: 10.4018/979-8-3693-1970-3.ch015

Omar, M., Nawawi, A., & Salin, A. (2016). The causes, impact and prevention of employee fraud: A case study of an automotive company. *Journal of Financial Crime*, *23*(4), 1012–1027. https://www.emerald.com/jfc/article-abstract/23/4/1012/446872/The-causes-impact-and-prevention-of-employee?redirectedFrom=fulltext. DOI: 10.1108/JFC-04-2015-0020

Orr, L. V., Fowler, A., & Huber, G. A. (2023). Is Affective Polarization Driven by Identity, Loyalty, or Substance? *American Journal of Political Science*, *67*(4), 948–962. DOI: 10.1111/ajps.12796

OSTP. (2022). Blueprint for an AI Bill of Rights: Making automated systems work for the American people. The White House. https://bidenwhitehouse.archives.gov/ostp/ai-bill-of-rights/

Overby, E., Bharadwaj, A., & Sambamurthy, V. (2006). Enterprise agility and the enabling role of information technology. *European Journal of Information Systems*, *15*(2), 120–131. DOI: 10.1057/palgrave.ejis.3000600

Özen, H., & Konucuk, E. (2024). *Global Citizenship Identity*. IGI Global., DOI: 10.4018/979-8-3373-0402-1.ch012

Parker, J. (2023). *80% of ransomware attacks now use artificial intelligence. MIT Sloan School of Management*. https://mitsloan.mit.edu/ideas-made-to-matter/80-ransomware-attacks-now-use-artificial-intelligence

Parker, N. (2009). From Borders to Margins: A Deleuzian Ontology for Identities in the Postinternational Environment. *Alternatives*, *34*(1), 17–39. DOI: 10.1177/030437540903400102

Pegalajar-Palomino, M. C. (2022). Implications of mobile learning for sustainable inclusive education: A systematic review. *Journal of Educational Technology & Society*, *20*(5), 538–553. https://files.eric.ed.gov/fulltext/EJ1373433.pdf

Peter, F. (2023). Political Legitimacy (pp. 3-C1P65). oxford university pressoxford. https://doi.org/DOI: 10.1093/oso/9780198872382.003.0001

Peter, F. (2020). The Grounds of Political Legitimacy. *Journal of the American Philosophical Association*, *6*(3), 372–390. DOI: 10.1017/apa.2020.6

Pew Research Center. (2020). Digital divide persists even as lower-income Americans make gains in tech adoption. Pew.

Pew Research Center. (2021). Mobile Technology and Home Broadband 2021. Pew.

Pierce, E. (2022). A Balanced Scorecard for Maximizing Data Performance. *Frontiers in Big Data*, *5*, 821103. DOI: 10.3389/fdata.2022.821103 PMID: 35434610

Podder, A., Roy, P., Ghosh, S., Sarkar, S. K., & Choudhury, R. R. (2025). *Citizen Engagement and Smart Governance*. IGI Global., DOI: 10.4018/979-8-3693-9030-6.ch002

Ponemon Institute. (2022). *Cost of a data breach report.* IBM Security. https://www.ibm.com/reports/data-breach

Popescu, C. R., & Popescu, V. A. (2015). The assessment methodology PDCA/PDSA – A methodology for coordinating the efforts to improve the organizational processes to achieve excellence. *Challenges of the Knowledge Society,* 693-696. https://www.proquest.com/openview/645eef907f691293b2009e53424df806/1?pq-origsite=gscholar&cbl=2036059&casa_token=MkyH-_I3fnIAAAAA:qanFrg_pA8NbSOrrSqH5zEK5gJBAJ5NsJe-0pXAihFa78gnoJKx5wCoyNSNf_PuRRTFPvIEWTUs

Pratt, T. C., Holtfreter, K., & Reisig, M. D. (2010). Routine online activity and internet fraud targeting: Extending the generality of routine activity theory. *Journal of Research in Crime and Delinquency*, *47*(3), 267–296. DOI: 10.1177/0022427810365903

Przegalińska, A., Triantoro, T., Kovbasiuk, A., Ciechanowski, L., Freeman, R. B., & Sowa, K. (2025). Collaborative AI in the workplace: Enhancing organizational performance through resource-based and task-technology fit perspectives. *International Journal of Information Management*, *81*, 102853. DOI: 10.1016/j.ijinfomgt.2024.102853

Pūraitė, A., Zuzevičiūtė, V., Bereikienė, D., Skrypko, T., & Shmorgun, L. (2020). Algorithmic governance in public sector: is digitization a key to effective management. Retrieved from http://www.ijmp.jor.br/index.php/ijmp/article/view/1400

Purohit, A. (2025). Breaking down barriers to AI accessibility. *InformationWeek.* https://www.informationweek.com/machine-learning-ai/breaking-down-barriers-to-ai-accessibility

Radanliev, P. (2025). AI ethics: Integrating transparency, fairness, and privacy in AI development. *Applied Artificial Intelligence, 39*(1), 2463722. Advance online publication. DOI: 10.1080/08839514.2025.2463722

Radha, C., Midunkumar, R., Muralibabu, S., Partheeban, V., & Praveenkumar, T. (2024). Role of artificial intelligence in big data analytics. *Int J Adv Res Sci Commu Technol, 4*, 586–591.

Radovanović, M. (2024). Political Power and Its Representation. *AM Journal of Art and Media Studies, 35*(35), 37–48. DOI: 10.25038/am.v0i28.603

Radware. (2022). *Supply chain attack trends and mitigation strategies in healthcare.* Radware Security Reports.

Raghavan, M., Barocas, S., Kleinberg, J., & Levy, K. (2020). Mitigating bias in algorithmic hiring: Evaluating claims and practices. *Proceedings of the 2020 Conference on Fairness, Accountability, and Transparency*, 469–481. https://doi.org/ DOI: 10.1145/3351095.3372828

Rainie, L., Funk, C., Anderson, M., & Tyson, A. (2022). AI and human enhancement: Americans' openness is tempered by a range of concerns. *Pew Research Center.* https://www.pewresearch.org/internet/2022/03/17/how-americans-think-about-artificial-intelligence/

Raisch, S., & Krakowski, S. (2021). Artificial intelligence and management: The automation augmentation paradox. *Academy of Management Review, 46*(1), 192–210. DOI: 10.5465/amr.2018.0072

Rajendra, R., Mishra, S., & Tripathi, S. (2022). Social isolation and digital connectedness: A study of Indian students during the COVID-19 pandemic. *Journal of Educational Technology Systems, 50*(4), 495–514.

Raji, I. D., Gebru, T., Mitchell, M., Boulamwini, J., Lee, J., & Denton, E. (2020). *Saving face: Investigating the ethical concerns of facial recognition auditing.* Proceedings of the 2020 AAAI/ACM Conference on AI, Ethics, and Society. DOI:DOI: 10.1145/3375627.3375820

Raji, I. D., Gebru, T., Mitchell, M., Buolamwini, J., Lee, J., & Denton, E. (2020). Saving face: Investigating the ethical concerns of facial recognition auditing. *Proceedings of the AAAI/ACM Conference on AI, Ethics, and Society*, 145-151. https://dl.acm.org/doi/pdf/10.1145/3375627.3375820

Raji, I. D., Scheuerman, M. K., & Amironesei, R. (2020). The fallacy of AI functionality. *Proceedings of the Conference on Fairness, Accountability, and Transparency* (FAT*20), 272–281.

Raji, I. D., & Buolamwini, J. (2019). Actionable auditing: Investigating the impact of publicly naming biased performance results of commercial AI products. *Proceedings of the 2019 AAAI/ACM Conference on AI, Ethics, and Society*, 429–435. https://doi.org/DOI: 10.1145/3306618.3314244

Ramezani, M., Takian, A., Bakhtiari, A., Rabiee, H. R., Ghazanfari, S., & Mostafavi, H. (2023). The application of artificial intelligence in health policy: A scoping review. *BMC Health Services Research*, *23*(1), 1416. DOI: 10.1186/s12913-023-10462-2 PMID: 38102620

Ramjit, D. (2022). *From Postinternationalism to Heterarchy: Turbulence and Distance Proximities in a World of Globalization and Fragmentation* (P. G. Cerny, Ed.). Heterarchy in World Politics. Routledge.

Reddy, D. H. (2022). An analysis of the supervised learning approach for online fraud detection. *Computational Intelligence and Machine Learning*, *3*(2), 47–56. DOI: 10.36647/CIML/03.02.A007

Reijers, W. (2019). *Practicing narrative virtue ethics of technology in research and innovation* (Doctoral dissertation, Dublin City University).

Reitstatter, L., & Galter, K. (2025). Learning From Listening To A Citizen Board. *Museological Review*, *27*(27), 174–191. DOI: 10.29311/mr.vi27.4894

Rest, J. (1979). *Development in judging moral issues*. University of Minnesota Press., https://www.amazon.com/Development-Judging-Moral-Issues-James/dp/0816608911

Reynald, D. M., Moir, E., Cook, A., & Vakhitova, Z. (2018). Changing perspectives on guardianship against crime: An examination of the importance of micro-level factors. *Crime Prevention and Community Safety*, *20*(4), 268–283. https://link.springer.com/article/10.1057/s41300-018-0049-4. DOI: 10.1057/s41300-018-0049-4

Rippling. (2025). Agentic AI security: *A guide to threats, risks & best practices*. Rippling Blog. https://www.rippling.com/blog/agentic-ai-security

Risk-Based Security. (2020). *Data breach quick view report.* Risk Based Security. https://www.riskbasedsecurity.com

Robbins, S., & Judge, T. (2017). *Organizational Behavior.* Person.

Roe, M. (2020). Polycentrism. In *Governance, Policy and Juxtaposition.* Springer., DOI: 10.1007/978-3-030-31848-2_5

Roopaei, M., Horst, J., Klaas, E., Foster, G., Salmon-Stephens, T. J., & Grunow, J. (2021). Women in AI: Barriers and solutions. *2021 IEEE World AI IoT Congress (AIIoT)*, 0497-0503. . https://ieeexplore.ieee.org/document/9454202DOI: 10.1109/AIIoT52608.2021.9454202

Rosenau, J. N. (2003). Distant proximities. In *Princeton University Press eBooks.* https://doi.org/DOI: 10.1515/9780691231112

Roumani, Y. (2021). Patching Zero-day vulnerabilities: An empirical analysis. *Journal of Cybersecurity*, *7*(1), tyab023. Advance online publication. DOI: 10.1093/cybsec/tyab023

Roy, J. (2008). Beyond Westminster Governance: Bringing Politics And Public Service Into The Networked Era. *Canadian Public Administration*, *51*(4), 541–568. DOI: 10.1111/j.1754-7121.2008.00041.x

Ruthvika, M. (2025). AI-Powered Data Analytics: A Game Changer. *International Journal of Advanced Research in Science. Tongxin Jishu*, •••, 97–102. DOI: 10.48175/IJARSCT-24409

Saaida, M. (2024). *The Role of External Actors in the Arab Spring*. Qeios., DOI: 10.32388/PPNEK0

Sahu, P. (2020). Closure of universities due to COVID-19: Impact on education and mental health. *Cureus*, *12*(4). PMID: 32377489

Saldaña, J. (2025). *The coding manual for qualitative researchers* (5th ed.). SAGE Publications Ltd. DOI: 10.4135/9781036235611

Saleem, A., Raza, M., & Deeba, F. (2022). Global Citizenship Education: A New Approach to Global Citizenship Development. *Perennial Journal of History*, 3(2), 392 409. https://doi.org/DOI: 10.52700/pjh.v3i2.131

Salifu, A., Mensah, H. N., Tchao, E. T., Acheampong, F. A., Agbemenu, A. S., & Kponyo, J. J. (2025). Enhancing speech recognition through diverse shared features accent classification. *International Journal of Speech Technology*, *28*(2), 461–481. Advance online publication. DOI: 10.1007/s10772-025-10198-w

Samarawickrama, M. (2022). AI Governance and Ethics Framework for Sustainable AI and Sustainability. Cornell University. https://doi.org//arxiv.2210.08984DOI: 10.48550

Sambasivan, N., Kapania, S., Highfill, H., Akrong, D., Paritosh, P., & Aroyo, L. (2021). Everyone wants to do the model work, not the data work: Data cascades in high-stakes AI. *Proceedings of the 2021 CHI Conference on Human Factors in Computing Systems*, 1–15. https://doi.org/DOI: 10.1145/3411764.3445518

Sarayreh, B. H., Khudair, H., & Barakat, E. A. (2013). Comparative study: The Kurt Lewin of change management. *International Journal of Computer and Information Technology*, *2*(4), 626–629. https://d1wqtxts1xzle7.cloudfront.net/33293215/Paper020413-libre.pdf?1395622098=&response-content-disposition=inline%3B+filename%3DComparative_Study_The_Kurt_Lewin_of_Chan.pdf&Expires=1770182492&Signature=P0VtSo-TcWR92-ie039dtlfSb56JOoOwNeIUa0YWE5sM-jsQA9rTK2kYWJedz9kK7HFvRQnpLPXI8mFHFvvE-4kO8f4jXZF7aU5rVC8Uw0pPgoeWyOwE9-b4SI3OI6tYWNxN2NnCkdREtv4caktFeu4mHIx8qS14LQD0l-JxNwzZBvheE7Sr6BaPjO1ZHu6S0ZNteVX3NEFbio~yaTBNEz-EGhMLufzyyF72TUyIkqNDQzLktgHCaNd6tjoW1QuRJNq-eJ40yGxCoGOf8o-pi5lHgQslIHazfQATW30RmQuxGCFsoqwjz-QbCxnnX6~--1CFZNIziAXusCxaR1nRXQ__&Key-Pair-Id=APKAJLOHF5GGSLRBV4ZA

Sartor, G. 2020. *The impact of the general data protection regulation (GDPR) on artificial intelligence*. European Parliament. European Parliamentary Research Service.

Scheerder, A., van Deursen, A., & van Dijk, J. (2017). Determinants of Internet skills, uses and outcomes. A systematic review of the second- and third-level digital divide. *Telematics and Informatics*, *34*(8), 1607–1624. DOI: 10.1016/j.tele.2017.07.007

Schein, E. H. (1995). The role of the founder in creating organizational culture. *Family Business Review*, *8*(3), 221–238. DOI: 10.1111/j.1741-6248.1995.00221.x

Scheuerman, M. K., Wade, K., Lustig, C., & Brubaker, J. R. (2020). How we've taught algorithms to see identity: Constructing race and gender in image databases for facial analysis. *Proceedings of the ACM on Human-Computer Interaction*, *4*(CSCW1), 1–35. DOI: 10.1145/3392866

Scotti, V. (2023). Women in engineering: AI and the empowerment of gender equality. *IEEE Instrumentation & Measurement Magazine*, *26*(9), 32–37. https://ieeexplore.ieee.org/document/10328674. DOI: 10.1109/MIM.2023.10328674

Security Standards. General Rules, 45 C.F.R. § 164.306 (2011). https://www.govinfo.gov/content/pkg/CFR-2011-title45-vol1/pdf/CFR-2011-title45-vol1-sec164-306.pdf

Seeber, I., Bittner, E., Briggs, R. O., de Vreede, T., de Vreede, G. J., Elkins, A., Maier, R., Merz, A. B., Oeste-Reiß, S., Randrup, N., Schwabe, G., & Söllner, M. (2020). Machines as teammates: A research agenda on AI in team collaboration. *Information & Management*, *57*(2), 103174. DOI: 10.1016/j.im.2019.103174

Selbst, A. D., Boyd, D., Friedler, S. A., Venkatasubramanian, S., & Vertesi, J. (2019). Fairness and abstraction in sociotechnical systems. *FAT '19: Conference on Fairness, Accountability, and Transparency,* 59–68. https://dl.acm.org/doi/10.1145/3287560.3287598

Selwyn, N. (2004). Reconsidering political and popular understandings of the digital divide. *New Media & Society*, *6*(3), 341–362. DOI: 10.1177/1461444804042519

Selwyn, N. (2021). *Education and Technology: Key Issues and Debates* (3rd ed.). Bloomsbury Academic.

Shabbir, N., & Porwal, S. (2025). Digital Literacy: A Necessity In The 21st Century For India. *Information Technologies and Learning Tools*, *105*(1), 222–231. DOI: 10.33407/itlt.v105i1.5883

Shacklett, M. (2021). The evolving cybersecurity threat landscape in healthcare. *Information Security Journal: A Global Perspective, 30*(4), 215–225. DOI: 10.1080/19393555.2021.1937999

Sharma, Y., Saha, A., & Goldsack, J. (2024). Defining the Dimensions of Diversity to Promote Inclusion in the Digital Era of Health Care: A Lexicon. *JMIR Public Health and Surveillance*, *10*, e51980. https://publichealth.jmir.org/2024/1/e51980. DOI: 10.2196/51980 PMID: 38335013

Shergill, P. S. (2025, April 18). AI can reshape enterprises—but the need for human involvement remains. *Forbes Human Resources Council.* https://www.forbes.com/councils/forbeshumanresourcescouncil/2025/04/18/ai-can-reshape-enterprises-but-the-need-for-human-involvement-remains/

Shrestha, S., & Das, S. (2022). Exploring gender biases in ML and AI academic research through systematic literature review. *Frontiers in Artificial Intelligence*, *5*, 976838. Advance online publication. DOI: 10.3389/frai.2022.976838

Shultz, L., & Karsgaard, C. (2023). Taming global citizenship education within twitter's attention economy. *Journal of Creative Communications*, *19*(1), 13–31. DOI: 10.1177/09732586231198960

Sibuea, N. (2025). Digital Innovation as the Key to Efficiency and Accountability of Public Administration in Medan City, Indonesia. *Golden Ratio of Data in Summary*, *5*(1), 24–31. DOI: 10.52970/grdis.v5i1.821

Simonite, T. (2018, August 17). AI Is the future — but where are the women? Wired. https://www.wired.com/story/artificial-intelligence-researchers-gender-imbalance/

Singh, J., & Singh, H. (2009). Kaizen philosophy: A review of literature. *The Icfai University Journal of Operations Management, 3*(2), 51–72. https://cdn.chools.in/LEAN_PDF/Kaizen%20Toolkit/Kaizen_Philosophy_A_Review_of_Literature.pdf

Skelton-Wilson, S., Sandoval-Lunn, M., Zhang, X., Stern, F., & Kendall, J. (2021). Methods and emerging strategies to engage people with lived experience: Improving federal research, policy, and practice. *Office of the Assistant Secretary for Planning and Evaluation, U.S. Department of Health and Human Services.* https://aspe.hhs.gov/sites/default/files/documents/62e7a64c60e10c47484b763aa9868f99/lived-experience-brief.pdf

Smallman, M. (2022). Multi scale ethics—Why we need to consider the ethics of AI in Healthcare at different scales. *Science and Engineering Ethics, 28*(6), 63. DOI: 10.1007/s11948-022-00396-z PMID: 36441282

Smith, S. M., Tate, M., Freeman, K., Walsh, A., Ballsun-Stanton, B., & Lane, M. (2025). A university framework for the responsible use of generative AI in research. *Journal of Higher Education Policy and Management, 47*(5), 623–639. DOI: 10.1080/1360080X.2025.2509187

Society for Human Resource Management [SHRM]. (2025). From adoption to empowerment: Shaping the AI-driven workforce of tomorrow. *Society for Human Resource Management [SHRM].* https://www.shrm.org/content/dam/en/shrm/topics-tools/research/from-adoption-to-empowerment-shaping-the-ai-driven-workforce-of-tomorrow.pdf

Song, F., & Yeung, S. H. F. (2024). A pluralist hybrid model for moral AIs. *AI & Society, 39*(3), 891–900. DOI: 10.1007/s00146-022-01601-0

Stanford Institute for Human-Centered Artificial Intelligence. (2025). AI index report 2025. *Stanford University.* https://aiindex.stanford.edu

Steerling, E., Houston, R., Gietzen, L. J., Ogilvie, S. J., de Ruiter, H. P., & Nygren, J. M. (2022). Examining how ethics in relation to health technology is described in the research literature: Scoping review. *Interactive Journal of Medical Research, 11*(2), e38745. DOI: 10.2196/38745 PMID: 35969434

Stokes, F., & Palmer, A. (2020). Artificial intelligence and robotics in nursing: Ethics of caring as a guide to dividing tasks between AI and humans. *Nursing Philosophy, 21*(4), e12306. DOI: 10.1111/nup.12306 PMID: 32609420

Strong, D. M. (2025). *Target data breach: What happened and how to prevent it.* https://www.strongdm.com/what-is/target-data-breach

Sujan, M. A., White, S., Habli, I., & Reynolds, N. (2022). Stakeholder perceptions of the safety and assurance of artificial intelligence in healthcare. *Safety Science, 155*, 105870. DOI: 10.1016/j.ssci.2022.105870

Suresh, H., & Guttag, J. (2019). A framework for understanding unintended consequences of machine learning. *Proceedings of EAAMO '21: 1st ACM Conference on Equity and Access in Algorithms, Mechanisms, and Optimization, 1–9.* https://dl.acm.org/doi/10.1145/3465416.3483305

Susnjara, P., & Smalley, T. (2024). *Machine learning for healthcare security integration*. Springer.

Swede, M. J., Scovetta, V., & Eugene-Colin, M. (2019). Protecting patient data is the new scope of practice: A recommended cybersecurity curricula for healthcare students to prepare for this challenge. *Journal of Allied Health, 48*(2), 148–156. https://www.ingentaconnect.com/content/asahp/jah/2019/00000048/00000002/art00013 PMID: 31167018

Swisher, L. L., & Davis, C. M. (2005). The realm-individual-process-situation (RIPS) model of ethical decision-making. HPA Resource, 5(3), 1-8.). https://www.semanticscholar.org/paper/The-Realm-Individual-Process-Situation-(-RIPS-)-of-Lee-Swisher/a83a548c3c59e7c7945ca3f0d4b42207dc46e1a4

Tadesse, S., & Muluye, W. (2020). The impact of COVID-19 pandemic on education system in developing countries: A review. *Open Journal of Social Sciences, 8*(10), 159–170. DOI: 10.4236/jss.2020.810011

Tamayo, S. G., & Petrelli, A. (2025). Work transformed: The promise and peril of artificial intelligence. ILO. https://www.ilo.org/sites/default/files/2025-07/ilo%20brief%20work%20transformed%20promise%20and%20peril%20of%20ai.pdf

Tambe, P., Cappelli, P., & Yakubovich, V. (2019). Artificial intelligence in human resources management: Challenges and a path forward. *California Management Review, 61*(4), 15–42. DOI: 10.1177/0008125619867910

Tanenbaum, S. J. (2014). Particularism in health care: Challenging the authority of the aggregate. *Journal of Evaluation in Clinical Practice, 20*(6), 934–941. DOI: 10.1111/jep.12249 PMID: 25406384

Tan, Z., Parambath, S. P., Anagnostopoulos, C., Singer, J., & Marnerides, A. K. (2025). Advanced Persistent Threats Based on Supply Chain Vulnerabilities: Challenges, Solutions, and Future Directions. *IEEE Internet of Things Journal*, *12*(6), 6371–6395. DOI: 10.1109/JIOT.2025.3528744

Tarafdar, R. (2025). Human-AI collaboration in workflow optimization: A framework for hybrid decision systems in automation-heavy industries. *International Journal of Scientific Research in Computer Science. Engineering and Information Technology*, *11*(1), 3594–3613. DOI: 10.32628/CSEIT251112384

Tavory, T. (2024). Regulating AI in mental health: Ethics of care perspective. *JMIR Mental Health*, *11*(1), e58493. DOI: 10.2196/58493 PMID: 39298759

The Nilson Report. (2025, January 6). *Payment card fraud losses approach $34 billion.* GlobeNewswire News Room. https://www.globenewswire.com/news-release/2025/01/06/3004931/0/en/Payment-Card-Fraud-Losses-Approach-34-Billion.html?utm_source=chatgpt.com

Thi Duyen, H. (2021). Digital transformation in higher education in Vietnam and its challenges nowadays. *Vinh University Journal of Science*, *50*(4B). Advance online publication. DOI: 10.56824/vujs.2021ed19

Thiel, A. (2023). *Polycentric Governing and Polycentric Governance*. Oxford University Press Oxford., DOI: 10.1093/oso/9780192866837.003.0005

Tin, D., Hata, R., Granholm, F., Ciottone, R. G., Staynings, R., & Ciottone, G. R. (2023). Cyberthreats: A primer for healthcare professionals. *The American Journal of Emergency Medicine*, *68*, 179–185. DOI: 10.1016/j.ajem.2023.04.001 PMID: 37061434

Tollon, F. (2024). Technology and the situationist challenge to virtue ethics. *Science and Engineering Ethics*, *30*(2), 10. DOI: 10.1007/s11948-024-00474-4 PMID: 38536486

Topol, E. J. (2019). High-performance medicine: The convergence of human and artificial intelligence. *Nature Medicine*, *25*(1), 44–56. DOI: 10.1038/s41591-018-0300-7 PMID: 30617339

Torraco, R. J. (2016). Writing integrative literature reviews: Using the past and present to explore the future. *Human Resource Development Review*, *15*(4), 404–428. https://journals.sagepub.com/doi/full/10.1177/1534484316671606?casa_token=QEKxwTdnxCoAAAAA%3ARowmT1h-GhD4p7Am6FffLJFOTm-IjNPDoQHiSifn3tiRXpTp2DOtBvW2EonEIRQeNFZq_-3pIlHwbQ. DOI: 10.1177/1534484316671606

Tripwire. (2020, October 25). *HIPAA breach notification – what you need to know.* https://www.tripwire.com/state-of-security/hipaa-breach-notification-what-need-know

Trist, E. L., & Bamforth, K. W. (1951). Some social and psychological consequences of the Longwall Method of coal-getting: An examination of the psychological situation and defences of a work group in relation to the social structure and technological content of the work system. *Human Relations, 4*(1), 3-38. (Original work published 1951)DOI: 10.1177/001872675100400101

Turner Lee, N., Resnick, P., & Barton, G. (2019). *Algorithmic bias detection and mitigation: Best practices and policies to reduce consumer harms*. Brooking Institute. https://www.brookings.edu/articles/algorithmic-bias-detection-and-mitigation-best-practices-and-policies-to-reduce-consumer-harms/

U.S. Department of Health and Human Services. (2021, January 14). *Insurer pays $5.1 million to settle data breach affecting over 9.3 million people.* U.S. Department of Health and Human Services. https://www.hhs.gov/hipaa/for-professionals/compliance-enforcement/agreements/excellus/index.html

U.S. Department of Health and Human Services. 2022, July 14). *Oklahoma State University – Center for Health Services pays $875,000 to settle hacking breach.* U.S. Department of Health and Human Services. https://www.hhs.gov/about/news/2022/07/14/oklahoma-state-university-center-health-services-pays-875000-settle-hacking-breach.html

U.S. Department of War. (2025, April 24). Defense officials outline AI's strategic role in national security. *Author.* https://www.defense.gov/News/News-Stories/Article/Article/4165279/defense-officials-outline-ais-strategic-role-in-national-security/

U.S. Equal Employment Opportunity Commission. (n.d.). *Title VII of the Civil Rights Act of 1964.* Retrieved from https://www.eeoc.gov/statutes/title-vii-civil-rights-act-1964

Ueno, K., Jackson, T. M., Ingram, R., Grace, J., & Šaras, E. D. (2020). Sexual minority young adults' construction of workplace acceptance in the era of diversity and inclusion. *Social Currents*, *7*(2), 91–108. https://journals.sagepub.com/doi/full/10.1177/2329496519888539?casa_token=SCmK8Sj-nI0AAAAA%3AaRVG1lUQJuoIMpisBGXSZEC4DOStjWvxbZM2kcTz4NT-bPJPbCuZn_TpMCj0ueAojUApl8oKZOUCqg. DOI: 10.1177/2329496519888539

UNESCO. (2018). *A global framework of reference on digital literacy skills for indicator 4.4.2*. UNESCO Institute for Statistics.

UNESCO. (2020). *Education in a post-COVID world: Nine ideas for public action*. UNESCO.

UNESCO. (2021). *Education and Digital Transformation Report*. United Nations Educational, Scientific and Cultural Organization.

UNESCO. (2024). *Global education monitoring report 2024. Gender report: Technology on her terms*. DOI: 10.54676/WVCF2762

UNESCO. (2024). Recommendation on the ethics of artificial intelligence. *UNESCO*. https://www.unesco.org/en/artificial-intelligence/recommendation-ethics

UNESCO. (n.d.). *HerAtlas: Monitoring the right to education for girls and women*. https://www.unesco.org/en/heratlas

United Nations Conference on Trade and Development [UNCTAD]. (2025). Technology and innovation report 2023: Opening green windows. *Author*. https://unctad.org/publication/technology-and-innovation-report-2023

United Nations. [UN]. (2023). Global digital compact: Open, free and secure digital future for all. *Author*. https://www.un.org/techenvoy/global-digital-compact

Valenzuela, A., Puntoni, S., Hoffman, D., Castelo, N., De Freitas, J., Dietvorst, B., Hildebrand, C., Huh, Y. E., Meyer, R., Sweeney, M. E., Talaifar, S., Tomaino, G., & Wertenbroch, K. (2024). How Artificial Intelligence Constrains the Human Experience. *Journal of the Association for Consumer Research*. https://www.journals.uchicago.edu/doi/full/10.1086/730709

Van Dijk, J. (2006). Digital divide research, achievements and shortcomings. *Poetics*, *34*(4–5), 221–235. DOI: 10.1016/j.poetic.2006.05.004

Vasant, M., Rahim, N. A., & Rani, A. M. A. (2025). Enhancing e-commerce security: A hybrid machine learning approach to fraud detection. *Security and Privacy*, *8*(1), e194. DOI: 10.1002/spy2.194

Vaudrin, C. J. (2019). Melting the Cultural Iceberg in Indigenizing Higher Education: Shifts to Accountability in Times of Reconciliation. *New Directions for Teaching and Learning*, *2019*(157), 105–118. DOI: 10.1002/tl.20333

Veale, M., & Binns, R. (2017). Fairer machine learning in the real world: Mitigating discrimination without collecting sensitive data. *Big Data & Society*, *4*(2), 1–17. DOI: 10.1177/2053951717743530

Verizon. (2020). *2020 Data breach investigations report (DBIR)*. Verizon Enterprise Solutions. https://www.verizon.com/business/resources/reports/dbir/

Verma, A., & Gupta, M. (2025). Harnessing the use of artificial intelligence in financial fraud detection. *International Journal of Education & Management Studies, 15*(1), 116–122.

Vielberth, M., & Pernul, G. (2018). A Security Information and Event Management pattern. *12th Latin American Conference on Pattern Languages of Programs.* HILLSIDE 978-1-941652-11-4. https://epub.uni-regensburg.de/41139/1/A%20Security%20Information%20and%20Event%20Management%20Pattern.pdf

Villegas-Galaviz, C., & Martin, K. (2024). Moral distance, AI, and the ethics of care. *AI & Society, 39*(4), 1695–1706. DOI: 10.1007/s00146-023-01642-z PMID: 37358944

Wachter, S., Mittelstadt, B. D., & Russell, C. (2021). Why fairness cannot be automated: Bridging the gap between EU non-discrimination law and AI. *Computer Law & Security Review, 37*, 105567. 2005.05906. DOI: 10.1016/j.clsr.2021.105567

Wachter, S., Mittelstadt, B., & Floridi, L. (2017). Transparent, explainable, and accountable AI for robotics. *Science Robotics, 2*(6), eaan6080. Advance online publication. DOI: 10.1126/scirobotics.aan6080 PMID: 33157874

Wang P, Boodraj M, Baskerville R (2025;), "Beyond passwords: A review of the hidden risks in two-factor authentication". *Journal of Systems and Information Technology*, Vol. ahead-of-print No. ahead-of-print. DOI: 10.1108/JSIT-03-2025-0140

Warschauer, M. (2003). *Technology and social inclusion: Rethinking the digital divide.* MIT Press. DOI: 10.7551/mitpress/6699.001.0001

Wazed, S. (2018, August 2). *Councilpost: Grow your organization with top talent using the iceberg interview model.* Forbes. Retrieved March 21, 2023, from https://www.forbes.com/sites/forbeshumanresourcescouncil/2018/08/02/grow-your-organization-with-top-talent-using-the-iceberg-interview-model/?sh=41d17c2175b8

WHO. (2021). Ethics and governance of artificial intelligence for health. World Health Organization. https://iris.who.int/server/api/core/bitstreams/f780d926-4ae3-42ce-a6d6-e898a5562621/content

Wiederhold, B. K. (2021). The Role of Psychology in Enhancing Cybersecurity. *Cyberpsychology, Behavior, and Social Networking, 24*(5), 291–292. PMID: 34003012

Williams, M. L. (2015). Guardians upon high: An application of routine activities theory to online identity theft in Europe at the country and individual level. *British Journal of Criminology, 56*(1), 21–48. DOI: 10.1093/bjc/azv011

Williamson, B., Eynon, R., & Potter, J. (2020). Pandemic politics, pedagogies and practices: Digital technologies and distance education during the coronavirus emergency. *Learning, Media and Technology*, *45*(2), 107–114. DOI: 10.1080/17439884.2020.1761641

Wilson, S., Mc Ardle, R., Slight, R., Slight, S., Hassan, N., & Tolley, C. (2024). Strategies To Advancing Digital Health Equity: Perspectives From Underserved Groups. *European Journal of Public Health*, *34*(Suppl 3), ckae144.1123. Advance online publication. DOI: 10.1093/eurpub/ckae144.1123

Wilson, T., Smith, A., & Jones, L. (2023). Algorithmic bias in health insurance claims: Legal exposure and governance strategies. *Journal of Health Law & Policy*, *18*(2), 45–72.

Workday. (2025). Elevating human potential: The AI skills revolution. *Workday*. https://forms.workday.com/en-us/reports/elevating-human-potential/form.html?_gl=1*kmr1eq*_up*MQ.*_gs*MQ.&gclid=Cj0KCQjw7IjO BhDyARIsAFzrWQwqvwHl_05zgUozuVr00I03541MfkNKcOEDP0GSIJSO wk5rwUJYtc0aArPeEALw_wcB&gclsrc=aw.ds&gbraid=0AAAAADgCFK diii6KzcTgvB6NEeSFnh--k&step=step1_default

World Bank. (2020). The COVID-19 pandemic: Shocks to education and policy responses. World Bank.

World Bank. (2021). World development report 2021: Data for better lives. *Author*. https://www.worldbank.org/en/publication/digital-progress-and-trends-report?utm_source=chatgpt.com

World Economic Forum. (2023). Global Gender Gap Report 2023. https://www3.weforum.org/docs/WEF_GGGR_2023.pdf

World Economic Forum. (2023, May). The future of jobs report 2023. *Author*. https://www.weforum.org/publications/the-future-of-jobs-report-2023/

World Economic Forum. (2024). Global Gender Gap Report 2024. https://www3.weforum.org/docs/WEF_GGGR_2024.pdf

World Economic Forum. (2025, January 21). Advancing AI transformation: A roadmap for businesses and governments. *Author*. https://www.weforum.org/press/2025/01/advancing-ai-transformation-a-roadmap-for-businesses-and-governments/

Wuthnow, R. (2023). *Religion and Political Power*. Oxford University Press New York., DOI: 10.1093/oso/9780197652534.001.0001

Xu, Z., Zhou, Z.-H., & Zhu, W. (2024). Machine learning automation. *National Science Review, 11*(8), nwae288. Advance online publication. DOI: 10.1093/nsr/nwae288 PMID: 39262924

Yazici, Y. (2020). Approaches to fraud detection on credit card transactions using artificial intelligence methods. *Computer Science and Information Technology*, •••, 235–244. DOI: 10.5121/csit.2020.101018

Yeo, L. H., & Banfield, J. (2022). Human factors in electronic health records cybersecurity breach: An exploratory analysis. *Perspectives in Health Information Management, 19*, •••. https://pubmed.ncbi.nlm.nih.gov/35692854/ PMID: 35692854

Yin, R. K. (2017). *Case study research and applications: Design and methods* (6th ed.). Sage Publications.

Yoldemir, T. (2020). Artificial intelligence and women's health. *Climacteric, 23*(1), 1–2. DOI: 10.1080/13697137.2019.1682804

Young, E., Wajcman, J., & Sprejer, L. (2021). *Where are the women? Mapping the gender job gap in AI.* The Alan Turing Institute. https://www.turing.ac.uk/sites/default/files/2021-03/where-are-the-women_public-policy_summary-report.pdf

Youssef, F. E. A. (2022). Industry 4.0 and its implications: Concept, opportunities, and future directions. In Bányai, T., Bányai, Á., & Kaczmar, I. (Eds.), *Supply Chain – Recent Advances and New Perspectives in the Industry 4.0 Era* (pp. 1–22). IntechOpen., DOI: 10.5772/intechopen.102520

Zapata, D. (2021, June). New study finds AI-enabled anti-Black bias in recruiting. Thomson Reuters. Retrieved from: https://www.thomsonreuters.com/en-us/posts/legal/ai-enabled-anti-black-bias/

Zawacki-Richter, O., Marin, V. I., Bond, M., & Gouverneur, F. (2019). Systematic review of research on artificial intelligence applications in higher education – where are the educators? *International Journal of Educational Technology in Higher Education, 16*(1), 39. DOI: 10.1186/s41239-019-0171-0

Zelny, A. (2025). Offloading Wisdom: Four Technological Relations that Mediate Phronesis. *Philosophy & Technology, 38*(2), 56. DOI: 10.1007/s13347-025-00889-2

Zeng, Q., Jin, Y., Liu, Y., & Xu, X. (2025). NNEnsLeG: A novel approach for e-commerce payment fraud detection using ensemble learning and neural networks. *Information Sciences, 646*, 17–32. DOI: 10.1016/j.ins.2023.119532

Zhao, J., Wang, T., Yatskar, M., Ordonez, V., & Chang, K. W. (2017). Men also like shopping: Reducing gender bias amplification using corpus-level constraints. *arXiv preprint arXiv:1707.09457*. https://arxiv.org/abs/1707.09457 DOI: 10.18653/v1/D17-1323

Zhou, E., & Lee, D. (2024). Generative artificial intelligence, human creativity, and art. *PNAS Nexus*, *3*(3), 52. DOI: 10.1093/pnasnexus/pgae052 PMID: 38444602

Zhou, Y., Li, H., Xiao, Z., & Qiu, J. (2023). A user-centered explainable artificial intelligence approach for financial fraud detection. *Finance Research Letters*, *58*, 104309. DOI: 10.1016/j.frl.2023.104309

Zoričić, D., Knežević, G., Miletić, M., Dolinar, D., & Sprčić, D. M. (2022). Integrated Risk Analysis of Aggregators: Policy Implications for the Development of the Competitive Aggregator Industry. *Energies (19961073)*, *15*(14), N.PAG. DOI: 10.3390/en15145076

Zuboff, S. (2022). Surveillance Capitalism or Democracy? The Death Match of Institutional Orders and the Politics of Knowledge in Our Information Civilization. *Organization Theory*, *3*(3). Advance online publication. DOI: 10.1177/26317877221129290

Zysman, J., & Nitzberg, M. (2020). Governing AI: Understanding the limits, possibility, and risks of AI in an era of intelligent tools and systems. *Berkeley Roundtable on the International Economy*. https://www.wilsoncenter.org/publication/governing-ai-understanding-limits-possibilities-and-risks-ai-era-intelligent-tools-and

About the Contributors

Darrell Norman Burrell is a visiting scholar at the Samuel DeWitt Proctor Institute for Leadership, Equity, and Justice at Rutgers University, where he is currently focusing his research on sustainability, health equity, and inclusive leadership. His work as a visiting researcher at the Pellegrino Center for Clinical Bioethics at the Georgetown University Medical Center in Washington, D.C., and as a post-doctoral public health researcher at the University of Maryland School of Pharmacy in Baltimore, MD, has provided him with a unique perspective on issues related to health disparities, health technology access, telehealth, adolescent health, and health literacy. For more than 12 years, he has also served in various roles as a doctoral faculty member, dissertation chair, and research panel participant at Marymount University, the Florida Institute of Technology, Capitol Technology University, the University of Liverpool in the U.K., and The Chicago School of Professional Psychology in Washington D.C. Dr. Burrell is a Certified Diversity Professional and a Certified Executive Coach. Dr. Burrell is an alumnus of the Presidential Management Fellows Program with the U.S. Federal Government and U.S. Nuclear Regulatory Commission, where he managed and developed leadership and diversity programs for professionals in Public Health, Environmental Health, Emergency Response, Technology, and Engineering. Academically, Dr. Burrell has three doctorate degrees and six graduate degrees, including a Master of Research in Artificial Intelligence Biotechnology Applications and Healthcare, along with additional graduate degrees in (H.R. Management, Management, Health Leadership, Sales and Marketing Management, Higher Education Administration, and Interfaith Action and Conflict Management). Dr. Burrell received his first doctoral degree in health education (DHEd), focusing on environmental public health and executive leadership coaching, at A.T. Still University in 2010. Dr. Burrell completed his 2nd doctorate, a Doctor of Philosophy (Ph.D.) in Cybersecurity Leadership at Capitol Technology University. In 2022, Dr. Burrell completed his 3rd Doctor of Business Administration (DBA) in Supply Chain Management at Capitol Technology

University. He has over 20 years of management, teaching, and training experience in academia, government, and private industry. Dr. Burrell has over 200 peer-reviewed publications and more than 1200 Google Scholar citations. Dr. Burrell can be reached at darrell.burrell@yahoo.com

Arthur D. Bradford, Jr. is a finance and operations executive with over 30 years of experience in higher education, Fortune 100 companies, and global retail organizations. Most recently, he served as the Chief Financial Officer and Executive Vice President for Administration at the University of North Texas at Dallas. His career encompasses significant leadership roles at Walmart, JCPenney, Conagra Brands, and Frito-Lay, where he excelled in financial planning and analysis, process improvement, and strategy. As a Certified Public Accountant, Arthur's financial acumen has driven measurable improvements in return on investment, operational efficiency, and organizational growth. He is also a dedicated mentor, committed to fostering talent and guiding teams toward achieving strategic goals. Arthur holds a Doctor of Business Administration from Marymount University, a Master of Business Administration from the McCombs School of Business at the University of Texas at Austin, a Master of Biblical and Theological Studies from Dallas Theological Seminary, and a Bachelor of Science in Accounting from Grambling State University. Arthur's leadership philosophy is rooted in his Christian faith, integrity, lifelong learning, and a passion for driving meaningful change. His diverse experience across sectors uniquely positions him as a thought leader in finance, strategy, and operations.

Sharon L. Burton leads in product management and development, Organizational Development Change Management, Cyber-Security/Technology, Process Improvement, Telemedicine/Telehealth and Learning & Development. Education includes: Ph.D. in Cybersecurity Leadership, and a DBA in Business Process Improvement; and two MBA degrees - Human Resources Management, and Management. Certifications in the following: AI Prompting Essentials; Project Management Essentials; Master Lean Six Sigma Black Belt; Kaizen Leader; Change Management Professional; Strategic Workforce Planning; Human Capital Strategist; Kirkpatrick Four Levels Evaluation; and Advanced Communicator Gold Toastmaster. As a facilitator and educator of audiences, she has more than 100 academic publications and has presented at over 30 professional conferences. Dr. Burton is available to present at conferences, participate in forums, and other initiatives. She may be reached at sharonlburton2@comcast.net and 302-547-8010.

Kylei Conti, aspiring forensic interviewer pursuing a M.A. in Legal and Forensic Psychology at Marymount University's Graduate Studies.

Maurice Dawson is an Associate Professor of Information Technology and Management within the College of Computing at Illinois Institute of Technology. Additionally, he serves as Director and Distinguished Member of the IIT Center for Cyber Security and Forensics Education (C2SAFE) and is responsible for working with the faculty who are members of this center. Before joining academia, he was an engineering manager for unmanned air systems and a senior program manager for rotary-wing aircraft. He has a Doctor of Computer Science from Colorado Technical University and a Doctor of Philosophy in Cyber Security from the Intelligent Systems Research Centre at London Metropolitan University. Additionally, he is the co-editor of Developing Next-Generation Countermeasures for Homeland Security Threat Prevention, and New Threats and Countermeasures in Digital Crime and Cyber Terrorism, published by IGI Global in 2017, and 2015 respectively. He has received four Fulbright Scholar Grants.

Hilda Eke is a nonprofit executive, certified Human Resources professional (SHRM-CP), and doctoral candidate at Marymount University. Her scholarly work examines leadership sustainability, psychological safety, and executive attrition in nonprofit organizations. She brings extensive experience in organizational operations, human resources administration, and systems development within mission-driven and community-based contexts. Hilda holds a Master's degree in Healthcare Administration from California State University, Long Beach, and a Bachelor's degree in Linguistics from the University of Benin. Her work integrates theory and practice to advance organizational effectiveness, workforce sustainability, and strategic leadership in nonprofit settings. Her contributions have been recognized through membership in Phi Beta Kappa and the Golden Key International Honour Society, as well as an award for service to nonprofit organizations in Northern Nigeria.

Natasha Harris is a doctoral researcher in Business Intelligence at Marymount University. Her interdisciplinary research examines human behavior and systems design across finance, organizational contexts, sustainability, and emerging technologies, with a focus on human-centered, capability-enhancing approaches to institutional decision-making and resilience in an ever-changing world.

Garrett W. Hart is a Doctor of Business Administration student in Business Intelligence at Marymount University and currently serves as Director of Training and Sales at Conequip Parts and Equipment, where he leads company-wide sales and workforce development initiatives across multiple departments. His research and professional work focus on how performance coaching strengthens autonomy, motivation, and retention, especially among Generation Z employees in customer-facing sales roles. He is an experienced educator and corporate trainer with extensive expertise in leadership development, instructional design, and applied organizational research.

Roderick Head is a doctoral candidate in Business Intelligence at Marymount University and Founder & Chief Intelligence Architect of Catalytix Holdings Inc., an emerging multidisciplinary strategy and insights firm focused on enterprise intelligence, ethical technology, and organizational performance. He holds an Executive MBA from the University of Memphis and an M.S. in Data Science from Indiana University Bloomington. Roderick brings over 20 years of experience across media, entertainment, consulting, and enterprise technology, applying systems thinking and analytical rigor to solve complex business challenges. His research and practice emphasize responsible AI, digital governance, and performance transformation. He also holds Lean Six Sigma, SAFe Product Owner/Product Manager (POPM), ITIL, and Technology Business Management (TBM) certifications.

Lawrence Iweriebor, Ph.D., is an educator and a researcher whose work spans artificial intelligence, Data Science, and fraud analytics. He earned a Ph.D. in Artificial Intelligence from Capitol Technology University. He also holds an M.S. in Data Science, an M.S. in Economics, and a B.S. in Statistics. He is currently pursuing a second Ph.D. in Financial Cybersecurity.

Laura Jones is an award-winning risk management thought leader, strategist, and practitioner. She specializes in cybersecurity risk, quality assurance, and artificial intelligence. She currently serves as an adjunct faculty member at Carnegie Mellon University, Wake Forest University, and Capitol Technology University. Dr. Jones earned a PhD in Cyber Leadership, a PhD in Product Management, an MS in Quality Systems Management, and a BS in Management Studies. She has completed executive education programs at Carnegie Mellon University (Chief Risk Officer Program), Harvard Kennedy School (Leadership Decision-Making), and UC Berkeley Haas (Business Strategies and Artificial Intelligence). Dr. Jones has numerous publications on cyber and risk management. She also speaks domestically and internationally about risk management and cybersecurity. Dr. Jones previously served as a graduate school Associate Dean of Student Academic Affairs.

Constantine M. Koursaris is an Associate Professor of Decision Science and Analytics at Embry-Riddle Aeronautical University. He holds a Ph.D. in Operations Research, is a Fellow of the Royal Aeronautical Society, and a Certified Professional in Engineering Management, with industry experience in logistics, supply chains, and aerospace operations

Eugene JM Lewis is a leading International Program Manager with an academic background in Information Systems, having taught in some Business areas such as Marketing, Management, and Information Systems. Dr. Lewis manages a portfolio of over 250 million dollars in the Foreign Military Sales (FMS) industry for the US Army. He is a leading expert in security assistance program management processes and competencies in total package approach (TPA) from hardware, training, case, financials, programmatic, contracting, technical support, logistics, and supply chain management. Currently, Dr. Lewis serves in the Aviation & Defense Industry, working in the Cargo CH-47 Helicopters Foreign Military Sales Program Office. Previously, he served as the Assistant Professor of Marketing at Oakwood University as a full-time and part-time instructor in Marketing, Management (Leadership), and Computer Information Systems. Moreover, lecturing students in areas such as advertising management, consumer behavior, global marketing, marketing management, organizational dynamics, project management, sales management, project management, logistics, and supply chain management integrating marketing methodologies. Dr. Lewis is a Practitioner and Consultant with education and experience in real-world examples of strategic integration within the business field. As an International Program Manager, he gives several briefings to dignitaries and foreign leadership around the world on logistics and supply chain management. Much of his employment experience consists of incorporating new innovative concepts to provide consumers with the requisite knowledge necessary to understand the value of emotional (EQ) and business intelligence (BI) by incorporating technology into the organizational workflow of operational planning. Dr. Lewis enjoys giving back to the community, spending much of his free time assisting young people in underprivileged areas and instructing them in Boxing. Dr. Lewis has been a Boxing Coach and Instructor for over 15 years. He is a registered Coach with the United States Boxing Association for the Southeastern Region. Dr. Lewis believes in the efficacy of developing young people. He is originally from Seattle, Washington. His family still resides in the Pacific Northwest. He enjoys every opportunity available to travel, write poetry, play guitar, and meet inspiring people.

Adina Lundy is the associate director of undergraduate psychology at a small New England Institution. A leading authority on the lasting effects of chattel slavery on poverty and the contemporary structure of the Black family; she brings deep historical insight and interdisciplinary expertise to her work as an expert witness for the Public Defender's Office of the New Jersey Family Court, a professor, and a multiculturalism scholar. A dedicated researcher on racism and systemic inequity, Dr. Lundy's work focuses on how structural barriers—including the lack of social capital, institutional bias, and uneven resource allocation—impact both students of color and faculty of color. Her scholarship illuminates how these inequities limit opportunity, influence academic pathways, and contribute to long-term disparities across disciplines. Through her research, workshops (with institutions such as Duke Medical school and the New Jersey Judiciary) testimony, and community advocacy, Dr. Lundy provides critical expertise at the intersection of history, policy, and lived experience, advancing efforts to create equitable systems and strengthen outcomes for children, families, and people of color. Dr. Lundy's research program centers the experiences of marginalized populations seeking to improve their socioeconomic status, with a particular focus on the transformative role of social capital and the strategic engagement of white allies committed to meaningful, equity-driven change. Her work interrogates how access to education, resources, and informed accomplices shapes the trajectories of communities striving for liberation and opportunity.

Teresa Manfreda-Foley is an accounting and business management professional with over 25 years of experience across industries, including construction, manufacturing, retail, higher education, and non-profit organizations. Driven by a quest for learning and a deep sense of integrity, she takes immense pride in analyzing situations and providing viable, financially sound options to achieve successful outcomes. Teresa has been with Brookdale Community College since 2013 and has held various management positions throughout her tenure. In 2019, she became the Vice President, Finance & Operations/CFO. Her goals are aligned with the Institution's strategic plan for the future while maintaining the College's financial health and realigning the organization for optimization. She serves on the President's Cabinet, the Executive Leadership Council, and the Information Technology Governance Steering Committee. She holds a BS in business administration/ accounting concentration from Monmouth University, an MBA in accounting from Southern New Hampshire University, and a Doctorate in Business Administration from Marymount University.

Quatavia McLester holds a PhD in Healthcare Technology from Capitol Technology University. She holds a Master of Science in Industrial/Organizational Psychology from Austin Peay State University. She holds a Bachelor of Science in Psychology and a minor in Applied Statistics and Data Analysis from Kennesaw State University. She is currently serving as a Board Certified Behavior Analyst for a mental healthcare service provider. Her research interests include processes and outcomes of organizational development and change at the individual, group, and systems levels within the healthcare field, the effects of destructive leadership within organizations, and the use of healthcare technology in the mental healthcare space.

Maria R. Mondala-Duncan serves as the Senior Management Analyst for the City of Simi Valley. Dr. Mondala-Duncan is a generalist and a business professional with over 18 years of combined management experience, 13 of which have been in the public sector. Her broad range of expertise entails the areas of labor negotiations, monitoring revenue and expenditures, review/analyze legislation for impact on the agency, building relationships with elected officials, and developing new ideas, in addition to operations and administration, organizational leadership/human resources, budgets, contracts, procurement, project management, accounting and finance, and law. Dr. Mondala-Duncan holds a BA in Sociology, an MBA with two concentrations in Organizational Leadership and Project Management, and a Doctor of Business Administration in Business Intelligence. She has published several journal articles, is a member of The Honor Society of Phi Kappa Phi, National Society of Leadership and Success, a 2024 Honored Listee in the Marquis Who's Who, and a recipient of the 2026 Baldrige Foundation Award for Leadership Excellence.

Stacey L. Morin is a Chief Financial Officer in the Financial Services industry, serving in the middle-market M&A advisory division of the world's fifth-largest financial institution. She brings over 25 years of experience in the sector, with deep expertise in corporate finance, banking, and capital markets. Dr. Morin holds a Bachelor's degree in Accounting from Eastern Michigan University (1995), an MBA in Finance from California State University, Northridge (2007), and a Doctor of Business Administration (DBA) from Marymount University (2025). She is currently completing a postdoctoral fellowship at Marymount University, where she continues to advance research in financial strategy and organizational performance. She also has multiple FINRA securities licenses required for her executive role. A dedicated pracademic, Dr. Morin bridges the gap between industry and academia by integrating real-world financial leadership experience with rigorous scholarly research. Her work informs and advances both financial theory and business practice. Throughout her career, she has championed inclusive, resilient, and data-driven organizational strategies. Her research and writing focus on corporate finance, banking, and strategic leadership within the business sector. Dr. Morin's unique blend of academic excellence and executive insight continues to shape her contributions to both professional and academic communities, and she is recognized as a financial data storyteller—translating complex financial information into narrative-driven insights that inform strategic decision-making.

Calvin Nobles is a cybersecurity professional and human factors engineer with more than 25 years of experience spanning military service, industry practice, and higher-education leadership. Dr. Nobles serves as Portfolio Vice President and Dean of the School of Cybersecurity and Information Technology at the University of Maryland Global Campus (UMGC), providing strategic and operational leadership for a large, workforce-aligned academic portfolio that advances cybersecurity education, applied partnerships, and innovation at scale. Dr. Nobles previously served as a Department Chair and Associate Professor at the Illinois Institute of Technology and completed a full career in the United States Navy before transitioning into roles within the financial services sector. Dr. Nobles is the author of a book focused on the integration of technologically advanced aircraft in general aviation and maintains active national service through advisory and professional bodies, including service on the National Cryptologic Foundation Board and the Cybersecurity Association Inc Board. Dr. Nobles is also a former Cybersecurity Fellow at Harvard University.

Stephen Olawoye is an experienced professional in Healthcare Cybersecurity with a Doctor of Philosophy degree. He has over ten years of experience, including malware threat research, asset security management, and secure configuration practices for the DoD Department of the Army and private sector organizations. His academic work focused on three main subjects during his PhD program, which included advanced malware detection, digital forensics, and compliance frameworks. Oladele holds an MBA (General); he also holds a BA in Logistics and Transportation Management, both from American Military (Public) University. The candidate demonstrates proven leadership abilities that qualify him to handle risk assessment, incident response, and regulatory compliance through NIST, HIPAA, and PCI DSS standards. Oladele utilizes his understanding to connect research findings with operational security needs, enabling him to create effective cyber threat protection systems for modern digital systems.

Chitra Perera is a financial leader with over 15 years of experience in budget administration, financial analysis, forecasting, and fund management. As Director of Business Services for the Collins College of Hospitality Management at California State Polytechnic University, Pomona, she oversees the strategic development and management of multi-million-dollar budgets. Her responsibilities include ensuring compliance with CSU policies and accreditation standards, supporting long-term financial planning, and advising on fiscal policy and resource allocation. Chitra is recognized for implementing robust internal controls and data-driven financial practices that increase transparency, improve cost control, and promote cross-departmental alignment. Her collaborative leadership and project management have supported academic programs, revenue operations, donor-funded initiatives, and major events, enhancing financial accountability and operational efficiency. Earlier in her career, Chitra worked in senior procurement and operations roles at well-known sports and entertainment venues. She managed large purchases, negotiated with vendors, oversaw inventory, and ensured compliance in busy hospitality environments. She holds a Master of Science in Finance and a Master of Science in Accounting from the University of La Verne, and a Bachelor of Science in Hospitality Management from Cal Poly Pomona. She is currently enrolled in a Doctor of Business Administration (DBA) program with a concentration in Business Intelligence at Marymount University. Chitra is known for her analytical, strategic approach and her commitment to fiscal stewardship in support of institutional mission, innovation, and long-term sustainability.

KerriLaine Prunella is an executive with experience in leadership development, organizational transformation, and human capital strategy across public sector, consulting, and nonprofit entities. As Founder and CEO of VINA79Group, she brings entrepreneurial vision and a deep commitment to leadership excellence, serving as a strategic advisor. As a board member, Ms. Prunella values collaboration and duty of care. She leads risk management and strategic oversight emphasizing opportunities for operational excellence. She is adept at CEO mentorship, guiding organizational transformations, fostering inclusivity, and aligning human capital strategies. She has demonstrated strong governance expertise to maximize stakeholder value through her leadership roles such as Healthcare Access Maryland, where she currently serves as Vice Chair of the Board, former chair of the Nominating Committee, and the Penn State Alumni Association, serving as Chair of Audit and Risk, and former Vice Chair for Governance and Finance Committees. Additionally, she served as a founding Board Member and Executive Secretary of the Management Advisory Council at George Mason University, Costello College of Business. Ms. Prunella formerly served as Chief Human Capital Officer with oversight of strategy and operations for Talent Management, Talent Development, and Executive Compensation across all office locations. As an Acting Assistant Inspector General for Administration, she led six divisions and a $65 million budget. A Big Four Alumni, she led strategies for human capital process re-engineering. Ms. Prunella earned a Bachelor's degree in International Politics from The Pennsylvania State University, a Master's degree in Business Administration from Trinity Washington University, and a Graduate Certificate in Organization Development from Marymount University. She is currently pursuing her Doctorate in Business Intelligence at Marymount.

William Quisenberry resides in Lexington, KY, and has a diverse background that includes studying and practicing within the field of business administration, coordinating implementation projects for Fortune 500 clients, managing and overseeing vendors/suppliers, operations management, project management, marketing, research analysis, consulting, and teaching at the collegiate level. Dr. Quisenberry has collaborated and worked on projects with a variety of major organizations in the marketplace that include: Lexmark International, Halliburton,

Branch Banking and Trust, The U.S. Department of Veterans Affairs, Wal-Mart, The U.S. Army Corps of Engineers, Accenture, IBM, Best Buy, Lockheed Martin, John Hancock Financial, and the World Trade Center Association. Dr. Quisenberry holds a Bachelor of Business Administration (BBA) degree in Finance, a BBA in Marketing, as well as a Master of Business Administration degree from Sullivan University's Graduate School of Business, and a Post-Graduate Certification in Forensic Accounting from Davenport University. He also possesses a Doctor of Business Administration (DBA) degree with a specialization in Leadership from Walden University.

Dana-Marie is an experienced scholar and researcher specializing in postinternational governance and multilevel politics. Dana-Marie's research explores the intricate dynamics between globalization, localization, and governance structures in a world marked by turbulence and complexity. With a focus on collaborative governance, heterarchy, and policy innovation, Dana-Marie has contributed significantly to understanding how states and non-state actors navigate the challenges of the modern political landscape.

Philip Reed, Strategic cybersecurity executive with expertise in building and maturing enterprise-wide cybersecurity capabilities, integrating cyber risk into corporate governance, and advising boards and executive leadership. Adjunct faculty teaching cybersecurity and cyber risk management.

Amalisha Sabie-Aridi, Ph.D., MBA, CMP-UNGGA, is an esteemed scholar, educator, and executive leader whose career spans over a decade of exceptional contributions to higher education, project management, organizational strategy, and leadership development. As a distinguished graduate professor and doctoral committee chair at multiple institutions, including Marymount University and Washington University of Science & Technology, she has guided countless doctoral candidates and shaped innovative curricula across disciplines such as technology, business, leadership, and project management. Dr. Sabie-Aridi's prolific scholarly output includes over 80 peer-reviewed publications covering diverse fields such as organizational behavior, artificial intelligence strategy, healthcare management, strategic leadership, diversity and inclusion, and cybersecurity. She is renowned for integrating research excellence with practical expertise drawn from her tenure as a senior project manager and executive operations leader, notably in high-stakes environments like NASA Engineering Inc. Internationally recognized, she holds honors including UN Global Goodwill Ambassador.

Gregory K. "GK" Smith is a Senior Principal Operations Research Analyst and Simulation Developer at Raytheon (RTX), leveraging more than thirty years of

Department of Defense experience to support complex modernization, modeling, and decision-analysis efforts. A West Point graduate with a Master's in Operations Research and Systems Analysis from the Naval Postgraduate School, he previously served in senior Army analytic and leadership roles across the Pentagon, Joint Staff, and deployed environments, including as the Military Deputy to the Director of the U.S. Army Combat Capabilities Development Command Analysis Center (DAC). He is currently a Doctor of Business Administration (DBA) candidate whose dissertation explores how professionals experience Generative AI pilot programs in capture and bid content management, and he remains active in the Central Arkansas community as President of the Douglas MacArthur Central Arkansas West Point Society and a lifetime member of Alpha Phi Alpha Fraternity, Inc.

Samantha Thibodeau is a Software Engineering Leader and DBA Candidate at Marymount University. She began her career in medical device design and transitioned to Software Engineering. For the last 10 years, she has held industry roles across Quality Engineering, Software Development, and Engineering Leadership, blending her academic interests within her roles. Academically, Samantha holds a Bachelor of Science in Biomedical Engineering from Florida Gulf Coast University and a Master of Engineering in Engineering Management from Ohio University. She is currently a DBA candidate with Marymount University. She also holds University certifications in Lean Six Sigma and Engineering Leadership, as well as technical certifications including AWS Certified Cloud Practitioner, ICAgile Certified Professional - Foundations of Artificial Intelligence, and the ISTQB Foundation Level Exam (CTFL) with distinction. Her research interests include Engineering Leadership, Leadership Cultural Shifts, Change Management, Cybersecurity, Operational and Business Risk, and Software Quality. Samantha's publications span a breadth of peer-reviewed journals, including those focused on business resiliency and operations, cybersecurity risk management, and engineering leadership.

Jason D. West is Senior Vice President, Strategy at The Bantam Group, where he leads qualitative and mixed-methods research for Fortune 500 and B2B organizations, translating complex consumer and market insights into actionable brand and business strategy. His work bridges academic rigor and applied practice, with a focus on culturally intelligent research, ethical decision-making, and human-centered strategy development. West is also a Lecturer in the Advanced Academic Programs at Johns Hopkins University, where he teaches research evaluation and strategic problem-solving in communication contexts. He is currently pursuing a Doctor of Business Administration at Marymount University. His scholarly work includes peer-reviewed research on Diversity, Equity, and Inclusion (DE&I)

strategies and the role of minority-owned advertising agencies in shaping authentic, trust-building marketing practices.

Index

A

B

C

D

E

F

G

H

I

M

O

P

R

S

T

U

W

X

www.ingramcontent.com/pod-product-compliance
Lightning Source LLC
LaVergne TN
LVHW062326300926
849161LV00007B/1588